Comments on the original *Real Lives*

"A wonderful book, a revolutionary book like *Uncle Tom's Cabin*, a book to set people free."
—John Taylor Gatto, former New York Teacher of the Year, author of *The Underground History of American Education* and *Dumbing Us Down*

"Buy this book! Like its predecessor, *The Teenage Liberation Handbook*, it may stun some teens—more likely their parents and their teachers—but it is a mind-expanding experience that belongs on all library shelves. Here, eleven... 'unschooled' teens write about...how they learn, socialize, study, and especially how their special interests and loves have directed their unconventional educations....These autodidacts' days embrace a challenging freedom unimagined by those of us bound by the limits and assumptions of the classroom....For those teens who always seem to travel to the beat of a different drummer, this fascinating book may point the way to a viable alternative. The rest of us should at least know that there are other roads to education and happiness than the traditional route. *Real Lives* is a consciousness-raising journey of a special kind."
—*Kliatt* Young Adult Paperback Book Guide

"Compelling stories....Don't be fooled by your personal memories of teenage writing. This is not a stack of high school English essays waiting to be graded. Instead it is a fascinating study in self-teaching....Each essay is unique, both in style and content."
—The Oregon Home Education Network *Network News*

"...[The profiles] are nicely varied and each student's personal voice shines through as he or she explains why traditional education was abandoned and what has replaced it...." —American Library Association *Booklist*

"These kids give me hope for a brighter future. Highly inspirational!"
—*Living Free* Newsletter

"Rich in-depth biographical and philosophical essays solicited from eleven teens who tell why they made the decision (with the help of their families) not to be 'tamed' or stifled by traditional schooling methodologies and regulations. The essays shed light on what happens during a typical day in the lives of homeschooled individuals, how the teens became as educated (and self-confident) as they appear to be, what motivates them to learn, their views on homeschooling versus traditional education, hopes for the future, etc. Many misconceptions about homeschooling are debunked..." —*Library Journal*

"I am unashamedly wild about this book; I think it's one of the most exciting things to happen to (or to come out of) the homeschooling movement in a long time.....These kids are learning from the world and they're contributing to it, too. It's impossible to read this book and not understand that homeschooling is more than just sitting at home with a textbook." —*Growing Without Schooling* magazine

by Grace Llewellyn

The Teenage Liberation Handbook: how to quit school and get a real life and education

by Grace Llewellyn and Amy Silver

Guerrilla Learning: How to Give Your Kids a Real Education With or Without School

edited by Grace Llewellyn

Freedom Challenge: African American Homeschoolers

Real Lives

Lowry House Publishers
Post Office Box 1014
Eugene, Oregon 97440
541-686-2315
www.LowryHousePublishers.com

SECOND EDITION
Printed in the United States of America

Publisher's Cataloging-In-Publication Data
(Prepared by The Donohue Group, Inc.)

Real lives : eleven teenagers who don't go to school tell their own stories / edited
and with an introduction by Grace Llewellyn. — 2nd ed.

p. : ill. ; cm.
Includes bibliographical references and index.
ISBN: 0-9629591-2-X

1. Self-culture. 2. Home schooling—United States. 3. Education, Secondary—
United States. 4. Teenagers' writings—United States. I. Llewellyn, Grace.

LC32 .R43 2005
371.3944

1 3 5 7 9 10 8 6 4 2

BOOK DESIGN BY TILKE ELKINS
WWW.ALLROUNDMAGAZINE.COM

Real Lives

eleven teenagers who don't go to school tell their own stories

eleven year anniversary edition, with updates by all the writers

edited and with an introduction by Grace Llewellyn

Lowry House Publishers
Eugene, Oregon

Tabitha Mountjoy with reconstructed animal skeletons

Photo by Amory Mountjoy

Contents

Acknowledgments

The creation of this book has been a joyous process, thanks to the helpful and creative involvement of dozens of people.

The essayists would like to publicly thank the following people for various kinds of help:

The Sellstrom family, Sue Taniguchi, Richard and Sandra Merrion, Deni Jacks, Cedrus Amphibian, Buff Puff Scruff, Jan Wetherell, Sandi Roberts, the Roberts family, Nick, Amy Mento, James and Kristin Williams, Henry Cleage, Pearl Cleage, the rest of the Williams and Cleage families, Susannah Sheffer, the Bergson-/Shilcock family, Sandra Morning Star, Kalista Mountjoy, Amory Mountjoy, Pam Gingold, Craig Gingold, Jarrod Almarode, Alice in Chains, Metallica, and the Raymonds: Dan, Kath, Seth, and Lydia.

As editor, I would like to thank:

The homeschooling community which has welcomed and encouraged me and my work.

The essayists whose work I could not include, due to the limitations of space and my own time and energy.

Susannah Sheffer, editor of *Growing Without Schooling* magazine. Susannah gave astute criticism on a near-final draft of the manuscript. Furthermore, her new book, *Writing Because We Love To: Homeschoolers at Work* (Heinemann/Boynton-Cook, 1992), is full of valuable insights which helped me make the shift from working with young writers as a schoolteacher to instead working with them as a respectful, real-world editor. And Susannah's encouragement and enthusiasm has often helped me continue to trust my own work.

Other people who read early drafts of the collection, especially Skip Bergin and Lesly Cormier.

Above all, my family and friends, without whose myriad forms of support and love I could not continue my work. I thank particularly Heather, Richard, Heather D., Ned, Colleen, Mark, Debbe, my parents, Lesly, Heiko, Jon, Tino, Caroline, and Skip.

Of course Tommy and Annika went to school. Each morning at eight o'clock they trotted off, hand in hand, swinging their schoolbags.

At that time Pippi was usually grooming her horse or dressing Mr. Nilsson in his little suit. Or else she was taking her morning exercises, which meant turning forty-three somersaults in a row. Then she would sit down on the kitchen table and, utterly happy, drink a large cup of coffee and eat a piece of bread and cheese.

Tommy and Annika always looked longingly toward [Pippi's house] as they started off to school.

—Astrid Lindgren, *Pippi Longstocking*

It often happens that the universal belief of one age, a belief from which no one...could be free without an extraordinary effort of genius or courage, becomes to a subsequent age, so palpable an absurdity that the only difficulty is, to imagine how such an idea could ever have appeared credible.

—John Stuart Mill, *Principles of Political Economy*

Preface to the second edition

At first I resisted the idea of publishing an update. It seemed almost crass—as if we had to *prove* that these people who lived richly as teenagers hadn't fallen off the edge of the known universe as adults.

But obviously I changed my mind, and this is how:

My own curiosity kicked in. With the notable exception of Kyla, who occupies a charming trailer in my driveway and spends many evenings laughing with me, I had lost track. I liked the idea of knowing in some depth what everyone was up to and how they've recently been thinking about their years as unschoolers, homeschoolers, rise-outs, and such.

Readers were also curious. They sent letters.

> We were wondering if you might ever do a "revisited" version of *Real Lives*? I know my husband and I would be fascinated to see how all of the kids are doing now that they are in their mid twenties. ... Now that they are adults, and maybe even parents themselves, it would be most interesting to see how they feel about the experience, and how they plan to raise their own children (should they choose to have any).

I took a deep breath and a more serious look at that question of "proving." I saw a subtle distinction: I don't care for defensiveness, but I certainly understand the need for role models. I knew that homeschoolers are often afraid when they first leap out of classrooms into the unknown. Although homeschooling is much *less* an unknown now than it was in 1993, it is still an unusual way of growing up—especially when engaged the way these eleven writers engaged it: not out of a box, not by taking orders, but by doing their best to listen to themselves, by generating their activities from their own affinities and from the context of living within their families and their neighborhoods and the natural and cultural world around them. (For thirty years, the shorthand term for this has been "unschooling," but from time to time it's good to name what it actually stands for.) We hunger for stories of people who've "made it"—not because we intellectually think that someone who leads trail rides and wins national 4-H competitions at fifteen will be lost at twenty-five, but because being part of a radical movement without a long proven history is just plain scary sometimes, and we long for reassurance. I got more letters:

> I wanted to know, since the pub date appears to be early nineties, if there was ever a follow-up done on the stories of the eleven teenagers profiled…. The profiles that captured my interest in particular were those on Patrick Meehan—I wondered whether he indeed landed a job in the computer game-design industry —and Kyla Wetherell. … I mainly ask my question for personal reasons, as [my husband] and I are seriously considering homeschooling our two now-extremely-young boys. I'd like to have a bit of outcomes information, although I pretty much buy the entire premise of home/unschooling. The more I learn the more dissatisfied I become with what I see around me in terms of conventional schooling—now *there* are outcomes that often seem iffy!

When I started Not Back to School Camp, my annual gathering for unschooled teenagers, *CBS This Morning* sent a crew. They aired their story, which included a soundbyte from me, a smidgen of camp footage, and vignettes of two campers' lives back at home. One boy was filmed saying, "I went to school for kindergarten and first grade and didn't like it. It wasn't what I wanted to do." After the segment, the anchorwoman said (to the correspondent), "It's really *upsetting*, Hattie—is it legal?….Amazing the little boy who said he just didn't like school so he dropped out after second grade—what if that kid decides he wants to go to college?" (Actually, five years later that particular kid did decide he wanted to go to college, and so at the age of seventeen he went. To Reed, one of the most selective schools in the U.S.)

They followed our snippet with commentary from a Virginia school board president. "It's probably one of the worst ideas I've ever heard," she said, "I suppose if they want to go off and—" she paused— "be a *potter* or something, that, you know, then they may be well enough prepared, but assuming these are kids who want to take their place, in some kind of career, they're going to need to know specific things."

Sadly, these reactions are typical of mainstream culture, which may feel it can give approving lip service to "doing what you love," but only as long as love stays in its place, which is to say on weekends, during vacations, just before you go to bed, and in your shopping cart. With this sternness all around us (and within us, too), anxiety is natural. It's no small thing to abandon a well-worn road and start bushwhacking through wilderness. Although in one way unschooling is the most normal thing in the universe, and allows a return to a non-industrial rhythm of life that we all intuit to be healthy and right, it's also a step into mystery. Of course, life *always* is one step after another into mystery, even for people who go to school. Showing up for class and studying for tests is no guarantee of success or—more important—inner peace and joy and the knowledge that one is contributing to the world. But it doesn't *seem* so mysterious when you're doing what everyone else around you is doing. True, there are hundreds of thousands more homeschoolers now than there were in 1993—and even then the movement was huge compared to its beginnings in the two previous decades—but it's still a bold undertaking. Boldness, naturally, often harbors insecurity and anxiety in its underbelly. We march on knowing in our hearts that it's right to build our lives and our learning around what calls to us, but when we're a small minority doing so, it feels immensely encouraging to hear voices from up ahead calling out, "We're doing fine! We're as alive as ever! We've been teaching people to build their own houses, and getting married and having babies, and going to college, and showing homeless children how to read and how to believe in themselves." And then we laugh and shrug our shoulders and we think, "Well, that's no surprise—after all, as kids they were teaching Civil War history to their siblings, or writing to pen-pals in India and Nigeria, or studying plankton down at the beach, or working a crisis hotline—I knew they'd be fine."

From time to time I forget about the possibility of this anxiety, because my own life is densely populated with grown unschoolers thriving on their own terms—tonight Kyla and I ate dinner with Carsie, who at nineteen washes dogs for money (dogs being pretty much her favorite thing ever) and devotes herself to writing the most stunning, poignant songs and singing them in the most stunning, poignant voice. And with Maya, who at twenty-three manages my office and is the competent and self-assured assistant director of Not Back to School Camp. And with Joe, twenty-two, who has developed more self-awareness than most sixty-year-olds and calls his own wholeness into service by leading teenagers in wilderness projects. I'm thinking also of Sarabeth, twenty-three, who runs a personal chef business and is one of the most inspiring mothers I've ever witnessed. Of Nicole, twenty-five, passionately dedicating her life to political activism and wearing her baby Lou in a sling. And of Evan, twenty-four, supervising volunteers who nurse wounded seals, and working to support other unschoolers on the cusp of adulthood—among other things, he directs a terrific annual self-educators' gathering called Quo Vadis. Those are just a few of my good friends. The web widens as I consider the Not Back to School Camp alums I get to see from time to time: Ruth, twenty-year-old firefighter and EMT. Dawn, twenty-two, working for an architect, building straw bale houses. Rick, innovative twenty-three-year-old computer wizard and designer of interactive web sites. Adrian, twenty-one, playing piano, violin, viola, and accordion all over Europe and North America as the youngest member of a much-acclaimed band called The Bills. Sarah, twenty-year-old commercial pilot (she transports injured people to hospitals), flight teacher, and professional marimba player.

Oh. And nineteen-year-old Roya, the *potter* who crafted the exquisite red mug out of which I sip my bedtime tea. By now it seems terribly obvious to me that unschoolers can grow up and choose not just to "take their place," but to *create* their own beautiful, personalized places to enjoy as adults.

I recall, though, the dismayed expression on that anchorwoman's face, and the tone of voice wielded by that school board president, and I know our work is not done. Many people do easily accept homeschooling, now, as a civilized alternative, but they *still* tend to envision parents teaching conventionally, relying on textbooks. They may think the practice is a little nerdy and isolationist, but they are likely to otherwise approve—after all, they've heard that homeschoolers can get into college and make babies just like everyone else. Imagining only such a small sliver of the truth cheats everyone—not only the unschoolers who continue to face disdain, but also the people doing the imagining: they miss out on a fat chunk of evidence that chasing our wildest dreams may not be so disastrous after all.

Yet, having said all that, I also want to say this: I don't feel that giving kids educational freedom should be rationalized only by hoping for a respectable "outcome." Occasionally in these pages—or perhaps when you meet other grown unschoolers—you'll find someone who hasn't yet settled into a satisfying work-niche. Where that occurs, I nevertheless find myself grateful that that person had great liberty, as a teenager, to learn and live *then* in the way he or she chose. Going to school certainly doesn't guarantee that life will offer up a gratifying career, as a glance behind the check-out counters of a Wal-Mart can remind us. Conversely, some of the writers here are successful (as adults) in unarguable ways, which is great, but certainly not intended as the whole point. So the one hesitation I still bring to this project is my fear that the reader's focus will shift too much to "how did they turn out" (as if we "turn out" by the time we are twenty-seven!) and somewhat away from fully enjoying the rich possibilities, represented here, for adolescence itself.

***

You'll notice that all of the essayists have in some way experimented with college or trade school, and their experiences run the gamut—from Ayanna thriving in a master's program (in a recent email she imagines continuing on for a Ph.D.); to Kyla deliberately taking a few classes to support her survey of literature and art history, and then nine months later, just as deliberately, deciding it's time to get back to having more time for her own writing; to Amanda deciding to try college *only* if she can do it without taking the SAT, which would compromise her ideals; to Rebecca enrolling in massage school and absolutely loving it; to Kevin starting college with one goal in mind, but that goal eventually changing to reflect his enthusiasm for the paid work he is doing with children. All of this echoes the sentiment, often expressed in homeschooling circles, that college choices can complement our temperaments in many ways—you can exercise imagination regarding, for example, not just what to study, but also where (and in what kind of institution) you study it, how you study it and for how long and with whom and toward what purpose, how fully you focus on it and what else you do in your life at the same time.

***

So much about this collection is solidly positive, but I'd feel incomplete if I didn't also address, here, the shadows that deepen a few of the essays. Although they rarely discuss it outright, it's no small thing for these eleven to have presented their lives as examples, as role models for others. While for the most part they have been glad to serve in this manner, some have also wrestled with the subtle ways that, as teenagers, they portrayed themselves as "successful"—not by telling lies, but by shaping their stories more around their achievements than around their difficulties and self-doubts. I've learned how important it is for humans to validate each other not only in our shining moments but also in our smallness. At Not Back to School Camp, which on the surface looks like a bumper crop of happiness, affection, and passion for learning, I've recently begun saying at each session: "Your *whole experience* is welcome here. Sometimes you may look around and imagine that everyone else is ecstatic all the time, and that only you have moments of self-criticism, jealousy, or loneliness. But the truth is that all of us have those moments, even here at camp, and there is nothing wrong with you or me for having them." Only to the extent that we are able to practice this deeper kind of acceptance and recognition of ourselves and each other, to tell the whole truth about our experience and listen to each other's whole truths, will we be able to also authentically celebrate and draw hope from each other's accomplishments.

So I am grateful for Jeremiah's update, in which he admits that he hasn't achieved as much as he would have liked, and feels some discomfort about that. (I think he's too hard on himself, but that's beside the point.) I appreciate Rebecca's essay, in which she reports that alongside her gratitude for her homeschooling experiences she also has regret, that she still wonders what it would have been like to at least *try* school. I appreciate Kyla for acknowledging that her exciting trip through South America had a dark side that she only briefly alluded to at the time, and that while she has never regretted her decision to leave school, she also sees, now, how that decision came partly from "a pretty messy and arrogant place." I appreciate Patrick for saying, simply, "I was a sensitive child, quick to take affront and escalate problems, so a lot of the problems I had or thought I had were my own doing." And I appreciate Anne for sharing that while she values the many unique experiences she had as a teenager, she can also see how she isolated herself through believing that homeschoolers were smarter and thus better than other teenagers, and that if she had to do it over again she'd take herself less seriously.

These are, I think, the hardest kinds of things to say, and they are so important—just as important as the easy stuff here, the stories of people following their dreams and achieving obviously wonderful things. I liked what Susannah Sheffer wrote in an email when we were discussing the struggles some of the writers were facing. She said she hoped the essayists would "raise some things that need to be raised—about the homeschooling community needing validation, reassurance, examples, and promotional material on the one hand, yet needing to understand the fullness of people's lives and stories, on the other. Probably the community could use some reflection on that."

Although I'm neither a grown-up unschooler nor an unschooling parent, I relate personally to all of these more difficult disclosures. In the writers' truthfulness they are faithful not only to themselves and their own experiences, but also to each of us in our times of doubt and self-criticism. What I take away from the overall collection here is something like this: "Cool! There are actual people out there living life in their own way, deciding what they want to do and doing it, and that helps me feel more able to live my life my own way too. Furthermore, they're human! Their motivations are not always pure. Sometimes they feel frustrated or insecure. And sometimes the processes that we choose to follow—like unschooling, like following our hearts in the larger sense—*are* difficult and confusing. So maybe I can forgive myself for all the mornings I don't wake up excited to carry out the work I've chosen....and for all the weeks I put off writing this preface!"

In the way these eleven writers illumine these two sides of the same coin, of the same mirror, I hope that you, like me, will find affirmation of the most helpful kind for your own journey.

***

A few comments on simple matters:

You may wonder about timing. "Eleven-year anniversary" is an arbitrary label: Some updates were written ten years after the originals, others twelve. It turns out that giving birth, moving, changing careers, and such—real lives, in short—tend to take priority over things like writing autobiographies. (So, as this book goes to press, Ayanna is nearly finished with her master's degree, and Rebecca is about to marry a man whose enthusiasm for math inspires her to have a new look at it herself, and I ran into Tabitha and her enchanting baby Ariel swimming in the river a few months ago, and Kyla's short stories have won several honorable mentions in nationwide contests.) "Eleven" makes a good average and happens to match our number of writers. I initially put their adult ages at the top of the new essays, but in the end that seemed wrong since updates-to-the-updates were occasionally made late in the game. It also felt odd to have one person who wrote at sixteen now be labeled "twenty-six," and another "twenty-eight."

I made a few changes to the original text: Many of the books that the essayists recommended in their first essays have become (or remained) classics, and many have been revised since 1993. So where a publisher and publication date were given, but that information is no longer the most current, I removed those details.

Similarly, where contact information for an organization or person was listed, but has since changed, I deleted it. In some cases I gave the new information in a footnote or in Appendix II. Of course, a quick Internet search can turn up current data on pretty much any organization or resource.

I killed off a few footnotes that no longer seemed relevant.

I changed some photo captions, and removed some photos in the interest of saving space.

***

Before I sign off, I want to say that I'm still grateful to all the people I originally acknowledged, and specifically, currently, to the following:

Maya Lester, miraculous blend of sweet, cute, strong, and efficient, for making my business run smoothly and thus protecting my time and sanity so that I can continue to work on projects like this one.

Tilke Elkins, creator of the brilliant, color-drenched, soul-sparking *All Round Magazine*, for saying, "I want to design all your books from now on!"

My parents, and my brothers and sister and their partners and children, and my dear friends at Suntop, for making my life feel rooted and whole.

Taber Shadburne and Kyla Wetherell, for the intimate, committed, unflinching, perceptive, all-embracing, and enduring love that helps me keep opening my heart and choosing to engage the world and my work in the world, day after day after day.

And once again thank you to Tabitha, Erin, Amanda, Kevin, Ayanna, Patrick, Anne, Rebecca, Jeremiah, Kyla, and Vallie: for your willingness to take this project on first as teenagers and now again as adults. I think it has taken great courage, perhaps even more this second time around, to offer your stories and your reflections in service to others who are finding their own trails through this mystery wilderness that we all inhabit.

Grace Llewellyn
Eugene, Oregon
November 2004

Introduction

I was a guest this morning on the Canadian Broadcast Corporation's *Early Edition*, talking up my brash ideas about education. ("Are you really suggesting to bored kids that they simply quit school?" "Well, *yes*.") One of the questions the host asked me was, "But if lots of teenagers quit school, how do you know that wouldn't lead to a rash of kids who did nothing but play Nintendo?"

I knew, I explained, not only because of the certainty in my gut that people are bigger than that, but also because I know the stories of hundreds of kids who do not go to school—not "dropouts" in the self-fulfilling-prophecy sense, and not unusually gifted geniuses either—but rather ordinary unschoolers, homeschoolers, "rise-outs," and other variously named autodidacts. These people find thousands of better ways to occupy their time than playing continual Nintendo. Because of the things unschooled teenagers have told me in letters and in person, and because of my other reading—especially all the back issues of *Growing Without Schooling*, a magazine overflowing with the details of unschoolers' lives—no, I don't worry at all about spawning a video game generation.

For the same reasons, I also do not worry that unschooled kids will shrivel into social outcasts, be turned away from college (when they want college), not find work, be unable to learn math or science (when they choose to learn these subjects), or fail to develop as healthy individuals prepared to contribute toward the health of their communities.

Now, I don't mean to be glib. I want to acknowledge two things. First, many kids who have spent more than a year in school definitely go through an initial strange, lethargic period upon quitting school. For a few days or maybe a whole year, they have no interest whatsoever in anything educational; rather, they overdose on teenage romance novels, TV, video games, food, hanging-out-at-the-mall, and such. Many people familiar with the homeschooling movement think of this as a necessary detoxification process, during which the psyche rebels against—and ultimately heals from—its years of submitting to external control. In every case I know of, *in time* something surfaces from within, and self-directed education starts happening, far more meaningful than any kind of prescribed or standardized education.

Second, I know that the lives of many "dropouts" seem to contradict my proclamation that kids are better off without school. To some degree, we all fulfill others' expectations of us, and kids who call themselves dropouts cannot help but absorb—to at least some degree—society's pessimistic judgments on their capabilities and futures. Yet, to transform millions of dead-ended "dropouts" into joyful independent learners, it would take no more—and no less—than convincing them to trust their own minds and desires.

But even though I am radiantly confident that unschooling works, my own generalizations and summaries of kids' lives are not enough. I constantly find myself wishing, during conversations like the one this morning, that the worried questioner could hear directly and substantially from kids who control their own lives and educations.

Hence, this book.

Another raison d'être for *Real Lives* has something to do with the general mystique surrounding unschoolers. When, at the age of twenty-three, I first stumbled across the work of John Holt, his ideas about unschooling and learning immediately echoed throughout my being. Next, I learned that there were people who had actually put his ideas to work in their own and their children's lives. I was intrigued and amazed to learn that there were thousands of kids in this country who didn't go to school—not because they had given up on themselves, not because their parents wanted to censor the information that came their way, but rather because they and their parents believed that the best way to get an education was simply through the joyful pursuit of a full, meaningful life.

I satisfied some of my own curiosity about these people in the next few years, especially during my work on *The Teenage Liberation Handbook*. With this second book, I hope both to awaken and partially satisfy your curiosity.

Why "awaken?"

I suspect that most Americans by this time have less sense of mystery about homeschooling than I did five years ago, because they probably already think they know what it is. They probably associate homeschooling mainly with fundamentalist Christianity, and to most of us there is nothing fascinatingly wonderful or inconceivable about the idea of a miniature school—complete with curriculum, parent-as-teacher-and-disciplinarian, rigid daily schedule, etc.—at home rather than in a school building. (Many fundamentalist Christian homeschoolers, actually, do not really homeschool this way. But enough do to support a significant industry of Christian homeschooling materials, and enough do that this sort of lifestyle dominates too much of the public and media perception of "what homeschoolers do.")

Anyway, if your definition of homeschooling is "school at home," you are partly right: For many people it is just that. But for thousands of others, it is nothing of the sort. Thousands of children in this country grow up without being told what to do, without being formally taught to read or write, without being required to study biology, algebra, and Ernest Hemingway, without ever *once* being forced to read a particular book or complete a particular worksheet—or any worksheet whatsoever. If you are imagining that all the people who live with such freedom are half-naked rural hippie-kids, you are wrong. In class background, lifestyle, appearance, religion, and most other respects, self-directed learners are diverse. (I don't mean to imply any prejudice against half-naked rural hippie-kids. My own future offspring will likely fit that description.)

The third reason for this book is personal. I used to teach school. While I could no longer justify—or enjoy—contributing to a structure which I believe is inherently harmful to its captives, I have deeply missed the habit of working closely with young writers. Through the synthesis of this book, I have been able to get to know these eleven people, to work with them to produce a serious piece of non-fiction rather than a cute bunch of useless exercises in essay writing. And as I edited this book written by free teenagers, I came full circle; the ex-teacher in me healed and found some redemption.

***

It is not every day that someone publishes a book written mainly by teenagers. Some of you will wonder how this book came into being, so:

I acquired most of the contributors to *Real Lives* by advertising in *Growing Without Schooling* magazine. A few others I contacted directly, since I already knew a little about their lives and knew that they enjoyed writing. They each wrote an essay about their lives and educations according to a set of guidelines I mailed out. ("The most ideal pieces will manage both to convey an overall sense of your unschooling experience and also to focus in depth on one or two specific topics that matter to you...Make sure you are honest and thoughtful and that your language feels good to you...If you have any recommendations or advice for new teenaged unschoolers, feel free to include that...")

After I received the first round of essays (and, unfortunately, eliminated some due to lack of space), we started the real work. Through the mail we went back and forth for five months.

(I would write, "Please explain briefly what pathwork psychology is," "Your closing doesn't feel quite right to me," "Why do you choose to study algebra with your aunt instead of on your own?" "I'd like you to explain a little more about your work with Susannah," "This is another of those places where I want a lot more detail," "Is *pace* the only way your approach to studies differs from school?")

The writers responded to my continual requests with alacrity, cheerfulness, and thorough attention to detail. In fact, the way this book came together is as indicative as anything of the way young people work *on projects of their own choosing*. Although these eleven teenagers are all self-directed, in other ways they are quite different from each other. Some hold themselves to a fairly regular academic schedule complete with at least one or two textbooks; others rarely, if ever, deliberately study *anything*.

Yet, all the writers for this book worked with me in a manner both exuberant and tirelessly professional. My letters to them were demanding and detailed, and yet no one backed out or shirked even my slightest request. The eleven main essays here range from 3,000 to 18,000 words, and average 9,000 words. The eldest writers are sixteen years old. At age sixteen, college bound high school students are usually required to write term papers of approximately 2,500 words—and this is generally perceived as a major ordeal. True, my eleven writers weren't simultaneously pressured to do math homework, study for finals, and read *Lord of the Flies*. But, hey, 1) that is part of the point, if you think about it: Unschoolers have time to do a few things well rather than a bunch of things frantically, and 2) anyway, these eleven kids have extravagantly full lives which were not dormant during the development of this book. I could write several thousand words on their professionalism, and how I think unschooling fosters such professionalism, but you didn't buy this book to read my lengthy analysis of the process behind it.

Occasionally we disagreed:

At times I felt uncomfortable with something in an essay—I am notoriously idealistic about making friends without school; about being able to study any subject, including science, better outside of school than in school; about kids not needing to study *anything* which doesn't interest them—unless it is *definitely, directly* necessary to accomplish a larger goal.

In a few of these essays, there are slight hints to the contrary. At first I squirmed at these hints, but censorship in any form repulses me, and I wanted not to be guilty of it. Sometimes I'd go back and forth in the mail with a particular writer about a particular subject. Usually, in the end we found that our disagreements were only misunderstandings, resolved by slight rewording. When we continued to disagree, though, I left the final outcome up to the writer, believing it was important for the kids to speak their own visions of the truth.

As a result, I can honestly claim that I did not slant or edit these essays to fit my hopes about self-directed learning. Although I did make small deletions to keep the essays focused, I did not remove anything negative anyone had to say about homeschooling. (The only negative material I removed described experiences the writers had had in *school.*) In the initial set of writers' guidelines I mailed out, I asked specifically for honesty, and for a *whole* perspective on homeschooling. I could not in good conscience publish a book which doctored or filtered the truth.

***

I want to make it clear that I do not intend or perceive the eleven self-portraits in this book as an accurate cross-section or survey of adolescents in the homeschooling movement. To be honest, there is a large subgroup of the homeschooling movement that hardly interests me at all—the aforementioned families who homeschool in a rigid schoollike way, usually with mother staying home to assign reports on the presidents of the United States and father as a back-up disciplinary vice-president and perhaps evening math teacher. Any-way, what I have chosen to portray in this book is not "homeschooling," per se, but rather *self-directed learning*.

Also, as it happens, slightly more than half of these writers live in rural areas. Just in case you didn't know, thousands of unschoolers live in cities, too. Cities obviously provide a particular set of advantages for the unschooler, just as rural areas and small towns provide other kinds of advantages.

***

Finally, I wish to turn this introduction over to you, the Dear Reader. Books being what they are—passive stacks of bound paper and ink—you can do whatever you like with this one. If you are a teenager you can read it in order to write a book report for English class. If you are a sociologist you can read it in order to acquaint yourself with an intriguing fringe of society. If you are a Pro-fessor or Student of Education, you can memorize bits of it to enliven your scholarly discussions of Intrinsic Motivation and Autodidactism. If you are a schoolteacher you can read it in order to make yourself feel useless and de-pressed. If you are Robinson Crusoe you can read it for entertainment.

But please don't stop there.

If you are any sort of adult you can also read it in order to see that your life might have gone very differently had you been allowed to direct your own education. Along with this depressing revelation, you can realize that now, in adulthood, your education—and, by extension, the larger scope of your entire life—is finally up to you.

If you are a dreamer or an activist, you can read it to imagine how we all might grow up in a freer, healthier society—and perhaps to begin working to-ward such a world.

If you are a teacher or school administrator you can let it spur you to change the school where you work, so that it gives significant amounts of power and self-control to students. This seems impossible, but perhaps it is not. (Or— you might read this book with the same radical receptivity that I read John Holt's books when I was a teacher. After those books and a few other influences, I quit teaching and started writing. No regrets, thus far.)

If you are a parent you can read it late at night instead of sitting up worrying about how your kids are doing in school.

And, most of all: *If you are a school-aged young person* you can read for inspiration, for a beginning sense of how your life might change if you turned your vocabulary worksheet into a paper airplane and skipped away down those grey halls, past the principal's office, out finally into the weather, the streets, the riverbanks, the workshops and observatories and art galleries, the whole strange lively world which looms waiting for you.

Erin Roberts, 15
Washington County, Maryland

My Favorite Teacher is a Horse

Photo by Amy Mento

"**Y**ou do *what?*"

Almost all my life I've been getting strange looks and even stranger questions when I tell people about my educational process. My favorite activities are horseback riding, soccer, 4-H, and reading. I get plenty of chances to do each of these because I don't go to school. No, I am not a dropout or a truant, I am an unschooler. I don't have to catch the school bus in the morning and I don't have to follow any certain schedule.

My typical day goes something like this: I get up between seven- thirty and eight and get dressed, usually in filthy dirty jeans and sweatshirt, and go out to take care of my animals. I have quite a few animals, which at the moment include goats, broiler chickens, sheep, and my favorite, horses. I feed grain to the chicks, water everyone, milk the goats, strain the milk, and, depending on the time of year, either hay the goats, sheep, and horses or move their electric fence so they have grass. Then, I eat breakfast and after that it is anybody's guess where my interests and desires lead me.

I am the eldest of five kids. My Dad, Craig, holds the official job in our family; he is a civil engineer who works in Washington, D.C. My Mom, Sandi, is a soccer coach, referee, cook, 4-H leader, chauffeur, etc. I live on a fifty-two acre farm in Washington County, Maryland.

When I first meet people I don't know, they always want to know what school I go to. When I tell them I don't go, I always get some strange looks and reactions like, "What do you mean, you don't go?" Then, when I explain that I am taught at home by my parents and *really* don't go to school, the responses range from, "Wow, I wish my parents would do that!" to "Is that allowed?" and "Don't you miss the social life?" After I answer their first questions everyone always wants to know *why* I don't go to school. My favorite response is, "I'm too smart."

Seriously, I have not met anyone yet who says they actually get educated at school. They go for the social life, for the activities and sports, because they think it will help them get into college, or because their parents make them. Nobody I have met goes to school to really learn.

How I got started

My mom loves to tell this story. I was about three and we were living in Germany at the time. I said to Mom, "I wanna go to school." She asked why and I said to learn to speak German. So she sent me to preschool. I went for three days and came home and said, "I don't want to go to school anymore." Mom asked why not, and I answered, "'Cause I didn't learn German."

My mom always wanted to homeschool us. However, she let us decide if we wanted to go to school. After my family moved back to the United States I went to a Montessori school in first and second grades. While I was in school she was going to homeschooling meetings!

I started homeschooling after second grade. In second grade I had a lousy teacher and all my class was doing, I felt, was repeating what we had learned last year. *Boring!* So, about halfway through the year my parents asked me if I wanted to quit. I said I would finish out the school year, and I have been homeschooling ever since.

When I say I am taught at home by my parents I don't mean I sit and listen to them talk all day. *Au Contraire.* My parents tell me where to find resources I need, then leave me to my own devices. They try to help me if a problem comes up, although in most cases I will try asking someone whom I know has a lot of knowledge on that particular subject. My parents, within reasonable limits, let me do just about anything I want. I haven't asked if I can dye my hair green yet so I don't know if they would let me do that. Probably not.

Most of the limits and goals I have, I set for myself. I enjoy setting challenges, then striving to meet them.

What I do

I live in Maryland (I think). It is sort of hard to tell for sure because I am ten minutes from West Virginia and Virginia. My address is Knoxville, Maryland, which is in Frederick County, and the farm I live on is actually ten minutes over the border into Washington County. My family moved here in 1985. When we moved here my family was the only homeschooling family in Washington County. Now, six and a half years later, there are over 125 families homeschooling in Washington County alone. In Maryland in 1990 there were approximately one thousand families homeschooling. Last year (1991) that number doubled. Someone figured that if that trend continues, every family in Maryland will be homeschooling by the year 2001.

In Maryland, homeschoolers use the portfolio system, which means that twice a year my Mom takes a notebook with samples of my and my siblings' work—like a bar graph I made using scores from a contest I competed in, or poems that I wrote, like these:

I have one bratty brother
I also have another
The big one is brattier than the other.
He always tries   A horse,
To tell big lies   Like a cloud
To our mother.   Moving with the wind
He hits and kicks and bites and punches,   Galloping
Doesn't eat his dinners and lunches.   Across the green field
Through his Game Boy he is hurled   The wind
To an imaginary world   Singing in my ears
Filled with blips and bleeps   We are one
Jumps and leaps.   Moving
And now his pride and joy   Running
Is beating this gray toy.   We are one
No longer does he ride his horse,   Running with the
His clothes and speech are very coarse.   wind
But what does this matter when
It only takes a while
Before he begins to smile.
"Look!" He says then
"I beat Super Mario Land
With just one hand!"

Mom also makes lists of activities we do and resources we have available which she submits to the local school board. The local board is very supportive of homeschooling. But boy, do they ever ask some dumb questions, especially about me since I am the oldest and high school age. They don't concentrate on our school work at all. They are more worried about other things—"Are they socializing?"—and they love to tell Mom, "Now, you realize Erin won't get a diploma, don't you?" Some other questions are, "Do you follow some kind of a schedule?" "Do you use a curriculum?" (Answer to both, NO!) But the question that takes the cake is, "How do you know they are learning if they don't take tests?"

Well, in the first place, everyone, even the littlest baby, is constantly learning, and you certainly don't see little babies taking tests, do you? Also, I *do* take tests, for example when I'm competing in a contest—and I do well on them. Still, the school board's question brings up an interesting subject. How do I learn?

Horsing around in school

When most people say they horse around, they mean goof off, act up, and generally misbehave. Not me, though! When I say horse around in school, I mean I literally horse around.

With my family's method of unschooling, everyone just does what interests them. Since my abiding interest is horses, I horse around. Now, I'll bet you are thinking, "But how can she learn anything by doing that?" Well, it all depends on what one wants to learn. *You* might not know the difference between a snaffle and a hackamore and might not care either, but you probably have a strong interest in something—maybe dogs, cats, crafts, reading books, or whatever—that you could learn a lot from. Mine is horses. I manage to cover most school subjects by doing work concerned with horses or two of my other main interests, 4-H and soccer.

I have always liked horses (what little girl hasn't?) and about a year after my family moved to our farm my parents bought two ponies, Brandy and Surprise, for us to learn on. Brandy was a real sweet old pony who had put up with lots of kids during her lifetime and knew exactly how to train them. At first all she would do was walk around the barnyard. When she decided we would not fall off, she would trot.

Brandy also believed in training adults. My dad decided to ride her one night. The field he rode her in was on a steep hill and there are four big, old apple trees with overhanging limbs in it so we call it the orchard. Dad told Brandy to "Giddy-up" and she did just that. She tore up the hill, ducked under the tree branches, and when my Dad ducked under the branches the saddle started to slip to one side. Dad couldn't get his balance and ended up underneath her belly as she galloped up the field with my whole family laughing our heads off (ha ha clunk) at the bottom.

So, you can certainly see what a good primary education I got. When I was eleven, I got a job offer from my neighbor, Tom Albrecht, who had opened a riding stable and needed someone to answer phones and help out around the place. He paid me two dollars an hour and for an eleven-year-old that was pretty good money. I started going down there on Friday afternoons to answer the phone and take messages. On the weekends, I would help out with the horses, schedule rides, bill customers, and do whatever else needed doing—which could be just about anything! By working there, I earned money to pay for my various projects and I also got to meet a lot of interesting people.

Also, I've learned a lot of valuable skills through my work there. When I first started, I thought, "There's no way I'll ever figure out what's going on." I mean, I didn't even know the names of the horses! But after about a month I knew all the names of the horses, where all the trails led to, what kind of riders to put on each horse, and how to get to Elk Mountain from D.C. I even learned how to figure the tax customers owe on each ride.

I learned a lot of my riding skills from working there, too. The guides and a few customers were excellent riders who were usually happy to share what they knew with me. Right from the beginning I got to go out on trail rides at least once a weekend, basically just for fun. After I had been working there about a year and a half, one of the guides broke his leg and I began leading trail rides on my own. Riding four to six different horses for seven to twelve hours straight, two days running, is bound to teach anyone how to ride!

Elk Mountain Trails is surrounded by woods and is about ten minutes from the C & O (Chesapeake and Ohio) Canal. I would take people out on hour-long rides through the woods, or a one-and-a-half or two hour ride on the C & O Canal towpath. When I talked to people over the phone to schedule them for rides, they obviously couldn't see me. Sometimes it came as a surprise to them that I was so young; when they met me, they could not believe I was the same person they had talked to on the phone. Then there were some people who simply did not realize my age, even after they met me. I have always tended to act older than I am and I guess they just didn't think someone my age would be taking people out on rides on their own. I mean, I had people asking me what *college* I went to at age twelve. Others thought I was a jockey, I guess because I was small. I can't begin to count the number of times people asked me if I rode at a nearby racetrack, CharlesTown Races.

Photo by Amy Mento

I also got asked a lot of interesting questions on trail rides. Usually, people just wanted to know about their horses or the canal or Harpers Ferry National Park which is right across the river. Every once in a while someone would ask a real oddball. The one I best remember was asked by a boy; I guess he was around fourteen or so. These groups of inner city youth were coming up on Friday afternoons and I would teach them how to groom a horse, how to feed it, and how to saddle it. Then we would go out on a ride which was always exciting. Try going riding with about ten teenagers and four adults, none of whom know anything about horses, and you will see what I mean. The equivalent is driving down the freeway at sixty-five miles per hour with everyone else on the road being a first time driver. Anyway, we were riding down the road to the canal and this guy asks, "Um, if I found a horse up in the woods just running around loose, would it just already know how to ride? I mean, could I just jump on its back?" It took me a while to answer that one, mainly because it is just so obvious to me that 1) there are no wild horses, to my knowledge anyway, running around Washington County, Maryland, and 2) I thought everyone knew horses had to be trained. Culture shock! But it works both ways. I would probably need directions to ride the Metro.

While I was working at Elk Mountain Trails, I was also growing and pretty soon my legs were long enough to wrap around Brandy's belly. I am not that tall but Brandy is a fairly small pony. So when I saw this ad in the 4-H newsletter, I thought it sounded great: "Will loan to an experienced rider, a nine-year-old Quarterhorse Gelding; Bay, 15 hands. English or Western, has not been worked in a year. Fat and needs conditioning. Would make a good 4-H Horse project."

I responded to the ad, and Nick came on February 8, 1989. My life has not been the same since! Nick is my favorite teacher and he has taught me many valuable lessons. He is blind in his left eye and has a tendency to spook at things he can't see. I worked with him at home with obstacles to help him overcome his fears. Last winter Nick and I took lessons (paid for with the money I had made working at Elk Mountain Trails) to learn to jump. Neither Nick nor I had any idea what we were doing, which made for some interesting experiences. This past year, I went to three shows with Nick. At the first two we got disqualified from our over-fences class because of too many refusals. (You are only allowed three chances to get your horse to jump over the fence and if he refuses to go, you are disqualified from that class.) But by the time county fair came around, Nick and I were working as a team and came in first. We ended up as year-end English high-point novices for Frederick County 4-H.

Nick's owners finally came up to visit him on the day after Christmas and they brought me a present. When I opened the red-ribboned box, I found his papers. They had given Nick to me! They said they thought I deserved to have him because I had done so much work with him. That was such a fantastic present.

I have learned many lasting and memorable lessons from Nick. He has taught me much about horses and safe riding in the almost three years that I have known him and he has taught me to work hard to accomplish my goals. Whether it is getting back on again after a fall, helping a timid rider become more confident, or writing a difficult speech, I know that if I take things one step at a time I can accomplish anything!

My other equine is Count Suleyn, an Arabian that I bought in November, 1989, and trained myself, teaching him to walk, trot, canter, back, move away from my legs, and all the other things he needed to know. The next summer I helped out on the farm that I bought him from, working with green horses, halter breaking foals, and doing whatever else they needed.

A lot of people ask me how I can stand to be around my parents all the time and have them teaching me everything. The answer is, they *don't*. I learn on my own or from other people quite a bit. My parents don't know anything about horses so I go to others. This spring, for instance, I worked with my riding instructor, helping her break green horses and work with spoiled ones. This was my "school work."

I could design a curriculum entirely around horses if I needed to. For example, English could be writing essays about horses, reading books and magazines about horses, doing book reports on the books and magazines I had read and giving oral reports on my horse.

Science is easy: I study the law of gravity by observing what happens when my horse goes one way and I go another. (Result: THUMP!) And don't forget the law of inverse relations (Murphy's Law) which states that the cleaner you are and the sooner you want to go riding and the more you want to impress someone, the filthier your horse will be. Behavioral psychology is studied hands on by working with my horses and younger siblings. (Okay, they are not horses but they are still animals, aren't they?) Convincing a three-year-old Arabian that a saddle does not bite and that no, that tree over there won't eat him, calls for some delicate handling. So does persuading a half-blind horse to jump strange looking fences when, really, it is much easier just to stop and go around them. Veterinary science: I have to know how to take care of my horse if something happens to him, and what to do to *prevent* anything from happening. Reproductive science is taken care of by learning about breeding mares, what to do at a foaling, etc.

Math: Now, admittedly we are not talking about calculus here, but some kind of math is involved in everything. I have to keep track of expenses, balance my checkbook, figure out how many hours I spend working with my horse for my 4-H records, and I also have to figure how much grain I am giving him.

History is full of equines. Pick up any book about history and there is bound to be some mention of horses, even if it is just, "This culture had not domesticated horses." From winning battles to starting feuds and helping people plow fields and get places, horses have had a lot to do with human history.

So you see, I could plan a whole curriculum around horses, but I have so many other interests I don't need to. Which brings me to...

Getting a kick out of school

Whapp! Bam! Thump!

No, I am not watching old *Batman* re-runs. I am playing soccer. I started playing when I was seven years old and have not stopped since! In addition to playing, I also coach a girls' team of six- and seven-year-olds and when I have time, I referee. I have played for Boonsboro American Youth Soccer Organization (AYSO) since I was nine. What is different about AYSO—as compared to more competitive teams where the only object is winning—is that every kid, no matter how good or bad, plays at least half of every game. Boonsboro is fairly small, and I basically played with the same group of kids since I started, so when they were old enough to play high school soccer, naturally, I wanted to too!

Photo by Sandi Roberts

My parents talked to the Junior Varsity coach and he did not have a problem with me playing, so then they talked to the varsity coach and athletic director, and they didn't have any problems with me playing either. Finally they talked to the principal, who said if the coaches didn't mind then he didn't care. So come first practice, I was out sweating and grunting with everyone else. There were times, like when we were doing a two mile run, running suicides, or doing an obstacle course, when I wondered if I was totally crazy. (The obstacle course consisted of six people getting in a line; on my turn I had to lay on my belly, then get up and jump three hurdles, crawl under a bench, move six soccer balls ten yards, then sprint back as fast as I could.) But most of it I enjoyed. The best part was that I got my own cheering section at the games.

I got a lot of attention not because I didn't go to school, but because I was the only girl. Being the only girl didn't bother me at all. I had been playing with these guys for years and most of that time I had been the only girl on the team. It did lead to some interesting situations though, like when we were playing an away game and the other team didn't unlock the girls' bathroom. Or when we were having a team meeting in the guys' locker room, and the entire football team came in.

After the season ended, Coach Scott, the athletic director, who also coached the track teams, asked me to run indoor track. When he put my name on his roster, someone at the state office saw it and decided that since I was not "physically attending school" I could not run and this fall I was not allowed to play high school soccer either.

But I continued to play high school *age* soccer, which basically means that the same high school teams play, but because of certain technical rules, they are coached by someone different. I played indoor soccer this winter, and this spring I am playing with the guys on the varsity team outdoors in a local non-school sponsored league. Plus, I am playing for an under-nineteen West Virginia-Maryland select team. I am the only girl there, too, and I am having a blast!

Physically speaking

A lot of the things I enjoy doing, and yes, much of my "schoolwork," involves outdoor, physical activities like soccer or horseback riding. Nobody has ever accused me of being a "dumb jock" (probably because I run my mouth too much!) but I have frequently been asked, "Don't you ever do any real schoolwork?" and "How can you learn stuff like math by just doing what you want?"

Well, hey! First off I *do* occasionally do "real" book work, when I see a need for it. And even though most of my favorite things to do are outside activities, I also enjoy many inside things. I like to do pencil drawings and various crafts, like decorated beeswax candles, painted T-shirts, etc.

My absolutely favorite, most enjoyed, best loved thing to do, though, is read. I love to read anything and everything! Books are everywhere in my house— on the floor, the chairs, the table, the bookcase. Sometimes what I read pertains to a project I'm working on; other times it's fiction. I read anything from science fiction to mysteries to horse stories to biographies.

I do wonder, though: What makes so many people think that the physical and mental must be separated?

A baby's first words and first steps are greeted with equal enthusiasm. You never hear a baby's parents say, "Now Johnny, you've been playing with your toes for half an hour. Don't you think you should practice saying 'Da Da'?" Babies don't make any distinction between physical and mental activities. It's all the same, just a new game, something else to learn and discover about life.

Babies learn about life hands-on, by looking, touching, and generally getting into everything. As a baby, I was allowed freedom to discover my surroundings without being confined to a playpen. As a teenager, I continue to learn in an uncoercive, unrestrained environment. Adults learn the same way, given the opportunity. I found a short article in the July 27, 1992 issue of *Newsweek*. It was written about the Olympics, but I think it reinforces the point I'm trying to make, that the physical and mental parts of life are not separate, but each very much a part of the other:

> The athletes of Barcelona may seem to be all brawn and speed, bulging quadriceps and blurred legs. But in fact they are much more. From the batter poised to let loose with his Louisville Slugger to the gymnast reaching back for an uneven bar she cannot even see, they are all Isaac Newtons in cleats or leotards, unconsciously calculating trajectories and forces and accelerations...

While I'm certainly no Olympic athlete, I do enjoy being outdoors, working with my animals, playing soccer, riding horses, etc. Doing all these things doesn't mean I'm not using my mind. Instead of sitting at a desk, working on math problems that have no meaning because they have been taken out of their context and reduced to meaningless scribbles on paper, I am working on what I want to work on, learning what I need to learn, in the best possible manner for me: an independent, self-directed study program that allows me to follow my interests, using a hands-on method of learning. Unschooling.

My friends

My friends are both older and younger than me. Through soccer and 4-H I get to meet a lot of friends my age. The friends I hang out with on a regular basis, though, tend to be people, both older and younger, who share a common *interest* rather than a common age.

One of my most interesting friends is Nancy Wright. She says she's my younger friend. I can't tell you her age, but she has two daughters in their twenties whom she homeschooled when they were younger. She also has a twelve-year-old son, Mike, who keeps trying to convince her to homeschool him. Nancy started her own saddlery business, North Shield Saddlery, a few years ago. I go over to help her with special projects, like making moccasin kits for girl scouts or custom designing saddle pads, or just to talk. Nancy knows a lot of interesting things, and anything she doesn't know she knows where to find out. This fall she is going to attend a local community college to get a degree in park management.

Nancy likes horses and has an Appaloosa mare, Rosie, whom she spoils rotten. When she has a question about horses she calls me since she hadn't been around them a lot until the last few years. She also likes to tell me that I'm not socializing enough and that I should go to school, "not to learn, because I know you're too smart for that, but just to meet more people." I have a very simple answer to that. I'm so busy meeting people, going places, and doing things, that I don't have time to waste on non-essentials like school.

With my soccer team I have played games in Pennsylvania, West Virginia, Virginia, Maryland, and New York. Through 4-H I have been all over Maryland, to Richmond, Virginia to compete in the National Bike Rodeo, and this December I get to go to the National 4-H congress in Chicago. This will be a great chance to meet even more new people from all across the nation and compete for college scholarships.

So anyway, Nancy, I don't think you need to worry any about my social life! In addition to my "younger" friends like Nancy I also have friends that are chronologically younger. One of these is Meagan Heneghan, a twelve-year-old, red headed, fun loving, positively crazy girl who started homeschooling last year. Meagan is in my 4-H club and raises dairy goats. We swap goat information and help each other get our goats ready for shows. We also like to talk about what obnoxious things our brothers have done lately, what so and so has been up to, and where the best places to go shopping are, not to mention all the absolutely have-to-tell-you's....like everything else that is going on!

Another friend of mine who is younger in years is Jed Dearing. Jed is ten and has been homeschooled all his life. He is really interested in horses, but hasn't been around them much. I've given him some riding lessons on my horse, Nick, and also on my sister's pony, Thunder. Jed also likes to read a lot of the same kinds of books that I used to read, like *Hardy Boys* books, as well as some of the ones I still like to read and re-read and re-read and re-read—*The Black Stallion, The Three Investigators, The Hobbit.*

Where I live there are not a lot of older homeschoolers. This year I went to a nine-week homeschoolers' co-op school on Tuesdays along with the rest of my family. It was the second time homeschoolers in the area had run a co-op school. How it worked was that parents and older kids volunteered to teach one or more classes. Then Ann Bearese, who coordinated, sent out registration forms listing class choices. Each family paid thirty dollars to attend, which helped to cover expenses.

We met one day a week for nine weeks. Each day was broken up into four classes of thirty-five minutes each. The first semester I taught a crafts class. Then the second, I taught two classes, one on safety and another on group singing. Some of the other classes offered were Family Math, French, Recorder playing, Machines, and Young Astronauts. The classes were divided into two age groups, six to nine (the one I taught) and nine and up. The age groups weren't hard and fast; some six-year-olds went in the nine and up classes, and some ten-year-olds went in the younger group, depending on how they felt about each class. The parents also took turns leading a play group for the very young children.

Anyone who didn't feel like going to class, as long as they weren't being disruptive, could just wander around or get together with friends. And since most of the classes were geared to a younger age group, for the last half of each day, all of the older kids (the number varied, but it usually ended up at about five) would go off in a room and play games, tell jokes, and listen to music like Bryan Adams (my choice) and NWA (not my choice) while we got away from various siblings and parents.

Concentration: Bicycle

Concentration. The letter B. Bike begins with the letter B.

Have you ever played concentration? You pick a letter and name all the things you can think of that start with that letter. Concentration, of course, is also being able to focus on one subject intently. Since I don't do "schoolwork" as such, when I do need to study something I can concentrate just on that subject without distractions. Sometimes it almost seems like cheating, having the advantage of being able to work on one particular project rather than nine different subjects at one time. A good example of how this works to my advantage is the National 4-H Bicycle Safety Rodeo.

Bicycle safety rodeos consist of contestants riding their bikes through a six-station obstacle course with penalty points given every time they mess up, plus a parts identification test and a written exam. These rodeos are excellent opportunities for everyone involved to learn about safe riding, rules of the road, and bike maintenance—and have a fun time doing it! I have been on the planning committee for our county rodeo for the last two years. I really enjoy working with the other 4-H'ers, helping them learn about bicycle safety. I feel like it is one way I can start to pay back 4-H for all it has done for me.

I have been participating in bicycle rodeos since I was eleven, when I saw a notice in the 4-H newsletter about a rodeo. I had no idea what a bike rodeo was but I like to ride my bike so my brothers and I went. The top 4-H'ers in the rodeo would get to go on to the 4-H state fair rodeo. (This local rodeo was sponsored by the Kiwanis club and was open to anyone, not just 4-H'ers.) Even though it was a freezing cold day, there were a lot of kids there. So imagine my surprise when a couple of weeks later, I got a letter saying I was one of only two 4-H'ers who had participated so I was going to get to compete in the state rodeo.

At the state rodeo, I still did not have any idea what I was doing but I ended up winning my class anyway. The next year I won again and missed my age group championship by five points, equivalent to one test question.

Photo by Amy Mento

The next year I wasn't going to let that happen to me so I read all the bike books I could get my hands on. I love to read anyway so it was just a matter of reading books on bicycle-related subjects instead of fiction. One of my favorite books is an older one, *Glenn's Book of Bicycle Maintenance.* Much of the information in it is outdated but it contains detailed blow ups of every part of the bike showing exactly what they do and how to fix them.

When the contest came around all my reading paid off. I won my age group plus I had the best total overall score the officials could remember.

Once you win your age group, you cannot compete again until you reach the next age group. (Juniors are ages eight to ten, Intermediates are eleven to thirteen, and Seniors are fourteen to eighteen as of January first of the current year.) Since I was no longer eligible to compete as an Intermediate and had another year to go until I was a Senior, my county extension agent got permission from the state office for me to go ahead and compete as a Senior. So I competed as a Senior and won against kids who were up to six years older than me. The Senior winner gets a free, all-expenses-paid trip to the national competition. I was filling out the form after the contest and I had to sign that yes, I was a member of 4-H over the age of fourteen and under nineteen as of January first. Well, I couldn't sign that. The upshot of it was that, even though they had said I could compete, I had to give my trophy back and they disqualified me. Just because I was too young. I was so mad.

I went back the next year and won the Senior age group again with, for the fifth year in a row, the best test score in my age group, and this time I was old enough to go to the Nationals. I thought everyone else there would be, like, pro riders, and then there would be *me*. So I totally immersed myself in bike books studying for the test, and went around to bicycle shops and asked them to show me the parts on my parts identification list. I practiced riding through obstacles for a couple of hours a day for a week while the Boonsboro soccer camp was going on. Afterward, I practiced forty-five minutes on the nights when I had to coach soccer, and an hour and a half on other nights.

When I got to the contest, which was an all-expenses-paid trip to Virginia, everyone was comparing what kind of make-up work they had been assigned for school. When I said I didn't have to do any make-up work, and that my school work for the last week and a half had consisted of getting ready for the bike rodeo, their faces turned green!

I ended up winning the contest which shocked me and everyone else too. A large part of my winning was all the studying I had done. The second place winner beat me by two points on the riding skills, but I ended up beating him by thirty-three points overall. I had a perfect score on the parts identification and only missed two questions on the test.

Now, the reason I made you sit through this dissertation is not just so I could brag. I also wanted to point out that even though I don't usually do structured schoolwork, I can nevertheless choose whenever I want to concentrate on one subject, take tests, and be "structured."

Photo by Sandi Roberts

A bicycle safety demonstration

I have a lot of freedom in my education by being able to learn what I want, when I want. I enjoy learning and since I have a reason to learn things in the first place, I remember them. I do eventually plan to go to college, possibly to become a lawyer, but in the meantime I am getting the very best education possible: *real life!*

Erin Cosgrove
Pittsburgh, Pennsylvania

In the Middle of Everything

What I'm Doing Now

Gosh, where to start? Well, I graduated from college, got married, bought a house, adopted two dogs and a cat, got my MBA, and have held a couple of different full-time jobs. I guess that makes me (almost) normal!

Erin and her favorite teacher, Nick

Photo by Allen Ellis

My husband, Ken, and I got married almost six years ago. We live in Pittsburgh, Pennsylvania with two retired racing greyhounds and a cat who thinks she's in charge of all of us. Ken is a political science professor, and I'm a product planning manager for Medrad, a medical device company.

Ken and I first met in 1995—only two years after the first *Real Lives* came out—and I think we're both amazed at how quickly this tenth anniversary has come up. It's a been a busy, crazy, fun and exciting time as I've transitioned from being an unschooling teenager, to a college student, to a working, married adult. Here's a little of what I've been up to for the past decade…

A Busy Ten Years

School

"Are you a genius or something?" The answer is no – unless it involves reasons to procrastinate! But I did get asked this a few times after I started taking classes at Hagerstown Community College in Maryland. Most people just assumed I was a normal college student, but every once in a while I'd be asked my age and got a few raised eyebrows when I said I was sixteen. In my family sixteen is a very important age—we lived in the middle of nowhere, so having a driver's license was the prerequisite to starting college!

I started with a few "just for fun" classes—drama and public speaking. It was a great way to meet people and get my feet wet without a lot of pressure. After the first semester, I went full-time and took overloads during a couple of semesters, plus tested out of some of the intro classes to graduate in three semesters with an Associates degree in communications. I was one of a half-dozen people to finish with straight A's.

After I finished at the community college, I wasn't sure where I wanted to transfer, so I took a year off and interned for my congressman in his district office, and at the National 4-H Center near Washington, D.C., before transferring to Bethany College in West Virginia.

Bethany had a strong communications program, and after spending time in Washington I was very interested in politics, so I decided to double major in communications and political science. Bethany was great about transferring all my credits and brought me in as a full junior, but the double major was a big commitment and I knew that I didn't want to spend more than another two years in school. So I worked out a schedule that let me overload by one class most semesters, and talked to a couple of professors about testing out of the intro history and political science classes. (I highly recommend this approach if your school is flexible—it's much cheaper and it lets you skip the boring intro classes.) Fortunately, they were open to the idea! With this boost to my credit hours, I finished in two years, and was second in my graduating class.

"The Attendance Hall of Shame"

When I was in 4-H, we had a motto that said "Learn by Doing". As an unschooler, I've always thought that made a lot of sense, and I carried that over into my college years.

I've always been involved in a lot of activities, but my senior year of college was really crazy. I was volunteering for a political campaign, serving on the Board of Trustees for the National 4-H Council, active in several campus groups, national secretary of Collegiate 4-H—you get the picture!

I decided that being involved in all this stuff was far more important to me than actually going to class. Luckily I was at a small school, and could talk to all my professors and explain what my schedule was going to be like, and that I was likely to miss at least a third of their classes. The professors I had were supportive and let me do a lot of creative tinkering with the class syllabi. I ended up writing several papers in airports and hotel rooms, and had to take tests before or after the rest of the class. I didn't get much sleep, but it was a terrific experience. I even managed to pull straight As for the semester! My friend Greg Slaby was in my economics class and loved to tease me about how little I was there. Right before graduation, he presented me with his very own "Attendance Hall of Shame" award for having managed to miss the most classes and still graduate!

"I Guess I Have to Do Math Now…"

After being out of college and working for a year, I decided to go back to grad school for my MBA. With Ken teaching at a nearby college, I wanted to stay in the Pittsburgh area, so Carnegie Mellon was my first choice. It has one of the top twenty MBA programs in the country and is renowned for its quantitative approach to teaching (read: lots and lots of math in *every* class!).

Thank goodness for persuasive public speaking classes! I managed to convince the admissions committee that despite the fact that my entire college math coursework had consisted of freshman Intro to Algebra, I could handle a program that is one of the two most quantitative in the country (right up there with MIT) and required two semesters of engineering calculus before starting. I did have to take those two calc classes, and the first really quantitative grad classes were a struggle, but by the time I finished, I was volunteering to do the number crunching in our group projects and could read a spreadsheet upside down and backwards.

Working

My grandmother always tells people that I'm the grandchild who has always known exactly what I wanted to do and figured out how to get there. That's absolutely right, but I've also changed my mind about what I wanted quite a few times along the way! And that's especially true when it comes to my career.

I started college thinking I'd become a lawyer, but after job shadowing one, I decided it wasn't the right career for me. I had enjoyed doing publicity and event planning for 4-H, so my next idea was to do public relations. I've always heard that you should try to get someone to pay you to do the things you'd do for free. Well, I'll certainly talk for free, and I'm happy to write, so my goal coming out of college was to find someone to pay me to write and talk!

My first full-time job after college was with Sony Electronics, doing public relations and corporate communications. I did a lot of writing, a lot of talking, and had a lot of fun for a few years. However, I also learned that the communications team in a major corporation almost never gets to actually make decisions—they just get to tell other people about them. I'd rather be in the middle of everything, so I started looking to see what it would take to move into a core marketing position. Most of the people in these positions had MBAs and understood a lot about finance and business in addition to marketing. I decided that if I wanted to move into one of these jobs, I needed those same skills—and the degree would make it a lot easier to get hired—so I started in the part-time program at Carnegie Mellon. I left Sony and worked as a product manager (basically the business/technical side of marketing) for a couple of small companies while going to grad school, then worked for Fisher Scientific before joining Medrad.

One nice benefit of homeschooling is that I had a lot of real world experience under my belt before I started working full-time. Having worked at least part-time since I was eleven, acclimating to an office environment was pretty easy. I've generally been the youngest person in my department, so spending time with people of all different ages while growing up was a huge help in making the transition from college to work.

My job at Medrad is to help plan and develop new products. This means working with a lot of different types of people—from customers, to salespeople, finance, hardware and software engineers, etc. Plus, I have to coordinate with the medical divisions of several large companies, like GE, Philips, Siemens, and Toshiba, to make sure our new products work with theirs. I think my background as a homeschooler has helped me on the job in a couple of ways. First, I grew up spending time with people from very different backgrounds and perspectives, who didn't always agree on the best way to do things (can anyone say "unschoolers and curriculum-driven homeschoolers?"). This is extremely helpful when I'm trying to coordinate (and frequently negotiate!) between an engineer, a salesperson and a customer. Secondly, because I did a lot of hands-on, informal learning, I don't get intimidated if I need to learn about a new technology or a new market and there's no formal training or information available. I just figure that if I ask enough questions, it'll eventually start to make sense!

As you can imagine, I'm keeping pretty busy these days (not that that's really changed…). I'm traveling a lot—I was recently in Europe with two of our R&D engineers to research a potential new product—but fortunately, I have a great relaxation technique when I'm home. It has four legs, a mane and tail, and never, never, never asks me for anything that doesn't involve food, grooming, or a chance to trail ride!

Horses

My horses were leased out while I was in college and starting to work. I missed them, but was busy and didn't have any place to keep them, so I contented myself with taking an occasional trail ride or lesson. About three years ago, the family that had leased them couldn't keep them any longer, and I started looking for a place near Pittsburgh where they could stay. Since our lawn is about the size of a postage stamp, keeping them at home wasn't really an option! Fortunately, I was able to find the Ellis family, who have nine acres and were willing to keep Nick and Suleyn for me in exchange for riding privileges. It's been fun—the Ellises are unschoolers too, and Laura, seventeen, is about as horse crazy as I am. The two of us have gone to shows and horse seminars together. (Ken wisely goes to baseball games instead.)

At twenty-four, Nick has become something of a senior citizen. I don't jump him anymore, but he still loves to trail ride, and the Ellises occasionally take lessons on him.

Erin and Suleyn   *Photo by Allen Ellis*

In addition to a lot of trail rides, Suleyn and I have been attempting to learn dressage, a style of riding that emphasizes balance and precision, and we've started jumping again. We're taking jumping and dressage lessons and even did a couple of schooling (low-level competition) mini-trials last year. These are based on an old military training test and require the horse and rider to perform a dressage test pattern from memory, jump cross-country obstacles, and finish with a show jumping course. We have a lot to learn, but we had a blast!

Where Will I Go From Here?

Having just finished grad school about three years ago, I'm in the process of building my career. I like marketing and plan to stay in similar types of jobs for a while. I'm probably done with formal school—the next step would be a Ph.D. and I don't have any plans to teach, so I doubt that I'll go back for more. One teacher in the family is enough, and I don't have Ken's patience!

Ken and I would like to have kids in a few years and we're already getting asked if we'll homeschool. We think it's up to the (future) kids, but we're certainly planning to! As a college professor, Ken sees the results of the public school system every time he walks in the classroom, so he's very much in favor of homeschooling.

What I'd Think About Doing Differently

Math

It might have been helpful, or at least easier, if I had consistently done some formal math while unschooling, rather than just jumping into it during college. Of course, I say this knowing full well that even if I could do it over again, I'd still avoid it! And even if I had done it, I suspect I would have forgotten most of it by the time I actually needed to use it in grad school.

I do think that despite my lack of rote knowledge, I built the skills to learn what I needed when I needed it—and that to me is a far more important skill than being able to find the area under a curve or some such nonsense. This holds true even for those people who do like math—my brother Brian will devour math problems (he recently finished a Master's degree in Computer Science and minored in math as an undergraduate), but detests writing papers and will do just about anything to avoid it. He's learned to write reasonably good papers, but like me with math, he's learned this on an "as-needed" basis.

College

Hindsight being twenty-twenty, I might have taken just a couple of courses at the community college and applied to four year schools as a freshman rather than a transfer student.

One of the things I didn't realize is how much tougher it is to get into the better four-year colleges as a transfer student. (Classes typically fill up with freshmen first, and then any available slots go to transfers.) I had really wanted to go to Carleton College in Minnesota, but got waitlisted. Not having come up with a good backup plan, I took a year off from school and did a couple of internships in the D.C. area before transferring to Bethany College. I'm very happy with how things turned out—I had a great time in D.C., met my husband at Bethany, and was admitted to a top tier grad school—but I do wish I'd known more about the admissions process ahead of time.

My Advice (for what it's worth…)

My one piece of advice is not to worry too much. I think a lot of homeschoolers (or at least homeschooling parents) tend to worry about whether they're doing enough of something—enough math, enough college preparation, enough socialization, etc. The homeschoolers I grew up with all took different routes to curriculum (or lack thereof), social activities, and college, but we've all managed to turn into semi-normal adults with jobs, families, and friends.

The Usual Questions

It's interesting how much public perception of homeschooling has changed in the last decade. Ten years ago, when I told people I homeschooled, it generally at least raised eyebrows. Now, it seems that almost everyone knows someone who is homeschooling. But since I've "graduated" from homeschooling, parents tend to ask me about what I did growing up. Here's a short list of some of their most frequent questions.

Q: But what about math?

A: I think that as long as you can do "real world" math you'll be okay. Everyone needs to know how to balance a checkbook, cook with fractions, and comparison shop. Beyond that, you can learn it when you need it. I spent the first three weeks of college algebra staring at the homework and crying because I didn't understand it. Fortunately, my dad could help me, but if you don't have a math-oriented parent, almost every school has a tutoring program. I struggled with adjustment, but was able to figure it out and get an A in the class.

Q: How about socialization?

A: This question and its variations (but what about the prom, yearbook, sports, etc.) is an oldie but goodie—lots of parents still seem to be concerned about this. Personally, I always thought that I had plenty of social opportunities through 4-H, co-op school and sports. I wasn't able to participate in high school sports after my freshman year, and I did miss that, but not enough to go back to school. Many states and school districts are more open to participation now, but it really depends on where you live. And even for kids who go to school, most socialization takes place outside of school—in clubs, teams, or just hanging out with friends. Homeschoolers have most of the same opportunities to meet and interact with people—as well as the time to do so during the day rather than sitting in a classroom.

Q: Can you get into college?

A: Absolutely! There are now lots of homeschoolers that have gone to college, and a few colleges have even started to recruit homeschoolers.

Q: But what if my kid doesn't want to do X...?

A: If it's not life threatening, I wouldn't worry about it. I prefer not to do abstract math, my brother Brian prefers not to write, and my sister Tara really doesn't like to spell. We'll all go to great lengths to avoid doing the things we dislike but we can do them when we have to. And if we can't, we figure out how to learn what we need when we need it.

Q: But what if my kid only wants to do X...?

A: Cool! Your kid has something they're interested in, and will probably manage to learn a little bit about lots of different subjects through this interest. As an unschooler, I was able to spend a lot of time focusing on the things I was interested in. This wasn't typically traditional academics—I was more likely to be riding my horses than working on a science project, but I think this opportunity to focus on my interests helped me learn to put diverse pieces of information together, and work through a project from start to finish without a lot of supervision. These skills came in handy when I went to college and began working full time.

Q: Will you homeschool your kids?

A: Well, the final decision is up to our (future) kids, but we certainly hope to!

Craig Roberts, Erin's father
Washington County, Maryland

When Can an Unschool Parent Declare Success?

In 1993, Grace asked the question of eleven teenagers and their parents, "Do you have to be a genius to unschool?" Everyone had the same answer, but each described in their own unique words why that answer was "no." Ten years later, as a parent of five highly educated unschoolers, I ask myself, "When can an unschool parent declare success?"

Parents who do school traditionally declare a kid's education a success at graduation—when the high school diploma or the college degree is presented as irrefutable proof. My mother (who never approved of unschooling) reluctantly acknowledged that unschooling must work when our third child graduated from community college with a 4.0 just like Erin had done five years earlier. While feeling proud of both the college degree and the grades, I think there is much more to define educational success than degrees or grades. A degree does not guarantee that one will be a happy, confident and competent individual who is able to get along in the world. A child who obtains neither good grades or a college degree can still be a tremendous success. An unschool education is far more than a terminal degree—it is just the beginning of a life filled with a love of learning.

In the last twenty years, we have had many unschooling moments when we could pause and declare "success." When your oldest daughter wins a national competition, your oldest son spends eighteen hours straight on a video game and masters that game, your middle son who loves soccer manages to excel on three soccer teams simultaneously, your youngest daughter takes off on a Puerto Rican vacation with a friend in the middle of the school year, and your youngest son gets a main part in a community theatre production; you say, if they weren't unschooled, it probably never would have happened. You also take pride in the fact that in each of these endeavors and hundreds of others, they were able to devote as much of their energies as they desired, without interfering with "studies", requiring extra work, having to make up for missed lessons, or sending a note to the teacher. It doesn't stop there. When they go out into the working world and get complemented on their good attitude, confidence, and competence, you know it may not have been that way if they had not unschooled. So, when can an unschool parent declare success? Almost immediately after they make the decision to unschool and many, many more times during the rest of their lives.

Jeremiah Gingold, 16
Midpines, California

Homeschooling for Peace and Justice

For some reason, most of my friends and family find it difficult to call me "Jeremiah," so I respond to a variety of nicknames ranging from "Miah" to "Jay." On the other hand, I tend to ignore people who refer to me as "Jerry" or "Jeremy"—I can't stand either one! I'm a fairly "normal" teenager, if that's not an oxymoron. I say *fairly* normal because I have homeschooled all my life except for very brief stints in school: three weeks in third grade, two months in junior high, and half a year attending an alternative public high school two to three days a week.

Photo by Pam Gingold

I live in Midpines, California, about forty miles west of Yosemite National Park. Midpines is so tiny that you can't accurately call it a town or even a village. To be exact, it consists of a Post Office, a small store where you can buy gas and snack foods, and a few paved roads. Most of the population lives off the main roads, on one-lane dirt roads. We live on a hill, a mile and a half from the highway (Scenic 140) in a very isolated area, with neighbors few and far between. We are about ten miles from the town of Mariposa, which was built during the Gold Rush (and hasn't progressed much since!).

I have a variety of interests and hobbies. I care deeply about peace and social justice, and my family publishes a newsletter for peace-oriented homeschoolers. I spend a lot of time reading science fiction, medieval fantasy, and computer technical books. I enjoy playing role-playing games, especially

Dungeons and Dragons. I love video games of all sorts, I'm a pretty good computer programmer, and I'm interested in electronics. I enjoy mountain biking and going on hikes, since I live in a perfect area for both of these activities. I'm especially into rock music, mostly heavy metal and alternative rock. I spend a lot of time folding intricate Origami models, and I also build airplane and helicopter models from kits. I like cooking and eating interesting foods, drawing, and designing computer graphics. Oh yes, and let's not forget girls!

My family

My family is very different from the families of most people I know (of course, that may be because I live in such a small, conservative community). I'd be hard put to say whether it's better or worse, but I can say that my family is far from average.

My sister, Serena, who is two and a half years younger than me, has also been homeschooled her entire life. Serena and I have very different personalities and interests, and as a result we don't often get along. This is rather unfortunate, since due to our circumstances of homeschooling and geographic isolation we are virtually constant companions.

My parents are both free-lance writers. They often write for *Cobblestone*, a history magazine for kids, as well as for several non-fiction homeschooling publications. They are also working on ideas for children's books, and my mom is in the planning stages of a book about homeschooling. They both serve on the Board of Directors for our state-wide homeschooling organization.

They were teenagers during the sixties and they're still sort of counter-cultural (as they put it). This led them to look into "radical" ideas such as home birth (I was born at home), breast-feeding (ditto), and homeschooling (naturally). My life is basically pretty different from that of my peers. My father doesn't go off to work every morning, and neither does my mother. We're not into strict schedules and rules that are carved in stone. (My dad has second thoughts about *that* sometimes!) Thanks to all of these things, I get along pretty well with my parents; I don't have a lot to rebel against. That's not to say that I *always* get along with them; we have our share of arguments, but at least we don't usually fight over the petty things my friends and *their* parents fight about.

Why homeschool?

Many people wonder, "Why homeschool?" Of course, every homeschooler has his or her own personal reasons for homeschooling. In my case, I have two basic reasons (there are more detailed and philosophical reasons—but they don't often come into play in my everyday life): Freedom and Time.

Having a lot of freedom in my life is a necessity. I need the freedom to learn things in my own way, at my own pace. I have my own unique way of learning, as does everyone, and I feel the public school system could not possibly accommodate my learning style.

For example, I learned to read in a way that was completely natural to me, but might have perplexed many teachers. Nobody ever told me that I should learn how to read by or at a certain age. Rather, when I was four years old, I decided, on my own, that reading was a skill that I needed and wanted. So, whenever my mom would read to me I would ask her what certain words said. I would also ask about rules of pronunciation and spelling, from "I before E, except after C," to silent letters. I already knew all of my letters, and how to pronounce them individually; I just didn't know the rules for stringing them together into actual words. My mom was a little puzzled as to why I wanted to know all these rules, when I didn't even know how to read yet, but she patiently answered every question.

Then one day I got a difficult puzzle at a yardsale. It was a challenge for me, as it consisted of 125 pieces and at that point I had never solved anything greater than a 24-piece Sesame Street one. For the next eight weeks, I worked on that puzzle every day, refusing to even look at a book or try to read. At the end of nearly two months of focusing on nothing but doing the puzzle over again and again, I picked up a "beginner" book and began reading out loud. I think that during the time that I was working on the puzzle I was also simultaneously working on the puzzle of reading in my subconscious mind, fitting together all the pieces I had organized into a cohesive whole. In fact, I progressed so quickly that one week after learning to read, I was reading a third grade level book, *The Story of Harriet Tubman*. It was this book that sparked my interest in social justice. I don't think I've been seen far from a book—or a social cause—ever since.

I still learn in much the same manner. I'm not quite so single-minded as I once was. But I often spend months during which I don't work on a given subject, such as algebra, and then come back to it at the end of those months and find that some concept that had previously eluded me now makes perfect sense. Obviously, this is not something that the public school system could allow me to "get away with," since it is based on the faulty notion that everybody learns by the same processes. No wonder I homeschool!

Another aspect of freedom that is very important to me is being allowed to do or learn what I want, when I want to. When I was thirteen I enrolled in junior high as a kind of experiment. Because I live in such an isolated rural area, it tends to be rather hard to meet and make friends with other kids my age. I went to school in order to socialize and have fun. I knew that if school did not measure up in any way, I would be free to leave, and go back to homeschooling the next day.

I actually did very well in school and enjoyed myself (as much as it is possible to enjoy oneself in school), making friends and such. But after a few weeks I quit—because I found that school was beginning to encroach too heavily on my time and freedom. I had recently bought a mountain bike, and I was trying to learn to ride. However, I didn't even have time to *read* (and that's something I *always* make time for!), let alone ride a bike, what with homework assignments and early bedtime.

My time is my most valuable asset. I only have a finite amount of time (like everyone else), and I want to make the best possible use of it. In school your time is under the control of practically everybody *but* yourself. That's definitely one of my major reasons for not attending school. I refuse to spend my time doing their busywork and taking their tests. I feel that I have better things to do with my time; learning things that are important to me personally, that will enhance my life.

The legal technicalities

From shortly after we moved to Mariposa County eight years ago, until a little over a year ago, I was enrolled in an Independent Study Program (ISP), which is one of the ways to homeschool legally in California. When we moved here, the school officials began harassing us almost immediately, trying to get my sister and me into a public school. (We had been homeschooling "underground" in Los Angeles all my life up until then.) At that time the school district here didn't have any provisions for homeschooling. Very bluntly, they lied to us and threatened us. Since my parents knew the law and knew many people in the homeschooling movement, they resisted, and eventually were put in touch with the local alternative public school. My parents demanded that the alternative school start an ISP program for K-8, and before we knew it, the school board had voted to okay it.

We always homeschooled on our own terms through the program, refusing to comply with any testing requirements or to use school textbooks (we mostly use real books, not textbooks). We became good friends with the ISP teacher and her husband, the alternative school principal, and they have always supported us in our endeavors, even letting us use the school Xerox machine to copy our newsletters. All we had to do was visit with the teacher at school every week or so, where we used the computers and did craft projects, and we were free to homeschool as we wished. My mom also filled out a form each month saying we did at least four hours of "educational activities" every day, so the school district could collect ADA money for us. (Average Daily Attendance is the money the school district gets from the state for each child attending school.)

This worked out fine until I was of high school age. Then we suddenly learned that I was required by law to earn high school credits through the ISP. Since I was enrolled in the alternative school's ISP, I had to use the same GED workbooks as the other students (most of whom didn't have any academic goals beyond passing the GED). The principal refused to give me regular credits for any of my real work. For instance, articles that I wrote for our newsletter were not counted for social studies or English, but rather as "extra credit." Reading books such as *Asimov on Chemistry* was considered extra credit at best, while filling in the blanks in a fifth-grade-level workbook was considered to be vital to my education. I spent hours every day reading, but to get even *extra* credit for that I would have had to document each book, writing a report about it. I found this terribly intrusive. I started falling further and further behind on my studies due to the boredom. One day I finally sat up and asked myself, "Falling behind *whom?* Why am I allowing other people to play games with *my* life?"

At this point, I decided to quit the ISP. I was angry that the school was collecting thousands of dollars of ADA money for me every year, but not providing me with an education when I asked for one. (We had petitioned the school board to let me take at least a science class at the regular high school, but they refused unless I would attend school full-time.) And they wouldn't even allow me the chance or time to educate myself. It also seemed incredibly stupid for the school to require even *more* busywork at the stage of life where people finally begin to have their own serious interests and are beginning to develop their talents. I consider this another point against the public schools, and a good reason for teenagers to take responsibility for their own lives.

So we filled out an R-4 form (private school affidavit), another way to homeschool legally in California. This is a very simple form requiring only the name and address of your "school," the persons designated as principal and teacher, and the number of students in each grade. There is no fee. Our whole family felt such a sense of freedom after filing this form! It turned our home into a private school, which we call "Natural High" (pun intended). We still have to keep attendance records and make sure we cover a "core curriculum," but now I have absolute freedom to do what I want with my education.

Autodidactism

With all of this freedom and time comes a lot of responsibility. The fact that I can choose what I want to do and when I want to do it also means that I'm taking on the responsibility for my own education. In school your work is graded; you know at all times whether you're "passing," "failing," or just scraping by. In other words, someone lets you know when you're supposedly sufficiently "educated." Because I don't follow a set curriculum, I have no such simple way of knowing when I know "enough" about a subject; no one grades me on my work. Thus, I am not misled by a false sense of security—but on the other hand I myself have to be aware of exactly what I need to learn in order to accomplish my goals. Sometimes I get a little worried that I'm not learning everything that I need to know. However, although I may not be getting your average, generic education, I am learning something all the time, *and* I know I'm capable of learning whatever I need to.

When I was younger my parents could easily help me with just about anything I wished to learn. However, as I grow older, I find I have more interests that differ from my parents' interests. When it comes to some of my non-academic interests, they sometimes have no expertise at all. When this happens, I generally have two choices: A) I can find other teachers or B) I can teach myself. Since I live in such a remote place, I usually choose the latter course of action (unless I just find that I'm not as interested in the subject as I had previously thought). Two examples of my autodidactism are in the areas of algebra and computer science.

My parents (especially my dad) have always been able to help me with mathematics, but lately I have become impatient with being taught. Especially in the past year or so, I have preferred to teach myself from textbooks with minimal outside help. I have found that learning from a textbook without the aid of a teacher is often more difficult, but I'm rewarded with a definite sense of accomplishment when I finally "get" a concept without help from any external source. Best of all, I have the knowledge that I fully understand anything which I have taught myself.

An even better example is computer science, since neither of my parents are really into computers. A couple of years ago, I inherited an Apple II+ personal computer from my grandfather, along with all of the computer manuals and several textbooks. I have always wanted to learn how to program, so I immediately set out to teach myself Applesoft Extended BASIC. At first I found the technical manuals and programming books to be dry and boring. However, I badly wanted to learn programming, so I persevered. I read and read until I achieved a rudimentary knowledge of programming. In fact, after a time I actually began to *enjoy* reading technical books, and then my programming skills began to progress by leaps and bounds. My first programs were rather simple, generally consisting of a few PRINT statements, FOR loops, etc. As the months passed, however, my programming skills improved dramatically until I was capable of writing complex programs for a variety of purposes. One of my favorites is a drawing program which is pretty sophisticated—considering that it's written in Applesoft BASIC, which doesn't have any of the convenient graphics commands.

My other favorite is a utility-type program which helps to generate characters for Dungeons and Dragons. I've originated some pretty neat algorithms for the D & D program, including a method of creating low-resolution (40x24) graphics in text mode (the Apple doesn't use graphics characters, so this isn't as easy as it sounds!) and a routine which allows free form input. At this point, I'm pretty satisfied with my BASIC programming, and now I feel ready to move on to a new language; the limits of BASIC are starting to frustrate me. For that matter, so are the limits of my current computer. I'd like to get a 386 or 486 IBM-compatible with Super VGA graphics, but that's somewhat out of my price range at this time.

I am really interested in programming advanced computer graphics (such as *can* be created on a decrepit and outdated microcomputer like the Apple II+). This is extremely difficult, involving a formidable amount of time. That's because BASIC is basically very slow. The only way to write programs that execute at high speed is by using machine language. Therefore I'm trying to teach myself 6502 assembly language. Learning assembly language is especially hard for two reasons: A) it is not a high-level language like BASIC—the commands consist of three-letter mnemonic codes (like "LDA") which stand for certain mathematical and program control operations, and B) one must be proficient in hexadecimal (base 16) arithmetic (sounds impressive, huh?!).

I am currently working out a contract with my friend Jarrod Almorode to edit a Dungeons and Dragons database that he is compiling. Although I'm not getting a lot of money or fame out of this deal, it's still worthwhile to me since I do get my name on the title screen, ninety cents per unit sold, and (most important) experience which will be useful for a job or college.

I'm seriously considering a major in computer science for college, and I'm also interested in exploring Artificial Intelligence and Virtual Reality. If you've seen *Lawnmower Man* you'll know what I'm talking about.

College

I tend to be pretty inclined toward academic subjects, so I've decided that I want to go to college. It's not prohibitively difficult for a homeschooler to get into college, although it *is* necessary to work hard at it. Most colleges consider SAT scores to be very important, so I've made up my mind to study for it, using several books I picked up at a library booksale. Although it goes against my principles to study for a *test*, as opposed to learning for the sake of knowledge, I feel that such an approach may be necessary in order to get an appropriately high score on the SAT. A really high score may be necessary for me, as I not only need complete financial assistance, but I'd like to be able to go to a top school like MIT or Caltech, and I'll be facing a phenomenal amount of competition. Not only should my test scores be extremely high, but I should probably do something fairly spectacular as well, like building a computer from scratch, or writing and marketing my own computer program. From what I understand, I also need to document a good deal of community service, and get several letters of recommendation.

Curriculum

I don't really follow a curriculum or schedule in my studies. Instead, I do my "school" work whenever and however I wish. I almost never actually sit down at a desk for six hours while I study each subject in turn. Usually I cover only one or two of the subjects that I'm currently studying. On one day I might feel like doing English and math, the next I may want to study math and science, and perhaps do nothing at all the day after that. I don't study at a specific time or for a specific length of time, either. I have been known to spend four straight hours on algebra, but sometimes it's only fifteen or twenty minutes. I may work at 9 A.M. or 11 P.M., whatever feels right to me. I work on weekends, holidays, and vacations in the same way. Somehow or other it all works out in the end.

Photo by Pam Gingold

I have five subjects that I'm trying to concentrate on right now. Every week, I try to get some time in on each: English, math, science, social studies, and "auto shop."

English

English is one subject that I spend a good deal of time on. This is partly due to the fact that my parents are writers, and therefore more than happy to provide me with advice and (when necessary) direction. But the real reason is that I love to read. My "curriculum" consists mostly of reading lots and lots of good books. My preferred genre is science fiction, although I'll read practically anything with the exception of romance novels and westerns. When I say science fiction, I'm not talking about space opera (i.e. *Star Wars* or *Battlestar Gallactica*)—although I admit, I enjoy that too, but rather "real" science fiction, by authors such as Asimov, Herbert, Benford, Huxley, etc. Among my favorite science fiction books are *Dune* and its sequels; also, *Brave New World*, and *Great Sky River*, just to name a few. I read a lot of classics, too. I especially love Shakespeare, Twain, and Dickens, and right now I'm working on Victor Hugo's *Les Miserables*, all twelve hundred pages of the unabridged edition.

I also do some writing—*real* writing, not school writing. I intend my writing to be read by others; for me writing is a form of communication, not just a "practice" in a necessary skill. I occasionally write letters to pen-pals, although not as often as I should. I write essays from time to time, on a variety of topics— like peace, the environment, and other major issues. I enter essay contests when I can, write pieces for *Growing Without Schooling* magazine and *Northern California Homeschool Association News* about homeschooling, and I've been writing articles for our newsletter for years.

During the Iraq War I wrote several extremely impassioned letters to my then-Congressperson, Gary Condit, letting him know just how disappointed

I was in him for voting in favor of the war. When a local boy was killed in combat and Condit didn't attend the funeral, I was even more incensed. I also wrote letters to the newspaper during a heated campaign for superintendent of schools. (Our friend, the principal of the alternative school, ran and won.)

Math

Mathematics is one of my favorite subjects. I appreciate its perfect logic and the idea that one can solve practically any problem that can be expressed numerically. All you need to do is use some general rules. So far algebra is my favorite branch of mathematics. At the moment, though, I'm working on geometry; I finished my algebra book a while back. I'm enjoying geometry too, mainly because I can apply everything I learn to computer graphics. As soon as I finish geometry I intend to begin algebra II/trigonometry. I can't wait to get started on calculus; I recently obtained a used calculus textbook, and it looks extremely interesting.

I do all my math studying from textbooks (math is the only subject where I take that approach). Of course, I make use of what I learn in my everyday life, too. Mathematics often comes in handy as a problem solving tool in many activities, including computer programming, art, and cooking.

I have never been able to understand why so many people dislike math. Perhaps this pervasive dislike has something to do with the way mathematics is taught in most schools. Teachers usually have their students learn by rote, instead of causing them to actually make sense of the beauty of the concepts involved. That's one of the things that bothers me most about school: They tend to make you learn by rote, rather than encouraging a deeper understanding of the subject.

Science

Science is another of my favorite subjects, for more or less the same reasons as mathematics. Actually, I like science better in some ways; science encourages creative thinking as well as following the rules. That's not to say that math doesn't ever encourage creative thinking—because it does. Once you get into algebra and geometry, it becomes obvious that creative thinking is a necessity. Still, there are many more unknowns in the world of science than in mathematics; it seems to me that it's much harder to turn all of mathematics on its head by discovering something new and mind-blowing. An example of creative thinking in science: Einstein didn't come up with his theories by sticking to the laws laid out by Newton; he did Newton's laws one better by using creative and provocative thinking to explain *why* Newton's laws worked.

I use three methods of studying science. For the most part, I study from all sorts of books. Right at the moment I'm using a really great textbook called *Conceptual Physics* by Paul B. Hewitt, but I also look into other textbooks, and read a lot of non-fiction science books by Isaac Asimov.

I also watch many science programs on PBS. My favorites include *Nova*, *Innovation*, *Discover: The World of Science*, *Infinite Voyage*, *The Nature of Things*, and *New Explorers*, and there are several others (mostly specials) that I watch from time to time. At the moment I'm really enjoying a series of programs about computers called *The Machine that Changed the World.*

Lastly, I sometimes learn by doing, i.e. experiments, observation, etc. However, as we don't get any ADA money from the state we can't afford to buy most of the equipment necessary for serious study in chemistry, biology, etc. Neither do I have access to any school facilities, as some homeschoolers do.

(I should note that I'm not any worse off in this respect than students at many high schools. The average school does not have much money, and probably does not place much value on serious science equipment—most would rather subsidize the football team! So, someone who is seriously interested in science might be better off homeschooling and trying to find their own equipment.)

I do have an old 300x microscope, a chemistry set, and a Radio Shack electronics "lab," which I fool around with from time to time. It's even possible to get computer software which simulates certain basic laboratory experiments and dissections.

Photo by Pam Gingold

Social Studies

Social studies is another subject that I spend a lot of time on, thanks to my parents' influence. I cover all areas, from history to geography to current events.

History sometimes seems like my least favorite subject. However, it's not really history itself that bothers me, but rather the dry, boring way that it is often presented. I can't stand history textbooks; I only look at them sometimes in order to gain a sense of perspective time-wise, or to see how separate events fit together. I've learned the majority of my historical knowledge by reading biographies and historical fiction. I really loved biographies when I was younger, everything from Thomas Jefferson to Martin Luther King, Jr. Now I'm more interested in historical fiction.

I've read many books by Howard Fast. One of my favorites is *My Glorious Brothers*, about the Maccabees. I also enjoyed *Citizen Tom Paine*. Besides more contemporary historical fiction, I've read some classical historical novels. My two all-time favorites are *The Three Musketeers* and *A Tale of Two Cities*.

I watch programs about history on PBS. I've learned a lot from programs such as *The American Experience*, *Eyes on the Prize*, and *The Civil War*, among dozens of others.

For the past two years I have participated in National History Day on the local level. In our town the contest is held at the junior high, where all the projects are displayed. The first year the topic was "Science and Technology in History," and I chose to build an exhibit on the history of solar energy. The second year I decided on a project I called "Conscientious Objection: The Right to Oppose War" for the theme of "Rights in History." History day projects require a lot of research, building a museum-type exhibit, and writing a paper complete with annotated bibliography. This is a complicated and exciting process which is well worth the work it takes. When I'm done I can revel in the knowledge that I have completed a difficult but worthwhile task, and built an aesthetically beautiful and academically solid project. This is an opportunity for me to delve more deeply into history than I would without an incentive. It is also fun for me to display and share my work, and see how it compares with that of others my age.

We have maps on our walls, and globes and atlases all over the place. (Perhaps this is why I'm one of the proud few in this country who can locate the United States on a map!) Because we try to stay on top of global affairs, as well as being interested in all cultures, my family talks a lot about other countries. I love to read *National Geographic*—we have a collection of hundreds of them, and they really broaden my horizons.

As a social activist, I try to stay aware of important issues in current events and government. My family has the radio on all the time for documentaries and news. We listen to KPFA, a Pacifica radio station out of Berkeley, and to National Public Radio's *All Things Considered* every day. We get a lot of information this way and always know what's going on in the world. Pacifica Radio is really wonderful—they present information, ideas, people, and points of view which are rarely heard on the mainstream media. Living where we do, without Pacifica it would be impossible for us to hear the kind of thought-provoking speeches and lectures that they broadcast.

On TV, I watch the network news most nights, as well as news magazine shows like *60 Minutes*, *20/20*, *Prime Time Live*, etc. And of course, PBS programs like Frontline.

Social Activism

My family has been involved in social activism for as long as I can remember. I clearly recall going to rallies and demonstrations at a very early age. When we lived in Los Angeles my parents belonged to an anti-nuclear group, Alliance For Survival; we went to demonstrations at Diablo Canyon and San Onofre. They helped put on a big show at the Hollywood Bowl called Survival Sunday. I used to carry signs and sing songs and have a great time.

As I grew older, I progressed from merely parroting my parents' views to forming ideas and opinions on my own. Because my parents are political activists and love to study many subjects, our house is full of resources: thousands of books, magazines, audio tapes, video tapes, maps, newspapers, etc.

My parents have always been major providers of information, either by directly answering my questions or by referring me to places where I can find my own answers. They always do their best to make sure that I get all sides of an issue. They are always teaching me that nothing is black and white, and that I must explore each subject thoroughly to develop my own opinions.

We often discuss issues as a family, and even after my views have been formed they are still subject to change, or at least modification. When I hear my opinions challenged, I am forced to re-identify them in my own mind, and clarify them by putting them into words. This has been a vital part of my education; I am working on developing very important skills in critical thinking and objectiveness (my dad says I always leap to conclusions!).

I am morally and politically opposed to war. Last year, while researching my History Day project on the history of conscientious objection, I learned a lot about the brave Americans who have opposed war since the founding of our country. This is a fascinating subject, and one which is especially important to me, as I expect to file C.O. papers if I am ever drafted. I got information about how to file the papers from a draft counseling center in San Francisco, and I have been working on them—very slowly—ever since. They demand a lot of soul-searching and extensive writing. During the war with Iraq I was involved in a fledgling local peace group (I was the only teen). We held candlelight vigils, wrote letters to our officials, and mostly talked a lot. I can't say that we actually affected anything directly, but it was a welcome change to get together with other people with similar views.

I am an avid environmentalist, especially since moving to my current locale. Living in this area makes me constantly aware of the beauty of our planet. Unfortunately the beauty also attracts logging companies and gold mining operations, so there are always opportunities for improvement. We have had our own little environmental disasters, such as when a local mining operation spilled cyanide into a nearby creek, contaminating the water. I would like to get involved with a group of people who are closer to me in age than the aforementioned peace group, people with more energy who are willing to take some risks and be more public. Unfortunately, none of the other teenagers in my town seem to be interested in activism at all (in fact, a lot of them are positively apathetic). I have never found any like-minded people of my age in the entire eight years that we've lived here! So all I can do at this time is learn about the problems our planet faces, and do my part to conserve and recycle. I'm also willing to write letters to government officials and newspaper editors when issues come up.

Homeschoolers For Peace

There are so many social/political issues that I am concerned about—and so little that I can truly affect at this stage in my life. In a couple of years I'll be allowed to vote, for whatever that's worth, but that's too far away anyway to be any real solace right now. This is where my newsletter comes in...

Originally the purpose of the *Pen Pal Network* was to provide me with a social life of sorts. When we first moved here from Los Angeles eight years ago I had no friends, and virtually no means of making friends. I eventually decided to send a newsletter (mostly jokes, puzzles, and a short letter) to several pen-pals, whom I found in *Growing Without Schooling* magazine. It quickly grew, both in content and in readership. It soon evolved from jokes and puzzles to articles on serious issues. We started calling ourselves *Homeschoolers For Peace* as we developed into a social action group, and carried out various projects. We created a peace quilt, sent letters as a group to a school in the Soviet Union, raised money to send school supplies to Nicaragua, etc.

Each issue, we publish articles by our readers on one subject (announced in the previous issue), sharing what we learn and providing a forum for homeschooled kids to share their views. Over the years we've explored such subjects as Apartheid in South Africa, the Israeli/Palestinian Conflict, Native American Treaty Rights, Labor History, African-American History, and Women in History, to list just a few. We have a mailing list of dozens of families, some of whom have subscribed for more than six years.

For many years the newsletter has been a central point in my education. It serves many purposes for me: It is a link to the outside world, a way to cultivate

Photo by Pam Gingold

Collating an issue of Homeschoolers for Peace

friendships, a valuable educational opportunity, and a forum for my opinions, feelings, and ideas on every imaginable subject. Through *Homeschoolers For Peace*, I have come to feel less isolated than I once did. Just knowing that there are other young people out there who share my political convictions has empowered me. Founding an organization and publishing a newsletter has given me a welcome sense of accomplishment and recognition, and has opened my mind to a lot of possibilities.

Auto Shop

I even have a home version of auto shop. I'm working on repairing and refurbishing a Chevy Vega station wagon, which is even older than I am. I have a general auto repair textbook which I'm teaching myself from, as well as the Vega repair manual, so that I can apply my newly acquired knowledge to the specific car. It's a pleasantly challenging job, as this is the first time I've ever attempted to work on a car. I have confidence that I'll be able to do it, though, because I've always loved fixing all sorts of things. Of course, the part that I'm really looking forward to is driving it. Unfortunately, even if I fix the car, I may have to wait to drive it, because I haven't taken driver's training yet; the schools around here don't offer it anymore. (Kids from Mariposa have to pay over a hundred dollars for professional driving lessons, and travel forty-five miles to the nearest large town to do it.)

Social contact

One potential drawback to homeschooling is the obvious difficulty with social-izing. Other kids are in school all day and when they come home they have to do homework. They are so caught up in the microcosm of school that they hardly acknowledge the outside world, including anyone who doesn't go to school. I'm not saying that *all* homeschoolers have difficulties with this, but I do, and I know that there are others with the same problems.

Socializing seems to get even more difficult as I get older; I guess I'm just getting more selective about my friends. When I was younger I would play with just about anyone; it hardly mattered if I really liked them or not. I live in such an isolated area that I seldom meet other teens, and when I do they're generally not homeschooling. This is not necessarily a drawback, but they have difficulty relating to homeschoolers. Even my friends have some problems in this department. This is not because they're stupid or insensitive or otherwise inherently deficient, but because they don't have any experience outside of school. When I relate problems that I have as a homeschooler, their invariable response is, "Then why don't you just go to school?" (as though that would take care of everything). I've managed to train them away from this mentality, but it still surfaces every so often. I think homeschoolers have to learn to be incredibly patient! I'm trying to alleviate my isolation by starting a teen support group through our state-wide homeschooling organization, NCHA (Northern California

Homeschool Association). I have some sense of how to go about doing this, thanks to my experiences with *Homeschoolers For Peace*, as well as some new ideas that I've never tried before. This will be a challenging task, as homeschooling teens in Northern California seem to be relatively few and far between.

Photo by Pam Gingold

I have already started a teen column for the *NCHA News*, and I would like to start a teen newsletter, dealing with issues relevant to older homeschoolers, which should be a good way for us to get to know one another. I'm also trying to organize various activities and means for us to get together physically, like campouts and conferences. Now that I'm old enough to travel alone, I would also like to visit with other homeschooling families, and have others come here. I think teenagers should become more involved in the homeschooling movement as a whole, so I'm trying to create a seat on the Board of Directors of NCHA for a teen delegate.

I recently attended the NCHA conference in Sacramento, which I helped to organize (we had teen workshops by Grace Llewellyn and the editor of *Growing Without Schooling* magazine, Susannah Sheffer!). I met quite a few California homeschoolers there who are also anxious to participate in this teen group, so I think I'm off to a good start.

The need for recognition

Something else that I find lacking in homeschooling is a built-in means of recognition. If a homeschooler writes an essay, builds a project, or does anything along these lines, he/she receives recognition from family and friends only. When you are younger this is perfectly satisfying, but when you mature, you develop a need for recognition from an external, objective source. I personally developed such a need around age ten or eleven. At this time I began to be less and less satisfied with the approval of my mother and father. I realized that they couldn't possibly be completely unbiased, and I felt that I needed approval from the outside world. I want to make it perfectly clear that I don't advocate a system of *false* recognition, such as one generally finds in the school system, in the form of gold stars, grades, and honor rolls. Rather, I feel that it is necessary to have one's work fairly appraised by a person for whom one feels respect and who is objective. I have managed to fulfill this need to a certain extent through *Homeschoolers For Peace*, National History Day projects, and (for a while) Boy Scouting.

Rebellion

There was another hole in my life, too, that Boy Scouts filled. Besides the obvious benefits of providing friends and a means of recognition, it gave me something to rebel against. In my opinion, every teenager needs something to rebel against; rebellion is a very healthy assertion of self. But at home I didn't have much to rebel against. I had plenty of freedom and I got along all right with my parents. Admittedly, this wasn't my original reason for joining Scouts; I joined in order to find friends and have fun. However, after being involved for a while, I found that I disagreed with many of the policies, rules, and precepts of Boy Scouting. To compound this, I developed an intense dislike for the Scoutmaster. His values differed strongly from mine, and for this and many diverse reasons it was difficult for me to respect him. He specifically and Boy Scouts in general were obvious targets.

I found that I actually enjoyed having something concrete and immediate to rebel against, after years of rebelling against "the system" by homeschooling, protesting war, etc. In Scouting, I rebelled in small ways, such as not wearing my uniform—a capital offense! (My Scoutmaster held that the uniform makes the Scout, while I thought that Scouthood is defined by actions, regardless of clothing.) I also voiced contrary opinions. Not that I was actively belligerent or anything, I merely stopped being acquiescent. After a while, the potential for rebellion was the only thing that kept me in Scouts. Once a week I could go to a meeting, see my friends, and assert my individuality—what better place to do so than in an organization that expects uniformity? I stayed for four years and quit a year ago when I finally decided that I had had enough.

Homeschooling and social change

I think the basic principle of homeschooling is summed up neatly in the words of Adlai Stevenson: "If we value the pursuit of knowledge, we must be free to follow wherever that search may lead."

That's what homeschooling is all about. How is it possible for anyone to truly engage in the pursuit of knowledge while being held prisoner behind a desk for six hours a day? Although a few scattered schools are beginning to ask this basic question, full-scale educational reform doesn't seem likely to happen anytime soon. In the meantime, the only real option would seem to be homeschooling.

However, I would like to think of homeschooling as it now exists as a stepping-stone to even more ambitious changes. I would like to see the whole community getting involved in education: children learning through apprenticeships rather than from dry, stuffy textbooks; mathematicians, scientists, writers, and other professionals actively involved in passing down the knowledge of one generation to the next. And I feel that only those of us who have had the experience of total freedom in education are likely to lead the way in bringing about such radical changes.

Resources

The following is a list of resources my family and I have found to be especially useful. May they prove as helpful to you as they have been to us.

Photo by Pam Gingold

Science

Asimov, Isaac, *Building Blocks of the Universe*
                Asimov on Chemistry
                The Sun Shines Bright
                and anything else.

Isaac Asimov is one of my favorite authors, fiction or non-fiction. He is also the most prolific writer I know of, having written upwards of four hundred books before he died earlier this year (1992). He has written books on virtually every imaginable subject, from science to history to theology, covering each with amazing lucidity. In the area of science, especially, one could probably get a basic education just by reading Asimov's books.

Hewitt, Paul G., *Conceptual Physics: a New Introduction to Your Environment*

This is by far the best science text I've ever used. Hewitt liberally laces his clear, interesting prose with diagrams, photos, and cartoons (most of which include everyday objects and situations), as well as incisive commentary on such subjects as pollution, conservation, energy consumption, overpopulation, and other important issues. As well, he does an excellent job of imparting the vital basic principles of contemporary physics, and infusing the reader/student with his obvious love of science.

Mathematics

Keedy, Mervin, and Marvin Bittinger, *Introductory Algebra*, Addison Wesley.

This book constitutes an entire self-contained course. If you want to teach *yourself* Algebra, this is the book to use. It was designed in such a way that it can easily be used by a single student studying on his or her own. Every concept involved is explained in depth so that the student will understand not only the mechanics of algebra, but also the reasoning behind the processes. It includes answer keys in the back, so a separate teacher's edition is not necessary (although I think one is available).

Math/Computer Science

Myers, Roy, *Microcomputer Graphics*, Addison Wesley, 1982.

This is a really great book on how to program advanced graphics in BASIC on your computer. The examples are for the Apple II line, but can be converted for use on other computers. The book covers topics from 3-D graphics through animation, with dozens of programs to illustrate the principles involved. In order to understand the concepts involved you have to have a good grasp of mathematics (mostly high-school level), so if you don't care for math you might not like the book. On the other hand, this book might give you an *incentive* to learn higher-level mathematics!

History

If you want more information on how to get your school district to set up a National History Day program, you can contact their organization directly. *

Davis, Kenneth C., *Don't Know Much About History*

I don't read much historical non-fiction, but I couldn't resist this book. *Don't Know Much About History* covers history from Columbus all the way up until the Iran-Contra scandal, exposing popular myths and generally livening up the same historical events that most other history texts render flavorless. For example, I find the "Crossing of the Delaware" a lot more interesting now that I know that, upon stepping into the boat, George Washington nudged General "Ox" Knox (weighing in at 280 lbs.) with his foot, and said, "Shift that fat ass, Harry. But slowly, or you'll swamp the damn boat." Whether or not you like history, this is one history book you'll want to read.

---

* Editor's note: see www.NationalHistoryDay.org.

Social Activism

Lewis, Barbara A., *The Kid's Guide to Social Action*

Don't let the "kid's" in the title put you off! This book is a valuable resource for anyone who would like to become involved in political action, but doesn't quite know what to do or how to go about it. It relates several inspiring success stories of kids and teens who have made a difference in their communities, as well as step by step instructions in how to carry out your own projects. From this book, you will learn how to get media coverage for your events, how to do fundraising and interviewing, how to conduct surveys, write speeches, change local and state laws, and more. In the back are resource lists and also tools, such as forms for petitions, news releases, grant applications, etc. Everyone who is serious about social action needs to own a copy of this book.

Teaching Tolerance Magazine, published by the Southern Poverty Law Center, 400 Washington Avenue, Montgomery, AL 36104.

This new magazine, free to educators (including homeschoolers), is a wonderful publication chock-full of resources for multi-cultural awareness. It is an inspiring collection of ways to teach/learn about how to stop racial, religious, and sexual discrimination. There are articles dealing with difficult subjects rarely covered extensively in schools: the Holocaust, Japanese internment camps, the Civil Rights movement, etc. There are projects to become involved in, mini-curriculums, and free stuff to order. This magazine is about building bridges and celebrating differences, which should be an important part of anyone's self-education.

Jeremiah Gingold
Boulder Creek, California

Unfettered and Responsible

When Grace first approached me to write an update for *Real Lives*, I admit to feeling some ambivalence. I would like nothing better than to relate some extraordinary accomplishments: earning my doctorate, founding my own successful business, producing critically acclaimed works of art, traveling the world, even starting a family of my own—but that's not the reality. I have yet to accomplish any of those things. Perhaps I will, in time; perhaps I won't. Life is an experience continuously unfolding, and should, with some luck, continue to be for as long as I continue to be.

Still, it's difficult not to feel some discomfort at this state of affairs, writing as I do with the knowledge that someone, somewhere, is reading these words, waiting with bated breath to see what heights of boundless achievement unschooling unlocked in *me*. I would be surprised if this were not the case, given that so much of homeschooling literature (this book included) seems founded, at least implicitly, upon the premise that the only thing required to unlock the genius and motivational drive buried within all children is to remove them from the confines of the public school system. I truly hate to disappoint that reader. Chances are that I won't, taken in context with the other essays in this book. For my own part, however, the last ten years have (in net result, if not in accrued experience) largely failed to distinguish me from the population at large of disaffected late twenty-somethings. Having been accepted into the

University of California at Santa Cruz in Fall of 1995, I've spent the last nine years of my life in and out of university, as I pursued degrees first in Computer & Information Sciences and then in Theatre Arts, settling ultimately on a major in Film and Digital Media with a minor in Technical Theatre—which, as of this writing, I have placed on indefinite hold, awaiting sufficient time and finances to complete my last units. I've worked, at various points over the years, as a theatrical technician, an independent computer consultant, an educational technology specialist and a web developer. At other times I've been virtually homeless and all but penniless. I've lived in Santa Cruz and San Jose, Oakland and Los Angeles—even spent a few short months in Brooklyn. I currently live in Boulder Creek, California, halfway between the Pacific Ocean and the Silicon Valley in the heart of the Santa Cruz Mountains, where I work from home as the webmaster of a Santa Cruz credit union. I have a wonderful girlfriend with whom I spend as much of my free time as possible. I express my urges toward creative weirdness as a member of You Are That Pig, a Burning Man theme camp, and have become involved with the formation of a non-profit artistic collective, the EvilAlien Foundation for the Arts. Life is good, if not on the whole particularly remarkable. If homeschooling was meant to have unleashed my limitless potential, it seems to have fallen a bit short, here.

Then again, maybe that was never really what homeschooling was about for most of us. It wasn't about making us special. It wasn't, and isn't, about producing musical child prodigies, or Harvard graduates at the age of sixteen. It was about allowing us to be who we were—who we are—as unfettered as possible, without apology or undue concession to external constraint. Even more importantly, perhaps, it was and continues to be as we grow older about taking control of, and responsibility for, our own lives and educations.

Serena Gingold, 13
Midpines, California

Another* Homeschooler for Peace

I love kids, plain and simple. One of the reasons I love being with kids (besides having fun) is that I'm thinking of going into a career of child development or psychology. Being in close contact with kids gives me the chance to observe them and learn about child behavior, which may help me in the future.

I also love to do things to make kids happy. I put on magic shows and skits, tell stories and jokes, and do face painting. I've also made several board games to teach kids about things like peace, the environment, and history. It's really fun making board games, because you can personalize them and tailor them to suit each child's needs. I may even sell my board games someday, or start my own company to make them.

A game Serena created
for a National History Day project

Photo by Pam Gingold

I spend a lot of my day reading books, since my house is *full* of them, and I really love to write: stories, articles, books! One of my goals in life is to write (and maybe illustrate) books for kids. I love books of all kinds, but I especially love mysteries. I'm particularly interested in black history, the Underground Railroad, and the Civil War era.

---

* Editor's note: In Jeremiah's first draft of *Homeschooling for Peace and Justice*, he described Serena's personality and activities. I asked whether Serena might like to speak for herself in a paragraph or two—and this short bonus essay is the result.
** See Susannah's book on her work with Serena and other young writers: *Writing Because We Love To: Homeschoolers at Work* (Heinemann-Boynton/Cook, 1992).

So many interesting and mysterious things happened on the Underground Railroad. My first book will probably be a historical fiction mystery, since that's my favorite kind. I have made several attempts at this already, and I've sent them to a special friend, Susannah Sheffer. She reads them and makes helpful comments on how to improve my work.**

I have always been interested in politics. Even when I was little I was aware of what was happening in the government. And I thought it was fun to learn the names of senators and congresspeople.

In 1984, when I was almost six, I watched my first Democratic National Convention and it changed my life. I "fell in love" with Jesse Jackson. After listening to his speech, I decided that my main goal in life (besides being a mother, writer, and other fantasies of a five-year-old) was to be a politician like Jesse Jackson. For several years I lived with this dream, and I got really excited when our Congressperson, Tony Coelho, told me I could be his page when I got older.

Then, in 1990, I realized what being a politician and being involved in politics was really like. One of my favorite adult friends, Sam Hill, decided he had to run for Superintendent of Schools in our county. He was the principal of the alternative high school and the Independent Study Program (for homeschoolers). His wife Kathy was the teacher of the ISP, and therefore my friend. The man who was currently superintendent was trying to get rid of the alternative education programs, and Sam felt the only way to stop him was to run for office and take over his job.

The whole town was divided and people argued all the time, through letters to the editor (I wrote some of them) and school board meetings. There was a tremendous amount of tension. I lost friends because we were on different sides. It was terrible when people began spreading bad rumors about the candidates and threatening people that they would lose their jobs or business if they voted for Sam. The whole thing made me sick, and I decided that I did not want to devote my life to politics after all—even though Sam did win. I'm still interested in world politics, but I've decided to take a different approach. Now I want to be an activist, fighting for children's and women's rights, and for peace and justice in the world. Besides, being a politician is limiting and I never want to be limited in my activism.

I have always been involved in peace work and activities, since that is of great interest to my entire family. I love being a member of *Homeschoolers For Peace*, my family's pen-pal network and newsletter. It is fun to share my writing, and interesting to read what the other kids have written about current events and history, peace and justice issues, and the environment—subjects that I am strongly interested in. I have made many friends this way. We write letters, exchange presents at birthdays and holidays, talk on the phone on special occasions, and sometimes get to meet. Several families have traveled across the country to visit us, and we've met others at homeschooling conferences.

I love networking with other people about how kids can be involved in social activism. I usually do this through *Homeschoolers For Peace*, but during the war with Iraq I had the opportunity to work with people on a local level. The Mariposa Peace Network was formed, and of course our family joined. It was the first peace group in the history of our town. I was excited to be a member, but unfortunately I was the youngest person in the group. I made the best of it, though, and quickly became friends with the adults. I like to talk to adults, sometimes more than to kids. We held candlelight vigils in front of the courthouse to protest the war, wrote letters to our congresspeople, and sent postcards each week to President Bush.

Photo by Pam Gingold

Serena works on a Homeschoolers for Peace environmental quilt for activist David Brower. On the wall hangs the HFP friendship/peace quilt.

I wanted to get more kids involved with the group, and later that year I had the chance. My idea was to have the Mariposa Peace Network sponsor a holiday peace party for kids. They agreed, and put me in charge. I wrote an article to advertise it in the paper, and I put up flyers around town, so that kids from all over the county could find out about it.

About twenty kids, between the ages of six and twelve, attended the party. My mom and I had co-written a short play about Sadako and the thousand paper cranes and made a small puppet theater and scenery. Almost all of the peace group members participated in the play. Afterwards my family taught the kids how to fold origami peace cranes (just like Sadako made) out of colored paper, which we used to decorate a small pine tree.

The kids all worked together to create a peace mural to present to the County Board of Supervisors. Then a juggler came to teach the kids to juggle, and we had party snacks contributed by members. Afterwards we planted the pine tree in a small lot in the center of town and had a ceremony, calling it a "Peace Tree." All in all it was a wonderful party and a wonderful way to share my love of peace with a group of kids. I would like to do more of these kinds of events, but the peace group is now defunct, so I'll have to find another way.

During the summer months I work on arts and crafts projects for the Mariposa County Fair. You might even say it's my summer job, because I win cash awards for most of my projects. I'm not exactly a genius where artwork is concerned, but I look at it as another way to express my feelings about social issues. I make all sorts of things, from posters about the environment, to peace mobiles, to projects that teach the community about homeschooling. The fair is an important part of my life, since it takes up so much of my time. I entered over a hundred projects this year. I not only have fun making these projects, but I also end up with a lot of presents to give away during the winter solstice holidays. And perhaps most important of all, I can share my work and feelings with others in a positive way.

Serena's update

In 1997 I was admitted to the University of California at Santa Cruz and graduated with a Bachelor of Arts in Cultural Anthropology in 2001. I spent the next few years managing a gourmet grocery store in Santa Cruz, where I still live, before re-entering college as a post-baccalaureate student in the Teacher Credential Program at California State University Monterey Bay. This May I will earn my teaching credential, and begin teaching elementary school in the fall— finally realizing my dream of so many years ago.

Vallie Raymond, 12
Port Townsend, Washington

Journal

Wednesday

One of the reasons it's cool to unschool is I like sleeping in in the morning. Again today I was the last in my family to wake up. My brother had already started drawing at the dining room table by the time I staggered out of bed and got myself downstairs. My mom and dad had left for a hike and my little sister was playing dolls. I got myself some breakfast.

Photo by Seth Raymond

My family has lived here in Port Townsend for the last seven years, but before that I lived in Michigan, Eastern Washington, and Minnesota. And I was born in Korea and lived there for four months until I was adopted by my parents. My brother, Seth, is four years older than me. We have been homeschooled all our lives, and Lydia, my younger sister who's five, will probably homeschool too.

After breakfast I got out the book I'm reading now, *Mr. God, This is Anna*, and sat in my favorite chair for reading, and read until my parents came home. As they walked through the door my little sister ran to greet them. While my mom got a drink of water I crossed the room to our school-book shelf and pulled out my math book and a pencil. I called my mom to come help me and sat down at the table where my brother had been drawing (by now, he had moved outside). My mom usually helps me for just a few minutes to make sure I understand everything.

After about an hour of reading word problems and multiplying and dividing fractions, I put my math away and got out my learning objectives to check off the math chapters I did. My learning objectives are something I've done for a few years. My parents help me plan out my goals for each quarter. Here's a peek at what my last quarter was like:

Vallie Raymond   *Winter quarter '92*   *7ᵗʰ grade*

Math

> *Saxon Math 76*
> Chapters: 46 through 90

World Geography

> Book: *National Geographic Picture Atlas of Our World*
> Quarter topic: Asia
> Will work on scrap book*
> Will take map test

Reading (I fill this in as I go)

> *Are You There God? It's Me, Margaret,* by Judy Blume
> *Fup,* by Jim Dodge
> *The Whipping Boy,* by Sid Fleischman
> *The Far Side Gallery,* by Gary Larson
> *Dog Song,* by Gary Paulsen
> *Snow Bound,* by Harry Mazer
> *What Could Go Wrong,* by W.D. Roberts

Writing

> Will write poems using ideas from *Beyond Words* by Elizabeth McKim
> Write to pen-pals
> Write about unschooling—send to Grace L. and Grandma

Science

> Will begin docent program at Marine Science Center in Feb.
> Will watch *Scientific American Frontiers*

Music

> Piano lessons weekly—teacher: Lisa Lanza
> Music Appreciation Class—teacher: Gwen Moore

---

* I usually study one continent at a time. Whenever I get interested in a particular country I take out our pile of new and old *National Geographics* and try to find an article about it. Then I cut out some of the pictures, draw a map of the country or state, and sometimes look up more information in the encyclopedia. Then I paste it all on sheets of paper and put them in a three-ring binder.

Physical Education
       Will prepare for Rhody Run—
       12k—in May[*]

Art (I fill this in as I do projects)
       Painting of tree
       Wax designs on candles
       Clay jewelry

Photo by Seth Raymond

Religion
       Will attend confirmation classes and youth group
       Teacher: David Housholder

Other Adventures
       Visited Seattle Art Museum (twice)
       Grand opening of The Barn at Arcadia Inn
       Kayaking (with Seth and my dad—I've gone out about four times now.
       We've gone to different bays in the area and once around a little island.)
       Dances—Valentine Formal, Sport Dance[**]
       Lisa Lanza's recital at Ravenscroft
       Saw movie *Wayne's World.*

I got out a piece of lined paper and started a letter to Brian. He's my Colorado pen-pal. I also have pen-pals in Washington, California, Massachusetts, Minnesota, Texas, Israel, and Japan. Most of the U.S. pen-pals I got from *Growing Without Schooling* magazine's pen-pal list. I have put off writing to Brian for a while because we recently started to play chess over the mail and I had to figure out my next move.

After lunch my dad headed off to one of his two jobs, carpentry. (After supper he cleans a school.) After my lunch I played the piano. The piano is one of my favorite subjects. I took lessons from my mom from when I was six until I was about ten. Then I thought I needed more variety and technique, so now every Tuesday I go to Lisa Lanza's house for a lesson. Lisa is a great pianist, and a very good teacher. In a couple of weeks she's going to play at the library's coffee hour and she asked me to play too. I think it will be a good opportunity for me to play in front of a crowd. I'm pretty sure I'm going to play "Piano Concerto in A Minor" by Edvard Grieg and "Cuban Mambo" by John W. Schaum.

I can tell when the school kids get out because the phone starts ringing for Seth and me. All my really close friends go to school, like Katie, Noa, and

[*] To train for the Rhody Run I'd run almost every day before lunch. I've done the race four other years and it's a tough race if you haven't trained.
[**] Our Rec Center hosted the Valentine Formal for seventh, eighth, and ninth graders, but I'm pretty sure a few eighth grade girls came up with the idea and their parents helped a lot. The other dances I've gone to were all sponsored by the school.

Melissa. Noa and Katie sometimes try to get me to go to school. They talk about all the cute guys and how much fun it would be if I was there, but they also talk about hating it themselves and wishing they could skip it. Their social life isn't that much different from mine. They might know a lot more people but we have the same amount of close friends. It doesn't seem to matter that I'm homeschooled. I'm glad I'm not in school because I often hear of situations that sound really embarrassing. And things like choosing up sides and getting angry at one person for not being as competitive, and teachers making an example of one kid in front of the whole class. I also hear that some kids really make it tough on new kids.

Today when the phone rang Katie was on the line wanting to do something. I headed off to meet her. Katie and I do almost everything together. One of our favorite hang outs is the local Rec Center, which is about a mile from our house. We go there to shoot hoops, play ping-pong, and try to play pool. Katie and I walk almost everywhere we go—downtown or Fort Worden, which is a state park just a few blocks from my house, where we hike the beach or go through the old bunkers or visit Katie's grandparents who work there.

It seems each of my friends is completely different, which is a hassle only when I plan a party. Melissa is my oldest friend; she just turned sixteen. I don't think age matters that much with friends. Our families are good friends. In fact, that's how I met her—our dads work together and we used to go to the same church. If I'm with Melissa you would most likely find us downtown spending all our money on food, magazines, make-up, or jewelry.

After their performance, *Photo by Seth Raymond* Vallie's team talks with officials

Noa, on the other hand, is someone I do more projects with. This year we're taking a music appreciation class together. Our teacher, Gwen Moore, helps us learn and enjoy classical music by playing a lot of pieces on the piano and telling about the composers. I met Noa when my mom started taking an art class from her mom. The first activity that Noa and I joined was O.M. (Odyssey of the Mind), which is group problem solving. Although I think O.M. is a school-sponsored activity, you don't have to be in school to join. We met after school hours up at the junior high. It was the first time I'd ever done O.M. and it was a lot of fun. Each group got to choose from a list of activities. Our group chose drama, and put together a play based on Alice in Wonderland. In the play we had to have something named Alice, a plant with human characteristics, a humorous invention, something that increased in size, an eccentric character, music, and poetry. Also, we had to make our own scenery and props. Even though our group didn't place well at the competition, most of us are planning to do it again next year. (Other groups built monuments, made balsa wood structures to hold as much weight as possible, and made cars that would run on five different kinds of power.)

I got home from the Rec Center about five o'clock. While my mom made dinner, I sat on a stool in the kitchen and told her about my afternoon at the Rec. Then I got up and helped her with the salad and set the table.

After dinner and when the dishes are done is when we are most likely to do our projects. Lately my mom's been doing sculpture, my brother chalk pastels and me, well, if I don't join one of them I go back to my trusty piano.

Thursday

Today I got up earlier than usual, in order to go baby-sit for a family that also homeschools. I noticed out the window that my mom and Seth were in the car and pulling out of the driveway. I figured that my mom was taking Seth to the bus stop. He takes an art class twice a week at a college in Port Angeles.

After I ate my breakfast I'd only played a couple of songs on the piano before the Watsons came to pick me up. Their home is a travel trailer that is parked in our local fairgrounds. It's really nice to baby-sit for people who live in a big open space. The kids and I like to take bikes and ride all around. Alissa (eight) and Gavin (four) are very inventive kids and we make up a lot of games together. Today we played Hot Lava Monster and made houses and tunnels for their gerbils. We don't really do any "school" type of work together, but I read books to them, we draw a lot, and we make things from clay.

I also baby-sit for three other families. Babysitting is the only way I'm making spending money right now. Most of my money I'm saving for a plane ticket to Minnesota. I want to visit some relatives of ours there. This will be the first trip I've ever taken alone.

When I came home about one-thirty, I found Mom and Lydia about to leave for the library. There was no reason I needed to stay home, so I went too. As I walked into the library I could smell that smell libraries have. Ours is an old Carnegie library that's been remodeled recently. Upstairs is a large meeting room where people have concerts, art shows, or meetings. Something different goes on there almost every day; it's fun to walk around and see what's happening.

Photo by Seth Raymond

Also upstairs is a room with a huge selection of new and old magazines. I remembered an article in *People* magazine I wanted to read, but as I was looking for it I came across a lot of big blue folders with issues of our local paper in them. I picked up one labeled 1924 and sat at one of the long conference tables. It was interesting to imagine Port Townsend back then. Most of the houses for sale are still here now. In one ad the house cost two hundred dollars. Phone numbers were only three digits long. One ad was for rooms in a hotel that is still downtown; rooms cost one dollar per night. The weird thing in that ad was their selling point: "This is not a Japanese-owned business."

What seemed like a half hour had turned into an hour. Mom came up to ask if I was ready to go home. I still hadn't looked for any books, so I said I'd walk home later. I went downstairs to the card catalog to see if they had more books by the author Gary Paulsen. I chose *Tracker* and went to find it on the shelf. Then I wandered around for a while; that's the way I find most of the books that interest me. Today my finds were: a book of photos from the first decade of *Life Magazine*, a Far Side book, and a book called *Paper-Maché Today*. I checked out the books and decided I'd better be getting home.

My dad beat me home by a few minutes. He had picked up Seth at the bus stop on his way. After dinner I went with my dad to his second job, to clean the Chimacum high school. I've gone with him a few other times. It's kind of funny how some of the people who go to school there make a mess for no reason. I helped him with wiping down tables, washing windows, and picking up candy wrappers. While he did the rest of his job I sat in the library and read the *Seventeen* magazine.

I go to the school with my dad because it gives me time alone with him. Also, it helps me to understand better when he talks about his job there. And, helping him is a lot of fun. I suppose going to help my dad is "educational" in ways, but I've never been required to go. Dividing up what's fun and what's educational is hard, because I don't often do things for my education that I don't find enjoyable.

Friday

Right now I'm sitting at a table on the Seattle to Winslow ferry. My family doesn't get to Seattle very often but today we wanted to go to the Seattle Art Museum. It's quite a ways from Port Townsend. We have to drive for about an hour and then catch a Washington State ferry which takes about half an hour to cross the Puget Sound.

We've been to the museum before but we were always in a hurry. Today we took all the time we wanted to look at everything.

I wanted to spend most of my time in the Northwest Coast Indian exhibit. I've been more interested in the local art since we went camping last summer near one of the major digs of a Native American village. We'd gone to the Neah Bay museum, which had a lot of objects from that dig. Today I saw a lot of things that were similar. My favorite was a set-up of many masks and head-dresses. It fascinated me to read the different stories of the occasions for which each was worn.

I also walked around the other floors and looked through rooms of pho-tography, paintings, and sculpture. I enjoy contemporary art. It sticks in my mind. There are no rules for it so it's wilder and further "out there."

When we left the art museum we started to hike across downtown. We passed a lot of different stores. There were cafes, art galleries, a photography shop, and a fancy toy store Lydie just had to go into. The one we all agreed on going into was a store about as big as its block, called Elliot Bay Books. You can get almost any book there that you can think of. Elliot Bay also has a little restau-rant in the basement. Since we hadn't eaten any lunch or dinner yet, we ate there. After we had eaten our soups and sandwiches we went back upstairs and looked for books. We stayed for two hours and then hiked back to the ferry terminal.

So here I am, sitting at this little table going back to Winslow with my family. It's been a really fun day in Seattle, but I'm sure glad I'm on my way back home.

Photo by Seth Raymond

Saturday

I just got home from my Marine Science class. It was my fifth session in the docent training program. I want to start working as a volunteer there this summer—show-ing visitors around the center and answer-ing any questions they might have, going out on the center's boat (the *Monty Python*), going water monitoring, and basically help-ing in any way I can. The class is mostly adults but there are a couple of high school students and some younger kids that come with their parents.

The Marine Science Center is a green building at the end of a pier in Fort Worden State Park. It attracts a lot of people. When you walk in the main entrance, there are four big touch tanks filled with sea stars, hermit crabs, sea cucumbers, anemo-nes, fish and more. People are allowed to touch everything except the fish, crab, and shrimp. Around the room are more aquariums to look at. In these are gun-nels, nudibranch, sculpin, perch, large crabs, octopus, and my personal favorite, the Pacific spiney lumpsucker. All the water for the aquariums and tanks is pumped right from under the pier so the temperature is the same as the ocean's. Other things in the main room are a small gift shop in the corner, woolly mammoth bones that were found in the bluffs along the beach, and shelves of fossils and different kinds of sea shells.

Today at class a geologist spoke and showed slides that were mostly about erosion and how our area has changed over the years. When he was done we all got to choose a M.S.C. T-shirt from the gift shop and fish print on it. Yup, that's really what fish printing is, you put paint on a dead fish and press your shirt over it. I chose a black shirt with white, green, and red ink. The print turned out really cool.

Class today was okay but I didn't enjoy it as much as the others. In our very first class, we learned about the eating habits of most of the animals there. That class was fun because our teachers, Ann and Judy, would ask us to compare a sea animal's habit of eating to some tool we use. Example: a drill snail and a hand drill—a drill snail will attach itself to a clam or something similar and then drill through the shell and suck out the body. Also that day, Ann took us through the main part of the building and helped us learn to identify the animals in the tanks.

Collecting plankton

In one class our group got to gather plankton from the water right outside. It was fascinating to see all the living creatures in a little drop of sea water. We stared into microscopes for about forty-five minutes, and everyone was looking in everyone else's microscopes. It's amazing to realize how much plankton is in the water and how many animals depend on it.

Another morning we went down to a beach and tidepooled. To tidepool, you have to wait until the tide goes out and leaves pools of water all around and under rocks. That's the best time to find life on a rocky beach. All different kinds of animals get stuck in the pools of water. I flipped over a few rocks and saw small crabs, snails, clingfish, gunnels, and small sea anemones. Everybody would pick up a different animal in a dish and run it over to Judy and ask, "What does this animal do?" or "What is this animal's name?" Judy also told us about ten different seaweed names, where each type grows, and how it protects some fish. We all had a great time.

Learning   Photo by Seth Raymond
to set up a plankton display

So back to today. Now that I'm home I've hung my fish print shirt on our clothesline to set the ink and to air out the fish smell. I'm really grateful for where we live because it's so much better to learn things about the sea at the sea instead of from a book.

Well, that's another "typical" day for Vallie Raymond. I don't have my future planned out yet because right now I'm concentrating on the present. I'm pretty sure that if I keep on doing what I'm doing and enjoying my life, all the activities I love doing now will reward me in the future.

Seth pulls together the first issue of Spoke   *Photo by Kath Raymond*

Seth, Vallie's seventeen-year-old unschooled brother, took the photographs for her essay. His interests include photography, drawing, sculpture, and outdoor activities. An avid freestyle bicyclist, he travels all over the northwest to compete in contests. In fact, he combines his interest in biking, photography, and art to produce his own zine, *Spoke*. You can read more about Seth in *The Teenage Liberation Handbook*.

Photo by Colin Robertson

Vallie Raymond
Seattle, Washington

Learning as a Way of Life

In the past ten years life has been exciting. In a nutshell, I homeschooled until I was sixteen, then received my GED and lived with my family in Port Townsend until I was eighteen. Five days after my eighteenth birthday I moved to Seattle to be on my own, and I still live there now.

In retrospect, when I was a teenager, everything from how I perceived myself, to how I perceived the world, to what I was interested in learning, changed rapidly from one end of a spectrum to the other and back again. I continued to docent at the Marine Science Center, and also did a research study project for three years that included videotape and drawings of plankton. I gave all my data to the science center and they used it for their own research and classes—I felt fantastic for my contribution! I took jazz piano lessons for a short while but when I was sixteen I quit piano lessons altogether to pursue other interests.

During those years I usually set weekly goals related to the areas I had chosen to study. During a typical day I might sleep in; study math, reading, and piano; read *National Geographic* until my friends from public school were home; and then I'd be out the door to hang out with them. My study worked as long as I was focused and interested, but finding things to be interested in grew more difficult for me, and it got harder for me to follow through since I loved walking around downtown with my friends and hanging out with other people my age.

Photo by Steve Jacobson

When I was fourteen my parents saw my disinterest in studying and asked me if I would rather go to public school or alternative high school. They had always been available if I needed help with studying or identifying interests to pursue, and now I appreciated their openness to whatever direction I wanted to take. And I did see public school as an easy way to socialize and be exposed to other kids from my small town, so I liked the idea of going, and I also liked the idea of having what to study decided for me. But my fantasies would dissipate every time I'd meet a friend at school and the bell would ring and the hall would be flooded with kids. Somehow it just didn't feel good to me to be there in the midst of that.

But I continued to feel not quite at ease, and adults and kids often asked how I learned and if I felt I was missing out on social activity by not going to school. So finally, frustrated with not really knowing how I felt about being homeschooled and curious about what public school would be like for me, when I was fifteen I decided to live in Sandstone, Minnesota with my grandmother and go to public school. I made friends, and I still liked to hang out as much as I could. But I found school to be more monotonous than I had expected, and too easy, and sitting down so much during the day made me restless. I did look forward to going to school to see my friends, but I missed the feeling of independence that homeschooling had given me, even though that same independence had once been overwhelming.

My biggest fears about going to school had been that I would not understand the material, and that I would come to realize that the way I had learned from homeschooling really hadn't taught me anything. But neither fear came true—I did very well academically in school. And after a semester I gladly returned to Washington and to homeschooling. I now felt that homeschooling gave me an exciting and fun outlook on life, learning, and understanding. I had a new appreciation for my freedom, and I no longer worried about not achieving enough, so I felt a weight lifted off my shoulders.

I started to use the same method of learning as before, but with a rejuvenated spirit. I had new enthusiasm and dedication. I began taking belly dance classes. I was also interested in taking the PSAT, and began to focus my study toward that by getting used PSAT workbooks from other people and the library. I started working at a vegan bed and breakfast as an assistant chef and housekeeper. Learning how to prepare each breakfast and learning about being vegan was a great experience. The owners gave me the responsibility of being their innkeeper while they were on vacation, so during that time I prepared breakfast on my own and greeted guests. I also started working for another bed and breakfast as an afternoon receptionist.

While reading an *Unschooling Ourselves* newsletter I noticed that Grace Llewellyn wanted to start a house in Eugene, Oregon, where homeschooled kids from across the country could live together. I thought this would be an interesting adventure for me to try. My parents and I discussed it and we decided I should take the GED test before I left so I could have the freedom to be out on my own and take college classes if I wanted. We needed the public school's superintendent to authorize me to take the GED, but she urged me to not take it, as then I would never be able to go to public high school should I change my mind and want to go. Finally, after a few months of aggressively trying to persuade her, she signed her approval. By this time it turned out that the house in Eugene did not come together, but I still wanted to take the GED. I took a drivers education class at the public high school and a GED preparation class through the community college. I received my GED in May and my driver's license in July of 1996.

Then, from age seventeen to eighteen I worked two part time jobs, one as bus staff, hostess, and wait staff at a downtown restaurant, and the other as afternoon receptionist at a bed and breakfast. I bought a car and still liked to hang out with friends whenever I could. I started considering studying food and nutrition at a community college. The closest community college with these classes, though, was an hour away and I didn't want to commute that far or move to that city. But I did decide to move to Seattle and go to a community college there.

A close friend joined me in moving to an area of Seattle called Capitol Hill, and I enrolled in Seattle Central Community College and started taking classes. I thought that would be a good way to give myself something to do while breaking myself into living in Seattle and to maybe meet some friends. I decided not to study food and nutrition, but just to take any class I thought might be fun. I also belly danced with a class a few blocks from my apartment, and I worked as head housekeeper for an inn. I stayed in school for a year, studying random subjects like philosophy, anthropology, sociology, art history, English, and math. I loved every class but I started to get impatient because school was costing me so much money and I wanted to travel and do other things.

The next summer I started a new job working for a small restaurant down the street from my apartment as a barista and wait staff. Shortly after I started, I ended up running the entire restaurant almost entirely alone. I had many responsibilities—to train staff, call in orders, and open and close the restaurant. I referred my friends to the job and they were hired immediately. Working there was a lot of work and a lot of fun.

A friend and I decided to take a trip to California in the winter of 1999. We moved to Long Beach, rented an apartment for about three months, and didn't work. I traveled to the other nearby beaches and to Los Angeles quite a bit. But we couldn't afford to live without working for much longer, and moved back to Seattle.

Another friend referred me to a job as an administrative assistant at a singles' match-making service. I got the job and worked part-time for about a year while also working as a receptionist for a large downtown hair salon. I then started to work full-time at the match-making service as front desk manager and bookkeeper for the business. The office consisted of the owner, who was also the matchmaker, a sales associate, and myself. I had much responsibility and was constantly a busybody. It was a very interesting place to work and I learned a lot of skills. During this time I took a painting class where we used acrylics but with oil-painting techniques, which I really enjoyed. I also started learning how to make my own music through ProTools audio production software, with a Korg synthesizer and turn tables.

As of now I am no longer working for the matchmaker service. I have been enjoying my time lately with painting, sewing, working out, and relaxing. I still love to play piano but don't get to play very often. I am living in a condo in downtown Seattle with my two cats and have been snowboarding whenever possible. At this time I am unsure about college because I do not know what I want to study. I do, however, see myself in a school of some kind in the next couple of years. My more immediate plans are to travel to Las Vegas and to Whistler, British Columbia, for vacation.

In conclusion, I have felt very fortunate to homeschool. If I had it all to do over again I would push myself further when I got interested in something, because it's so easy to procrastinate. As an adult, I'll think of skills or knowledge I want and how I could have learned them when I was younger. For example, playing electric guitar is my next big learning project, and it was something I was always around while I was growing up, yet I never got past learning a couple chords. I would have also tried to meet and keep in touch with my pen pals, done more small art projects, and I would have learned to snowboard sooner.

My advice for parents who homeschool is to be open with your kids about your own experiences with school and life. Let them know what you've benefited from, and what you would do if you could do it over again. Take them—or let them go on—as many learning trips or opportunities as you possibly can, because their interests will be changing all the time. The expeditions my parents made possible for me always taught me

Photo by Steve Jacobson

new things and opened my mind to start new ideas and projects. My advice for homeschooling kids is to keep yourself busy and follow your spur-of-the-moment interests, while also keeping an open mind about your parents' ideas and suggestions. I have never felt different—better or worse—because of being homeschooled. I view learning as a way of life and I am very pleased with mine, and with what I have accomplished so far.

Editor's note: While *Real Lives* was getting ready for press, much more happened in Vallie's life. She adds: "I enrolled in a Real Estate Fundamentals course, received a Real Estate Sales Agent certificate, and will be taking the state exam soon. Instead of going to Las Vegas, my boyfriend and I went snowboarding in Austria and toured around Zurich, Switzerland (which was the most exciting, beautiful, and romantic place I have ever seen—I cannot wait to go again!). Recently, he proposed to me at an aquarium here in Seattle and I was completely surprised. We had met at the Port Townsend Marine Science Center back when I was doing my plankton research—he was working in the gift shop while I was looking at petri dishes under the microscope. We talked one day but never saw each other again until I was living in Seattle and going to school with a mutual friend, who re-introduced us. We will be married next August, and for the moment I am enjoying planning a wedding and playing electric guitar."

Rebecca Merrion, 15
Danville, Indiana

Giving My Time

This essay is dedicated to my parents
for bringing me into this world and choosing to homeschool me.

Photo by Sandra Merrion

When we walked in the door of the homeless shelter, eleven preschool children were running everywhere. The fifteen teens and parents from our homeschool group felt a little awkward until one child ran up and said, "Hi, my name is Dominique," and proceeded to give everyone a big hug. Not all of the kids were as friendly as he was, though: One kid hid in a cupboard and it took some encouragement to get him to come and join us.

Several months before, our group had worked in the food pantry and had volunteered to have a party for the little kids. So now we decorated T-shirts with them and wrote their names on the backs of the T-shirts, played basketball (using a little foam ball and a trash can as the hoop), and played ring-around-the-rosie. We also bought pizza and made cookies and cake. Though the children had little, they had big hearts—and tried to give away what little they did have. They all got in the toybox and tried to give us lego and dolls' arms. When it was time for us to clean up and go down and help with lunch in the kitchen, they begged to go with us. It was so much fun to know that we were bringing joy and to discover that we were crazy about these kids.

Volunteer service is one reason why I am not going to school. I like the feeling I get from giving my time to less fortunate people. If I was in school I would not have enough time for my volunteer work, and I think that volunteer work should be a part of everyone's lives whether they are young, old, or a teenager like myself. I have volunteered with homeless shelters, with Habitat for Humanity, and I visit several elderly ladies who live in our community—like my ninety-seven-year-old friend Beaulah, a spry lady who learned to drive when she was seventy-one!

I live in Danville, a town of four thousand, which is a bedroom commu-nity of Indianapolis. My parents moved here from Detroit, Michigan twenty years ago in hopes of getting away from some of the noise and air pollution of Detroit. I have two older sisters, two older brothers, and one younger sister. All of my older brothers and sisters went to school so I was the first one to be com-pletely homeschooled. My little sister is also homeschooled and hopefully she will choose, when she gets old enough to have her own choice, to stay homeschooled.

My brother Rob, who is seventeen, left school at the end of second grade but went back in tenth grade because he wanted to play soccer, and the school won't let anyone who is not enrolled play sports on their teams. Rob seems tired of most of the teachers but he also likes to be with his friends. I cannot see him sitting inside in a building all day long; he could never stand it when he had to stay inside for even an hour.

Indiana must be the freest homeschooling state in the union—there aren't many regulations that we have to comply with, state or local. The only thing that my parents have to do is register as a private school with the attendance officer at the state board of education. I can take an achievement test if I want to, but it is not required. I have taken achievement tests about three times in my homeschooling life to see how I was progressing and to see what subjects I needed to work on.

I have thought of going to school because some of my friends have tried to convince me that school is a lot of fun. Then I have other friends who say, "Why would you even consider it? You have a much better deal than what we have." I have even convinced a few of my friends that they should homeschool but their parents say no, even if their kids are unhappy at school.

Also, I think of how long you have to stay in school to graduate and I think, "Naaah." Why stay in school until you are eighteen when there are alter-natives? I have a better arrangement than that: I am going to graduate early as a homeschooler* so that I have a few years to work, travel, and get myself ready

---

* I'm with Clonlara Home Based Education Program. Clonlara will issue me a high school diploma after I complete its required study in two or more years. As a teenager I have to keep my own records of time spent on education-related activities. Clonlara has a suggested reading list that you can use as a loose guideline or that you can follow exactly. All they really want is for you to have a good overview of different literature. The program also suggests that you have three hundred hours of volunteer work, which can be with one organization, your church, a homeless shelter, or a variety of places.

for college—*if* I decide on college. To me, life means a whole lot more than just going through school, taking academic courses, and then getting a degree. My goal is to not only hear about events but to know and experience life.

I know some kids who are pushed into going to college right after they get out of school and they end up not knowing what they really want to do, so they get into a field that they don't even like. Then, when they graduate from college, all of the people in the same field race to get the best job and be the most financially successful. Once they earn some money they get married, buy a big house, and then they have one kid. Their first and only child is then put into daycare (dayorphanage) and spoiled with material things instead of being spoiled with love.

In fact, here is a true story from Tony Campolo's book, *Wake Up America!* There was a couple who married and they had dreams that they would be the perfect couple and spend all their time with their kids. They would take long walks and have long talks together. When their first baby was born, they wanted the best for it, including all material advantages. Of course, the mother had to start working so they could afford the best, including the best daycare. Pretty soon they no longer had time for the long walks, and then they no longer had time for the long talks. Communication soon dwindled between the parents and the marriage ended in divorce. If that does not show the commercialism of this world that we live in, I don't know what does.

I don't think that homeschooled teenagers get into the commercialism of the world nearly as much as teenagers who go to school. For some reason, everyone in school wears and does the same thing that everyone else does, be it Guess jeans, punk hair, or continually hanging out at the mall. I am glad that some homeschoolers feel they can be anyone that they want to be, unlike most of the kids that go to school and feel that they all have to be alike, or else they don't fit in and are called weird. Not only individual spirit and taste are lost in school, but responsibility also, because in school kids hardly ever have to do anything for themselves except spit back memorized information. And yet they put up with it for thirteen years—not including college.

My mom and dad leave me pretty much responsible for myself. That way if I screw up or get a story (like this) in late, I can blame only myself and learn from my own mistakes. I am glad that my parents made me responsible for myself because I have seen so many irresponsible people who are always relying on other people to tell them what to do.

I spend my time throughout the year helping around the house, baby-sitting, going on field trips, book learning, and vacationing. A great thing about homeschooling is that you can go on vacation anytime you want without waiting for school vacations. Many of our vacations have been to Florida to see our grandparents, but we have also gone to Oregon, Mexico, Texas, Washington, D.C., Philadelphia, and numerous other places.

For English I have read a lot of books and literature, but I also use workbooks. For science I do experiments, read books, visit museums related to science, and also watch science-related TV programs. History, government, and geography are learned on field trips, vacations, everyday life, and through books. Math is the only subject that I spend any real time learning out of a textbook. When I was younger, though, we used a lot of games to teach me the basics of math.

When I am at home, I sometimes sit down for several hours with my algebra book and then maybe I won't do algebra all the rest of the week. Not like in school where you have to do an hour each day. After writing this essay I will be able to count many hours of English, typing, and computer on my records for Clonlara. Each month for my hours spent on all subjects I average between one hundred and two hundred hours. My hours consist of everything from the normal academic subjects to ballet class. In fact, I can count almost everything I do as a credit.

Over our homeschooling years we have belonged to several different support groups. Most of these were Christian but welcomed anyone who wanted to join. Last year we had a teen group that met once a month and had around fifteen people when everyone attended. I have two close friends in the group; we have known each other all of our lives and have been in many homeschool groups together. We used to have a pretty big teen group until a lot of the teens went to school.

My mother is as involved or more involved with the group than I am. She leads the teen group and also participates in some of the things that the little kids do. Unlike some people, my mom doesn't try to set everything up for us and tell us what we are going to do every time. She lets us pick our activities and doesn't always try to force us to do something "educational." This is good because we learn to not rely on somebody else to arrange stuff for us; we have to come up with what we want to do and make sure that everyone agrees to what we have planned. It is a wonderful way to give us some responsibility.

Our group has done everything from cooking a whole Thanksgiving dinner (the type that the pilgrims would have had at the first Thanksgiving, outside on an open fire) to making bead bracelets and working at a family homeless shelter. For the Thanksgiving dinner we all had to research what the pilgrims would have had at the first Thanksgiving. We came up with some pretty weird stuff, and also with some stuff that tasted pretty good. We killed, plucked, and cooked a chicken, made venison stew, had cornmeal mush (just cornmeal and water mixed together), cranberry pudding (cooked mushed cranberries), and also a cow's tongue (which was not part of what the pilgrims had but we cooked it anyway). We joined with another homeschooling group to learn how to make

Indian bead bracelets, and even though a few months have passed since then, many kids are still beading away, including myself. At the shelter we washed dishes, stacked food in the pantry, folded clothes, and played with the little kids.

I have never wanted to play any sports connected with high school; in fact, I have never liked any competitive sports, especially on an organized team. Competitive sports remind me of training our youth for war, not peace. And I don't like the idea of some people being turned away because they are not as good as somebody else. Somebody should tell the coaches that not everyone's abilities are on the same level and that kids, especially young ones, should not have to experience rejection.

I have taken ballet for around three years, going to class twice a week. I've been in four performances, plus a series of performances I did while on tour for the *Nutcracker* with the Indianapolis Ballet Theatre when I was twelve. (The tour lasted about twelve days. It was nice not having homework like the other seven children on tour did. After practice, when they were doing their homework, I could be reading a book or doing whatever I wanted to do. Altogether, we performed about twenty times. The tour was a great learning experience, not to mention all the exercise we got while dancing our parts over and over again. It also gave us a feel of what professional dancers go through when they are performing all over the place.)

Ballet is a good way to use the muscles in your body and to keep yourself in shape, but I have no real desire to continue on and become professional. I don't think I'd like to be a professional dancer or even an actress, because it is such lonely work. Taking ballet, though, makes me realize why it is more than just a way of dancing. It is a beautiful way of dancing and also a very beautiful art. When you are dancing, you are working as hard as, say, a football player would at winning a game for his team. Yet when performing for an audience it all appears so effortless. Right before I go out on the stage I think, "Oh God, I'm not going to be able to do this." But then when I get out on the stage and hear my music I get lost in what I'm doing and I feel like I'm on a different planet than everyone else. I am brought back to reality by either the sounds of the audience or the people backstage telling me that I did a good job. Then I realize how hard I had worked my body to show people what I could do.

I admire other dancers—students, teachers, and professionals—because everyone expresses themselves in a different way and it is interesting to see both how different dancers express themselves and also how the audience responds to certain techniques. When you are dancing you can let your spirit free to dance inside of you and for you, and you are able to show people another side of yourself that they otherwise might not see. To express yourself, you also have to be able to put yourself in the audience's place and think, "If I could see myself dancing up on the stage right now, what would it look like? Would it look like I would want it to?" This way, it is easier to tell what actions I should be doing or what expression to have on my face.

I enjoy using my summers as part of my schooling because I am not stuck doing it in an unpleasant way. I can choose to do whatever I want, whenever and however I want to do it. During the school year, a school student is forced to do stuff, and has to learn it all out of a textbook, which if you ask most people is pretty boring. If I went to school I probably wouldn't want to do anything involving school during the summer. I would have always been taught everything that everyone thought I needed to know at school—and why do it on your own if you might just have to learn it in school again anyway? But much of my own "schooling" has come from real life experiences rather than from books, and I think that is one of the best ways to learn.

Almost every summer we have had a foreign exchange student from Japan or Spain. We have chosen not to have exchange students during the school year because we don't want to be tied down to the school schedule.

In past years we have had two boys and one girl as foreign exchange students. Miguel, our Spanish student, came to see us twice—the first time through an exchange program, and the second time on his own because he had so much fun the first time. We picked up some Spanish history from Miguel. During the Spanish Civil War (1936-1939), his family had been very wealthy but his grandfather was captured by the loyalist, communist forces and the family gave up all their worldly wealth for his release.

The first year that we had a Japanese student, Junichi, Miguel also came back to stay with us for the second time. The day after they both got here, we packed up and drove to Florida to go to Disney World and to see my grandparents and my older sister Michelle. We played lots of games and had a lot of pillow fights that week.

Our last Japanese visitor, Shiho, filled her suitcase with American candy to take back to all of her friends. She left some of her clothes with us so that she would have more room for candy—but I'm not sure if any of that candy made it back to Japan!

Eric, a fifteen-year-old French student, is with us now. His Dad works for Allison Gas Turbine in France and since my Dad works for Allison in this country, he has gone to France a few times on business. On one of these business trips he was at Eric's family's house for dinner when the topic of visiting the United States came up. They asked if Eric could come and stay with us for his summer break from school. So he will be with us for about six weeks and then he has to go home because he has to go back to school in September.

Rebecca and her sister   *Photo by Sandra Merrion*
Tiffany with French exchange student Eric

We find that all of our foreign exchange students' schooling is much more intense than in the United States. You can tell how important academics are in other countries by the amount of time that students go to school. Both of our Japanese students were sent here with major amounts of homework to do; it had to be finished before they went home. Neither one quite got their homework finished and their mothers wrote to us and explained that the kids couldn't write because they were too busy trying to finish the work that they didn't get done while they were here!*

Last summer my time was filled up with Habitat For Humanity. Wherever I turned, it seemed to be calling out my name saying, "Come help us build houses." It is a great opportunity to learn carpentry skills and make new friends. I love Habitat because it builds houses for God's people in need, people who otherwise would not be able to afford a decent house—just as I love the homeless shelters because they help people who don't have a house get temporary living quarters.

My family and my friend Naomi (who is seventeen and also a homeschooler) headed down to Kentucky for our first Habitat For Humanity experience. We got to the headquarters on a Sunday night at around eleven- thirty. Thank goodness there were some girls at a gas station who offered to take us to the town that the headquarters were in, or we probably would have never got there. Everyone was still up when we arrived, so we got to meet our close companions for the

Photo by Betty Phelps

---

* Editor's note: Many homeschoolers set up foreign exchanges informally through pen-pals or friends' relatives, but others go through programs such as the Council on International Educational Exchange, www.ciee.org.

week, who were from all different parts of Indiana and Ohio. There was one other teenager besides Naomi and me; he was fifteen and the grandson of the couple who organized the week. The rest of our group were adults between thirty and fifty, but we all became very good friends. After meeting everyone, we retired to bed because we had to get up in the morning and get started on our Habitat work.

For the next week, we did everything from painting walls and porches, to pounding in nails, tearing down a small concrete building and rebuilding it, and tearing a porch off of a house on a hill and building a new one. We also took out enough time to get to know one another and to do some fun things like going to see a pet monkey, or hearing about the bloody Hatfield-McCoy feud enough times that it seemed like we could retell it perfectly if we wanted to. Learning history in this way is much more exciting than if you are just reading about it in a history book.

Taking a break from
building trusses and walls

Photo by Betty Phelps

We took the time to have potluck dinners with the people of the community and to watch a couple of movies and play some games. There were also opportunities to just sit and talk with our companions, mostly at breakfast and dinner because those were the two meals that we ate together. We all took turns making dinner so that one person was not always stuck with the cooking. At the end of the week, Habitat sent us home exhausted and with new knowledge of many things.

After we got home and settled back into our daily routine, Habitat suddenly entered our lives again. A man from my father's work told him that Habitat was going to blitz build (build a house in a week) a house in Frankfort, Indiana. He invited us to come and see how a blitz house was done. We did not think it would be possible to get a house built in five days, but we did go on the last two days, and we were surprised both at how much they had gotten done and also how much more there was to do.

Pulling nails out of old factory boards

Photo by Duke Merrion

On both Friday and Saturday we tore up and replaced the sidewalk, landscaped the lawn, and tried to get the inside of the house finished up by Saturday night. The crew of workers were totally exhausted Saturday night, and although some trimming and finishing work still needed to be done, the house dedication was held as scheduled. I had fun helping out and learned many new skills. Along with other things, I learned how to smooth out a sidewalk and make curbs. And I got to sign my name on the sidewalk since I was the only girl helping with it.

Although the blitz team was mostly made up of twenty- to sixty-year-old people, I was able to join them while they were working in the Indianapolis area. We built another house in Lebanon, Indiana, and then went to Indianapolis to help finish up some blitz houses that had already mostly been built. The team then went to Martinsville to build trusses and walls. (We used wood from the crates that the ammunition from the Gulf War was shipped back in.)

Having volunteer experience will help when I'm looking for a job; I will be able to say, "Hey, I know how to do that." Of course, *everything* is not going to necessarily help; it is not going to help to know how to smooth out a sidewalk if I get a job caring for the elderly. But I am trying to decide what field I want to go into, so I am trying to experience many things to help me decide.

Also, I think that being homeschooled, and having time to give, has helped me realize the importance of many of the subjects that I am now concerned about. Through my work with Habitat For Humanity and homeless shelters, I care about those with inadequate housing. Seeing and living in our natural environment makes me want to recycle and care about the earth. I never expected to develop such a concern for the environment, but I have decided that if somebody isn't concerned, then we are in pretty bad shape. If more people don't try to be earth-conscious it will be too late and I hate to think of what would happen then. I try to recycle as much as I can and reuse stuff that can be reused. I also try to recycle other people's trash by picking it up from the side of the road. I read about the environment and what I can do to help save it; there is so much information out there and yet the people who most need to read it aren't reading it. I have also planted 150 trees on our property and I am looking for places to plant more.

My dad and my siblings were gone for most of last summer, and our usually full house seemed like it would be pretty empty. So I came up with the idea of having swimming lessons in our family's pool for the little kids in our homeschool group. Boy, did I get a better turnout than I expected. I had around fifteen kids and was I busy! In the two and a half months that I taught swimming, I had to rescue kids about six times. Twice it was the same little boy. I figured that he would be scared from then on, but in about ten minutes he was back in the pool and heading for the deep end again. Other times the kids were just chasing balls or rafts and slipped on the slope that goes down into the deep end. None of them got really scared and I was thankful for that. The mothers must have appreciated what I did, because they have been asking me when I'm going to start lessons again. It makes me feel good that maybe I was able to teach them something that someday might save their lives or even somebody else's.

I make many of my friends through our homeschool group and through my brother and his friends and, of course, through the friends I already have. I meet their friends and pretty soon I have more friends than I can keep up with. I have made a lot of friends through my volunteer work also; the opportunities are endless. I get along better with people older than me but I also get along with people my age or younger. I do not turn away anyone who wants to be my friend just because they are younger.

I have friends who go to school whom I met through other people or through an activity, such as ballet. Sometimes it is hard to keep in touch with your friends who go to school, because they see their school friends every day.

I have met some homeschooled teens who have gone to school before and are shy. I think this is mainly because a lot of them were rejected at school since they didn't fit in. But I have also met a lot of homeschooled teenagers who are very open people and very friendly. If you talk to them you learn that they quit school because of all the mental abuse caused by the school situation.

I actually used to be one of those people who could never do anything by myself. I always had to have a friend go along with me everywhere so that I wouldn't feel left out. Now I realize that that is foolish, because you can never find anyone who has exactly the same interests as you. What helped me to become more outgoing was that I just told myself that we were all created equal, and that I was just as nice as everyone else, and who cares if I wasn't as pretty as some other girl? Also, if other people could be outgoing, why couldn't I? I told myself that outer beauty is only skin deep, and that there are a lot of people who are pretty on the outside but who wouldn't be too good looking if they were turned inside out. I decided that I wanted to be one of the people that would be good looking if someone cared to turn me inside out. I personally want to be remembered for what I have on the inside rather than how pretty I am on the outside.

One key to a full social life when you are a homeschooler is being able to make your own fun. If you wait around for the fun to come to you, you'll be waiting for a long time, unless the fun just tends to flock to you. I have learned to make my own fun and that is one of the reasons I am so busy with friends. With my different friends, I have hung out at the mall, gone to movies, gone fishing in the rain, slept out under the stars when it was too cold to go outside without a coat on, and gone swimming when we should have been in pants and long sleeved shirts.

I have said a lot about how good homeschooling is, and I know that some of you are probably saying that it couldn't be always fun and enjoyable. What are the bad things about homeschooling? People ask me if I get sick of my mom, dad, and little sister, and of course there are times when I wish that I could just get away for the day like school kids do. (I'm sure that they also get sick of me, especially when I'm in a bad mood.)

Sometimes peers don't accept the fact that you're homeschooling. I had a homeschooling friend who went back to school. Her "friends" had started rumors that she couldn't make it in school, so she had to drop out. She ended up going back to school because she is shy and didn't like the rumors. If I went to school and then decided to homeschool, and people started rumors about me, I would have to say to them that they must not realize how much better than them I had it. I would also explain to them how responsible you have to be to homeschool, and how busy I am.

Homeschooling is something that you have to *want* to do. If you are thinking about it, you should talk to another homeschooler personally, because then you can ask questions and they can ask you why you are thinking about homeschooling, and whether you would be ready for the responsibility. Besides talking to a variety of people who are homeschooled, read all you can find about the different styles of homeschooling. The only way that I have homeschooled is very unstructured, but I know a lot of people who more or less run a school in their home. I think that the better way is unstructured, yet I can't really judge them since I have never tried homeschooling in their way. Being unstructured, you are able to experience a lot of things that you would not be able to experience if you were in a structured setting.

If you are a new homeschooler and you are not meeting any other homeschoolers, try to find a support group in your area; you will be a lot better off than if you were just trying to make it on your own. You will find as you continue homeschooling that different ideas work for different teenagers. Some things will work for you, and some things won't. As you make friends that are homeschooled you will become more secure with homeschooling and will like it more and more. One thing I have heard many homeschooled teenagers say is that they are thankful that they don't have to eat any more school lunches!

Rebecca Merrion
Danville, Indiana

Gratitude and Regret

Staring at my blank screen, I wonder where to begin. I *loved* homeschooling—I loved the vast and varied opportunities it offered me. And I *hated* homeschooling—I hated feeling that I didn't have the choice *not* to homeschool. Whew! Okay, having said that scary mouthful, let me try to explain these extremes. Years after my homeschool career I can finally sit and reflect both on what I missed and what I received.

My parents had the courage to make an incredible decision in homeschooling me, and also the perseverance and generosity to follow through on that decision day after day, year after year. They helped bring to life math, history, science, reading and other subjects, not only through books, but also through vivid experiences. For example, as we were learning about the constitution and the forming of the United States we traveled east and saw the Liberty Bell, Constitutional Hall, Betsy Ross's house and the Benjamin Franklin museum. While studying the planets, we got some idea of the immensity of outer space by taking different-sized objects and arranging them, to scale, according to their placement in the solar system. Most wonderfully, when I was sixteen my parents took us on a four-month adventure through Australia and New Zealand. They invested a lot of time, patience, and even money into providing me with the greatest learning experience they felt I could have. I appreciated the sacrifices they made and I savored the opportunities I was given.

I also loved being able to learn things in different ways and at my own pace. And during my high school years, I did many things that I imagine other kids would have been jealous of. I spent hours with friends wandering the city of Indianapolis. Museums, monuments, libraries—you name it, we explored it. We watched plays and ballets, discovered parks, and basically spent hours quenching our thirst for knowledge. It was a wonderful feeling to wake up and ask myself what I wanted to do that day. I felt a freedom that most people don't experience until far later in life. And I loved homeschooling for giving me this freedom.

On the other hand, I grew up and formed views of my own that didn't exactly mirror my parents', and I know this has been hard for them at times—how could it not be, after all they poured of themselves into my upbringing? So, although I hate the thought of hurting their feelings, it also feels important to speak truthfully. And the truth is that I do have some regrets. I regret that I never went to a high-school dance, or belonged to a debate team or even ate a school lunch giggling with girlfriends about cute guys. At one time, I wanted to be part of an alternative learning environment that *wasn't* taught by my own Mom or Dad. I wanted to know what the other kids did that I was missing out on. I wanted, at least once, to feel the panic of running down the hall being late for class. At some point, I tentatively brought up the subject of trying out school, but my parents weren't enthusiastic, and I didn't press, and we all dropped the subject. Because I never really pushed, I don't know how they would have responded if I had. So, perhaps I *should* have fought harder for that experience. Perhaps I should have tried to communicate more clearly that just because they thought it was great that I didn't have to experience any of the "horrors" of school, I would have liked to see and judge them for myself. And I do still wonder what I missed out on. I wonder whether my longings are just the remnants of an unrealistic teenage fantasy, or would school have indeed been everything I sometimes imagined it was? I'll never know, and I hated homeschooling for not giving me the chance to find out.

So those are the feelings that I've carried with me, and that I'm still resolving. But let me back up and just touch on what became of a few of the things I described in my first essay, and give you a little update. After I returned home from Australia, the world looked full of new things I wanted to try. So while I still enjoyed ballet, it felt less important than making room for new opportunities, and I let it go. But I still benefit from my dance training. My sisters laugh that I might be the only member of my family with grace and poise. I'm not sure I can agree with the grace and poise part, but my training did give me a deep appreciation for the arts.

I am proud to say that my involvement in Habitat for Humanity inspired my father to start a local chapter. I served on the board, and in numerous other capacities, and saw many families into new homes. I learned some important lessons that have helped me in many situations since. Life has taken on a busier tone and Habitat is one of the things that I put on the back burner, but I expect that one day I will go back and get the same enjoyment and satisfaction that I always did. Until then I have fond memories of all of the families that I spent time with, and I remember lessons learned from each one.

I still bead and read. Not at the same time, of course! But these are two of my favorite "me" things to do. And I try to challenge myself each day, whether by looking things up on the Internet or in an encyclopedia, or taking a class, or just talking to someone wiser than me. I tend to look at most situations as learning experiences. I nurture and protect my excitement about learning new things, and I believe it comes from my homeschool experience.

After an "illustrious" four-year career as an assistant manager in the camping department of a local outdoor store, I recently quit. I came away with an expanded knowledge of the outdoor industry. I am now comfortable entering the woods, confident that I know more about the outdoors than the chicks on *Survivor*! Along with enjoying hiking and backpacking, I've also discovered that I love kayaking, and the peace of being on the water by myself. Ironically, I realized that my job, although I loved it, couldn't support the new interests it had inspired, since it didn't pay very well or, more importantly, provide enough time off. So I enrolled in massage therapy school, another unexplored-yet-close-to-my-heart intrigue.

Massage school provided me with my first real glimpse of conventional schooling, so I was nervous and apprehensive at first. However, I found it to be refreshing and fun. I enjoyed being in an environment where I was subjected to multiple opinions, all of which were right in their own way. I reveled in having many different instructors, all from different backgrounds, who provided us with diverse personal experiences. I loved being in class with people with whom I shared common interests, and yet were so varied in their views. I discovered that I thrived in a classroom and delighted in having so many friends to argue amicably with. My experience in massage school satiated my desire for conventional schooling a little, but I do still encounter that feeling of having missed out whenever high school is being discussed. It's almost like coming from another country and having no idea about the American way of life.

Anyway, since completing my certificate in massage therapy, I have taken numerous continuing education classes to keep learning about the body-work field. Shortly after graduation, I got to spend a week in Jamaica learning water massage and celebrating. Not only do I love my new work, but—because of the good pay and flexible hours—it also offers me the opportunity to travel, another passion that my parents instilled in me. I have taken several trips, some to get more massage training, and some for other reasons altogether. I am now applying my skills in a busy salon where I am able to work only three days a week and leave plenty of time for my other interests.

So, having voiced the spectrum of my feelings on homeschooling, what will I choose for my own children? I do feel an alternative learning environment provides a healthier setting both mentally and spiritually than does conventional schooling. I do hope to give my children some of the same great experiences that my parents bestowed upon me—and by that I mean not only educational experiences, but also having a strongly bonded, loving family. The one different choice I will probably make is to provide my future children with the freedom of choice, when or if they should choose a different path than the one that I have imagined for them.

Kyla Wetherell, 16
Corvallis, Oregon

Rising Out

At the time I wrote the following journal entries, I was still in public high school, at the top of the junior class, editor of the school newspaper, former exchange student to Thailand, active club member, etc.—not a person anyone would expect to drop out of school.

Photo by Weston Becker

Monday January 6, 1992

After my first day back at school, I want more than anything to just leave—even possibly to be finished with formal education altogether. I can think of no good reason why I should remain in a situation I loathe, except long-run financial problems. There simply is no motivation to continue.

Not that school today was anything out of the ordinary, but I resented the ordinary more. I resented sitting, conforming, and being told what to do by teachers who pride themselves on being the authority. I resented that force which kept me inside classrooms, doing and learning absolutely nothing when I could see the sun outside, and I especially resented having to work up the motivation to try to motivate the newspaper staff after a numbing day of school.

School is such a farce. I'm sure I learned more reading and writing at my own leisure for the two weeks of winter break than I did the whole first semester of school!

What I *want* to do is drop out, but what I probably will do is graduate a semester early. I'll have enough credits by the semester break next year, and I can use the time during the second semester to study on my own, read, write, and just do what I want to do.

Even just one more year of boredom and disgust seems like an eternity, though. There just isn't any reason why I should have to sit in school all day—or, for that matter, why anyone should.

Monday January 27, 1992

My first thought this morning when the alarm went off at 6:30 was, "Why should I get up? There's nothing to look forward to in a day of school."

But I did get up. It was the first day of second semester so I went to my new classes. Speech is going to be one of those phony "let's get to know each other" classes. Physics used to be the only class I liked, but now there are so many students in the class that I wouldn't know if I was enjoying it. Health—eight years of the same required curriculum, this class speaks for itself. Advanced algebra is just math—I'll do as little of the busywork as I can all semester and then memorize a few equations at the end so I can pass the final. Short story writing—I was really excited about this class, but I should have guessed that school can turn any subject into just another waste of time—another class to contemplate skipping every day. We're "learning" for the zillionth time what verbs and adjectives are. Then there's advanced placement U.S. History. There's nothing advanced about this class. For the first couple weeks we wrote essays and held discussions, but since then the bulk of the class has been boring lectures and time-consuming worksheets of busywork. I don't know what I think of the newspaper anymore. I certainly put more effort into it than any other part of school, but it's becoming tedious and because it represents the school there are limitations everywhere.

I spent the next few weeks in school, dreading each day, becoming more and more bitter, and letting it drain all the energy and excitement out of me.

There's something Dr. Seuss calls "The Waiting Place" in his story, *Oh, The Places You'll Go!* (my favorite children's book). That's what school was for me: just a place to sit and wait for my life to begin. Even though I liked working on the paper, and occasionally enjoyed a class—or, more often, a break—it was frustrating to sit in classes, too aware of their wastefulness and encouragement of mediocrity.

English was always my greatest interest so it was the subject I hated most in school. I didn't even *want* to understand why teachers used multiple choice questions to gauge a student's understanding of a poem, why most insisted that every student in the class come to the same conclusion regarding the theme of a play, or how writing could be graded on a numerical scale. I found that even in advanced classes in subjects I was interested in, teachers spent a lot of time baby-sitting bored students and regurgitating textbook drivel.

I'd sit in algebra class making all kinds of plans, thinking about biking across the country or just looking up something interesting in the library, but by the time that last bell rang I was usually so disgusted and drained that I just went home and did nothing, or went out with friends and tried to forget it all.

By February, I was taking every possible short cut in school. I switched my schedule around, and talked about graduating early and resigning as editor. I was searching for a positive way out and finally found it on a Monday morning break when my newspaper advisor told me he had a book I would want to "steal away" from him. It was Grace Llewellyn's *Teenage Liberation Handbook: how to quit school and get a real life and education*—the perfect catalyst for an idea that had been developing in me for a long time. By the end of the day I was pretty sure I would quit school. What really convinced me was the revelation that I didn't need a high school diploma to go to a good college or do any number of other things. I sat down with my mom that evening and tried to explain it all very carefully—why I wanted to leave school, that it wouldn't ruin my future, and what I wanted to do instead. I think she was much more relieved than she was worried (since she knew what a negative impact school was having on me), and she gave me her total support.

I spent that week reading the book, thinking about it and talking to people. Amazingly enough, I couldn't find even one good reason why I should keep wasting my time in school. This is not to say, of course, that I had no doubts. A few times I was momentarily stunned with an uncertainty about my life and future that I had not previously had to face, but it was more a reaction to such a big change than it was a logical concern.

So on Friday morning, I marched into the main office, sat down with the vice principal and told her that I would no longer be coming to school and that I needed to know what would have to be done in terms of signing papers, etc. I don't think she quite believed me. She looked almost amused, as though she knew "kids like me" don't drop out of school, and it would be easy enough to talk me out of it. The first thing she said was, "You can't; it's illegal." She told me that the law had recently changed and it was illegal for a sixteen-year-old to drop out. I had a few options, she said. To be legal, I had to 1) be employed full time, 2) be enrolled in an alternative school full time, or 3) be employed part time and enrolled in school part time. I laughed and said none of those options would be acceptable so she suggested that I simply stop coming to school, and in ten days she would call the truancy office.

I asked about homeschooling then, and at that point the principal walked in. He said something implying that he thought I was just interviewing for a newspaper article. The vice principal said, "We're not writing an article here, we're exploring options for Kyla." He whirled around with a shocked expression on his face and told me I needed to "think about this more carefully." I just smiled and said I already had.

The whole experience was worthwhile only in its amusement value for me and its shock value for them. Sure enough, by reading the law myself (which, ironically, the principal had photocopied for me) and talking with people who were not in authority positions—especially a friend whose expertise is in law and education—I found that it is perfectly legal. All I had to do was spend a couple days taking the GED.

(I should add here that registering as a homeschooler was also an option, but I decided that it would be easier to simply bypass the periodic achievement tests and whatever check-ups from the school that are required of homeschoolers. I don't stay at home and I don't spend my time doing things I did in school so it didn't seem like an accurate term anyway.)

So I was out! I wrote in my journal on the first day when there was school and I didn't have to go,

Tuesday February 18, 1992

My first day of freedom!

I rode my bike through buckets of rain downtown to CNIP [Center for National Independence in Politics where I volunteered, doing clerical work, desktop publishing, and some writing] and interviewed a few of the coordinators for a part of the newsletter I'm writing.

I talked to Judith last, and she asked me, "Isn't there school today?"

"There is," I said.

I told her that I had quit and briefly explained why. She was happy for me. (I'm starting to wonder if anyone is going to tell me I'm stupid or try to talk me out of it!) She also gave me the copy for a pamphlet, and I get the freedom to design it. It's nice not to have to turn down things like that because of a lack of time caused by school!

I rode my bike around some more, weaving through all the college students hurrying to their classes under umbrellas, and I visited with the man in the bead store.

By then it was noon so I had to go to school for newspaper. I'll continue going to newspaper for three weeks—one issue—to train the new editors and help out. The administration agreed that even though my name could not appear on the paper as editor I would be allowed to come and help for one more issue.

I walked into the newspaper office and saw my friends sprawled out eating their lunches. It kind of hit me then how free I am. I realized that I would be sitting there with them and probably look just as drained and annoyed if only I had made a different decision, or, worse yet, if I hadn't even been allowed a choice at all.

My whole life I've been waiting and looking forward to something that seemed far away. Whether it was the weekend or graduation, I was always waiting for life to happen, impatient to get through school so I could do what I wanted. Finally, I realize that life comes when you bring it, and my life is now!

The reactions I got from most people were that of astonishment but also of acceptance and often even envy. Though everyone was surprised, my friends at school said I was "so lucky" while neighbors, my mom's co-workers, and other friends called me "brave" and seemed to think that because of my decision I would "go far in life." Of course, there were one or two people who tried to commiserate with my mom, saying things like, "It's okay, even real smart kids can get in trouble." For the most part, though, the responses were positive; it seemed that those who I was sure would harass me for my decision were the first to applaud it. Even my grandpa said, "Way to go!"

I talked with my physics and history teachers and asked for their support since I planned to pursue both subjects independently and take tests come the end of the school year. With college and my future at what I considered to be some degree of risk, I wanted something concrete that I could point out to skeptics to make my intentions in quitting school clearer. I also figured that completed courses and test scores might be easier for college admissions officers to relate to than, say, a log that shows I practiced my guitar every day. And I thought that following a "curriculum" would be a good way to soften the shock from quitting school by giving my life a bit of structure. Both teachers were not only supportive but even offered to spend time tutoring me if I so desired.

During those first three weeks without school, while I still went to help on the school newspaper every day, I also spent a lot of time just doing what I wanted to do from one moment to the next. After that first week of rain it got really sunny and warm so I lived outdoors during the day. I wrote:

Monday February 24, 1992

Another wonderful day!

I finished the pamphlet for CNIP, rode my bike around under an almost hot spring sun, ate lunch in the gazebo in Central Park, stopped by a few shops I'd never been in, and sat in the doorway of Grassroots bookstore reading magazines. It's amazing—the activity of Corvallis on a sunny day when all of the still trapped and confused people are closed up in schools or offices! It's beautiful. People sit on porches strumming guitars. The parks are full. I rode my bike without destination. I smiled, and I felt alive.

This evening I worked through half of the next chapter in physics, drew up study plans for the next thirteen weeks in physics, U.S. history, and Spanish, and read the first two chapters in Steven Hawking's *A Brief History of Time*.

(When I first got out of school I was anxious to make sure that I wouldn't abandon my studies just because the structure I was used to had disappeared. Fortunately though, as I adjusted to my new life, I got out of the old mode of making lists and rigid plans. Gradually, I found that by giving myself the freedom of spontaneity, I didn't at all jeopardize my self-made education, but actually increased the enjoyment and diversity of learning.)

I started volunteering more at CNIP and CATF (Central American Task Force); I found four interesting books with different slants and viewpoints to help me study for the advanced placement history test, starting over with the colonists because I hadn't learned anything in class; I got a guitar and started learning to play, teaching myself with some help from friends; I continued to work at the *Corvallis Gazette Times* newspaper as a paste-up artist, a job I had been hired for in February; and I also spent some time those first three weeks working on a column that would be published in the school newspaper about "rising out" of school and "dropping into life." Thanks to my friends who succeeded me as co-editors, to an advisor who doesn't restrict students in creating their own paper, and to an administration that doesn't insist on seeing the paper before it goes to press, my column wasn't censored.

So on March sixth the legitimate school paper came out endorsing the wastefulness of the very existence of school. I was accused by some teachers of "dropping out of school and then abusing the privilege of the paper by encouraging other students to drop out too," but for the most part the reactions I got were surprisingly positive. Teachers, students, and parents respected my decision and told me it sounded like I was doing what was right for me. Unfortunately, the compliments were always followed by a "*but...*" and something about most kids not having the self-motivation I have. It makes me cringe every time. Just that kind of thinking is what keeps the whole system going. People are born with the motivation to do what is important to them, but by discouraging "unrealistic" dreams society has inevitably produced so called "unmotivated" people. An encouraging and accepting environment breeds self motivation, whereas the atmosphere of school has made so many people dependent and uninterested. Given freedom and opportunity, wouldn't every person figure out what it is she loves to do and do just that? And isn't it doing what one loves that brings happiness and thus success? Anyone leaving school because that's what they want to do can be happy and successful by their own standards. No one else's standards should be relevant anyway.

I was, however, more than satisfied with the overall attention the article got and the discussion it provoked. I was told that some classes spent entire periods talking about it and about what could be changed in the school to make it a place that people like me could feel satisfied with. A faculty committee spent a whole meeting discussing my rising out of school. The consensus there seemed to be that I probably made a good decision for myself but that 1) other kids "might try to rise out of school and fall right on their face" and 2) didn't I feel any obligation to remain in school in an attempt to make it a better place??

Frankly, no. Does a wrongly accused prisoner choose to prolong his sentence so he can try to make the penitentiary a more valuable and productive experience for other inmates? Do refugees voluntarily remain in abusive camps because their presence might better the situation? School is forced on us. If we follow the path, through school and society, which is cut out for us from the beginning, we have very little say in how we spend the first eighteen years of our lives. For a time, I put a lot of wasted energy into improving my school experience and that of others. I wrote editorials suggesting greater student involvement, presented ideas to the principal about conserving in the cafeteria, and helped organize recycling projects, Earth Day celebrations, etc. What it all comes down to, though, is that school is mandatory (well, of course, like everything else there are ways around it, but in the minds of most it *is* strictly mandatory), and as long as it remains in that state it is an inherently bad place.

With my allotted time to help with the school newspaper over, I had full days of freedom.

Monday March 9, 1992

I stayed at the library today from opening to closing. It was great to have the time and the freedom to browse, to read whatever I wanted for however long I wished. I skimmed or read parts of books that caught my interest. Philosophy turned out to be the main theme today. I read some of Einstein's essays in *Ideas and Opinions*, looked through some books on the Gaia theory, was delighted by a comic-style book about Marxism and a collection of essays about the philosophy of human perception and thought called *Metamagical Themas*, and started reading Thoreau's *Walden*.

I also found a good book to help me with U.S. history and checked out a couple of Studs Terkel's oral histories to complement my studies.

I had to tear myself away when the library closed. I think I'd be happy spending all day, every day there. If only there weren't so many other things I want to do too! One of the biggest differences between life in and out of school is that in school I was always wishing I could fast forward time until I was through with school altogether, but, instead, time dragged on and on. Now there's so much I want to do that I wish I could put time into slow motion, but, of course, it feels like just the opposite: My days go by so quickly that I don't have time for even half the things I want to do.

I feel so inspired and optimistic about the present and the future now that school isn't looming over me every day and holding me back. I wish, on the one hand, that I could have been taking advantage of all the years of my life while I'm still young and not financially responsible for myself. I feel cheated in a sense from all the years I spent in school that could have been years of learning and growing and happiness without restriction. Not that I didn't have a wonderful childhood. I just remember the story of the first time I was taken to a big library: The moment I walked in with my mom and got a look at all those books, I yelled into the silence of the library, at the top of my fourteen-month-old lungs, *"PLEASE READ!"* It makes me sad to think that if I never went to school I could have lived with that excitement for learning throughout my growing-up years. On the other hand, I am glad that I figured it out for myself, that I made the decision to leave school by my own will.

The vast majority of my days during those first few weeks as I was just tasting my freedom were as wonderful as that first day. I was happy and never once regretted leaving school—even the tiniest bit, although sometimes I would get this feeling that in a year and a half I'd be eighteen, having to support myself without even a high school diploma. I was so satisfied with teaching myself at that point (and still at this point) that I couldn't imagine wanting to go to college and sit in a classroom again, being told what is and is not important to learn. Worse yet (actually now I would say that it's better yet, but it seemed like another problem at the time), I couldn't think of a single job I would be happy submitting to. So once in a while I felt a little trapped and uncertain about my goals and my future. Recently, however, I have realized that options will be open to me regardless of the decisions I make about college, "careers" and lifestyle. In fact, I feel quite certain that I will be personally successful *because* I've risen out of school, not in spite of it.

I'm often asked to describe my typical day now that I'm out of school, but one of the things I like best is that there's nothing typical about my days. Sometimes I stay home all day writing at my computer and taking breaks to play my guitar, while other days I hop on my bike and end up looking through the arts center, meeting new people, reading Ayn Rand at the library, renting a movie that goes along with what I'm studying in history, taking a roll of film of "a day in the life of Central Park," *and* going to work. It just all depends.

Photo by Weston Becker

Sometimes I wake up in the morning and feel like getting out of town for the day or even for the week. As of yet it hasn't stopped amazing me that I do have that choice. Of course, there are small logistics to work out, such as access to the car and my work schedule, but if I'm in the mood to leave—to go camping or whatever—I can do that. Recently, I spent a few days staying with friends in Portland in their apartment downtown. This is an entry in my log book during one of my days there:

8:00-12:30 P.M. 22-mile bike ride, picnic, and photography at Forest Park, a five thousand acre forest here in Portland

1:00-3:00 P.M. explored Portland, talked with street musician who showed me how to play his African drums

3:00-5:00 P.M. Portland Art Museum: Native American, Cameroonian, Himalayan, and Japanese exhibits, plus European paintings and sculptures

6:00-7:00 P.M. read three chapters in *One Flew Over the Cuckoo's Nest*

8:00-10:30 P.M. saw modern theatrical production of *Richard II*

11:00 P.M.—12:30 A.M. read articles about the historical reign of Richard II and Henry IV.

I also do some things regularly. I study U.S. history on a schedule because I have to be ready for the AP test in May. I'm teaching myself linguistics, working twenty hours a week as a paste-up artist, volunteering for CNIP and CATF. The current project I'm working on with CATF is a demonstration for tax day to show people that their tax dollars aren't being spent by the government in the way they would choose to spend them, if it were up to them. I also volunteer at the library and am in charge of reshelving and organizing the travel and history shelves. When I applied, I wrote "autodidact" on the application instead of specifying the completion of a grade level.

My mom works at the community college in our area so I get three free classes a term. Even though classes don't sound especially appealing to me these days, I signed up for a photography class this term. I love it because it's really just an open lab with darkroom materials and an instructor and other students who help only when asked. I just got a Nikon manual camera, and I've been experimenting with it, developing film, printing enlargements, etc. It's great fun!

I go on mountain biking trips a lot, usually just in the hills around Corvallis but I do some longer trips too. When my friend, Cedar, was on spring break we put our mountain bikes on the back of the car and drove off to the high desert of eastern Oregon. It was great to ride our bikes on the trails around our campsite and explore the barren land and even a few ghost towns we happened upon. Biking, both on and off road, is one of my favorite things to do. Not only have I discovered beautiful areas right around Corvallis that I had never seen before, but the speed of a bike is perfect for exploring and it serves almost as a meditative activity. There's nothing like a few hours of biking to give me a new perspective on an idea or inspire me to write a story or an essay.

I write essays about everything I think about, sometimes just in my journal as it comes to mind and other times as a formal opinion piece. Before I left school, I had them published in the school newspaper. Now, I have just recently been appointed assistant editor of a local alternative paper called *Medicine Fish* so I can have columns published without trying to appeal to a high school audience. I've also had more time for creative writing since I left school, have found that I really like writing poetry, and as soon as I get a little better on the guitar, I want to start writing my own songs. Cedar and I are now working on writing and illustrating a children's book called *Run Free Little School Children!*

With all the time I have without school, I've been reading so much more. Before, I had to spend so much time reading textbooks and other worthless materials that I had to let all of the books I wanted to read pile up in a stack by my bed. I've diminished that pile now, and every day I find more books at the library that I want to read. Right now I'm trying to get through everything that Carson McCullers and Thoreau ever wrote.

Being out of school during the day, I've met some interesting people. I was always really disgusted with the social circles and games in high school so meeting people of all kinds is a nice change. Just the other day, I made friends with an elderly woman who was out doing her gardening. I ended up helping her out, and I think we really brightened each other's days. I have friends whom I've met from various things I've been involved in, have had more time to keep in touch with people I know outside of school, and I also have had no trouble continuing my friendships with people still in school.

I feel bad, though, for my friends in school. It seems that so many are trying to figure out ways to spend the least possible amount of time there. Most parents won't even listen to talk about "dropping out," and I find it so incredibly frustrating that their fear of something they don't understand has so much power that their kids must continue to be unhappy and waste their time.

Although I'd like to think that I would have left school regardless, I owe a lot to my mom for listening to me, keeping an open mind, and supporting me all the way. She understands that I know myself and my goals better than anyone else and that I need the freedom to make my own decisions. She doesn't monitor my behavior and activities, but she is interested in what I'm doing and helps me if I ask. We talk about the various books we're reading, and she helps proofread my writing sometimes, but because she works during the day and I enjoy my independence, our involvement in each other's activities is minimal. In my journal:

Tuesday March 17, 1992

It feels like, in the past month, I have gone from being a high school kid to a working, living adult. I don't necessarily feel that I'm any more mature or that I have changed so much, but now I am treated like a human being full-time instead of part-time, and I have control over myself and my life.

I don't have school degrading me every day, but also, adults and especially my mom seem to have started trusting me even more than before. I'm treated like just another adult living in the house. For the first time in my life, I feel like I have total control over my decisions.

Between now and August I plan to continue with all the things I'm doing now and prepare for some of the long term goals I have set. Then, starting in August or September—the time I would have begun my senior year of high school—I hope to embark on a biking adventure in South America.

Most people don't really understand or believe me when I tell them that I want to fly down to the Southern tip of South America and ride my bike back up to the U.S., taking photographs and writing about my experiences. I get a lot of laughter and responses like "Reality check" when I tell about this, but I always figure that if I want to do something I'm going to find a great way to do it regardless of how far-fetched it sounds. I've been researching South America and thinking about a rural biking excursion through wilderness and village areas. By writing to some organizations—including American Youth Hostels and the South American Explorers Club—and reading about others' experiences, I'm hoping to find a cheap, safe way to carry out my plan. I have also just started apprenticing at a local bike shop so I can learn as much about bike repair as possible before my departure. Eventually, I'd love to write and publish a book about my journey.

Although I am leaving the return time open—so there's room for a bit of wanderlust—I have a vague idea that I might return in about a year, at which point there are many things I want to do. Eventually, I want to spend some time doing apprentice work with subsistence farming. I'm interested in spending a few years early on learning the skills I might need if ever I want

Photo by Weston Becker

to build a house, live on a farm, sail away on a boat, or just start my own organic garden.

Sometime, I also intend to go on another biking trip—this time with Cedar in Europe. We've been planning to go there to travel and meet our numerous pen friends for quite a while now, and we will probably work on a cruise ship or at the Alaska fisheries for a few months to earn the necessary money. We want to spend an unplanned amount of time in Europe just doing whatever comes up, staying in youth hostels, living with pen friends, and biking the backroads.

By this time I will doubtless have enough experience and "maturity" so that I can get into college—if I decide that's what I want to do—or get a job using my skills and doing something I really enjoy. Or, ideally, I will have the faculties to become self-employed. I'm not so naive as to think that it will all happen just as I've crafted it in my mind, or even that I'll want to do exactly the same things in six months that seem so exciting to me now. It's fun to make plans, though, and it's even more amazing that I *can* do these things. As the time between myself and school widens it seems that I'm constantly becoming aware of more and more opportunities. It's almost scary to think that under slightly different circumstances I might still be sitting in school, graduating, going straight to a prestigious college, getting a degree, etc., and probably assuming that I was doing the best possible thing I could do with my life.

The world is full of options for all kinds of people. The fact that a person doesn't need a formal education to be happy or to do great things is like a best kept secret by parents, schools, and society in general. For those who want to go to college, it's so much better to spend a lifetime doing what one wants and two days taking an easy test (the GED) than it is to endure years and years of school. I'm constantly amazed by how many opportunities are open to people even without a high school diploma or a college degree. The possibilities are truly endless.

The only things I was taught in school that I couldn't have learned faster and better outside of school were to conform, to be blindly patriotic and accept all the stereotypes presented in textbooks, to submit to patronizing treatment from adults, to suppress my own ideas and dreams and go along with the norm. Good thing they weren't successful in teaching me even that!

For me, leaving school was not only a great idea for my own personal benefit; it was also a statement, a protest against an oppressive institution. Why people have chosen such a means to achieve status and "education" I don't understand, but I do know that it is not something I ever wished to condone. As Thoreau put it, "Cold and hunger seem more friendly to my nature than those methods which men have adopted and advise to ward them off."

He also wrote, "What old people say you cannot do, you try and find that you can."

Kyla Wetherell, 16
Corvallis, Oregon

Notes on Finding Work

Before I left school, I had already been hired at the *Gazette Times* and done work with both the Center for National Independence in Politics and the Central American Task Force. I found a job opening at the GT while browsing the classified ads (during a particularly mind-numbing classroom lecture, I might add) and applied even though I was pretty sure I wouldn't be considered because of my age and inexperience. Well, I was rejected at first, but when another opening for the position of newspaper paste-up artist opened, I was interviewed and hired.

I got involved with CATF over a year ago when my opposition to the Gulf War put me in touch with community activists of all kinds. Activist groups are always grateful for volunteers, and all it takes to join most groups is checking out campus or community bulletin boards, finding a group that fits your interests, and showing up at one of their meetings. Your possible ignorance or inexperience shouldn't be a problem because much of what needs to get done is often busy-work, *but* by attending meetings and participating you will learn from the experience and, no doubt, be given more thoughtful jobs to do as you learn more.

Community sections in local and alternative newspapers are good places to look also. That's where I found an article about CNIP. I went to their office and asked if they could use a volunteer. In a few weeks I was stuffing envelopes; later, the position developed into work with database, page design, and writing.

I want to add here that I eventually stopped volunteering at CNIP and at CATF because during those first months out of school my ideas and views changed; I came to question the value of both organizations and realized that the work was no longer meaningful to me. I don't, however, regret working with either: The volunteers are hard-working groups of people and I learned much from the experiences.

Because I spent a lot of time at the library once I was out of school, the idea of volunteering there surfaced, and I simply asked for an application at the reference desk. Weeks later, I was called in and given first an orientation, then the simple job of organizing the travel and history shelves. It took only about an hour a week—not an especially "important" job, but I was told that if at any time I wanted more responsibility, all I had to do was ask. I never did because this was at an especially busy time with my other activities, but I assume that had I been really interested and wanted to put more time and energy into it I could have acquired a much more educational position.

The process of becoming assistant editor, and now editor, of *Medicine Fish* newspaper was similar to the others in that I picked up a copy of the paper and wrote to the editor, saying that I was impressed by the publication and would like to help out. I met with Chris, the editor, and found that not only was he editor and manager of the paper, but he made up the entire permanent staff. So, given my experience and willingness to help, I was automatically appointed assistant editor. A few weeks later, when we were about midway through putting out the third issue of *MF*, Chris called me to say that he was moving and the paper was all mine. This was a mixed blessing since I was already busy, but I found a few more people to help and promoted myself to editor!

Finally, in acquiring my apprenticeship at the bike shop I sort of went out on a limb. I just knew that I wanted to learn bike repair and that I didn't want to take a class. (I'd tried a bike class through the community college and didn't enjoy it.) So I walked into a few of the bike shops in town and asked to speak with the manager. I simply said that I wanted to observe and help with repairing bikes and that I would gladly do some of their grunge work in return. I was turned down two times before the idea was accepted. The first two managers told me that they had enough help and someone with little experience would just be in the way. The third manager agreed, however, and the apprenticeship worked out better even than I expected.

In general, by staying alert and just being willing to work for experience instead of money, it is fairly easy to find valuable volunteer positions. One of the most important things to keep in mind that I've found, is that often you'll be rejected at first, but if you know what you want to do and you're stubborn enough, you'll find what you're looking for.

Photo by Weston Becker

Kyla Wetherell, 17
Quito, Ecuador

La Gringa y La Bicicleta

I wake to sleep and take my waking slow.
I feel my fate in what I cannot fear.
I learn by going where I have to go.
Theodore Roethke, *Words for the Wind*

Monday, October 5, 1992

I'm about seventy-five miles deep into Ecuador, and what a day!

Exchanged goodbyes with the López family who so generously opened their home to me in Ipiales, and bade farewell to Colombia too, with promises to both that yes, someday I would return. Rode steeply downhill to the frontier, crossed the border into Ecuador, and landed in chaos.

It seems that my four-day delay in Ipiales, Colombia was due to some sort of uprising or strike concerning commercial trade between Colombia and Ecuador. When I reached the border this morning, cars were still unable to pass, but the police allowed me to slide my bicycle under the barricade.

So welcome me to Ecuador! Trees laying across the road, hoards of people walking to the border and all asking me what the situation was like. All I could tell them, as I lugged my loaded-down bike over the trees and other ingenious barricades, was that I had been allowed to pass, as had two Ecuadorian pedestrians now dragging four gigantic suitcases up the hills.

Then the town of Tulcán—to my dismay the strike had caused everything to close down, meaning no banks or exchange houses were open, and I had only Colombian money and U.S. dollars. It took some looking, but I finally found a street changer to take my pesos in return for sucres at a reasonable commission.

But there was something else unusual, too, about my first Ecuadorian town. I couldn't pinpoint it until I sat down to eat my breakfast orange in the town square and took a good look around me: Everyone was moving slower! Ecuadorians are more leisurely than Colombians?! Also, before I left town, I met an English couple who were envious of my independent style of transport—they've been stuck in Tulcán four days and still haven't found a way to leave!

Then came a relentless steep climb—the great Andes come to test my good humor once again. But with no traffic on the road save an occasional motorbike or friendly bicyclist, and with the weather overcast and cool, I quite enjoyed myself. Also, I made an Ecuadorian friend traveling on a dirt bike, and we talked and laughed throughout an hour's worth of hills.

I waved goodbye to my dirt bike companion as he turned off to his village, and sped down hills which made me shiver enough to wear my winter coat here on the Equator! In Ecuador, the Pan American highway runs mostly along the valley between the Eastern and Western Cordilleras of the Andes, but this valley is interspersed with intermontane basins, thus providing me with harsh mountain climbs and downhill glides, hillsides quilted with farms—occasionally brightened by Indians working in their traditional colorful dress, and deep gorges which eventually led me down into the tropical Chota Valley. As I was descending into the valley, six Swiss men on motorcycles, whom I had encountered previously in Colombia, surprised me from behind. When we reached Juncal at a mere fifteen hundred meters we attracted the attention of just about the entire town. This area is inhabited mostly by black people—descendants of the African slaves who were brought over in the seventeenth century. They gathered around us and made jokes about the girl working hard on a bicycle while the big men relaxed on motorcycles! One of the locals bit off the sides of a stalk of sugarcane and we all tasted the sweet cane.

Pedaled back up to an altitude of 2,225 meters and found a cheap hotel here in Ibarra.

I flew to Caracas, Venezuela one month ago, took buses to Cartago, Colombia (west of Bogotá) and have been pedaling ever since. I do believe this is the first time in my life I've given myself the chance to just live—the first time I have no plans for the future so I'm able to enjoy living in the present. And I'm so very full! Full of the jerks and bumps and near-deaths of Latin American buses on Latin American roads; full of the hospitality and liveliness of all the people I've met; full of the dark, formidable presence of the Andes; full of triumph and frustration, but mostly just full. Happily full...full but still hungry.

Back at home, I encountered a lot of discouragement and doubt (both within myself and from others) during the summer, as I attempted to organize my trip. There were phases when I was sure I wanted to do the trip exactly as I had originally planned, without stopping to wonder if the idea made sense as a whole or if it would even be enjoyable. At these times, it seemed I was faced with the most opposition: jealously scoffing adults, skeptical and patronizing discouragement. People are scared of anything that is outside of the obvious and generally followed "road of life." We've been taught that any travel in foreign countries is at least slightly risky (in terms of future financial security, lack of structure, or actual personal harm), let alone a young female biking alone in South America! It was hard to explain and justify myself when even I didn't feel wholly confident that my trip would be possible and safe. I was concerned that I might be subconsciously censoring valid warnings in order to support my hesitant hope that my journey could be fun and safe.

But there were other times when something would inspire me and I would speed over to the library on my bike and come home, triumphant, with an overflowing backpack of books and my mind swarming with new ideas. I often found that people's skepticism stemmed from ignorance, while encouragement came from those with experience and knowledge about what I would be doing. Also, as the time for my departure grew near and people realized that I was really going regardless of their warnings, I actually started receiving a lot of warm and admiring responses.

Fortunately, my experiences thus far in Colombia and Ecuador have proved any insecurities I had to be quite unfounded. The widely-held belief that Colombia is a dangerous place for foreigners to travel—a land of rampant crime and dominating drug trade—is yet another myth. Wherever I happened to be in Colombia at any given time, the local people told me that I was safe in that place, but that my next destination was extremely dangerous, full of criminals (who would steal my bike or plant drugs in my bags) and guerillas (who would slit my throat). At this point, the storyteller would take out his own machete to illustrate! But somehow I never reached the fabled land of danger, though I traversed Colombia North to South.

Instead, the Colombians I met were consistently friendly and gracious. Perhaps it was *because* I was alone and female that I was invited into homes so often. I stayed in a Colombian hotel only once; otherwise I was able to camp or stay with families. In one town, I asked around for a place to camp and every time was pointed in the direction of the police station. Due to my natural aversion to police, I was reluctant but in fact I received a warm welcome, a free shower, dinner, and breakfast! Another time I spent the night in the home of three nuns—one from New Zealand, one French, and one Colombian. During the day we helped haul wheelbarrows of bricks to the building site of a house and went around the village visiting the old people—then we stayed up half the night laughing. Kyla joins in a slumber party with three lively nuns—very strange!

I spent a lot of my summer in Oregon reading, writing, drawing, and hiking or biking. I found that I was able to write before I thought, instead of the other way around, so that writing became a way to learn about myself rather than to express a formerly processed idea. I no longer retained any interest in finding a magazine for which to write about my trip, or in keeping track of miles and being able to say that I rode this far in that amount of time. I knew that the trip was for *me*, and that I didn't need any expensive, fancy gear in order to sleep outside, or a male companion in order to keep me safe, or a lot of money in order to learn and to live.

After many letters written, conversations with travelers and friends, books skimmed and read, and plenty of deliberation, I realized that beginning in Santiago or Buenos Aires as I had initially planned and riding my bike north all the way back to the U.S. was incompatible with my hopes of leisurely spending time living and working in different places, and also with my objective of seeing and learning a lot about the Andean countries specifically. I was generally more interested in living and learning in South America at whatever pace felt right than in completing a long distance, and probably somewhat grueling, traverse of a continent. The South American Explorers Club was extremely helpful in making suggestions for traveling alone, and made it possible for me to feel confident organizing my own adventure.

I also did a lot of research on my own, looking for information that would be necessary in planning a fun, safe adventure but also searching for a more general knowledge of the continent's natural, cultural, and political history in order to enhance my experience. How much more exciting it was to study geography, language, ecology, social studies, etc. because it was relevant to my coming journey, not because a teacher said it was important!

Mid-summer, I took six days off of work and went on a bikecamping trip through the Cascade mountains alone. If there's one thing I would suggest to someone abandoning the structure and oppression in their life (namely school), it would be to take some kind of solo trip for as long as it's possible to get away. I had no tent and only ten dollars, a stove, dried food, tarps, sleeping bag, etc. I was anything but experienced in that kind of outdoor living, but I *wanted* to be experienced, and I did just fine.

As far as academic pursuits, the summer proved again and again how irrelevant school could be to even the most scholarly future—not that this is necessarily what I have in mind! But I received the results from the AP U.S. History exam on which I scored a perfect five, having taken only half of the class which the test was based on. I also easily passed the GED and opted out of taking the SAT since I wouldn't need it for the only college that has of yet caught my interest.

I wrote a letter to Hampshire College (located in Amherst, Massachusetts and lacking any grades, tests, required courses, and other structural restraints) explaining my situation, my plans, and why Hampshire interested me. I received a prompt reply: In a nutshell, no high school diploma is perfectly fine and no need for me to take the SAT; it sounded like I would do well at Hampshire, they wrote. However, I don't plan to go to college anytime in the near future. I do think that attending college for a year or two will be an experience, just like anything else, that I'd like to try. At this point, though, I'm fairly sure that spending four years in classrooms and collecting a degree would feel just as artificial as earning a high school diploma.

Because of my apprenticeship at the bike shop, I had access to the help and equipment I needed to rebuild and upgrade my bike for the many miles and the abuse it would take in the coming months. This and other opportunities—both incidental and planned—made it possible for me to pay for the entire expense of my travels with my own money, which I earned mostly from working for six months at the newspaper. Youths (under twenty-four years) get reduced airfare (especially low in South America) so I was able to fly to Caracas, Venezuela for only $250, and the cost of traveling here in South America is significantly cheaper than just living in the U.S. (I'm spending an average of $3.50 per day.) My biggest expense ended up being custom-made bike bags which convert into an internal frame backpack and have allowed me to ditch my bike when I tire of it and trek some. The flexibility was worth the cost, no doubt.

I pretty much cycled directly through Colombia along the Pan American Highway, although I did spend a few days in wayside villages and four days in the picturesque colonial town of Popayan. I stayed with a family there, strolled down narrow cobbled roads bordered by stark white cement houses, visited ornate churches and cathedrals, and took day trips into the surrounding countryside.

Pedaling on to Pasto, then Ipiales—the border town—was challenging but spectacular. The Pan Am actually goes up and over one of Colombia's three parallel cordilleras (mountain ranges) here. Just south of a town called El Bordo the road dipped into a dry, parched valley. This stretch was sad and difficult, with no water, barefoot emaciated children lining the road begging for pesos, and an unprecedented amount of Colombian policemen armed with gigantic machine guns. My bags were searched twice—ostensibly for drugs, but more likely out of a simple curiosity about "the young blond gringa on a bike."

Otherwise, my experience was as rewarding as elsewhere in Colombia. I was joined off and on by companions of all kinds—everything from a *campesino* (peasant) on horseback to a group of *mestizos* with slick bicycles and lycra racing shorts. I stopped at roadside foodstalls for my meals, tasting local fruits and dishes. Always I was greeted with kindness and curiosity; I often repaid the generosity by simply allowing the local children to ride my bicycle!

I am sitting now against a eucalyptus tree in La Esperanza, Ecuador. It's Sunday morning and I'm waiting for the first of a series of buses which will, eventually, return me to Quito. This is Latin America—who knows how long I'll be waiting here!

Friday morning I took a bus from Quito to Cayambe, a small town dominated by a mountain of the same name which is the highest point in the world directly on the Equator. I started off hiking along an old Inca road which winds and climbs and falls amid the shadows of the Andes.

I walked much of the morning with two indigenous women, on their way to Olmedo. Striking in their full, bright skirts, white embroidered blouses and dozens of strands of gold beads piled up to their chins, the women told me a story about the jagged volcano Imbabura. Their eyes widened in disbelief when I told them I had climbed Imbabura with a British woman one week earlier.

Ate lunch with a family in a wayside home, then delighted the two young boys with my frisbee. I'd stopped so much along the way and marveled so much at my surroundings that night caught me by surprise long before I reached La Esperanza—the first town with a hostel. For an hour or so, I walked happily under a brilliant canopy of stars, but having left my tent and sleeping bag in Quito, I was lucky to catch a ride on horseback with two *campesinos* to Zuleta and even luckier to find a pick-up going from Zuleta to La Esperanza.

Ah, here comes my bus...I am staying now in Quito during the week and traveling on weekends. I made a friend who tutors me two hours each day in Spanish, and I'm living at a hotel with cooking and laundry facilities for $1.75 per night. I arrived in Latin America one month ago with practically no Spanish, believing as I do that the only way to really learn a language is to go where it's spoken. Sure enough, I was effectively communicating in "guerilla Spanish" within a week, although I had a long way to go from there. Although it has been frustrating at times, I think it would be much worse to have spent three years studying Spanish in a classroom, only to arrive in Latin America unable to communicate anyway. I've met plenty of disappointed travelers in this position.

I want to spend two to three weeks studying with my Ecuadorian tutor in order to form a basic understanding of the grammar, but I have and will continue to learn mostly by simply *communicating* daily. The locals have been understanding and helpful, and have made the experience of learning Spanish much more fun than it would be if I were sitting down and memorizing vocabulary words.

Though my plans for the immediate future are completely flexible, I'm thinking of remaining in Quito at least through October. The hotel I'm staying at is popular with travelers and locals alike, making it ideal for meeting interesting people. I also spend quite a bit of time at the South American Explorers Club Clubhouse in Quito. Available to members is a small library with books in English on Latin American politics, poetry, birds, environment, culture, natural history, etc.; files with information on everything from exotic butterflies to travelers' reports on excursions all over the continent; a bulletin board full of opportunities for travelers, a fairly comprehensive map room, and a book exchange. It's also very comfortable—a wonderful atmosphere in which to relax and talk with fellow travelers.

Through SAEC, I've found a housesitting job which may open up in November. If that works out, I'll have a large rural house—in a small community twenty kilometers from Quito—all to myself for free! From there, I can make local friends to speed the process of learning Spanish, and continue to travel around Ecuador. This country is a cheap and beautiful place in which to do jungle excursions, mountain climbing, etc. My budget doesn't allow for the price of guides here, but I'm finding ways around spending so much money, and this often makes the experience inherently more original and exciting anyway. Another opportunity I may take advantage of is a retreat on the southern coast called Alandaluz. Workshops in organic agriculture, ecological architecture, and appropriate technology are offered in addition to ocean, rainforest, and mountain excursions. At about seven dollars per day it's cheap but still beyond my budget so I'm considering offering to work in exchange for living and learning there for a few weeks. It might work—who knows?

Plans beyond that are sketchy. Pedal on to Peru and Bolivia—probably not Chile, but maybe—then I want to take an Amazonian tributary north to Manaus, Brazil, then back through Venezuela, Colombia, Central America, and finally, I'd like to pedal on up to the States. If I run out of money or decide I'd like to increase my budget a bit, it's quite easy to find work tutoring English informally for a while. Money isn't a formidable obstacle in the least. It's quite possible to travel in South America (and elsewhere, I'm sure) indefinitely, if one is only creative enough!

Traveling is an incredible bundle of extremes. It's exuberant triumph and uncontainable excitement one day and overwhelming difficulties and frustration the next. But it's consistently rewarding and generally a whole lot of fun. And educationally speaking, could anyone honestly tell me I'd be learning more attending my senior year of high school, trading in these beautiful Andes mornings for a stuffy classroom?

One last note: I've now met three fellow travelers who already knew my story. In each case I've explained a bit about my trip, and then they've interrupted: "Oh yeah, I heard about you when we were talking about the craziest people we've met. Aren't you the girl who rode a bicycle through Colombia *alone??*...How old *are* you, anyway?"

***

November 4, 1992

I wake with a tropical sun, prepare breakfast in my little open-air cabin, and an hour later we're off, trudging into the jungle, laden with nets, jars, bananas (bait), and notebooks. We'll be gone the entire day: checking traps, marking butterflies, and walking...*lots* of walking. From rich primary forest to the forest edge, where the tangle of vines and diversity of trees suddenly stops and cattle-grazing land takes over; from this pasture on to second-growth forest; and finally to "high-graded" forest—meaning forest with the big commercial trees removed, but the rest relatively undisturbed. Each of these habitats contains ten simple traps equipped with fermented bananas which attract butterflies and beetles.

It's all part of a study, and I'm a sort of research assistant. I ended up here at Jatun Sacha after following up on a list of organizations needing volunteers, which I found at the Explorers Club. Jatun Sacha is a biological reserve and research station situated just south of the Rio Napo, about two hours on a bumpy bus from Tena. I volunteer my time in return for lodging and learning.

Our daily rounds take us through only a fraction of the 1,235 acres (seventy percent of which is primary forest) that make up Jatun Sacha. This week, my companions are Deborah, a peace corps volunteer and the only other foreigner currently here, and Gabriel, a local Quichua man. As we walk, Deborah explains the ways of the great strangler fig we just passed—how it begins life as a mere epiphyte on a huge, thriving tree, how it sends roots down to the forest floor from its tall perch and eventually surrounds the original tree, and how the tree rots while the now-enormous, but hollow, strangler fig takes its place.

We talk about the mating grasshoppers, brightly colored poisonous frogs, and butterfly larval host plants as we climb up muddy slopes, wade through brownish streams, and make our way through the vertical labyrinth of vines. We stop in our tracks to watch two large weasels scurry away, to peer upwards toward the canopy at the sound of monkeys—and once, to allow a boa the right-of-way. A birdlike noise echoes through the forest, somewhere nearby; simultaneously Deborah says, "Toucan," and Gabriel says, "Quail." We wait for the call to come again and follow it silently. This time we realize Gabriel is probably right since the noise is coming from a niche near the shallow leaf-covering of the forest floor.

It's just this sort of thing that makes the rainforest so intriguing to me. While it disappears at the notorious rate of fifty acres a minute, even some of the most basic aspects of the ecosystem remain a mystery to science. Deborah has been studying butterflies at Jatun Sacha for two and a half years, but at least once every day she swipes one up in her net and announces that she's never seen its kind before.

Strangely enough, after my first day of work I was relatively unimpressed by my contact with the tropical forest—it seemed a monotonous concentration of green. By the end of the second day, though, I was completely overwhelmed by its complexity and diversity. I could pick out a tree early in the morning, then not see another of the same species for the entire day. Inspection of the underside of almost any leaf showed it to be teeming with life. A closer look at almost any plant revealed what seemed to be completely out-of-place colors and shapes. Sometimes the strange things I saw could be explained by Deborah or Gabriel, or by books that I found in the small library and read by candlelight. Other times the mysteries remained intact, and I decided nature must be having fun with all the possibilities in such a humid, lush environment.

November 8, 1992

The seven days of hard work are over now, the beetles are counted and classified according to habitat and species, but no visible pattern emerges. No one is surprised!

Now I have a choice as to what project I will volunteer for next. I can continue working for Deborah, studying butterflies and their larval host plants; I can work with some Ecuadorian university students in a botanical garden, cultivating medicinal plants; or I can help with a survey of mammals at Jatun Sacha. I haven't decided.

The weekend of my seventeenth birthday found me biking with three companions (one of which, I might add, turned out to be a happy high school dropout, now working six months of each year for the Explorers Club and traveling for free) on a strange and spectacular dirt path near the volcano Chimborazo.

Another weekend I spent with two of the Swiss motorcyclists mentioned earlier. We took a "train" (actually a cargo truck mounted on tracks) from Ibarra—high in the Andes—down to San Lorenzo, a port on the Pacific coast in northern Ecuador. Along with a couple dozen locals, we sat atop potatoes and onions for an exciting eleven-hour journey out of the mountains, through *paramo*, desert, and eventually the coastal lowland rainforest. We ducked through tunnels, dodged bats and flying lizards, hauled rocks off the tracks, were drenched by warm rain, and sang with our fellow travelers.

The coastal towns of the north, accessible only by train or boat, resembled the towns in old Wild West movies, and the people seemed to spend day and night in the street—dancing to salsa and marimba music, playing checkers with bottle caps, etc.—a very festive atmosphere. We took canoes from San Lorenzo, surrounded by mangrove swamps and hunting pelicans, to the mouth of the Rio Santiago, then up the river to a village called Borbon, where a very black-skinned local greeted our canoe by announcing, "Welcome to Africa!"

Now I am welcome at Jatun Sacha as long as I wish to stay. (Incidentally, I'm renting my bicycle to a couple in the town of Baños for more money per week than I could ever spend on the food I cook—my only expense.) I have a job offer in Quito teaching English, another in Baños waitressing and learning to bake bread, a dozen open volunteer positions all over Ecuador...but I also hear the call of the road, the road and its increasingly southern destinations.

Kyla Wetherell
Eugene, Oregon

Improvising

Spring 1999

The sun sinks into the Babokeivari mountains. A covey of quail chants and pecks in the dust nearby. I am kneading the last handfuls of cob into the waist-high walls of the "cobbage"—an improvisation on an age-old architectural form, a soon-to-be studio space on our small plot of land in the desert west of Tucson, Arizona. The sky is a cupola of color, the temperature dropping fast, but the mud in my hands and between my toes, caked halfway up my legs, is warm still. I can see the crouched shape of my partner through the red blooms of our living ocotillo fence, picking greens to accompany the stew that's been simmering all afternoon in the solar oven. She and I dug the gardens basin-style, to catch what little rain falls here, and the sandy soil we extracted now disappears daily into the walls of the cobbage.

For three years I have been teaching workshops and taking contract work on cob (a mixture of clay, sand and straw) and straw-bale house-building projects, loving to work with my hands and bare feet, to envision and design living spaces, sculpt them into being, to share the work and simple knowledge with others.

The walls of the cobbage creep skyward. We teach a workshop and they shoot up—a couple feet in a day; then weeks go by, one meditating handful at a time, finding solutions as we sculpt—for instance, how to get an arched home-made door to swing correctly and close tightly on a hand-formed curving frame?

The cobbage is a cylinder, a tower of sorts with diamond and arch-shaped windows which we cut ourselves out of an old sliding glass door, and colored bottles set into the wall (some containing time capsules), letting in blue and yellow light along the floor. An earthen oven set half-way into the wall will be fed from the outside and used for bread-baking and for heating the interior space. Juniper logs placed into the wall as we build it, form a simple spiral staircase leading up to a flat roof. Nearby, leaves from a resinous local plant steep in hemp oil donated by Women Build Houses, a local nonprofit which sponsors our workshops. We'll paint the steeped oil over the final coat of plaster and hope it will protect our cobbage from the annual monsoons.

Soon I'll be sleeping on the roof of this small abode I built with my hands and my friends. When summer has come and our straw-bale cottage absorbs too much heat to stay cool all night, I'll dream under the shifting stars of the enormous night, with the acrobatic night hawks and the loyal moon.

Photo by Kyla Wetherell

Winter 2001

On the insides of my eyelids colors dash and spread and vanish. I am dancing and alone. My limbs are tides. I am a starfish flung like a discus out over panting tongues of surf.

A voice calls, "Shift."

I open my eyes. I am on my knees in a white room with a worn wood floor. I am still yet still moving. There are two other bodies in the room. One ebbs along the wall; in the edge of my eye she looks like winter unfurling the hands of fall from a brick building I once knew, where a vine loosed its leaves and retreated, dying back. I am the vine myself now, in another season, scrolling up from thawed soil, twining toward the sky. The other body is a bird. It soars the space. Its wing dives between my shoulder and my ear.

"Shift," I say.

The three of us have been calling this "The School." We will meet around thirty hours per week for about six months, coming up with scores—loosely choreographed structures—to guide and illuminate our improvisation. We will begin with the intention to become a performance dance group and end with very individual and differing directions. But for now, we are interested not in learning someone else's movement style but in creating or discovering (we're not sure which) our own. We are interested in the subtle shifts of consciousness that happen when our focus changes from internal to peripheral to external; in expanding our options as movers and improvisers and being aware enough to choose among them in a high-stimulus situation; in embodying imagery from our lives and our dreams; in challenging the relationship between performer and audience; in bringing expressive movement into public space. We dance in the studio, but we also dance downtown, in parks, cemeteries, on the bus. We facilitate a weekly improv night, collaborating with poets, musicians and visual artists.

"Shift."

Spring 2003

I live now in a screened dome at the edge of a jungle on the windward eastern slope of the Big Island of Hawaii. The ocean is less than two miles away. I can hear its pulse now, steady on the rocks at Wai'ele. A waning half-moon sets between a swath of cumulous and a deep green billow of mango leaves on the western sky. Flitting between palm fronds: a hoop-eyed blink of a bird.

For my rent and my pleasure I work on this land, keeping back the jungle, growing taro, sweet potatoes, ginger, various fruit, and a vegetable garden which is just beginning to outwit its pests. I've long dreamed of growing and gathering all my own food, and for the first time that feels like a realistic goal. I help milk the neighbor's goats and recently acquired a fishing spear.

I do landscaping one day per week for money; participate in a neighborhood association endeavoring to build local economy; swim daily in tidepools, ocean or a nearby crater lake; ride my bike everywhere I go. I am studying mbira (African thumb piano) with a master of Shona music who lives up the hill, and less than a mile away I have my trapeze rigged, where I dance with friends and teach a class for neighborhood kids.

Primarily though, I live alone, study literature, and write. It is a pared-down time in my life,

a time of much solitude and of creative exploration into the written word. For the past ten years, I have focused where I felt most malnourished after ten years in public school—in the fundamental realms of body, earth and relationship. I have studied organic farming and permaculture in the Midwest, the Northwest and the South Pacific; co-managed a community-owned food store; researched, designed, and built experimental solar ovens and fuel-efficient wood stoves; learned to tan hides, weave cordage, make baskets, gather wild edibles and medicinals and make salves and tinctures; co-created a non-profit which salvaged building materials from condemned houses and returned them to the inner-city; birthed my own non-profit to educate and empower women and girls in sustainable living skills; conceived and organized and taught natural building classes, workshops and camps; studied, performed and taught dance improvisation and aerial dance on low-flying trapezes. And now I return, to my most stubborn and long-standing vision for myself: to write fiction.

I have written in this year roughly half of a first draft of a novel, various poetry, and now mostly short stories, which I am getting to second and third draft stages on. I read hungrily, and though I have always been a big reader, the depth and delight I find in it is mushrooming. It is like the mbira music I listened to a year ago, which was then a pretty melody and is now a rich texture, infinite with relationships, interwoven with movement and meaning. It is like the way, when you begin to sense into your body, you become aware of all sorts of sensations and rhythms you didn't even know you had, though you've been living inside them all your life. What is art, if not a luring oneself to look (and listen and sense) more closely?

Working in isolation for almost a year now has given me space to gestate, allowed me to work with great abandon, trying on voices and styles and forms. Fiction feels like a way to get close to what is Other, to let differing aspects of the world bump up against one another and to get honest about what I think would happen; to look at these lenses we all have over our eyes and at how determined we are to defend them. Working in isolation, lolling in my apprenticeship with a legacy of writers I have access to even here in the jungle, through the little branch library in Pahoa, what I have in abundance is time. I have silence, beauty, the space to honor the sometimes-swerving, sometimes-stuck process that is uniquely mine, and to keep reclaiming responsibility for the fulfillment of my basic needs, one of which is learning.

1992

As I reflect on that time of a decade ago, I am aware that I wrote the preceding chapter at a time in my life when I had a lot to prove. I still believed that if I didn't achieve some form of stardom, my life would be a failure. In a certain way, ironically, quitting school was an expression of this deeply school-installed belief. Both my rising out and my journey to South America were attempts to push past confusion quickly and deliver myself directly into some imagined lap of glory.

And I'm sure that was exactly what I needed to go through—that in order to shed that skin entirely, I needed to play it out on my own terms and by my own initiative. My time in South America was everything I wrote it to be, but also accompanied by a deep shadow which I did not then know how to acknowledge: a subtext of running away, isolation, illness. That journey accelerated my process of growing up and stranded me in the terrifying gulf between my ideals and my actual circumstance. Maybe that's just what travel is for—to bring us right to the edge of who we think we are   But it certainly wasn't comfortable, or carefree, and I struggled a lot with the way I presented myself in this book—not wanting my life to be championing a certain path, or to have exposed myself so publicly and so one-dimensionally, no longer wanting to call my choices superior, or to be acknowledged as a role model for something that, while it ultimately led me to maturity and growth, was, at the time, still coming from a pretty messy and arrogant place.

My decision to leave school was absolutely right for me. It was a transformative choice, and, like most transformations, it brought me to crisis and darkness before it returned me to the light. I can easily trace all my explorations since then to that one turning point, when I decided to try something different, to tear up the map and turn instead toward the cusp of my own current, to inquiry rather than profession (literally, to ask more than I tell), and success by my own standards: the cobbage blooming brown against the sky; the uncomfortable contact dance where I neither merge nor exit but stay and dance what's mine, leaning up against what's hers; the story that, as I write it, causes me to ask a new question.

Winter 2004

After almost two years of writing retreat in Hawaii, I have returned to the mainland, and to my home state of Oregon, where I feel finally ready to settle. I am living in a sweet and cozy trailer in Grace's lusciously vegetated driveway, keeping my expenses low, while I work very part-time at a non-profit human service agency, and write and dance and study yoga, and . . . go to school.

At first, attending community college came from two places: I wanted a solid foundation in literature to support my own writing, and questions about career and money were surfacing strong as I contemplated my income-producing options as a person who most wants to write fiction. I thought perhaps I would get a degree so I could teach. Now though, as I find myself perfectly content (as I have always been) living very minimally (as I always have); as I find myself still, more than anything else, devoted to my writing, and wanting the other activities in my life to balance that out by being physically active, socially interactive, and out-of-doors; as I find myself in another job I love, which may not be my most central life's work, but which nevertheless feeds a part of me that would otherwise be hungry, I return to my own trajectory, and going to school becomes not a means to an end, but just another sojourn along the way. I am learning the canon of Western thought, and whatever I might think about how that came to be, it is still the common language of the writers and thinkers I am in continuous conversation with through books. All of this means so much more to me than it would have ten years ago, or even five years ago. I needed to write my own stories before classical literature could genuinely fascinate me. I needed to build houses out of mud before ancient art and architecture could really come to life.

So I am devoting a year to eke what edification I can from college. In a few months, I will return to my own apprenticeship as a writer. Even now, I continue to write my own stories (if slowly), share them with friends and receive feedback, and recently, I sent several stories out for potential publication. I am getting trained at my workplace as a crisis worker and counselor, which I can imagine being a portion of my eventual income. I am seeking a place in town where I can set up my trapezes and teach classes, and next summer I plan to do a yoga teacher training and add that to my patchwork of meaningful work.

If this essay-in-intervals tells any story, it tells of how drastically and unexpectedly my plans and visions change. Still, sitting at my writing desk, I work as though I can see some end. What I am doing is never quite what I think it is though, and in a world like that, I'll keep on improvising.

Anne Brosnan, 15
Northern Kentucky

Sweet Kentucky Home: Honeybees and a Bluegrass Banjo

dedicated to the memory of John Holt

Photo by Claudia Brosnan

It is the first part of April. The black walnut, cherry, and ash trees have begun to bud, the grass to green, and a few flowers to appear in the pastures and by the roadside. The dandelions are out and on the warpath, determined to take over this continent, or at least our small farm in Northern Kentucky. Near the road, facing east, and positioned near the fence on top of the hill, six beehives have been recently placed, and their inhabitants have begun to emerge after winter and find themselves in new surroundings. Some of the hives need a new coat of paint, and a lot of the equipment needs total replacement.

It is late morning, and my father and I have been working in the garage since we awoke. Inside, amid my sister's gym equipment and my mother's easel and paintings, we have been building new hive stands and supers (individual boxes that are stacked together to form a hive), sorting out frames, cleaning off wax and propolis (bee glue, which the bees make out of tree resin), and getting ready to reverse our hives.

Finally, we begin to suit up. We wear light colored clothing—a person who wears dark colors is more prone to be stung since bees have evolved to attack dark furry objects like bears. We attach veils to ourselves through our belt loops, making sure that there is no opening for a bee to get in. As Dad hauls some of the equipment up near the hives, I put on my gloves, which are my most prized possession: They are elbow-length and of thick material, yet they fit perfectly.

I find the old smoker, which is blackened with rust and fire. A corncob is used to plug the smoke hole when it is not in use. I take it out and open the top, stir the ashes up, and add a handful of rotten wood, twine, and small bits of newspaper. I light a match, and soon I add more wood. As I pump the bellows, smoke emerges and I know I have a fire going in there somewhere, so I close the top, stuff a few pieces of burlap in my pockets, grab as much of the morning's equipment as I can, and follow Dad out to the hives, skirting around Mom's freshly plowed vegetable garden.

We puff a little smoke in the hive entrance near the bottom and also under the outer cover, which we have lifted up a crack. As we stand back and wait, the bees, stimulated by the smoke, go back in the hive and begin gorging themselves on the honey. There are many theories for why they do this, and also as to why being gorged on the honey makes them more docile. All I know is that as we begin our work, we use smoke as beekeepers have always done. And even before beekeepers, native peoples harvested wild honey using smoking torches.

Someone in a pickup slows down a bit to watch, probably thinking we are insane, yet very much interested. They drive off, and after a few minutes, we open the hive. Now we are looking into the top of a brood box, which has vertical frames hanging down intended for the queen to lay her eggs in. Bees are everywhere. They have not begun to fly around much but there are many of them, *thousands* of them, in the hive. As we remove the frames we try to find the queen, but in the end, she never appears.

We can see some of the bees still going about their business, head first into a cell of honey, drinking away with abdomens wiggling in the air. Sometimes we can see bees hatching right out of their cell—in seconds they emerge and right away they begin their hive chores of feeding and taking care of larvae—just as they were taken care of not long before. Dad works slowly, and the bees have begun to gather together in the air. A few of them inspect me, crawling on my veil, shirt, and gloves.

We start the reversing process, working as smoothly as we can. We switch the brood boxes around, placing the bottom on the top, and the top on the bottom. At the same time, we replace one of the old supers with a new one, remove old frames full of empty, dark comb, and give the bees a

Photo by Claudia Brosnan

Extracting honey

freshly painted hive stand and new bottom board. The purpose of reversing is to prevent the bees from getting too crowded and *swarming*, or leaving the hive. Putting the bottom super, which is basically empty, on top gives the queen more room to lay eggs. She is not very intelligent; all she does is lay eggs—hundreds each day. She tends to work upwards, and when she gets to the top she won't go back down, so she thinks she has no more room to lay eggs. We are fooling her, yet at the same time we are making the hive a healthier place.

We finally finish at around two o'clock in the afternoon and we begin to collect the old equipment and go back down to the garage. We didn't get stung this time, so we are lucky. After a while, the bees will settle down again, and go back to their business. As the sun sets, the worker bees come in from the fields and the bees will huddle together to keep the brood (and themselves) warm. Numerous messages go back and forth among the colony; some bees report their exploits, giving directions to the other bees to a good source of pollen or nectar—many of them, I'm sure, are discussing the wonderful wild plum tree that is blooming up the road at the Huffs' farm.

Dad and I go inside after cleaning up and painting some of the equipment, and we talk about the new equipment we will have to buy in order to keep the hives in good shape and get them ready for the spring honey flow. Later on, when we go to bed, the blossoms outside close up, ready to open again when the sun rises and the honeybees fly out again to gather their nectar and pollen.

Until the day I die I'll be grateful to my parents because they decided to keep me out of school and let me make all kinds of decisions for myself so I could lead a self-directed, self-educated life. I have never attended any school of any kind, and it is sometimes hard for me to compare my life to one I might have had if I had gone to any kind of institution. I like the way I live and cannot imagine living any other way. I have never known the meaning of a Saturday or a Sunday, because to me every day is like a weekend or a summer vacation. But I never stop my schooling on Saturdays or when the summer comes, because my school goes wherever I go—I am my own teacher, and I feed my own education into my own brain.

The world is full of interesting things. So much is happening everywhere and so much has happened through history, that I can't understand why kids are made to sit in classrooms and have everything interpreted to them through other people. Volcanoes erupt in the Pacific Ocean, in cities people write books full of revolutionary ideas, in the Amazon people still discover new species of insects, and in your own neighborhood people build things and work at their jobs. Yet, from the littlest kindergartner to the high school senior, the younger generation is shut off in buildings behind closed doors listening to the teacher *tell* them about all these things happening. They don't get to experience it until they graduate—*then* maybe they will decide to explore the Amazon, but they will have already wasted so many years in school. Yes, I simply think that school is above all things a waste of time.

I have my whole life in my own hands to do whatever I want, and that includes *right now*—I don't have to wait until spring break or until I get my college education. My parents, too, share this philosophy in many ways: They have always let me choose my own interests and supported me in them, but not "taught" me. They have their own things that they like to do, and by not having to teach me all the time and give me lessons as if our home was some kind of fake school, they have time to live their own lives as well. I do have chores and requirements (take out the paper and the trash, or I don't get no spending cash), and I am limited in some areas; for instance I depend on my parents for transportation since I can't drive yet, so I pretty much only get to go places if my parents are willing to drive me. But most of the time we either do things together as equals or pursue our own interests separately and try to run a democratic, happy household.

At present it is Spring of 1992 and I am living with my family on an eight-acre horse farm in northern Kentucky. My father works here as a pilot for an international airline that flies packages and documents out of the Greater Cincinnati Airport. Even though the airport serves Cincinnati, Ohio, it is actually located in Kentucky, and we live deep in the hills neighboring the Ohio River which separates the two states.

I have many interests, but my two greatest loves are nature and music. I spent the first part of my life in northern Minnesota, where we lived in a small cabin without electricity, running water, or telephone near the Chippewa National Forest. I grew up with hundreds of animal and plant species outside my door, and with the skies above filled with stars and the Northern Lights. Since then, I haven't always lived where the wilderness has been so abundant, but it has always stayed inside me. From my earliest childhood, I have been sensitive to nature, and I think this is because for a time we lived in New York, and there I experienced what could happen to an area where there were many people living together among huge masses of buildings and technology. We lived in the suburbs of Long Island, not in the city; yet even there, there wasn't any great expanse of land—nowhere to walk or run, and no places where native animals and plant species survived as they had before the Europeans came.

Right now, I live in a rural hill area where everybody has at least a few acres and almost everybody has a horse or two. We moved here in the winter and now, as the warm weather comes, we have begun to work on the farm and enjoy all the space and freedom. We have plowed up gardens, and planted trees, shrubs, bushes, berry orchards, and asparagus beds. The fish in the pond have begun to bite and we have bluebirds as well as hawks, kestrels, killdeer, and eagles using the skyway above the pastures. At night, rabbits and opossums walk along the road and any time of day you can see whitetail deer if you search hard enough. We don't have any farm animals or livestock yet so we are not as busy as some farmers.

We are starting out doing a lot of organic gardening and also have started an apple orchard, which combines nicely with the honeybees. Mom does most of the gardening but I help her when asked; my sister is into herbs and flowers so she handles those areas. I do all of the fishing in the pond—it's a manmade pond so it needs to be fished out to keep the ecology balanced. Water snakes, different kinds of turtles, and frogs live near the pond as well, and we keep some of the bank wild so that they have a place to live. Later on we are going to get animals for the pasture—Mom wants burros, and we have also been considering goats and sheep, as well as horses. Four or five of our acres are in pasture, so unless we have an animal to keep the pasture down, we will have to mow it. I would really like to have a dairy goat operation, but the rest of the family is not equally enthusiastic.

The more open land I have around me, the better; I love sports like canoeing, hiking, cross-country skiing, and running. We go back to Minnesota frequently, which in the summer gives me a chance to canoe and fish, and in the winter, a chance to ski. Last winter we spent two or three months there, and skied a lot. Since we have no school schedule, I could stay there as long as I wanted without having to worry about getting back. Also, every summer we go to the Boundary Waters Canoe Area in Northern Minnesota near Canada, and go canoe-camping for a week. When I was littler I would just ride in the canoe, but now I have to do my share of the paddling and portaging. Our cabin is south of the Boundary Waters and we live on a chain of lakes, so we can go canoeing there too. I like to live using a canoe for transportation and with a lake to get my dinner out of. It's not always possible, but sometimes it works for a little while. In the winter I can cross-country ski on the snow-covered frozen lakes, and although I began skiing just last winter, I already love it. Living in Kentucky is harder in that respect because the winters don't have much snow and it is hard to cross-country ski up and down all these hills!

My own special project on the farm is going to be apiculture—the keeping and raising of honeybees. Honeybees fascinate me. In general, I am interested in social, working animals or insects. Part of this interest stems from the fact that as an intelligent, social mammal, humans are in the process of destroying their world rather than living in harmony with it. I am interested in different species of animals—whales, wolves, bees—which live together and behave in ways similar to humans but exist harmoniously in their environments. I also became interested in bees because of Dad's interest in apple orchards, for which bees are useful in pollination.

Before moving to the farm, I read up on apiculture and found out that it is not as simple as I thought it was. Many problems and diseases threaten bees, and year-round you have to both manage the hives and equipment and also worry about things such as bees starving or swarming. But after we moved and began talking about what kinds of things we wanted to be doing on the farm, Dad became interested in beekeeping as well, and as he has said: "It's nice to be *doing* something." This spring we started the apiary and have yet to see how the first spring honey flow turns out.

We bought bees and six hives from a few local beekeepers who advertised in the paper. Each hive cost about a hundred dollars but they came with some extra equipment and supers. Dad paid for all of the equipment and hives, but we have yet to work out all the financial details. It pretty much depends on how much we get for the honey and how much of it we sell. I receive an allowance, but with my hobbies I sometimes have to buy expensive things. Dad says that I can use the money I get from selling honey to buy some things I want—a new Gibson five-string banjo, for instance. Some of the money I might have to use to pay him back for some of the bee equipment; the extractor (a machine that spins the comb to get the honey out) is one of the most expensive things we may have to buy.

At first, we didn't know a lot about what we were doing. Dad wasn't really into it yet and I had only read a little bit. Then, Dad started reading a lot of library books, and we became a little more familiar with what we were getting into. We went to a local beekeeping school, which was a one-day program at a local vocational college. The fee was small, but the classes were conducted by master beekeepers and we learned a lot. It was a strange experience for me since I had never before sat in a classroom and listened to somebody talking and drawing pictures on a blackboard. But I enjoyed it since the "teachers" were really just people who loved beekeeping and were willing to share their knowledge with other people, and the "students" were all kinds of people, young and old, male and female, who had freely chosen to learn about the subject. Afterwards, we went to a meeting of a local beekeeper's association and we plan to attend the rest as soon as they come up.

Beekeeping is not really a regular farm hobby similar to raising livestock, because it does not require daily attention (vs. milking the cows or slopping the pigs every day). It revolves around the seasons, and beekeepers are people who know a lot about nature. They can feel the seasons change, they make note of the weather, and they know all kinds of plants and flowers. Also, honeybees have not really ever been domesticated although they are sometimes called "the domestic honeybee." They are wild insects and can survive on their own without human intervention. Wild bees in a log in the forest are no different than the ones you may raise in your apiary. Of course, one *species* of bee is different from another, but many beekeepers establish their apiaries from swarms they have found in the woods.

When we work with bees, our only objective in the end is honey production, but along the way, we help the bees out in certain areas. In the spring we reverse the hives which keeps the bees from swarming—an occurrence that produces another colony of bees, similar to a cell splitting in two. Beekeepers don't like swarming because we need as many bees as we can get to stay together, be a big, strong hive, and produce a lot of honey. Beekeepers can also help prevent certain diseases like European foulbrood, which destroys the brood. And bees often get infested with mites, which are one of the biggest worries for beekeepers. None of our bees have shown signs of mites, but we are pretty confident that we can deal with them if they appear. In winter, we help bees survive the cold temperatures by insulating the hives and making sure they have enough honey. As the weather then begins to warm up, we can help the bees at the point where they are most likely to starve, by feeding them with sugar water.

The busiest time for a beekeeper is in late July or early August when the bees are at their peak of honey production and we can collect the surplus. At about the first of May, we put on the honey supers, which are designed to hold honey. We have to watch for certain things—if we put the supers on when the dandelions are still blooming then we will get dandelion honey, which is pretty bad. But if we put them on at the right time we will get honey from certain choice spring flowers—basswood blooms and buckwheat, roses and raspberries. Also, we have to be sure to take off the honey at the right time. It if is too soon, we may not have enough ready, capped honey. If it is too late, the honey may have darkened and the bees may also not have enough time to refill their own supply of honey from the fall flowers. The bees have a spring honey crop and a fall honey crop, just as nature has a burst of spring flowers, and then in fall goldenrod blooms along the roadsides. If we leave the bees the fall honey, they can survive the winter.

So far, my experience with beekeeping has involved a lot of carpentry. We order the equipment from a beekeepers' supply company in Kentucky, and when it comes it needs to be glued and nailed by hand. Dad and I do this work together. If we need more supers, bottom boards, outer covers, or other pieces of equipment, now that we have more time Dad is going to build them all from scratch with his table saw. The frames, which are smaller and trickier, we will probably always have to buy from a supply store. After they are assembled, using little nails and little hammers, we have to install the sheet of wax foundation which provides the bees with a base for building the combs.

After this first year, everything will be much easier since we will know more and also have all the equipment already built. I think we will be beekeepers for a long time, especially if later on Dad goes into apple orchards full time. It's pretty uncommon for a young girl or even a female of any age to be a beekeeper, but I am not intimidated by that. At times the work may be hard—a full super of honey is extremely heavy, and we already had a bad experience dropping one of the hives as we carried it up the steep hill behind the garage. I have been stung about seven times since we got the bees, but still I find them fascinating and I want to continue to keep them as long as I can.

I love living on a farm, but eventually I just want to live among nature and not try to control it. The time I have spent in Minnesota, especially northern Minnesota, has convinced me that it is one of the most beautiful places on earth. The boreal forest is one of my favorite ecosystems—the thousands of lakes, the pine and spruce trees, the rocky ground and the lichens. The animals that live there, too, are among my favorites: moose, bear, raccoon, owl, squirrel, jay, deer, many kinds of fish, and in particular the gray wolf. Like bees, wolves are social, loving, highly intelligent animals. But wolves have for centuries been one of man's worst enemies, although their bad reputation has been partially turned around in this century by the work of such biologists as Adolph Murie, L. David Mech, R.D. Lawrence, and Farley Mowat.

I'm not sure why I became interested in wolves specifically, but the areas of northern Minnesota, Michigan, and Canada are among the few places where gray wolves still survive in the wild in substantial numbers. I have never seen or heard a wolf while canoeing or staying at the cabin, but the fact that they live there, and nowhere else in the contiguous United States, has always intrigued me. One of the first movies I ever remember seeing was *Never Cry Wolf*, based on the book by Farley Mowat. As I got older, I read magazine articles, books, and reports on the wolf's status in the wild and as an endangered species. Everything about the ecology of the regions where wolves live is interesting to me, and in particular I like wolves because of their role as one of the top predators in those ecosystems. I grew to want to see wolves be introduced back to areas where they had originally thrived but now were driven away or killed by ranchers or farmers.

I guess I first got the idea that it is possible to concentrate on studying wolves and their specific ecology and behavior by becoming familiar with David Mech and his books and studies. Although he has studied many other animals too, his main focus is wolves, and through his work I gradually came to the idea that I too would like to focus on wolves.

When I was seven or eight and living in New York I had the ambition to be a scientist. At the time I read avidly, and I had consumed practically all the books in the children's library covering any branch of science. For a while we rented a house that had eight or so bedrooms and I converted one of them into a "museum" where I displayed hundreds of shells (we were two houses away from the beach) as well as rocks, berries, owl pellets, feathers, natural history books, and all kinds of other things. My most interesting exhibit was the skeleton of a turkey (minus the skull but otherwise complete) which I had bleached and attempted to reassemble. During moving from house to house and further away from the beach, most of my collection was eventually lost and I never returned to that type of collecting as a naturalist. For the next few years I went into my literary stage and started a career as a writer and a poet.

Last year, though, Dad started talking about my college education and in the course of the financial planning and philosophical discussions (I wasn't so sure I wanted to go to college at all) we started to think about what I actually wanted to do as a career. Most of the time, I get seriously involved in things that are close to home and that I can do right now, on my own, by experimentation and self-education. I don't usually need to think beyond that, or have to say, "Well, I can't do that until I'm a grown-up" or "It's too hard to learn that right now." But I have finally begun to think of what I would like to do when I'm old enough to travel and work on my own.

I think I have always known that I want to go back to Minnesota, and I have decided that I would like to study wolves there, and make a living off of it if I could, as a scientist, park ranger, or as an employee of the Fish and Wildlife Department. I am not sure yet as to exactly what kind of work I want to have or will end up having. But I know that if I can, I would like to spend as much time as possible out in the forest rather than in a classroom studying biology or ecology. I probably wouldn't mind going to college—that is my parents' hope, because they enjoyed college and they think that I will too.

In Ely, Minnesota, the Vermillion Community College specializes in classes on wildlife biology and outdoor resources. (I imagine people graduating from there go on to be guides or rangers for the BWCA, as well as biologists.) The writer and naturalist Sigurd Olson taught there—wildlife biology and ecology—and the college is connected with the International Wolf Center, also in Ely. The Center has wolf research programs open to the public and by taking part in an expedition (for a fee of about three hundred dollars) you get credit for the college.

I know I will certainly learn a lot and benefit from my time there, but above all I don't want to spend too much time there studying to do or be something I could be out in life already doing or being. As much as I can do ahead of time—before I'm old enough to leave my family—I'm going to try to do. My father is qualified to be a flight instructor, and from him I'm going to learn to fly airplanes; maybe I could get work helping other scientists tracking wolves. I can't know exactly what's going to turn up but I'd like to be ready for it when it comes. I don't like to be involved in something unless I can do it as fully and as well as I can. I've found that the clichés, "Whatever you want to be, you can be" or "Whatever you want to do, you can do" are absolutely true.

Living by my own rules and not (in any way whatsoever) by what other people think makes it easier for me to think about doing big things that are important to me. I have no pressure on me to eventually go to law school and to "succeed" in life and make lots of money, and as for the present, I have no immediate pressure to wake up and haul myself to school tomorrow and finish a report by Tuesday. Not going to school opens up all kinds of doors. It shows you that there are all sorts of things to do and you really *don't* have to wait until you are older or have all kinds of special skills.

A lot of kids dream of being astronauts, major league baseball players, race car drivers, or President of the United States, but later they dismiss these ideas as unrealistic fantasies. They were probably laughed at and not really encouraged to keep trying to do things they wanted to. For me, I can think somewhat nonchalantly, yet seriously, about doing things that I really want to do—no matter how far out of the mainstream. I am not really sure why this is, but it may be because I have never been graded, classed, or compared in a school atmosphere. This is a process that makes kids (and adults) think kids must work hard in competition with their peers to prepare for the "real world," a place where you do what other people wish you to do and act the way other people wish you to—in order to get a promotion or a raise. According to this way of thinking, they definitely must *not* quit school and climb Mount McKinley, instead. I know what I want to do, and I know that I will have to work if I want to do it. But I also know that I can and will accomplish my goals by myself, without depending on an institution or a diploma.

Slung over my shoulders is a Kay model five-string banjo—a round white head with a few scratch marks here and there, a sign that a banjo is loved by someone. The neck, with simple block inlay, is strung with five steel strings, medium gauge. I'm hoping they're in tune. One might be a little flat, but this is not the New York Philharmonic. I guess they're tuned enough for bluegrass. On my fingers, three picks: two steel Dunlop finger picks and one white National thumbpick. I brush across the strings in open G, and gradually move up the neck in chords—a C here, an F there, a D way up high.

"Play something, Anne," suggests a guitar player, ready to strum along the rhythm to whatever I decide to play.

"Well, what?" I say.

"Do a little Cripple Creek."

I start off kind of slow, but then I get going and go back and forth from melody to verse, over and over, not knowing when to stop.

> *Goin' up Cripple Creek, goin' in a whirl,*
> *Goin' up Cripple Creek to see my girl.*
> *I got a gal at the head of the creek,*
> *Go on up to see her 'bout twice a week.*
> *She's got eyes of pearly blue,*
> *Makes my gun shoot straight and true....*

The tune sounds better played clawhammer style, but I'm only a Scruggs style picker. A mandolin player comes in for a break—he takes the lead while I revert to back-up and the bell-like tones of his instrument ripple through the song as if they were the real waters of Cripple Creek. The bass player picks up the rhythm and that wonderful rock hard timing moves in, connecting everybody together. There is not a sheet of music anywhere, no books or papers, only instruments and people, and the music comes directly from the people's memory and imagination.

I begin another song; this time it's "Cumberland Gap." The guitar players have an easy time of it, only one chord or two to follow. Someone else takes a break while I rest, chunking chords in a banjo player's style of back-up. I take a break again, moving somewhat absentmindedly into the rhythm and having to search for the bass to get myself established, but then I begin again, and as my little finger slides from the eleventh to tenth fret, I can tell I've managed to connect with the bass and the guitar players can follow me. I smile and in my happiness almost lose it again, but then we keep on going.

Me an' my wife an' my wife's pap,
We all live down in Cumberland Gap.
Cumberland Gap, Cumberland Gap,
Way down yonder in Cumberland Gap.
Lay down boys, and take a little nap,
Fo'teen miles to Cumberland Gap.

The room is beginning to fill and people walk in the door, some with instrument cases, many without—they've come just to sit and listen to the music and talk to each other. This is a weekly jam session, a Friday night pickin', and many of the people are regulars. The crowd is mixed, older couples, single men and women, sometimes families. Some of them have not been out to jam for a while, and when they walk in the door, they are greeted with a medley of voices from inside the room.

"Still pickin' that banjer?" someone will ask me.

"Yeah, I'm trying," is my answer. They laugh and tell me I'm doing fine; in fact, a lot of them tell me that I'm improving faster than they've ever seen anybody else improve. Some even tell me that if I keep it up, I could be "one of the best around." Now it's my turn to laugh, but I promise them I'll keep on pickin'.

A few people step up to the microphones and switch them on, ready to play and sing no matter how crowded or empty the room may be. A guitar player or two may begin and lead off a song, and then everybody joins in on the chorus. There is a fiddle player, a mandolin, and a bass, usually, in the background. Some of the time they'll get a good banjo player to come up to the mikes. I usually am the only one there, and I stand in the background and play a little back-up while watching the intricacies of the band. Someone forgets a line of the song, another one is daydreaming and forgets to take his break, or there is some mix up about who *is* going to take the break and lead. But they are sounding good tonight, and I listen so hard I sometimes forget what I am doing with the instrument held in my hands.

I am jerked out of my reverie when I hear someone telling me to come up to the mikes and play a song. I smile—I am not nervous, but I do wish they had given me a little more warning. I walk up to the middle microphone; it has been empty, waiting for a banjo. The microphone is adjusted, turned on, and ready; I am ready; the band is ready. I lead off, and at the first beat, everybody kicks in. I hear the bass player and I try to keep the beat always with me. I don't know whether I am listening to it with my mind or my heart—or perhaps I simply feel it vibrating through the air. The guitar and the mandolin produce a steady strum, helping me along, trying to follow me, and the fiddle weaves in and out, all around. I am doing well, I think, the best I have ever played. I love the song, my fingers know exactly what to do, my right hand's fingers playing as hard as they can, the music driving hard, beating like a hammer, my fingers sliding along the steel strings and bringing out the melody.

Gonna whup that steel on down, Lord, Lord,
Gonna whup that steel on down.

Well, John Henry told the captain,
A man ain't nothin' but a man
Before I let that steam drill beat me
Gonna die with a hammer in my hand, Lord, Lord,
Gonna die with a hammer in my hand.

I was first introduced to classical music by my parents. But I don't remember listening to it (or any kind of music) very much at home when I was little, because most of the time we didn't have radios or stereo equipment. (We didn't have electricity, and batteries were expensive.) And neither of my parents played a classical or other musical instrument. But I remember that every year we used to go see Tchaikovsky's ballet, *The Nutcracker*, at Christmastime; in fact we still see it every year. That was my introduction to classical music, as well as to the ballet. Of course I developed a strong urge to be a ballerina, as is pretty much common with small girls.

When we moved to New York, I had a chance to try out for ballet at Lincoln Center. Mom gave me the choice of going or not going, and for some reason I chose not to. I'm glad I made that decision because I don't think I could have stood the hard work and dedication to a single art and the long rides to Lincoln Center every day on the train—and I couldn't have lived long with nothing more to inspire me than the grey streets of New York City. More recently, I had an option to stay in New York and try to get a scholarship to Julliard to study piano there. Dad had said that if I wanted to stay in New York City, he would find a way for me to do that. But I never did audition for Julliard or any other music school. The rest of the family was on their way here to Kentucky, and I really did want to live on a farm and not in New York City.

When I was nine we had bought a small Lowry spinet piano, and for four years I taught myself to play classical piano. I developed a strong interest in classical music and did much of my playing by ear—I would listen to recordings all the time and try to incorporate what I could into my own music. Because I was never pressured to take lessons or made to like classical music because it was "good for me," I built my own ideas and feelings toward the music and the piano that made it possible for me to love it in my own way, with interpretations of the music that were different from anybody else's.

But although I had a deep *love* for the music I was missing a lot of musical knowledge that would have made it possible for me to play the piano in a way that fully *expressed* that love. I could feel the music, but in most cases I couldn't play it well enough to show my feeling, because I would stumble over scales or chords. Rhythm was one of my stumbling blocks too, because I didn't know how to read it—I had no concept of half-notes, quarter-notes, beats or measures; I simply put the rhythm into the piece from the way I had heard it played by other people and sources. I didn't know how much I was missing, since I was virtually playing in a closet with no help from other people, no thoughts and opinions from other piano players. I didn't even go to many piano concerts or see other pianists in action.

Finally I decided that I would like to play piano *with* someone else. I wasn't sure that I was ready for *lessons*, as it would be the first kind of formal instruction I had ever had, in any subject. But I thought that I would at least prefer to take lessons from someone near my own age, since it would be more informal than taking them from an elderly lady in a house full of cats (no offense, really, but some of you must know what I mean). By luck we heard of a summer music program at the Town of Babylon Department of Parks and Recreation, where high school age kids taught music as a summer job. They got paid, but the lessons were free for anyone who wanted to take them. It wasn't very high-class, and most of the kids who signed up were very much beginners.

I'm sure that I was kind of a challenge for my teacher, a high school senior by the name of Dave, but we did manage to work a lot on the music and although in some areas we were both equal in skill, there was still a lot he could teach me. At the end of eight weeks of lessons, he had convinced me that lessons weren't all bad, and that it was a shame for me to be sitting around at home not progressing in areas that I needed instruction for. He convinced me to take lessons from his former piano teacher, and so I did, later on in the fall.

I liked my new teacher very much. He almost exclusively taught technique to young piano students, and this is what I needed the most. The parts of my playing that were missing, and what I needed to become an all-around piano player, were exactly what he was willing to teach me: rhythm, timing, how to work with the metronome. We also worked on finger structure and fingering (numbering your fingers so that you play each note with a certain finger) as well as a whole realm of technical stuff that I had to learn starting from the very basics, and try to incorporate into the complicated music I was playing (or attempting to play) at the time. Throughout the lessons, he didn't give me any kind of opinions on what to *think* about the piece of music, or how to play it *mentally*, so I could still do this myself and continue to be something of a self-taught musician. I was just getting to the point where the technical aspect was beginning to solidify, where my fingers did have some kind of structure as I played and weren't "dead" or "strands of spaghetti."

But then my family made the move to Kentucky, and I couldn't continue with my teacher. I am left with a terrible feeling of having started something that remains unfinished, and so I have started a half-hearted search for a new piano teacher in hopes of continuing work on technique. Of course, I really wanted to move to Kentucky, to the country, and that came first in my mind. I never really fell in love with the piano enough to devote my whole life to it and not care how or where I lived. But I did love improving, getting my mistakes corrected, and feeling everything solidify, and this is why I was sorry to lose a teacher who I was able to work well with. I know now that the kind of teacher I want teaches in a specific way and that I'm not going to go out and take lessons from just anybody. So it may be a while before I take lessons again. When I do, I think it will be just for my enjoyment, and I will not try to make a career of it. Sometimes, that is the best way to learn something. I do love the music and would like to be able to play the piano well, and I think that is enough.

When I was playing piano, I became interested in many different styles of music that had nothing to do with the music I heard around the house or that my parents liked. One of these was ragtime piano. Interspersed with the classical, I had always been playing simple folk songs and Christmas carols that found their way into my musical library. In one songbook, *Best Loved Songs of the American People*, edited by Denes Agay, I stumbled upon a simplified version of Scott Joplin's "Maple Leaf Rag." Before this I had been playing many show tunes from that era as well as some "boogie" tunes. But when I found the "Maple Leaf Rag," I found a whole realm of new music, different from classical yet pleasing to my ear and challenging (very much so) to my fingers. This was Ragtime—the great age of syncopated piano rhythms.

I spent a lot of time finding the music, because it isn't very accessible. There was a ragtime revival in the seventies after the movie *The Sting* came out, but it was not being played very much in the late eighties. I didn't have opportunities to hear it being played, because there aren't even ragtime recordings in many music stores. Yet I found the music, usually in big collections such as Rudi Blesch's *Classic Piano Rags*. Then I set to work playing it, which took a lot of work as I was a twelve- or thirteen-year-old girl playing music written in the early 1900s by men with huge hands and years of experience! Somehow, I worked around the obstacles.

By searching through a lot of the music, I was able to find relatively simple works that sounded good and were written by contemporaries of Joplin, whose familiar works, "Maple Leaf Rag," and "The Entertainer," are pretty well known but are two of the hardest pieces to play. I think these pieces might be discouraging to some people who are encountering ragtime for the first time, and who have to play simplified versions of Joplin's works and then get discouraged when they meet the real thing. There are quite a few other, easier pieces that are good to start out with, and that way you get the nice feeling that you are starting out with real ragtime. There are certain composers in particular—one of my favorites is Tom Turpin, who wrote quite a few wonderful ragtime pieces which are relatively easy to play. He must have had small hands, because the music fits me perfectly, and I can only reach a comfortable octave. His two pieces, "Bowery Buck" and "Rag Time Nightmare" (a lot more innocent than the title suggests) are easy favorites of mine. He also wrote "The St. Louis Rag" which is a well known piece and can be played if you spend some time working on it. Some of the lesser-known but easier rags by Joplin include "Elite Syncopations" and "Swipesy Cakewalk," my all-time favorite rag.

I worked hard at learning the history of ragtime and played as much of it as I could. I have been able to perform it at concerts (recitals) put on by my teacher, complete with tapping feet, a big grin, and a sinister looking felt fedora. Through ragtime I turned to many different "boogie" styles, more toward modern jazz, except always with a good beat.

About this time my interests broadened to other musical instruments besides piano. Through my encounters with hundreds of pieces of written music and recordings, as well as by my keeping my ears open and exploring new things, folk music started to intrigue me. Throughout all my music making I found songs that would reappear in different, unexpected places. I found folk music in classical, in ragtime, in boogie, in blues. I found folk music everywhere—but that's the way it's meant to be: If folk music is truly "the music of the people," then anybody who makes music, makes folk music. I began to collect more music and more songs. Anytime I saw a new version of the words to a song written down I would copy it, and if I had the music to that version I would record that as well, playing it on the piano and tape recording it so I would always have an idea of how the tune went. Whenever I could, I searched out and bought old songbooks or musical paraphernalia. I had an obsession (and still do) for tracking down and recording as many versions of folk songs as I could.

It was fascinating to me the way a song changed as it traveled through a country, and passed down through generations. Also, I began to find out that there were regional differences in songs that you could sometimes detect—one song would be sung differently by a folk singer from the Adirondack mountains than by somebody down in the Appalachians. I would spend hours researching the original roots of a song. Then, of course, I would eventually find out that many songs came from England or Scotland or Ireland hundreds of years ago.

I have always liked history but I never really thought of it as a school subject; to me, history can't be taught that way. To let everything that happened in the past be grouped into a single subject, to be studied and then more or less forgotten, is not only heartless, but unrealistic. I have never felt that I have "studied" history, only encountered it in other areas, and in that way it meant a lot more to me than it would have through a class or a textbook. In the words of hundreds of songs—songs that can be played and sung today as if they were written yesterday—people's lives and happenings can be preserved, better than through any written record or document. How many people remember who John Brown was, and what he did during the Civil War years? Probably only those who are familiar with the song, "John Brown's Body."

We would not know very much about the working people in history if their songs had not survived. Most times, they had nothing to pass on to further generations except songs—many of them had no birth certificates, and were buried in nameless graves. Yet songs about them still survive and now they are larger-than-life heroes, such as in the case of John Henry, who was an actual black man who died driving steel by hand for the railroad. For me, history would not come alive and mean anything if it weren't for music and songs.

When I was around fourteen and becoming interested in folk music, we had a banjo that belonged to my uncle which I would sometimes play as a diversion from the piano. I had no idea what I was doing at the time, as I was learning only from a small book called *Bluegrass Banjo* by Dick Weissman. I was unfamiliar with different banjo styles, and I had no idea what made "bluegrass" banjo different from anything else. I knew that the songs I played were folk songs—Appalachian folk songs mostly, so I figured I must be playing Appalachian folk banjo. But as I began to get interested in folk music styles I spent more time with that banjo. I still had little idea of what bluegrass was, because although by that time I did have a knowledge of many folk styles, bluegrass was not one of them. I did not hear it on the radio, and there were no recordings of it in the music stores. And there definitely weren't any local bluegrass bands, because I would have found out.

After a while, though, I did begin to realize how bluegrass banjo was different from other styles. There is a style of playing that originated in the Appalachians that is called "frailing" or "clawhammer," which uses the whole hand and the fingernails to strum or "hammer" the banjo strings. The bluegrass style is done with three fingers on the right hand that pluck or "pick" the strings in different patterns or rolls while the left hand plays chords on the neck. You use metal finger picks on your fingers and thumb to play bluegrass. The style was popularized by a musician named Earl Scruggs. So, I of course wanted to know, *who was Earl Scruggs?* So I found out Earl Scruggs is a bluegrass musician. *But what was bluegrass?*

We moved to Kentucky just before Christmas. I had a remote notion that we were moving to the "bluegrass state" and that there would be this kind of music here, but I wasn't exactly sure what it was like and what to expect. Now I think it must have been a stroke of luck that we moved to this area just as I was beginning to get interested in bluegrass.

About a week or so after we moved, I heard of a place in the nearby town of Hebron where some people got together to play bluegrass. It was in the basement of the Hebron Masonic Lodge, and we happened to walk into the middle of their annual Christmas party with all kinds of food and a couple of different bands. I don't remember who the first band was or who was playing in it, but as soon as I walked in the door I saw the microphones lined up on the floor and with their backs to the door were the musicians.

I can't describe the feeling I got the very second I heard a chord of that music. I don't know if I had even heard it at all before, but when the music hit my ears, I grinned so wide and I knew that if I got to know these people, and everybody else involved with bluegrass, I too would be able to play this music—the wild fiddling and fast banjo-picking, as well as the slow love songs and the lonesome sounding dobro guitar.

At first we were met by Gene Thompson, who pretty much runs the whole show and also leads the home band, Mixed Company. We talked a little about the banjo—he wanted me to come back next week and bring it. Then, when I explained that I had hardly played it at all, he mentioned a banjo teacher that I should take lessons from. The next week, I did bring my banjo, and Gene taught me a little bit of what he knew about it. Most important, he taught me the chords up on the neck, which are used a lot in back-up playing.

A couple of weeks afterward, I took his advice and went to Buddy Rodger's Music to meet my banjo teacher, and everything has grown from then on. It is hard to define what a bluegrass song is. The truth is that bluegrass is really nothing except a *style* of playing. I've heard bluegrass bands play country western songs written in the last half of this century, Appalachian folk songs (originally of European descent), all kinds of gospel songs, spirituals, fiddle tunes for square dancing and clogging—songs like "I've Been Workin' on the Railroad," "She'll be Comin' Round the Mountain," "When the Saints Go Marching In," and "You are my Sunshine," that almost every American knows, no matter how young they are or how unmusical. Mostly, bluegrass has been known as a style of country music, and has been grouped with "Traditional Country" by the media.

One of the most basic things that sets bluegrass apart from other kinds of music is that the instruments are all non-electric or acoustic instruments. Of course, there *is* cheating—many people use electric guitar or drums as a substitute for the bass fiddle to keep the constant background rhythm. But usually electric instruments are frowned upon. There is a saying that goes: "It takes four bluegrass musicians to change a light bulb: one to change it, and three to complain because it's electric."

Bluegrass is also different from most country western music because it has a faster tempo for most songs and plays dance music that is incorporated into the fast, intricate dance style of clogging—which, by the way, is done in tennis shoes by a lot of people—actual "clogs" are unheard of. The feet of the dancers go as fast or faster than the fingers of the banjo player or the bowstrings of the fiddler, and it is fun to watch.

Bluegrass is definitely hard to explain, but if you love your particular instrument and it fits into the band and you can play at least some songs that everybody else knows, then you can consider yourself a bluegrass musician.

Since I encountered that first jam session, I have attended many more. All across Northern Kentucky and Southern Ohio, in music stores or small scale "opry houses," in basements everywhere, amateurs and professionals get together and jam. Every night of the week there is a jam session somewhere. Many people are loyal to one place—you can see them at the same jam at the same place almost every single week. I have become like that, going to Hebron. But if I were to go somewhere else, I would be certain to find people I knew there, and if not, would meet them real quick.

The people involved in bluegrass are among the most warm and friendly people I have ever known. Nobody is ever downhearted about anything, or if they are, they don't show it. Every jam session is complete with jokes and laughter and smiles and people kidding one another. Everybody has had a lot of patience with me, as I am learning, and it is the most friendly and helpful encouragement I have ever had. Many of the other musicians have been playing bluegrass for years and I think they like to see a younger generation become interested. I think also that it is different since I am a girl, and that is really a rarity, in bluegrass music. Most bands consist of middle-aged men. This is also true of many jam sessions, although you *can* find mixed groups of people, young and old, male and female, jamming together.

Photo by Claudia Brosnan

Back when bluegrass was being born in the mountains, before it ever came to the stage, many women and mothers were the main musicians in the family. In many cases, a mother passed her knowledge of the music on to her sons and they grew up to be leaders in the history of bluegrass. Today, there are a few bands with women in them, and some, like the Coon Creek Girls and Petticoat Junction, consist of women only. But it is still kind of rare, and I can think of few girls my age who are as serious about learning as I am.

My banjo teacher, Jeff Roberts, plays with two different bands, and is probably known by almost everybody in bluegrass. At one time he belonged to the Charlie Sizemore band, which is a pretty big name. He also played on Garrison Keillor's public radio show, *A Prairie Home Companion*, when it was still being aired from St. Paul, Minnesota. Constantly people give him compliments when I mention who I get my lessons from; it gets tiring sometimes, but somewhere in there they usually end up complimenting *me* as well! I haven't taken banjo lessons from anyone else, but I'm pretty content as it is and I don't think I will ever look for another teacher. We have a lot in common, liking the same type of music and both trying to achieve the ultimate banjo sound: smooth, rhythmic, solid timing, yet with enough force to make that hard-driving bluegrass banjo sound.

Banjo lessons are a lot different than piano, a lot less formal and serious. We may spend some time concentrating on a part of the music that I'm having trouble with, but for the most part Jeff lets me work it out on my own, at home.

One of the biggest differences between classical piano and bluegrass banjo is that most music for the piano was meant to be played exactly as it was written, and you spend much time going over small details and trying to interpret exactly what the composer wrote. With bluegrass, many times there are no composers for the songs. The objective is actually to try and *change* the music to find new ways of playing it. Nobody wants to hear everybody playing the same song the same way. It is very important that somewhere down the line, you develop your own style. Earl Scruggs, who made popular the three-finger roll style played by everybody in bluegrass today, is still alive, and still playing. Everything is still changing, and the musicians are expected to change it.

When we look at a piece of music for the banjo, which my banjo teacher has written out and is most of the time his own interpretation of the song, I try to play it exactly as it is written at first, but this is only to make sure I have the tune and the timing right. After that, the doors are opened and anything I want to change or do differently, I can do, as long as it fits in with the tune and the timing is still there. I can change the roll, or do anything else. Sometimes I ask Jeff to teach me a song, and he'll ask me to figure it out by myself—sometimes because even he is not sure yet how to play it or write it down.

Sometimes it's hard for me, because with the piano, I was trying to be broken of that very habit of improvising, changing the rhythm or the melody to suit me. My piano teacher called them "Anneisms," little things I would add to the music, that weren't really supposed to be there. So while I learned the piano, I was taught to follow the music exactly, and not improvise or syncopate at all. Now, with banjo, improvising is *exactly* what I am supposed to do, and I have to unlearn what I learned with piano. It's frustrating, but I know that I am going back to something that was natural for me at first.

During the summer months, everybody in bluegrass gets together for the festivals, either to perform, to listen, or to jam around backstage or under the trees. I have only been able to attend one festival so far this year, in California, Kentucky, but there are still other opportunities. In California, I saw almost everybody I know well, and had a really great time listening to the bands. The Taylor Farley Band was there, and their banjo player (Taylor Farley) dedicated a song to me. In July, I'll be spending three straight days in nearby Burlington at the Boone County Bluegrass Festival.

Through meeting all kinds of people, listening to bluegrass on the radio, and getting together and jamming, I have immersed myself in the music so much that my banjo playing has been improving as fast as the days go by. I've found that this area is full of hidden musicians, bands, jam sessions, concerts, contests, and festivals playing good old bluegrass, and I feel privileged to be a part of it. From what other people have told me, in the short time I've been here and even shorter time that I've been having lessons, I've learned more quickly than most people. I went from not even getting my banjo out of the case to playing simple rhythmic background with the band, and now sometimes taking a shaky spot in the band as a lead banjo player. I practice well enough, but I think it's just my wholehearted enjoyment of bluegrass music and of playing it that makes everything go so well for me. I know that if I can keep it going, in a year or two I'll be as good as I ever hope to get, but I don't think I'll stop there. If I do move away, or follow a different occupation in life, I think my banjo will always go with me wherever I go. For a while, at least, I'll have known the feeling of being a dedicated banjo picker surrounded by some really good bluegrass musicians and bands.

There have been quite a few academic things in my life that I'd have trouble with right now if I were in school. Mathematics is the main one—I did a lot of it in workbooks when I was younger but then as I got into other interests I left math behind. For some reason it did not carry into my other interests. I've read the opinions of many people who say that mathematics goes far, far beyond the mimeographed sheets of multiplication problems—that you can find math in many fascinating places: in music, astronomy, cooking, building, navigating, and tying your shoes. Yet I seem not to have found it.

If there is math in music I do not see it because I don't use it—I wouldn't think of *counting* or using *mathematics* when I'm rippling through "John Henry" or "Foggy Mountain Breakdown" on the banjo—I just let the guitars and the bass set the pace, gather it up into my feet and set one of them tapping, let it go to my fingers, and usually, everything fits right in. (I did use some math in timing when I played the piano, but that was only because I was trying to follow written sheet music.)

I guess I'm just an ignorant and ornery kind of person about things I don't understand—but I still don't see what I need math for. If I went back to my old math books, and started over again, I think I would just be wasting my time. The furthest I ever got was long division, and I spent most of the time correcting the simple adding and subtracting mistakes I made while trying to do the division.

Dad says that if I am to be a scientist, then to know advanced math like algebra, trigonometry, geometry, and calculus, is a necessity. He says it's possible to pursue a career in life without knowing advanced math, but it helps in any field of science, and it wouldn't hurt me to try and learn as much of it as I could. *I* think it would be wasting my time, especially if it makes me miserable, as it usually does when I sit in front of a page of problems. "But," he says, "You may be wasting your time now, but later on when you realize it would be helpful to know algebra, you'll wish you had learned it when you had the chance." Even though I don't like it, I see his point, and I'm always curious to learn how to do things I've never done before, so I guess this counts for algebra as well. I'm going to have Dad explain as much of it to me as he can when we both have the time and patience to sit down and do it together, because I find that I like learning from people rather than from books—something I've learned from my musical exploits.

I have really enjoyed my life without school so far and I don't think I would choose to change any of it. One of the things that I have come to appreciate most is that I am free to roam about the world and be a hobo, both physically and mentally. I've spent a lot of time on the road—sometimes in small cars, some-times in big trucks—as we traveled from place to place. When I was little, this was sometimes torture. But now it has become inbred in me so that I usually get the urge to wander if I stay in one place too long. We travel a lot in connection with our interests as well as with Dad's job. In the winter we go up north to ski, and in the summer, to canoe. As I write this, I am getting ready to hop in the truck and go up to work on the cabin with Dad. When we lived in New York, we'd often go to Washington, D.C. when Dad had work in Maryland. We got used to the city and saw a lot of the attractions—except the White House, which really doesn't interest me anyway. It's a strange city, but fun. In April 1990 we were in Washington for the twentieth anniversary Earth Day Celebration; we never got anywhere near the stages to hear the music or the speeches but the atmosphere of the whole city and the people there expressing their love for the earth was something to remember.

Some people do other things to calm their minds and get away from their hectic lifestyles, but me, I'd rather be out on the highway reading roadsigns and eating fast food—even if being a vegetarian does make it a bit hard at times. It's hard on my environmentalist side too, because in general I am against all motor vehicles and the highways that are built on the fields and through the forests of the country. But sometimes I just like to forget all of my little preju-dices and hop in a truck and head west.

I love playing team sports, and have never really found it hard to be admitted on teams even though I don't go to school. I've never played on a public school sports team, but I had good experiences playing on a parochial school's track and basketball teams when I was in New York, and now in Kentucky I play softball for Boone County parks and recreation teams. Track is an individual sport, and from running mile and half-mile races I have grown to love running, usually alone, or with my Dad. The racing itself became a little too much for me after a while. I don't like sprint racing; it is too fast and competitive for me. I don't have the reflexes to burst off at the sound of a gun, but on the other hand I do have good endurance and the mental stamina needed for longer races. I haven't joined a track team here in Kentucky and I don't think I will; to me running is now something to do alone, in the country or somewhere else where there is a lot of space, so you don't have to go around in circles.

Playing basketball was my first introduction to team sports. We weren't a good *team*—we were unorganized, the coaching wasn't professional, and we won only one game. Nevertheless, I had a good *experience*. Being on a team with a bunch of kids means a lot to me since I'd never really felt a part of anything like that anywhere else. I got along well with the other kids in New York, but I find that here in Kentucky on the softball team, I have been able to make friends more easily: There are more kids who are a lot like me. A few of them express a dedication to the game. They are willing to work and learn with an extremely optimistic attitude that I respect since I don't see that quality in many other kids.

Baseball and softball are among my favorite sports, and for a long time I have waited for this opportunity to be on a team. It's an all-girl team, called the Hebron cougars, and we practice at a beautiful field in Petersburg, down by the river. I'm the catcher, and one of my best friends is pitcher, and we're just starting out in the season trying to prove we can make something of our team. Being the catcher is a kind of funny position for me—I'm supposed to keep the team's enthusiasm up, and help the pitcher, and always, *always* be aware of every single thing that goes on. Fortunately with my own enthusiasm for the team and knowledge of the sport, it's not that hard, although I'm not the greatest catcher there ever was!

Photo by Claudia Brosnan

My sister Gaea is two years younger than me. When we were little, we played together constantly. Now, we have different interests, but still talk to each other and agree on a lot of things; we rarely fight. She likes gymnastics and also plays softball, but sometimes has a different outlook on sports than I do. She's been doing gymnastics for a couple of years now, and doesn't seem to mind that she doesn't always practice or work hard at getting better. I sometimes perceive that as a lack of dedication, but she still loves doing gymnastics and does work at it—slowly but surely. It took me a while to convince her to play softball with the same Boone County league that I play with—she's shyer than me—but now that she is playing, she's on a good team and is improving faster than I am. She has other interests that I don't share—dancing, theater, and costume. She has never been in any play or worked with a theater company, or ever taken dance lessons, just pursued a casual interest at home—in that way, too, she's different from me! She does all sorts of crafts, embroidery, and needlework. She can knit Irish fisherman sweaters using complicated patterns—something I would never have the patience for.

Though most of my time I have spent with just my sister for a companion and haven't had any kind of social life outside of my family, I have known quite a few kids my age growing up—just enough to know that it's hard to find a really good friend anyway. Like most people who don't go to school or who are advocates of homeschooling, I get annoyed by people who ask about my social life out of school. This is not merely because I think that you can have a good social life out of school—that's been said enough now by enough people that it should be quite obvious. The thing that counts is that it shouldn't *matter* whether you have the sort of social life people acquire in school. Yes, you should be a friendly person and get along well with other people, but I don't think it's necessary to have gobs of acquaintances or belong to clubs, or even know somebody your own age, at all times. If I had to go to movies or the mall or be answering all kinds of gossipy phone calls, I wouldn't have time to live the kind of life that matters to me, so I don't *want* friends who think those things are important.

But this is not to conclude that I don't have any friends or that I don't have a social life. I meet different kinds of people through my interests; we become friends simply because we can do things together that matter to both of us. This happens not only with music and by jamming with other musicians, but also through the mail with people who are interested in writing and poetry. Some of my pen-pals and I have visited each other and we're just as good of friends in person as through the mail. And I am friends with kids near my age who like things I do—the environment, sports, fishing, farming.

Gaea and Anne with homeschooled friend Ariella (center),
visiting for a month

Photo by Claudia Brosnan

A lot of people think, and they're probably right in some ways, that it's important for kids to know lots of other kids or else they'll grow up backwards and unable to fit into society. I think it's true that if you grow up without kids your age around you every day, you won't turn out like all those other kids who are growing up to fit into society. Why everyone *wants* you to be like other kids, and why they want you to fit into society, is what I don't understand. There are billions of people and everybody is different, hundreds of societies and each one of those is different, too. If you live in the suburbs of America, but you are not like all the other American suburban kids, it's no big deal. You could always go and live in a hut in the Andes and you might just fit in down there.

Nobody needs to belong to any social group, or dress in fashionable clothes, or go to school, or watch TV, or eat Frosted Flakes for breakfast, as long as they're living the way they want to, somewhere on Planet Earth. Down here in the hills of Kentucky, there are a lot of kids who don't go to school, and I am one of them. The school board hardly knows about us, and it doesn't really care. It's a great feeling—we don't have to take tests or be evaluated or judged by anyone. We never had any trouble in New York, but the laws were different. Here, there are no requirements. We can be and do whatever we like.

This whole country has its problems: the economy, the environment, education. But still the United States is the sweet land of liberty. I know, because I have had the right to reject compulsory education and grow up thinking and acting as I want to. It isn't necessarily in the interest of the United States to let its citizens grow up as free and independent thinkers—what if I turned against my country someday? But really, if the United States government were to educate each and every citizen in exactly the same way, we would have a lot more problems than we do now. We would turn into one of those science-fiction societies where the whole population has been programmed to act the same and do everything in a dreamlike, robotic state. Actually, that is pretty much exactly what this country *is* working toward, with standardized tests, grades, lessons, studies, required courses and exams. The government's goal seems to be for all the children in America to learn exactly the same thing and learn it at the same level.

But if this were different, if each student was free—self-directed, self-educated, self-taught—then the world would be filled with so many wonderful people. There would be more harmony and fewer wars, because people would be happy with themselves; they would be in charge of their own lives, and thus would be able to care more for others. We would be able to live equally with others, and in turn all societies would have respect for each other, and this would lead to what we all ultimately need: a greater respect for the earth, and the ability to live in harmony with this, our mother planet.

Anne Lawson
Berea, Kentucky

Fulfilling God's Call

The past ten years have been the most glorious of my existence so far. I thought life was an adventure when I was sixteen; I didn't know I hadn't even boarded the ship. In ten years I have done three very important things. The first and most important thing is I gave my heart and my life to Jesus Christ. The second, I married the other half of myself, Tim Lawson. And the third: I had two beautiful, smart and talented little children named Jessie Grace and Timothy Judah.

Some other nonessential but fascinating things I have done along the way:
- Moved to Idaho with my family where I worked in the huge downtown library in Boise. At age seventeen I drove the city transport car taking books to a branch library—until they found out I wasn't old enough to drive the city car! I occasionally worked alone at the branch and dealt with all aspects of the library.
- Moved to Berea, Kentucky on my own when I was seventeen, lived with a Christian homeschooling family and helped with the five kids and lots of housecleaning.
- At eighteen I was working in Renfro Valley, Kentucky, a small, touristy town that revolves around country music. I became the editor of their newspaper, running an office and having an assistant, writing and editing a monthly newspaper that circulated all over the U.S. I was put on salary and drove a silver

Jaguar. I had my own apartment and began volunteer work in youth ministry.

• At nineteen, I went on a missions trip to Israel and began taking classes at Berea College in English and theater.

• At twenty, completely stressed out from journalism, I took a break and planned on going to college full-time, but ended up working in a hand-woven textile factory weaving throws and blankets on hundred-year-old looms.

• This whole time I continued to play bluegrass banjo, joining a gospel band called Narrow Road and performing in churches all over Kentucky.

• The day before my twenty-first birthday I married my husband, Tim. Ten months later we had a baby girl. At twenty-two I became the youth pastor at our church. And at twenty-three my son was born.

Now, at twenty-six, I look back and wonder how I fit all that stuff in. The past five years have been the most maturing years of my life, and the most important for me spiritually. I realize now that puzzle pieces are fitting together; and through all the unusual things that happened to me, God had a big plan. Some things I look at and wonder, "What was the purpose for having done all that?" Eventually, I find that God used all things to bring me to the place where I could find my purpose and destiny for living.

At twenty-six, I am a mom and a wife, a Bible college student and a youth pastor, a disciple of Jesus. I live in Berea, Kentucky in a little green house in the suburbs. My husband is a pastor, a worship leader and a music teacher. My two little blonde-headed, blue-eyed children have demanded a lot of time in the past four years. My teenage adventures turned into twenty-something adventures with diapers and crayons. None of which I regret, of course, but I could have done without the morning sickness.

Most importantly, I have found my passion: fulfilling God's call upon my life as a youth pastor. Although I have worked in different areas and followed one career path after another, nothing satisfied me as much as working with teenagers. No matter how talented I was in writing, music, or even just being a housewife, nothing is more fulfilling to me than making an eternal impact on the life of another person.

I work as a youth pastor at an unconventional church based in Mt. Vernon, Kentucky called River of Faith. (It's unconventional in several ways, one of the main ones being that the people of the church are trained to do the actual work of the ministry; everyone who has something in their heart that they want to do is encouraged to try it.) I pastor high-school age youth and oversee a middle-school ministry (which is pastored by a teenager!). My vision for teenagers is to help them overcome the enormous difficulties they face today: In our particular area, drug abuse is a huge problem, as are poverty and lack of opportunities for higher education. In general, teenagers today are growing up with more divorced parents, more substance and physical abuse, and more need for positive role models. In other words, they desperately need to hear the message that God loves them, that they can overcome problems because of what Jesus has done, and that they can have a sense of belonging when they become a child of God. This is my life's work, and although it is demanding and challenging, it is very rewarding.

I am very fulfilled in my life as it is. But some things that I hope to accomplish in the future are: finishing my degree in ministry, which I am working on through correspondence with Trinity Bible College. I am dedicated to being the best youth pastor I can be, and as a family we are dedicated to working in the ministry. I would like to take teenagers all over the world doing missions work, and possibly write books on youth ministry as I get older and wiser. Another challenge will be homeschooling my own children.

I also look forward to opening a teen center in our community to help teenagers not only spiritually but in many other ways. I envision a "safe" place where they could hang out after school, spend time with mentors or counselors, get a meal if they weren't going to get one at home. Our area is not exactly poverty-stricken but is definitely rural and low-income. If teenagers needed food, clothing, or other practical things we would have a clothing closet, etc. One way that this could be especially attractive is if we were able to stock fashionable clothes and give out cologne, nice jewelry, and other things that their parents couldn't get at Goodwill. It's very difficult to be a poor teenager when the demand for nice things is so great in high school.

There would also be access to computers and Internet resources so that kids who didn't have computers at home could study. Tutoring could be provided... or classes in computers, typing, and other subjects. Of course, because libraries are close to my heart, I would provide lots of books and resources. We also really need an effective drug counseling program.

Although these resources are available in schools, I find that there is a need for not just resources, but *relationships*. For example, kids in high school are now required to select a career path before graduating, and apparently aren't really getting the adequate counseling to do this. I have kids coming to me asking if I can do career counseling. I ask, "Don't they do this in your school?" The answer is yes, but it usually involves computer-assisted questionnaires that never match their hearts. One kid told me that he kept taking these profiles and came up with everything from a circus performer to a rabbi. What he really needed was someone to just sit down with him for a couple hours and say, "What is really in your heart to do?" Teenagers are starving for relationships, and I believe a center that was staffed with adults who really cared about teens could fill this void.

Looking back ten years: Nature and farming were very important to me when I wrote my first essay for *Real Lives*, but they became less so. For one thing, my family moved to Idaho, and having left our farm, we could no longer keep bees or horses. I also started working in libraries, and then soon was out on my own. But I think the major reason that my focus changed was that I became a Christian. Before that, in many ways, nature was more important to me than people. Afterward, I came to understand that although God loves the natural world (after all, He created it, and it is beautiful), people are His passion. And because His heart is in mine, my focus has turned more toward people instead of away from them. When I was fifteen, I was a loner, and could spend days just camped out in our pasture. Now I know my ministry is to work with teenagers and to minister the gospel to them, and this has become first priority in my life. I still enjoy spending time outdoors because even nature reveals God: "The heavens declare the glory of God, and the firmament shows His handiwork" (Psalm 19:1). But my focus is on worshipping the Creator, not the created.

Looking back again—if I had to do it all over again? I wouldn't change much. Everything that I did has helped shape the person that I am today, and every situation I faced has taught me a lesson that I pass on to the young people I work with.

One thing I do regret is that I never went to college at the same time as my peers. When the time came to think about college, I had this idea that I would homeschool my way through college like I did through high school. But when I was working in Renfro Valley I took some work-related courses, really liked the experience, and got good grades! Marriage and children, though, delayed my going full-time. Then, when the opportunity arose to go back as a full-time student, I realized that my life's work was in youth ministry. It turned out that at the only local college that really interested me, nothing I could major in was relevant to what I wanted to do. I am now working on a degree in youth ministry through correspondence and this fulfills my desire to learn and grow academically.

However, when I was in my early twenties, I would drive through the middle of our college town with my two babies in their car seats. I would stop at the crosswalk and watch the students walk by, going to study, to eat, to rehearse in the theater or the band or the choir. I would realize that they were all my age. I would sit there and think, what a life. Someone else cooks your meals and when you get sick you have a school nurse and all you have to do is learn and learn and do cool stuff with a bunch of other people your age who are all growing up and figuring out who they are. Cool. It wasn't that I didn't want my husband and kids or that I resented the place where I was at. It was just that I was frustrated with myself for thinking, at age eighteen, that I didn't want to do what everybody else was doing. I just *had* to be independent and *different*, and I realized that, if I had just given it a chance, I would have really had a lot of fun.

Here's the lesson I learned that I feel is important for homeschoolers to understand. I think that we (homeschooled teens) tend to develop intellectually and independently faster than schooled teenagers. If the research has proven correct, many homeschooled teenagers *can* be smarter and more creative than schooled teenagers. And it is true that the opportunities are endless for homeschoolers, and I believe it is wonderful to see the world and do unusual things and take advantage of the opportunities that schooled teenagers do not have.

However, one of the traps that older teenage homeschoolers can fall into is one that I found myself in. We have the opportunities to excel in our areas of interest, way beyond what is normal. And so, we may we enter a career at a young age, and although we are brilliant and creative, we burn out and are ready to retire before we reach twenty.

When I was an eighteen-year old newspaper editor, playing in a bluegrass band on the weekends, living in my own apartment, driving my third car, paying my own bills, people called me the "female Doogie Howser" (the TV show high school genius doctor). I think I robbed myself of some time that I could have spent just making friends and having fun and doing normal teenage things. In other words, I made myself grow up too fast. Because I was intelligent and independent, I wanted to show the world that young people can do anything an adult can. My favorite statement was, "Why do I need to go to college to learn how to do what I am already doing?" or "Why do I need to get a degree to get a good job?" I was making more money without a college degree than my boyfriend, who worked for the same company and did have a college degree. So I felt I was on a mission to show the world I didn't need a college education to make it in life—all I needed was talent and experience, and I had both.

But what I didn't realize is that, at that moment, many of my peers were relaxing in the cafeteria, some of them discussing the great mysteries of life, while I was alone in my apartment, tearing out my hair trying to proofread articles and design sales brochures at two in the morning. It wasn't so much that I needed the degree. What I needed, and what I would miss a few years later, is just the freedom of spending a few years learning about the world and about myself, without the pressures of having a career and a family. One thing that I did not have growing up was a lot of friends my age. For one thing, I thought that the things that other teenagers were doing were stupid. Going to the mall? I mean, come on. I had poems to write.

I think because I was different from most teenagers I thought I was better than them. This is also a trap that homeschoolers have to look out for. I was raised with a slight prejudice that homeschoolers were smarter than schooled kids, therefore better, and that everything that schooled kids did was stupid. Other teenage girls were into clothes and hair and boys. I loved books and science and *life*. They screamed for New Kids on the Block, I was into Beethoven. So I distanced myself from my peers, and this attitude prevailed in me for a long time. Then I got older and realized I was full of pride. Not only was I not all that and a bag of chips, but I had spent my teenage years shut up in my own little world and had missed some great opportunities just to let my hair down and have some good times with friends.

In retrospect, I'm grateful for all the awesome and unusual things I got to do as a homeschooled teenager. I've gone dogsledding in Michigan and walked along the shores of the Dead Sea. I've been a librarian, an editor, a housekeeper,

Anne getting ready for a day of painting in Bethlehem

a weaver, a missionary, a musician, a church secretary. And I would do all those things over again if I had the chance. But along the way, I would try not to take myself so seriously. Homeschooling worked for me, but I have seen people that it did not work for. And there are many, many talented and intelligent teenagers out there, both in school and out of school. When I was a teenager I needed to understand that how intelligent you were did not determine your worth as a human, and that there were many people worthy of my friendship regardless of whether they were young geniuses or just the average sleepy teenager. That some stereotypical experiences, like hanging out at the mall, are okay. That I really didn't have to prove that I could "make it" without any formal schooling. Everybody would have liked me just the same whether I had been a performance-driven autodidact or just another bright girl who worked her way through the educational system. In some ways, they might have liked the latter better, because I likely wouldn't have been so uptight!

My advice to homeschooled teenagers today is to go for your dreams—have all the awesome adventures you want to in high school. But I would urge you as you get older not to ignore college or other traditional things that your peers are doing, not to dismiss things like this too quickly, without considering their value. Everyone will go on many different paths in their lives. Some are traditional, some are untraditional. Homeschooled teenagers often assume they *must* travel down untraditional paths, because homeschooling in itself is (although more and more popular) untraditional.

As a grown-up homeschooler, I can truly say I am grateful for my education. Self-directed learning worked for me because of my drive and self-discipline. I have worked with teenagers who were out of school for the wrong reasons—sometimes to *escape* school rather than to *do something better* than what school can offer—and homeschooling did not work for them because their parents let them lay on the couch all day. So I cannot say this is true for everyone, but for me, homeschooling was the best choice and has allowed me to do wonderful things I couldn't have done if I had been in public school. If I didn't believe it works, I wouldn't be homeschooling my own children!*

---

* Anne says: Any homeschooled teenagers or schooled teens who are struggling are welcome to contact me for long-distance mentoring or any other kind of support. I can be reached at tajtj@earthlink.net, or at 328 Kings Trace Drive, Berea, KY 40403-8752, or c/o Lowry House Publishers.

Ayanna Pearl Williams, 16
Idlewild, Michigan

Fifty Pen-Pals

This essay is dedicated to the kids I used to go to school with,
especially the kids who couldn't—or didn't—make it in the system.

Winter, 1991

Dear Letter Box,

I am a fifteen-year-old African American girl. I have four sisters and two brothers. I live in a very small town in the U.S.A. I am a homeschooler, but I have only been homeschooling for the past two years. We started homeschooling because of the many problems in the U.S.A.'s school system. I am very interested in the world at large, but especially Africa and Latin America. I enjoy reading, writing pen-pals, listening to short wave radio, cooking, and drawing. I would like to have my address read on the air for people who want a pen-pal.

Sincerely,
Ayanna Williams

It all started after this letter was read over the air on the *Christian Science Monitor*'s radio program, *Letter Box*. I already had some pen-pals I'd gotten from Clonlara* and some from a multi-cultural magazine called *Skipping Stones*. My pen-pals from Skipping Stones were Nigerian, Indian, Cameroonian, and Mexican-American. Even so, I wanted more pen-pals, and I'd written a lot of letters that were never answered.

I had no idea that my *Letter Box* letter would get so many replies! For about a month after it was aired, I got letters from a new person every day. My few pen-pals have now turned into over fifty correspondents worldwide. I have pen-pals on every continent except Europe.

Sometimes fifty pen-pals does seem a little overwhelming, but it is really interesting. I've found out a lot of new things. Most of my pen-pals are guys in Africa. I do have girl pen-pals too, though. One is a homeschooler who

---
* Clonlara is an alternative school with a program for homeschoolers.

lives in New Zealand. And my best friend in the world is Denise, a Mexican-American in Colorado.

One guy in Ghana writes a little story at the end of each letter, about things he sees or makes up. One of my favorites seems to illustrate a few of the reasons some people choose to homeschool:

Photo by Tulani Williams

There was this poor fisherman, who supplemented his little income by carrying people across the river to the other side in his canoe for a fee. One day a pompous, stiff-necked scholar from one of the most prestigious universities in the country came along and demanded to be taken across the river. The fisherman agreed to take him and the two of them sat in the canoe and paddled off. Halfway to the shore, the scholar pulled out a huge book from his belongings and started reading. A few minutes afterwards he looked up and asked the laboring fisherman if he knew anything about what "Communism" was.

The fisherman said between gasps of breath, "Nothing."

"How pathetic," said the scholar, looking down his nose. He asked if he had any idea at all about "Capitalism."

"No," said the sweating fisherman, puffing from all the rowing he was doing.

"Pathetic," said the scholar with thinly concealed disgust, "Surely you must at least know something, some tiny little thing about 'Fascism,' don't you?"

The fisherman sighed and said, "No, I don't."

"Well, what are you good for, then?" shouted the enraged scholar and turned his back on the poor fisherman.

The fisherman's patience finally snapped. He turned the canoe upside down and they both fell into the deep river. The scholar immediately began to drown.

"Save me, I'm drowning!" cried the scholar as he gulped down mouthfuls of the river.

"Well, well, well, my clever friend," said the fisherman as he did a few back strokes around the scholar, "What do you know about 'swimmism?'"

"Nothing! Oh do save me, I have a wife and kids at home, please."

"What ignorance," said the fisherman, "What, if anything, do you know about 'save-your-lifeism?'"

"Nothing, please, nothing, do give me a hand please," cried the scholar as he went down for the second time.

"Incredible, absolutely pathetic!" exclaimed the fisherman as he did some laps of breast stroke around the drowning man, "Now surely you must have some tiny little idea about 'floatism?'"

"No, I don't," came the almost inaudible reply, "Please help me!"

"Well, what are you good for then?!!!" shouted the fisherman to the almost-gone scholar. Then he dived and brought the limp but still-breathing body up, turned the canoe upright and put the scholar into it. "That," said the fisherman as the exhausted scholar's tears mixed with the river, "Was your first lesson for today!"

—Richard Sammuel Essah, Ghana, 11/27/91

I have a pen-pal in South Africa in his forties who teaches people about my age. He writes long interesting letters and illustrates them. I have another pen-pal who is a native of Ghana, went to school for a year in Cuba, and now works in Libya. In Nigeria I have many pen-pals, one of whom is an eighteen-year-old Igbo:

The Christmas celebration was very dull this year in Enugu state. The reason was that many people moved out of the state since the creation of new states recently. During Christmas day everywhere was so dull that it looked like a ghost town. The masquerades that usually chase people around were nowhere to be seen. I went out that afternoon with my brother in our car. We drove to some of the places that are usually congested with people and masquerades, but no one was seen. Only a few people loitering around. Back home we celebrated happily with our family. After prayers, we dined on rice cooked with coconut juice, stew with chicken, and goat meat and some drinks. Celebrating Christmas in Enugu state is usually very enjoyable, especially when watching different masquerades passing by, sometimes chasing people around.

—Chionye Alisigwe, Nigeria, 1/20/92

When I write to my pen-pals, I tell them about Idlewild, my family, the activities I am involved in, my plans and ideas, the things I like and dislike. I answer their questions and I ask my own. On all of my letters I draw people, and my drawing is getting better, I think, from all this practice.

Dear Mamta,

Idlewild used to be a booming black resort. There were night clubs, skating rinks, hotels, and riding stables. The great black entertainers performed in the clubs. Since integration in the U.S., Idlewild has really gone downhill. People used to come from the nearby cities of Detroit and Chicago. Now, some people come on the weekend but Idlewild is more of a retirement community. And people from the city send their children up here to get them out of the city. Since most of the people here are from the city, Idlewild has city problems. It has a city atmosphere, drugs, bad schools, unemployment, teen pregnancies, juvenile delinquence, etc...But

Idlewild's problems are on a much smaller scale than in the city, so it is really not that bad. We have no gang problems and not much violence. Tell me about where you live in India. I got to go.

Your pen-pal,
Ayanna

I met three of my pen-pals—all in the same family—when we drove to their farm in Illinois this winter to get one of their rottweiler/labrador puppies. When my family got there they showed us the puppies and the rest of the farm. We ate lunch and dinner with the family and then watched a video, *Robin Hood*. We stayed overnight, sleeping on sleeping bags on the floor. We'd planned to leave early but ended up staying late, eating breakfast and watching another video before we left. It was fun meeting them; we plan to go visit them again soon and hope to have some of them come to Idlewild. I will probably meet some of my foreign pen-pals too—many plan to come to the U.S., and I am hoping to go to Ghana or Nigeria sometime in the not-too-distant future!

When we first started homeschooling, we were the only homeschoolers around. Now more people are starting to take their children out of school, and also some homeschoolers have moved here from Flint (Michigan) and from Oregon. Most of the homeschoolers here are younger than high-school age, though.

I don't homeschool for religious reasons. The reason I homeschool is because I can get a better education without the school system. I like homeschooling because it gives me control over my life and time to do things that are important to me.

None of my years in public school were good experiences, but my last year was the worst. My teachers were not good—in English and reading, the teacher was really boring. For the two hours of class we would do poorly copied worksheets. For math and social studies, I had a teacher who confused me when he tried to explain anything, even something I already knew! In science class, I had substitute teachers most of the year because of teacher layoffs. One sub who was there for a long time would show us horror movies and have us watch game shows in class.

Another problem was that my two best friends had moved out of the state. No one that I was even sort of friendly with was in my classes that year. I never had many friends in school anyway and those that I had, I never felt the need to spend time with outside of school. The first year of homeschooling I did not see much of the people I used to go to school with. As a matter of fact, I did not really spend any time with people my age at all. But I was not lonely because, like I said, I had never spent much time with kids my age in the first place.

Also, in the last three years that I was in school there were lots of bomb threats—sometimes two or three in one day. Students called in the threats. If the weather was nice and I was in a boring class, then I was glad to leave the building. I remember once it was snowing big, wet snow flakes and a bomb threat was called in. We stood out in the wet snow for at least an hour. Then the buses arrived and we piled on to wait for the school to be checked. Sometimes we would go home early after a bomb threat; other times we just had to wait it out. After a while, my mother started listening to our police radio (my father is a volunteer fireman), and would come pick us up when there was a bomb threat.

My family lives about five miles away from the town of Baldwin, where the high school and elementary school are, so we rode the bus. When they cut out busing one year, it was a problem. That summer we decided to homeschool. I did not miss school at all.

3/21/91

Dear Shawn,

Do you like home school? I like it more now than I did last year. We are less structured than when we started. Now I am involved in more out-of-the-house stuff. I started homeschooling because 1) I wasn't learning anything at school. 2) All of my friends moved the year before. Well, my real friends anyway. So I didn't really enjoy school. 3) The whole school was just really bad. I didn't need it and I didn't have to have it, so now my younger sister and brother and I homeschool. We will probably all homeschool through high school.

Your pen-pal,
Ayanna

When I first started homeschooling my life was more structured than it is now. That first year, we went to a lot of things out of town. We went to a play, concert, or museum every month, and we always had to drive for at least an hour. I remember seeing *Three Blind Mice* by Agatha Christie. We saw it twice, performed by different groups. One was a group of high school students at Interlochen Arts Academy and the other was a community theater group. We also saw *Twelfth Night* by Shakespeare. My three-year-old brother, Cabral, thought it was scary, but I liked it. It was not at all what I would have expected after hearing about what a hard time people have when studying Shakespeare. I especially remember the costumes and scenery, which were really well done. Sometimes we'd go to art shows at Interlochen Arts Academy where my older sister, Ife, was going to school. She often had a drawing, painting, or weaving in the show.

That first year, my father taught me to play the recorder a little. I learned the scale, "Mary had a Little Lamb," and a few other songs. I can play a recorder duet with my mother playing the alto recorder.

My mother taught us some Spanish. We would make puppets and have them speak the little Spanish we had learned. We also played bingo and sang songs in Spanish.

Also, the first year of homeschooling, we enrolled in Clonlara's Home Based Education Program. We figured that if the public school gave us trouble, we would at least be registered at another school. Clonlara is an alternative school, based in Ann Arbor, Michigan. For an enrollment fee, they send you a curriculum and deal as a middleman with the school system. You don't get books or assignments, but they will make you a transcript if you send them your grades[*] and a report of what you have been doing.

In Michigan, you have to have contact with a certified teacher to homeschool legally. Neither of my parents are certified teachers, so we were just playing it safe by enrolling with Clonlara. (I do not think that certified teachers should be required for homeschooling. If a homeschooler feels that they need the help of a teacher, that is fine, but not everyone does.)

6/10/91

Dear Omar,

You mentioned in your letter how you worked so hard on your Clonlara requirements. Do you think you could tell me in a little more detail what you do? I don't do much...well, not as much as I should anyway. One thing I don't do enough of is Spanish. Do you know any Spanish? My mother was teaching all of us (me and my younger brothers and sisters) and then I got this correspondence course. It only has eleven lessons and it's not that hard, but this is the second year I have been working on it. I only have two lessons left. Another thing I have been working on is U.S. history of Native Americans, African Americans, and Latinos. It is really hard, around here anyway, to find any trace of Latinos in U.S. history. Do you know anything about it? Native Americans I can find in many books. My parents have a lot on African Americans.

Your pen-pal,
Ayanna

As a high-school student with Clonlara, I was supposed to record my work on grids, which helped keep track of how many hours I spent on each "subject." When you complete so many hours, pass a test covering the basic subject areas, and present a portfolio of what you have been doing for the past four years or so, they give you a diploma. I always sent my grids in about a month late, and I never looked forward to filling them in. I don't know how I always ended up with so few hours on my grids—I never sat around doing nothing, yet I couldn't come up with much to mark down.

---

[*] Clonlara combines the grades you give yourself with the grades your parents give you.

I am not homeschooling through or with Clonlara anymore; we didn't feel that we were getting enough help from them. For instance, I wrote to the woman who was supposed to be my family's contact person. I asked her if she had any suggestions as to how I could incorporate some science into my life. She told me that a project I was working on in 4-H with videos was science. She either must have thought I was doing something other than the *Voices of Youth* project (in which teenagers were interviewed about what they needed from adults), or else she got me mixed up with someone else.* So, this year is our first on our own. We don't really have a curriculum, but we never used Clonlara's anyway. We've also met a certified teacher who signs our state reporting form.

After the first year of homeschooling we gradually relaxed so that by now it is nothing like school. It's just life. I spend my time learning about different cultures through music, books, cooking, and pen-pals. I do a little math out of a book but most of the math I do is figuring how many stamps I can get with my money, or how much money I need to make to travel around the USA. Science is an everyday thing taking care of the growing number of pets my family has, and growing some of the vegetables I use to make dishes from around the world. I do not have the feeling of waiting for life to begin that many young people seem to have.

Learning about worldwide cultures

On Saturday night from 11 P.M. to 1 A.M., a local public radio station plays African and Caribbean music. I try to stay up and tape it so I can listen later when I am more alert. Also, I wrote a research paper on West Africa. I've become very interested in Africa after exchanging letters with so many people there.

Lately, I have been reading books by Camara Laye, Mongo Beti and other African writers. My favorite books now are *African Child*, by Camara Laye and *Mission to Kala* by Mongo Beti. I like these books because they give me a vivid picture of life in some West African countries before colonization had taken its toll. I have also been enjoying books like *The Autobiography of Malcolm X* and *The Ways of White Folks* by Langston Hughes. We have a lot of books written by black people in the house.

I cook dinner a lot. I love to cook and can cook almost anything. The dishes I used to make most often were fried chicken, potatoes, rice, lasagna, stew, hamburgers, and pizza. Now, I try to look for international recipes. In this last week I have cooked dishes from Jamaica, Madagascar, the Philippines, and Ethiopia. My family sometimes thinks the combination of ingredients sounds awful, but it always ends up edible and usually even tastes good. Our favorite so far is Ethiopian beef wat on Ethiopian flat bread.

---

* Editor's note: Although the Williams family had a negative experience, many homeschoolers recommend Clonlara.

For social studies, we used to find places we read about or heard about on the news on a world map. The map was blank, so after finding a country, we'd color it in. Also, we'd play board games called "Where in the World," and "Global Pursuit." It was very hard, at first, to find countries on maps and to answer questions about them. But I started listening to the news a lot and discussed it with my family. I did a research report on Central America. (It was not an assignment—I was interested in Central America after hearing so much about it on the news.) And I wrote to my pen-pals about what is going on around the world:

March, 1991

Dear Aubree,

    You're a "good old American"—what is that supposed to mean???? You asked me what I thought about the war in the Gulf. Well, I don't support it. The U.S. invaded Panama last year, they gave Iraq aid not so long ago (with the "madman" Hussain in power). The U.S., in my opinion, is terrorizing the world in the name of peace and democracy. (You asked what I thought.)

         Your pen-pal,
         Ayanna

Through these activities, I gradually became more familiar with the location of places—especially places in Africa. I could tell you with no problem where Sierra Leone is, and that its capital is Freetown. But I don't know what the capital of Norway is, or where Germany is in Europe!

Reading, writing

Every Saturday we used to go to the library. I read about all types of things. I especially liked books about orphan girls where everything turned out good in the end, and books that were written a long time ago. Some of my favorites were *Dicey's Song, Anne of Green Gables, Lydia of the Pines, The Witch of Black Bird Pond, All Over Town*, and *Emily of New Moon*. I read the *All-of-a-Kind Family* books and *Gone Away Lake*. And as I mentioned above, I have more recently been seeking out books by black writers.

    I write articles every month for my family's newsletter, *Ruff Draft*. The *Ruff Draft* has been going almost as long as we have homeschooled. My sister Tulani, my brother James, and I write most of the articles. Lately, my two older sisters have been contributing some articles too. We send the *Ruff Draft* to our family and friends. We mostly write about what's going on in the family, and sometimes explain our opinions on different topics. In our first issue, I wrote:

Socialization

It seems that some people worry that I won't get socialized. I have only been out of school for one year. If they were going to socialize me, I should be pretty socialized after eight years. What is this thing that I am supposedly lacking? It couldn't be working with other people. I was always under the impression that you should look at your own paper. It couldn't be to communicate. At my school you were not supposed to talk in class unless you were called on. "Talk at lunch, recess"—then you sit quietly for three hours. It surely isn't to obey, they couldn't really believe you would do some of the things they tell you to do, like not talking unless you are acknowledged by the authority....I can do all the above when I choose. I can't figure out what socialization is, and if I did, would I want to be socialized?

Math

This year I studied geometry. I would like to do math without a book and to have it simply be a real part of my life but, so far, I have not been able to find anything that I *do* that is related to the higher forms of math. I tried to learn algebra, but I was not really interested and it made no sense to me. My father tried to help in the evening when he got home from work. Often, my pen-pals ask what I am studying.

Dear Ayanna,

I am glad that you are doing pretty well in geometry. Now, put on a "thinking cap" and ask why they teach geometry. It is not to teach you about right angles, bisecting, etc.; it is to get you thinking logically and to think through a problem to its conclusion. That way you will handle all of life's problems in a better manner than if you do not think. I remember when I took algebra in ninth and tenth grades...the first year was kind of "what's going on here???" But later, after the summer vacation passed, I found that I was "ready for it"...it just took me an extra year to mature, I guess. Remember: More things are achieved by TENACITY and PERSISTENCE than by "just wishing!"
—John, Costa Rica, 2/29/92

Science

The whole time I have homeschooled, I have had a small problem with science. I do keep animals and plants and I suppose that is somewhat related to science. We have two puppies—a rottweiler-German shepherd mix that promises to be really big, and a rottweiler/black lab that is already big. We also have rabbits, six cats, and two goldfish. We have a garden, and I raise house plants. But sometimes I feel like I should do more in the way of science. I don't know if I will ever need science, and if I do I have no idea what kind. I do not know much about science, but I might be interested if I did. Also, I admit that part of the reason I would like to know something about science is simply that it is expected of me! But in spite of all this, I don't spend much time on it.

Ayanna and
her brother Cabral

Photo by James A. Williams

I did collect insects, flowers and leaves last summer, but I never labeled or did anything with them besides send them to pen-pals. Every once in a great while I will do some experiments. For a few weeks, I did physics experiments. They were sort of fun, but usually I either forget, don't have the time, or just am not interested. When it is warm and I spend more time outside, I feel that I do more science. I watch birds, and see the leaves and ferns come out. The Gypsy moth caterpillars seem to be everywhere. Maybe I learn a lot of science without trying!

Work

This summer I am working on a project to record the history of Idlewild as told by the people who lived it. It involves talking to elderly people and videotaping, and is paid for by a job training program funded by the school district. (The program assigned me to the Idlewild library, and the library designed the actual project.) I spend at least three hours each day at the local meals program in Baldwin. Old timers come to spend time with their friends and eat. They tell me about Idlewild in the fifties. I find it fascinating hearing their stories. I heard one story, for example, about coming to Idlewild fifty years ago with a suitcase, a box, a little girl, and a greasy bag that used to have chicken in it. This job is more interesting than most I've had.

I like to listen to the elderly talk to each other about growing up in the days of big families, home grown food, and even homeschooling! One lady told me that when she was growing up there was no school to go to. They were taught arithmetic, reading, and writing at home

Ayanna asks about the old days   *Photo by Tulani Williams*

by mothers, fathers, grandparents, aunts, uncles, and any other adult around. They tell me if I stick around they will learn *me* something. They also tell me that it is a good thing, what I am doing. And they say I should talk to some *really* old people before they die or forget what they know.

6/10/91

Dear Omar,

You wrote that you have a job landscaping; what do you do? I rake leaves and mow lawns. Would that, by any chance, be the type of landscaping that you do? If so, there is a terrible $300 job up here I wish you could do! This guy wants his leaves raked, grass cut, beach rototilled and a building torn down. There are so many leaves in the yard, it must not have been raked for awhile. I hate raking leaves!

Your pen-pal,
Ayanna

I have had jobs outside my home since I was about seven years old and delivered newspapers. I learn something from every job I have had, just like I learn from all experiences. I learn a lot about people because all my jobs have been dealing with people in one way or another. The first summer after I started homeschooling I had a job working at the local high school. It was called a basketball day camp. Many of the planned activities never happened. Usually all I did was sit on the bleachers with the other "workers" and watch the kids play ball.

That winter, I worked at a Catholic church helping to teach a preschool religion class. But the woman that I worked with was very bad with children, always telling them to color inside the lines and that they had to do this and that to get ready to go to school. She did a lot of things for the kids that they could have done by themselves. They were supposed to sit in their chairs all the time, and sing and answer silly questions when asked. I was supposed to help her, but there was not much I could do.

The summer I was fifteen, I worked at Ferris State University library, about an hour's bus ride away. Along with about ten other young people, I rode a school bus provided by the summer job program. I had gone to school with four of the girls on the bus and I knew the other people too. They talked a lot about who was going with whom and who was pregnant. Many of the girls I had gone to school with were pregnant or had already had babies. The guys were starting to get in trouble with the law and stuff. Often during that summer I was really glad I didn't still go to the local school. The girl that worked with me in the library was a quiet person, and we got to be friendly by the end of the summer.

Since I worked this winter at the township office, I could afford to go visit my sister Jilo at Northwestern University near Chicago during her spring break. I went down on the train and stayed for two weeks. While there, I went to some of Jilo's new classes for the spring semester. One class was about computers, taught by a woman who seemed unorganized and self-conscious. I went twice and it was very boring. The things covered in the class were the same as the things I was supposed to learn in my fifth grade computer class at the Baldwin schools.

The other class was about writing. The professor asked the class if they spoke Greek or Latin. No one did, but still he would throw in foreign words as if the class should know them. He was very condescending. He said many things that I did not agree with, but even if I had been taking the class I would not have bothered to argue with him. He was the type of person who would not listen to reason.

I went to the university library, which was the biggest library I have ever been in. There I watched *The Battle Of Algiers*, a movie made in the sixties about the Algerian revolution. I also saw *Salaam Bombay*. It was sad, because at the end nothing had been solved or even bettered through all the pain and suffering.

At the student rec center, I learned how to play a little pool. I went with Jilo to her job at The Third World Press—they have a lot of interesting books in the bookstore. And I went to a play called *Solitude* about a black woman with a white boyfriend.

It was interesting being on a college campus. I think I will go to college, but I am considering a smaller school like Berea, in Kentucky. But I want to study languages (Igbo, Hausa, Chinese, or Arabic) and study abroad for a year, so for that reason I might go to a big school like the University of Wisconsin, Milwaukee. When I am through with school I want to work with children. Doing what, I am not really sure, but I don't think I want to teach in public schools.

4-H

I joined 4-H a few years ago in order to get out of the house and be around more people. My first 4-H group used to go out of town for the weekend about once every two months. It was a Peer Plus Club, supposed to be promoting positive peer pressure. But the people in the club were just in it for the trips. After a few meetings I realized that I didn't have a lot in common with them. I convinced my younger sister to come with me once or twice, but she didn't like it and stopped coming. The reason I still went was because I enjoyed watching the other kids and thought it would make a good story one day. Sometimes they talked about the people I knew from school. From what they said, school sounded like it had only gotten worse.

It was almost spring when our leader told our group about a video project called *Voices of Youth*. We were supposed to make a video from our point of view, to explain what teens need from adults who work with them. But we took too long and the adults ended up making the video; we were just interviewed about our opinions. I had not planned to talk about homeschooling, but the leader told the interviewer that I was a homeschooler and she was really interested. She had never met someone that really homeschooled!

Voices of Youth was presented at a conference of adults with our 4-H group giving a rap for the introduction. It was well received and we were asked to do it many more times. But I didn't like the rap routine, was getting tired of the leader, and had better things to do with my time.

That summer I went to Michigan State University for a weekend 4-H program called Exploration Days. 4-H'ers from all over Michigan come to Expo-Days. I took two classes. One was on developing foreign friendships, and I got the address of my pen-pal in Belize there. The other was supposed to teach games that I could use with people of all ages, but it wasn't very good. I had gone to Expo-Days the year before, also, and taken cooking and tie-dyeing workshops. I think Expo-Days is the best 4-H activity I have been to.

I never went to another meeting with that 4-H group after a week-long trip to Washington, D.C. We went from Michigan to Washington by bus and the bus broke down! We had to wait at a rest area on the Ohio turnpike for hours. We were always rushed once we got there. We went mostly to the "important" monuments and to other planned, boring events. Our Michigan group was the first group with black people that had come all summer to the program. In general, the trip was not what I expected and I think a lot of other people in my group, too, had not imagined it as it turned out.

After I quit that 4-H group, I didn't have a place where I saw people my own age every week, but I was really tired of them after the summer. I am not at all sorry that I stopped going to the meetings. I am happier now as a teen leader in a 4-H club that was recently started in the neighborhood. This club has younger people, mostly ten- to twelve-year-old boys. We cook, play games, and they especially like to go to the gym to play basketball. The club has been spending a lot of time raking leaves to raise money to go to Exploration Days this year.

***

My family is close. We have always been close, even before we started homeschooling, and I have always lived with both my mother and father. For most of my life my mother has not worked outside the home. My family eats all meals together around the dining room table, and we talk about the day or discuss world events while eating. My sisters, brothers, and I spend a lot of time together. We travel, play ball, talk, and just hang out. I do not know any other families as close as mine, whether Black, Asian, Latino, or White. Of course, we are not perfect; we do argue and have our problems.

Being Black affects my whole life so, of course, it affects my homeschooling experience too. I think that people of color are likely to have good homeschooling experiences compared to the bad experiences we have in the public schools. People of color homeschool for some of the same reasons that white people homeschool—for religious reasons, because

Part of the Williams clan, clockwise from top: Ayanna's father James, cousin Steven, sister Tulani, brother Cabral, Ayanna, and brother James

of bad experiences with a school system, and because of the need for more than schools can provide.

I think anything you can learn in school you can learn better without school. Homeschooling is especially good for those of us who don't see why we need to go to school anyway and/or don't feel like we are learning anything in school. Homeschooling gives you the opportunity to learn things from people that you might never meet if you were in school for eight hours each day. And homeschooling is different with every person; at its best, I believe, it reflects our individual interests and personalities.

Often it is hard to explain to my pen-pals what homeschooling is. Like many people, they don't have any experience with it, and they are not sure what to make of it. I think they eventually come to understand what I am doing, but their initial reactions are sometimes amusing:

Dear Ayanna,
...I think homeschooling is a nice idea. No striking teachers, syllabus will be covered more fully, and students will be able to ask more kinds of questions in your case, since it is your parents teaching you...
—Femi Olarinoye, Nigeria, 3/4/92

Dear Friend,
...What do you mean by homeschooling? I can't make out what it is. But from context I guess that it is schooling via computers. I mean by logging into computer network of school with the help of a computer and a modem you thus attend class sitting in the confines of your sweet home. Am I right?....
—Annesh Thandassery, India, 12/31/91

Ayanna Pearl Williams
Atlanta, Georgia

A Purpose Beyond Myself

"As we live, so we learn." –Yiddish Proverb

Photo by Kristin Williams

I don't write to fifty pen pals any more—but I still write lots of letters! My letters today are to nonprofits and other organizations that serve families and build communities. I send out about twenty a week—requests for general information on programs, cover letters for job applications, and letters to friends and family asking for advice and connections. Although writing to pen pals helped me learn and develop letter writing skills, that was not my motivation for writing. Pen pals were an opportunity to express my ideas and connect with a diverse group of individuals. And over the past ten years I have continued to seek experiences that allow me to interact with generationally, culturally, and economically diverse people. These experiences have helped me to formulate opinions on a wide spectrum of topics. Consequently, I have been motivated to commit my time and energy to making the word a better place. In my apartment I have a quote from Ralph Waldo Emerson that illustrates what has become my philosophy for life:

> To laugh often and much; to win the respect of intelligent people and the affection of children; to earn the appreciation of honest critics and endure the betrayal of false friends; to appreciate beauty; to find the best in others; to leave the world a bit better, whether by a healthy child, a garden patch, a redeemed social condition; to know that even one life breathed easier because you have lived. This is to have succeeded.

I am the product of a childhood filled with dinner conversations in which my parents worked through complex social issues, discussing everything from why problems exist to what ordinary people could do to precipitate change. I considered myself to be socially aware, but little did I know how much further that awareness could develop. Nothing had forced me to analyze poverty like the experience I'd later have of trying to convince a three-year-old that he had something to live for. At the age of fifteen I thought I would travel and see the world. Well, in ten years I have gone no further than Canada, which isn't saying much in Michigan. But instead of discovering new worlds in foreign lands, I found direction and purpose in the social disparities of America's urban landscape.

I moved to Atlanta the fall after my eighteenth birthday, and my first job was as a preschool teacher's assistant. At the time I didn't know that this job would change my life by opening my eyes to concrete issues that I would feel compelled to tackle. I worked with homeless children and those in the surrounding community, kids who had seen more in their three or four years than anyone should see in a lifetime. I found myself overwhelmed by their needs. One three-year-old would run for the street, crying that he wanted to kill himself, whenever he was mad, sad, or upset. The families these children came from were not just strapped for cash—this was chronic, multi-generational, abject poverty; the kind where there is never enough of anything and life is a struggle to just barely survive. I went to work at the preschool believing I could change the world. Reality knocked the wind out of my sails as I realized that in a world that tears away at the innocence of children I needed to provide more than nursery rhymes and happy songs. Knowing I did not have the skills or training to precipitate meaningful change, I set out to find them.

"If you are planning for a year, sow rice; if you are planning for a decade, plant trees; if you are planning for a lifetime, educate people." –Chinese Proverb

So in 1995, when I was nineteen, I moved to Houston and became involved with a community-based, child-centered, church-run youth program called Alkebulan. These children were poor too, but their families had hope that they and their children would not always be in poverty. Alkebulan provided staff with the tools to effect change—we were trained in a phonics-based reading program, an arithmetic teaching program, and a vocabulary and comprehension-building program. We also met weekly to discuss our program and how we could better serve our children's individual needs—we really paid attention to cultivating their minds, bodies, and spirits. My repertoire grew from those nursery rhymes and happy songs to skills and values the children could build on for a lifetime. I was now teaching them to read, add, subtract, write their names, and tie their shoes. And through games and more loosely structured activities, I was helping them learn basic social skills—how to play together, share, and use their growing vocabulary to communicate with both children and adults.

As a member of this community committed to raising well-adjusted, happy, intelligent children, I connected with parents from a variety of socio-economic backgrounds. My most vivid memories are of the children who came in with painful issues but blossomed into happy children, believing they could do anything they put their mind to. I was invigorated to see the difference I was making in the lives of the children, their families, and the community. I spent over four years with Alkebulan—I was a phonics-based reading teacher, a house parent, summer camp counselor, project coordinator of the young adult fellowship, president of the community college social activist chapter, and much more. I worked just for room and board, often putting in well over forty hours a week.

It was hard work—hard in the long hours, hard in the emotional commitment that it required, hard in the daily tasks themselves. And hard to allow myself to be a part of something bigger than myself—to step outside of my comfort zone, to take my focus off of me and put it on other people. Yet, it was also a wonderful feeling to have a purpose beyond myself. It was good to be needed, to be missed when I was gone, and to feel like I was a part of something important. I saw that if I did not do my part and give in the ways that were uniquely mine to give, somebody else's life would be harder. I began to feel that my life had direction, purpose, and meaning; to sense that I had a calling. I decided that I would like to learn more about working with children, and I enrolled in Houston Community College with a major in education.

"There are many paths to the top of the mountain, but the view is always the same."
–Chinese Proverb

I was not confident in my intellectual ability when I started at Houston Community College in 1997. I had worked for three years at that point, and had not been in a classroom setting in about eight years. I had no way to gauge my intellectual ability in scholastic terms. I had taken the standardized tests but they did not tell me whether I could hold my own in a classroom. In all honesty, as a homeschooler I did not cover everything that is taught in high school. I learned more of some areas and not that much of others. For example, I loved to read, so I learned a lot through books. But I have no patience for math so I learned little beyond basic algebra. (I now know that few students in traditional school learn all that is presented to them either, although some waste time pretending to know, ignoring lessons that do not reach them, or studying random facts they'll forget after a test.) The most important thing I learned as a homeschooler, though, was how to learn. I really believe that anything I do not know I can learn in a book or by spending time with someone who knows the subject well. (Cooking, for example—I'm a great cook. I can cook anything: Pizza, lemon squares, barbeque ribs, you name it, I can make it. I learned through cookbooks, which I used to read like novels, and by cooking with really great cooks.)

When I tell people that I homeschooled, I try to explain the experience of having had five years of freedom to explore my interests. I had spent much of my "senior year" looking at colleges and preparing essays and explanations for my nontraditional high school education. I compiled a list of books I'd read and wrote a detailed description of how I met the requirements of each subject I studied. I took the SAT, ACT, and the GED. I did very well on the verbal portions of each test but not so great on the math. At that time I could not understand why I needed to know math and did not have the patience or desire to spend time learning geometry or algebra. I researched and applied to several small liberal arts colleges with strong co-op programs. (Co-op programs give college credit for life experience, and the ones I looked at tended to alternate a semester in the classroom with a semester out in the world.) I also applied to a midsize state school in Michigan. And I was accepted into every school to which I applied. But I didn't want to go just for the sake of going, and since I didn't yet have a true reason to go, I decided not to. This was definitely going against the family norm—my parents and both of my older sisters had gone to college—but they supported me, even though I didn't even have a solid plan of what I wanted to do instead. They helped me financially, and I moved in with my sister and contributed minimally to her household expenses. And they provided emotional support, through stimulating conversations and suggestions of opportunities. So I was not only the first in my family to homeschool, but also the first not to go straight to college.

But now I had a reason to go to college, and I was starting at Houston Community College. I went to every class, I sat in the front, I smiled at the teachers, and I answered their questions. I read the textbooks and came to classes with a basic understanding of the material. I learned how to take notes during a lecture. I think that I did well because I took the time to learn what the teachers wanted and I did my best to give them that. I have a terrible memory when it comes to regurgitating facts but I am great at synthesizing information. I can find an answer on a multiple-choice test and I coherently argue anything in an essay question. Spanish, algebra, and physics gave me the most problems, but I learned to arrange my schedule so that I simultaneously took one class that was really hard for me and three classes that I enjoyed and could easily excel in. One of the best things that I did was to become very organized. I was going from homeschooling, where the day was mine to do with as I pleased, to a very tight schedule that involved forty hours of community work and twelve to fifteen credit hours (four to five classes). I bought a planner and then whenever I received a class syllabus I would sit down with the planner and a wall calendar, and write down each test, quiz, paper, and special project on both. Depending on the classes I might also make a reading schedule to ensure that I kept up. I was a child who hated school, but as a woman I came to enjoy the intellectual stimulation of college.

In 1999 I moved back to Michigan to be closer to my family. I worked with a youth group for about a year and transferred to Wayne State University. I began to expand my interest from youth work to the broader work of community building. And I changed my major from education to sociology. As a sociology major I became part of a community that looked at the way that groups of people interact with societal institutions (like educational, religious, and correctional institutions).

I was also selected to participate in Wayne State's National Institute of Mental Health Career Opportunities in Research Program, which helped me take my education to a whole new level. In NIMH-COR, I was asked to bring my unique outlook and experience to the table in a community of socially aware, intelligent young people. Discussions in structured classes and beyond stimulated my love of learning and reawakened my natural tendency to question the nuances of societal issues. The program had a social science lab, where I gained invaluable hands-on experience. And I delivered presentations at research colloquiums—never having considered myself to be a public speaker, this was a new and rewarding experience. Through NIMH-COR I was made aware of opportunities which combined my desire to help people with my intellectual ability, allowing me to make a larger impact on the lives of children. By the end of this program and my undergraduate education my dreams of changing the world by helping one child at a time had transformed into a desire to influence policy through program development and analysis.

"A society grows great when old men plant trees
whose shade they know they shall never sit in." –Greek Proverb

A Million Youth   *Photo by Kristin Williams*
Movement rally in Atlanta

I now work as an AmeriCorps team leader with elementary children, supervising literacy and math tutoring to the lowest thirty percent of the children in one of the poorest performing schools in the Atlanta public school system. The first four months of this job were challenging, frustrating, and in all honesty the most difficult learning experience I have ever endured. There are still days when I hate my job, and wonder if we are doing more harm than good for the children. I question my ability to lead and my willingness to continue in a position of leadership in an organization that I do not always agree with. I am not well paid or well appreciated by the staff or teachers.

Yet I stay because I believe there is a lesson for me in this experience. I stay for the moments of validation, a day that runs smoothly, a volunteer who has a meaningful experience, a service leader who grasps a concept that has eluded them for months. I stay because I know that I can leave the children better and see the team grow. It is hard to see in the day-to-day struggle, but when I take a minute and step back I know that I am providing a valuable service. I am motivating people to do a job that is difficult with few tangible rewards. I am there for the children every day from 8:30 A.M. to 5:30 P.M. because I believe that I can make a difference for them. I believe that in their otherwise basically miserable lives they will remember the book I gave them. I believe they get something from our exchange of smiles and from the kind words that I dole out like candy. I know I won't see them in fifteen or twenty years and I'll never know what impact I make on their lives, but it gets me up in the morning and helps me through the hard days to believe that I am making some difference in their lives... and this belief is supported by the stories I hear about famous people who were pushed to do great things because one person believed in them or challenged them when they had no hope and it looked like they would never achieve anything.

"Today is the first day of the rest of your life." –North American Saying

As I navigate the future and try to chart a course for my career, I am looking for a position that will allow me to use my caring and compassionate nature as well as my mind in an environment that is focused on making the world a better place. I was accepted into the University of Michigan Masters of Social Work program in May and will begin in September. This is a sixteen-month program from which I hope to learn grant writing, budgeting for a research project or organization, and program planning experience. I want to go back to school for two reasons—first, to become better qualified to get the kind of job that I want, and second, to once again be in an environment of thinking people. I want to analyze and synthesize information, I want to engage in intellectual conversations, I want to be challenged mentally every day. And, I am still looking for opportunities for the future, such as internships, jobs, or PhD programs. I have found great validation working with nonprofit organizations, and plan to continue doing so.

I am looking for a group of people who love children, respect the elderly, and believe in using their skills and God-given gifts to make the world a better place. I have found everywhere I go little pockets of what I am looking for—a person here, a person there. This search brought me to Atlanta at the age of eighteen, where I worked at a preschool that served homeless children. It led me to Houston where I spent five years as a youth worker at an urban Christian mission and started my college career. My search for this community brought me to Detroit, where I earned a B.A. in Sociology. And now this same search takes me back to Atlanta one more time.

Patrick Meehan, 16
Orlando, Florida

Ascent from a nightmare

Prelude

All my life, school has been abhorrent to me, a prison where my mind was put in shackles to keep it from escaping. I'm out now, and have been, quite happily, for three years. I became what is known as a "homeschooler" in 1989, after an eight-year struggle with traditional education, both public and private. In Orlando very few people have heard about homeschooling as an alternative. That's why it took so long to find a way out.

Photo by Christy Beckert

By the time I left school, the summer after the seventh grade, I was a nervous wreck. All of my "friends," save two, had turned against me. I had virtually no self esteem. Everyone whom I met seemed to become my enemy. Now it is just the opposite. While I don't strive for popularity, I have developed a close circle of friends; people whom I should know seem to seek me out. It's ironic, given people's worries about how homeschoolers will socialize, that only now that I am outside of school I have found some true friends.

Above all, homeschooling has given me time to think. I have time away from the constant social pressures and traumas associated with the school environment. If I want to spend the day listening to music, drawing, or working out, it's my right. My time is my own to develop as I please. I have not attempted to create a formal education for myself; rather, I have taken a completely free-form approach, living and learning according to my own natural lifestyle.

This method frees me to identify my interests and develop them in my own way. For example, if I want I may devote all my time to a single subject, like math. I may learn it so thoroughly that it becomes intrinsic, second nature. I may study it fully without being interrupted constantly and forced to change gears. And I may do this when it seems to me to be the appropriate time in my development. I am not forced to learn something for which I do not yet see any connection to my life, nor forced to wait to learn something until someone else decides that it is convenient.

I get so many different reactions when I tell my peers that I homeschool. Most really can't comprehend that life could exist outside the safely reinforced boundaries of the bureaucratic school system. They go away assuming that I am really a "drop out," or maybe in a special education program.

Admittedly, "homeschooler" is a misnomer. I haven't the faintest idea who coined it, but the word "home" suggests something inferior, primitive, "home-made." People may think, "I suppose that is good enough for some, but really...how can a homeschooler expect to get along in the modern world?" Perhaps "independently educated" would be more accurate, because after all, the way I have chosen is not a "school" concept at all—at home or otherwise. For that matter, I don't necessarily learn at home. I learn everywhere. I even go back into a physical school building when I see fit.

Also, the concept of homeschooling is too new for an exact explanation. It has as many meanings and purposes as it has names and students. Some parents take their children out of school for religious reasons, not wanting their young to be exposed to attitudes different from their own. Others take their children out of school simply because they understand the American school system only too well, having been through it themselves. And some parents allow their children to leave school for the one and only reason that they can't bear to watch their children's lives being crushed. My family lies in this category.

Of course, there are plenty of books available on the problems of school and plenty more that suggest better systems. But I don't believe in one ideal system. Like so many religions, the school system is trying to provide a set, mechanical, irrefutable method of education. That's fine if we want to turn out set, mechanical, unthinking people. The very nature of any system seems to destroy the concept of "individual."

It is my opinion that those in the school system realize that any intelligent child in today's schools is going to be very unhappy. School is designed to mold things that should not be molded, like young minds, and to simply dispose of the parts that don't fit. Let me demonstrate with part of a worksheet given to me in third grade, which shows the narrow-gauge creativity that schools allow. (This is quoted exactly; my mother still has the original.)

The story below has some unfinished sentences. You can make either a fantasy or a realistic story just by using different words in those sentences. Decide which kind of story you want to make—a fantasy or a realistic story. Then finish the story by writing on each line one of the two words below that line.

Eliza woke up one morning and noticed a _____

bird   dragon

sitting outside her window.

"Wow," cried Eliza. "That's the first _____ I've

bird   dragon

seen this spring!"

Suddenly, the creature began to _____.   It

roar   sing

_____ so _____ that Eliza called to

roared   sang   sweetly   loudly

her mother. "Did you ever hear such _____?"

an awful noise   beautiful music

asked Eliza.

Just then the _____ went over to a tree.

dragon   bird

"I wonder what's in that tree," said Eliza. When the _____

dragon   bird

left, Eliza walked over to the tree.

There she saw a little _____.

nest   gold box

I chose "dragon," "dragon," "sing," "sang," "sweetly," "beautiful music," "dragon," "dragon," and "gold box." I got a D. Need I say more about what the schools think of creativity and imagination?

School people realize that while most students will obediently swallow garbage like that, free-thinkers are profoundly disturbed by it. So it must be ensured that the latter are forced, *by themselves and their peers*, to stay in school long enough to be brainwashed.

To make an analogy, all schools have a great big door with the word "OUT" written on it. But according to the schools, the only way to be allowed to use this door is to tattoo permanently a big "L" on your head. "L" for "Loser." And the schools warn: "Don't use the door! Don't drop out!"

Let me take this opportunity to discuss "dropping out" (the thing that the celebrities warn against on TV). As a "drop out" you're of course considered a loser with no future—which may or may not be the case at all. But leaving school as a legitimate homeschooler is something else again. It is a little-known way through the out door with no tattoo, and furthermore you can do it long before the legal dropout age.

Anyway, I think that this little mechanism, of manipulating students to force *themselves* to stay in school, is one of the most ingenious traps our schools have set for us. Pure genius! People are so much easier to manage when they can't (or don't dare) think. No wonder so few great leaders are produced in today's schools.

But I'm getting ahead of myself. What, in particular, would make a student want to leave? Let me tell you what caused me to become a homeschooler.

The nightmare

Although my story might seem extreme, you've probably already met someone like me. In fact you might be very much like me yourself. The first few years of school weren't as bad as the later years. If it had not been for what happened in the fourth grade, I probably would have stayed in school. I would have continued to be dissatisfied, but not downright miserable—like having a low-grade infection rather than an acute, painful one.

But even from the very beginning I did not like the way we were being taught. How pointless: sitting around all day with a bunch of other children being told about how one plastic bear plus another makes two, and being graded on foolishness like how well we could skip, run, or walk. Even in the first grade it was obvious to me how inadequate my teacher was. She knew from the first day that she would be leaving in March, and she showed little interest in us. The person who followed her was of course a substitute. The system was against all of us. I could see that the way things were set up, it would be difficult to learn.

I thought that my first grade teacher was somewhat sadistic, too. I used to have very sensitive ears, and a few seconds of the school's fire alarm bell were enough to give me a splitting headache that could last for days. Of course at that age, all I could really manage to convey was that the fire alarm was abhorrent to me. So the teacher took it upon herself to rid me of my silly notion.

One day the fire alarm was having extensive work done and it would go off at random every minute or two. So I kept my sweaty fingers plugged in my ears, and when the end of the day rolled around, my lovely teacher decided not to allow me to leave until I had endured five minutes of the noise. I swear to you, she literally pulled my hands away from my ears and fought me down, until she eventually pinned me to her desk. I staggered out of school that day with my ears ringing.

Before second grade, the school tested me to see if I qualified for the gifted program. I passed and was assigned to a class that was held at another school. I was bussed away every Wednesday and spent the entire day doing what seemed to me to be nothing in particular. This was helpful in some ways but caused problems in others. For example, my second grade teacher insisted I make up every bit of work I missed on the "lost" day. This was abuse against the countywide school policy, but she continued even after the principal and my parents told her to stop. It made a struggle of the entire year.

By this time I was getting restless with the whole school routine. I'd often finish an assignment while the teacher was talking (she'd go over it like we were morons or something) and then have to sit until the slowest child in the class had finished. Sometimes I'd draw, secretly, but eventually the teacher made it clear to me that this was not allowed, and provided me with some ditto work sheets (those faded blue jobs) and a microscopic box of crayons. The dittos weren't even interesting, mostly cartoon animals and festive icons. To add insult to injury, she would then grade me on my coloring job. I'll never forget the time that I put a little yellow glow around the picture of a candle flame, and a bit of blue at the base of the orange flame. I was reprimanded. First for coloring outside the lines with the yellow glow, second because she claimed not to be able to *see* yellow—so I therefore shouldn't use it, and third, flames are red and ice is blue, and, dammit, I was going to learn to use the proper colors. All this for work that was not even assigned to begin with.

I always had respect for my teachers, but for the wrong reasons. Teachers have the power to punish, and constantly remind their students of that power, even in off-hand ways. Kids would literally wet their pants rather than ask for permission to use the hall pass. Whenever you would ask, the teacher would always sort of look at you like you were stupid and deliberately causing trouble.

The third grade was great, though it had its imperfections like the previously displayed creativity worksheet. The calm before the storm, I suppose. I can truly say that I had an excellent teacher, Mrs. Yvonne Carter. I will always be grateful to her. She was a wonderful person, with a warm, open, southern way of talking. Most importantly, she read. Every day, for fifteen minutes before lunch, and sometimes for fifteen minutes afterwards, she would turn out several of the glaring overhead lights, open the windows, and read aloud to us...and it wasn't "Dick and Jane," either. The book that I remember the most vividly was

Moby Dick. I also recall her reading *Where the Red Fern Grows* and *A Day no Pigs Would Die.* Her audience was spellbound. She never tested or quizzed us on the books, but students would often take it upon themselves to illustrate their favorite characters or events in the story.

Fourth grade proved to be the storm. I was taken completely out of normal schooling and put into a special program, the Academically Accelerated Individualized Model (AAIM). It was supposed to give me the freedom to progress at my own speed. It was limited to students who were identified as "profoundly gifted."

The program selected its students based on unusually high IQ and a strong, individual interest in progressing academically. They also considered unusual talent in a particular area; mine was art. Although they did not stress each person's personal interest particularly, there was supposed to be more sensitivity to it than one would find in an ordinary classroom setting. I was thrilled and thought my troubles were over.

Soon, though, we found that the teacher had little idea what she was doing. Studies such as plane geometry and plate tectonics obviously were designed to impress parents and visiting dignitaries. History, in particular, consisted of in-depth trivia study ("more is less"). This held true with most of the rest of the work as well. While I had expected to be able to study independently and move at my own speed, I found instead simply an advanced curriculum with no support system. In other words, we were handed material far beyond what we should have been given at the time and told to figure it out for ourselves. My reading skills were advanced, but my math skills needed to progress in a more structured way. I liked plane geometry, but we had skipped ahead and left out multiplication, division, fractions, etc. Essentially, it was more garbage in a nicer package.

And in addition to academics gone awry, I had to suffer the incredible jealousy of my previous "gifted" (but not "*profoundly*") pals, and the general ridicule of the "normal" students. The other kids called AAIM "gifted-gifted." It was a term of derision.

Unfortunately, AAIM was housed in the elementary school I had attended up to that time. All the other students, except for one girl, were bussed from around the county. It was particularly difficult for the two of us; we even had to go home to ostracism since our tormentors were also our neighbors.

To make things even worse, at the beginning of the year the "gifted-gifted" teacher paraded the entire class all around the school, telling everyone, even the sixth graders, that they should respect us because we were special. "Special" is a dangerous word.

AAIM seemed a disaster in every aspect. Hindered more than helped, I left the program at the end of fourth grade. Incidentally, the other students had problems similar to mine. Their parents, though, would do nothing about it. My parents and I suspected that they were enjoying crowing to friends about their child being in a program for the *"profoundly* gifted" and just too, too terribly bright to be in ordinary classes. School administrators and teachers are not the only culprits. Even our fellow students and their parents use "education" for all the wrong reasons: competition, competition, competition.

The concept of leaving school and learning at home occurred to me at this point. I asked my mother about it, but she had never heard of homeschooling as a legal alternative, and dismissed the idea immediately.

When I returned to the regular fifth grade, I was labeled a defective by my former friends. They could not believe that anyone would voluntarily leave such a prestigious position and I suspect they secretly could not forgive me for qualifying for AAIM in the first place. Two people, who were formerly my best friends, spent the entire year making my life miserable. They managed some-how to turn almost every other student, including *every* "gifted" student, against me. And because I was behind in math, I was defenseless against their accusa-tions that I was *thrown* out of gifted-gifted for being stupid.

Of course, the fact that I had missed an important year of regular fourth grade math did not help. I had not needed multiplication or division at all in AAIM. As a result, I returned without the essential mathematical backbone.

That lack destroyed completely any hope of learning the subject under normal classroom conditions. It had been assumed that I was a mathematical genius. (Apparently it is taken for granted that if your IQ is high enough, you're automatically gifted across-the-board.) So I was started out in the most advanced class. By Christmas my deficiency was obvious and I was transferred into the math "pit"—accompanied by my classmates' ridicule.

All of the fifth grade was quite terrible. Our whole family limped through together. Were it not for the fact that I had some excellent teachers, I think that I would have literally died.

When I realized after several weeks that I was not going to be accepted by other kids again after being tainted by AAIM, I became very depressed and despondent. I even made a serious suicide threat, which almost got me hospital-ized. Luckily that did not happen—not because of any change of plans on my parents' or the doctor's part, but because the hospital was full.

(Thank God! Recent events have shown me that I was saved from what was probably a terrible fate, something from which I might never have escaped. Because of the nature of how I learned this—somebody else's secret—I can't really elaborate, but whatever you do, no matter how depressed you feel, *be very careful* about psychiatric hospitals and other places that claim to rehabilitate teenagers. They may things worse than you ever dreamed possible.)

We all knew that I would be going to middle school next and a change of some kind could be expected. I was concerned, though, because I knew that many of my old antagonists would go along with me to poison new opportunities and keep the torture alive.

So, we sidestepped. I wanted a clean slate and a new order. I went into a popular private preparatory school here in Orlando that I will call Prep H. That year and a half in prep school would make my elementary school look like a relaxed learning environment, filled with kind, loving people.

I first laid eyes on Prep H in the summer before sixth grade; my mom and I had driven over for a private tour. Our guide was a ditzy preppy cheerleader-type who, during the process of showing us around, greeted every other ditzy preppy cheerleader-type with gratuitous physical affection. My mom and I went home numb. It was so gushingly insincere. When asked if I wanted to attend, I responded with an emphatic *"No!"*

But, no other opportunities appeared. I reluctantly enrolled.

At Prep H I was given the opportunity to be a member of the patrol, assigned to guard the safety of the younger children waiting to be picked up by their parents. I was truly honored and intended to take my responsibility quite seriously, expecting the adult administrators to back me up the way they would have at the public elementary school I had left. But I discovered that what they said at Prep H and what they meant were two different things.

I had anticipated an easy job. I was wrong. Never have I encountered such a group of brats. They (I'm talking about third graders here) shouted obscenities, played in the traffic (which I probably should have encouraged) and threw rocks at cars. They stole and buried each other's bookbags, and sometimes they would disappear for a half hour at a time.

All this would have been fine and dandy with me, as long as it wasn't my responsibility, and as long as it wasn't considered *my fault*. But the fact remained that I was supposed to make sure that the kids stayed out of trouble. Incidentally, no adult teacher or administrator remained outside while I was there. They left very quickly, leaving me alone to watch many children.

Now, I personally have no problem with dragging an uncontrollable kid to the office every now and then, but this was becoming a daily routine: Get out of class, go to the parking lot, watch after the kids, try to talk them out of throwing rocks or playing in traffic, be flagrantly disobeyed, drag the offender to the office, turn him over to the lower-school principal.

Then I found out that I wasn't supposed to do this. It was my job to simply stand there and watch the kids, even if they *were* playing in traffic. And lo! One of the children was hurt! There were countless letters from angry parents, and I was beaten up several times by older brothers.

One day, relatively early in my tenure on the patrol, some of the much older, upper-school students came up to me on their way back into the gym from P.E. They forced me to take off my patrol belt, throw it in the dirt, and stamp on it. They did this in front of the children whose respect I needed so badly. Then they called me a few names, laughed at their terribly clever joke, and went off into the gym. My mother saw this, but at my request said nothing to the officials because I knew that if it were reported, I would get worse next time—in some other area and some other way.

All of this is the *happy* side of the sixth grade. I can't even begin to convey to you the feelings of hate that permeated the school environment. The endless snobbish hypocrisy boggled the mind.

For a while I thought it was just me they picked on, but I learned as the year passed that there were many others. (I guess there was a little respite in the knowledge that their cruelty was directed to everyone, not just me.) I think I was singled out especially because I was new. I learned that all of the new kids were similarly ostracized in one way or another. In fact, I was surprised when I found out that even those new kids I thought were getting along fine were miserable inside because they feared that the pack would turn on them at any moment. It became clear that certain people, who had been there since first grade, were the ring leaders—and their fringe group joined in on any little horrors they cared to inflict on their victims with sadness but willingness. These fringe people were terrified that if they did not join in, they would be singled out and cut from the pack. They were simply too weak to stand the pain they knew would come to them if they revolted.

I was an easy target in other ways too, besides newness. I was not athletic. My parents had never cultivated Orlando "society." I wanted to learn. I did homework. I wanted to ask questions. Being part of the students' hierarchy was of no interest to me; I only wanted to be left alone and allowed to work.

Their cruelty left me in a state of awe. I remember one girl who walked up to me, sweetly said "hello," and then proceeded to empty an entire can of cinnamon-flavored Binaca (an acidic breath freshener that comes in tiny aerosol cans) into my unsuspecting eyes. Several hours later, when my vision had finally returned to normal, she apologized.

Another time, a group of seventh graders came into the art room, where a friend of mine was carrying a sculptural piece of art, ingeniously constructed out of cardboard and poster paper, across to the table where he intended to work. The piece had taken him several months to build and was one of the best in the school.

After he had set it down, one of the seventh graders took his math textbook and smashed my friend's art completely flat. Then they chastised him for his clumsiness at allowing his art to be destroyed, and locked him out of the building. He never came back to art again.

I did make one important friend in sixth grade. The first student I noticed, and the only person who was consistently tolerant toward me, was Justin Page (one of the few people in this essay who appears in glorious Real-Name). I was eager to be friends with Justin; he seemed to be almost exactly like me, and indeed throughout the year we seemed to be leading duplicate lives. Unfortunately, Justin was a member of a clique which, for some reason, detested me. But, every morning before school, while we waited in a massive courtyard, we talked together like the best of friends.

My family hoped that sixth grade would end my "initiation" and that the next year, when I went into the middle school on the upper-school campus, I might be considered part of the group and allowed to assume a lower profile on the hit list. Dreamers.

I can't say that seventh grade was completely worthless. There was lots to do. We sometimes used to play dodge ball in the afternoon. I also remember finding a dead cat in the lake, dismembered and, apparently, disposed of courtesy of the senior science class as a result of their dissecting activities.

I had enjoyed my sixth grade art teacher very much. She did as much as she could to encourage me, taking my art work seriously. I was devastated to learn that there would be no art in the seventh and eighth grades. I asked her if I could take art anyway—maybe she'd be willing to work a little with me and allow me to do independent study. She thought this was a great idea.

My parents talked to the school administrators about this opportunity. At first they balked because it had never been done, but we pointed out that they allowed math high-achievers to move ahead. There was really no difference, or difficulty. If the teacher approved—after all she was the one who would have the extra work to do—then it should be all right. Prep H lured prospective students and their parents by claiming to offer tailor-made classes, and we called them on this. They decided in my favor and I was allowed to take art.

Anyway, approaching seventh grade was a big step for all the sixth graders. Suddenly we were expected to range all over a large campus—changing classes, carrying heavy bookbags, using lockers, and so forth. It was scary. We were all small and absolutely at the mercy of the upperclassmen.

Going to my locker was always a time of trial and danger. There were rarely teachers or other adults to monitor behavior, so the upperclassmen took advantage of this opportunity to haze us younger students. Sometimes they would hold small seventh graders over the rail and threaten to drop them down below. While I was there, they did drop one boy over and broke his arm. It got so that I carried everything all day long in a huge, heavy bookbag so that I could avoid the terror of the locker halls.

Also, we were required to wear ties. The change time between classes became a gantlet we had to run to try to get through without being strangled by an older student who might take offense at the kind of tie we wore. My ties were ruined again and again because no matter what I had on, it never pleased those who had decided it was their right to decide.

Just to give you an idea of how progressive this prep school was, and how considerate they were of their students' development, several months into school the principal of the upper school had the brilliant idea of starting the "senior counselors" program. It worked like this: The seventh grade was divided into several groups of about twelve each. There were two senior counselors, one male and one female, assigned to each group. They were to be role models for us and help us adapt.

I remember the "counselors" asked us what we wanted to be when we grew up. When my turn came, rather than letting me speak, they said, "Oh, you want to be a sumo wrestler, just like in the Timex ads," and moved on to the next person. Naturally everyone thought that was high humor. Yup, yup, yup, that's me: Mr. Sumo, Sumo-san.

Earlier I mentioned the special art class I was allowed to take. In itself it helped me a great deal. But it also became an almost unbearable difficulty: Unfortunately, the only way to schedule it was to remove me from P.E. This caused hard feelings among other students and they satisfied themselves by calling me a wimp, and, predictably, "gay." Too much of a weenie to take P.E. so I took AAARRRTTT instead. I was devastated to learn that the ringleader in this particular case turned out to be my supposed best friend.

At this point my parents moved to take me out of school. But the administrator called the offending students in, and we "resolved" the situation to the point where I was persuaded to stay on.

My geography teacher proved to be the pivotal point. She was, perhaps, the largest contributor to my choosing homeschooling. I feel safe saying that she was the worst teacher I ever had.

At the beginning of the year I had felt encouraged by her. This was her first year of teaching, although she was at least forty years old. She had been almost everywhere in the world, including Africa and Haiti.

Now, please remember that we were seventh graders, just out of a very protected period of our lives, suddenly exposed to a whole new way of functioning in school. I suspect this woman was all puffed up with her dream of being a *teacher*. Perhaps she had been given the impression that she was going to be working with a bunch of well-prepared, committed students with a background in academic excellence. What a joke! This was a school where other students made fun of you if you did your homework. And if you asked a question in class: "Ohhhhh, Patrick, you're SOOOOO stupid!"

The work she assigned to us was far beyond anything we had ever faced before, and on top of it, the woman seemed to be a chronic liar. I was not the only student who had problems with this teacher. Virtually every other seventh grader detested her unfairness and capriciousness. I soon learned that if you ever missed any of her classes, as I did because of a bad case of bronchitis, you were going to fail. It was simply impossible to catch up. To make matters worse, somehow I lost my geography folder which contained the completed assignments for the first nine weeks, and most of the second. Capital offense for sure.

After much tearing of hair and posturing, the teacher agreed to quiz me in lieu of having me turn in my folder. I did well on the quiz, only to find out that she *still* wanted the folder; the quiz only counted for part of it. Again and again she would agree that if I completed this or that extra assignment, she would consider me caught up—and each time, she would change her mind. This always seemed to happen the day after she had talked to my mother on the phone, reassuring her that all was well and that I was, indeed, caught up. Then, the next thing I knew, I still "owed" her something I had never heard about. I was so confused by then I didn't know what was right and what was wrong.

Finally my parents arranged a meeting with the dean and the guidance counselor, who both gave us the impression that they were on our side. We learned from them that there were many complaints about this teacher and that not even the other teachers could stand her.

The very next day I was called into the guidance counselor's office alone. She took me into the dean's office, where he was waiting. There they told me quite a different story than they had told my parents. Not only was I a "disgrace to the school," I was a lousy student, and responsible for *all* the problems they had been having with the geography teacher. They accused me of disrupting her class and they accused my parents, whom they would not let me contact, of calling the other parents, and, get this, "turning them against the school." For the record, it was the other way around. The other parents had told *my* parents about the problems that many of their children were having.

I zombie-walked through the rest of the day, and when I got home, I told my parents the whole story. They were furious and offered to take me out of school right then. But, for some reason, I decided not to quit just yet. I kept hoping that somehow I could get through it.

Several days later, one of the teachers said something that was the last straw. I stood up, gathered my books, told her to go to hell, and walked out of her class. I went straight to the office and, completely unannounced, walked in, picked up the phone, called my parents and declared my freedom from Prep H.

(At the end of the year, we heard that the geography teacher had continued to cause trouble. Many students were disciplined by their parents for being unable to do the work in that class; many were grounded for weeks on end; many were scheduled to repeat the class the next year. But in the end, she was not invited to return, and all those who "failed" were allowed to go forward with no problem. I don't know whether the bad grades were taken off their records or not; it was satisfaction enough to know that I had avoided the continuing pain the others had to suffer.)

I went into the public middle school I had sought to avoid when I left fifth grade; it was all we could see to do. By then I was a wreck. I had virtually no self-esteem, only one friend—Justin—and my health was suffering.

Speaking of health, this is probably a good time to mention that subject. Before I went into school, I was rarely sick. But, beginning with the first grade, I was sick often. My tonsils were removed after the fourth grade. I had headaches, nausea, and nose bleeds. My eyes bothered me. I suffered anxiety and depression.

In the third grade I was put into glasses and told to expect to wear them forever. Because of all my desk work, my eyes would supposedly get progressively worse. But the glasses did not improve my condition. The doctor said I'd get used to them. He changed the prescription somewhere along the line. But I never did get used to them and stopped wearing them entirely.

Eventually I went to another doctor. He said I did not need glasses at all and couldn't understand why I was put in them ($$$$??). He said that my problems were psychosomatic and that I would get better results from a psychologist than an ophthalmologist. Yes!

Anyway, being back in the public school was a challenge. I was particularly interested in doing something about my math weakness and maybe meeting new friends. But the sharks were circling in the form of all those good buddies from elementary school, still as cruel as ever.

As for math, that stint in AAIM had left a big hole. The tests I had taken, including the SAT (as part of the Duke Talent Search program) plainly showed that I understood the concepts but was weak in application. However, I was so debilitated and depressed that I could not catch up. This worried me because I knew that I needed that information.

Before we go any further, I would like to say that not all the school people I have met were negative. There were several along the way who took genuine interest in me and wanted to do everything they could to help. It is a shame, though, that there is such a lack of knowledge among them about homeschooling. When teachers and administrators know of a student who is having extreme difficulty, and when they can see that the student's parents could likely facilitate homeschooling, they should suggest it. They should even offer to be of help. (Of course, it's possible that their well-meaning "guidance" could end up being stifling, and might short-circuit the very freedom that homeschooling offers.)

Glimpse of a new land

Toward the end of the 1988-1989 school year, I met someone who not only lived near me, but shared many interests. He introduced me to the Amiga computer, and he had been homeschooled at one time. Not only did he know that it was possible to school legally at home, he was anxious to return to it himself. We even toyed with the idea of homeschooling together, but my family and I shied away from that because of his family's overpowering religious fanaticism.

But the seed was planted. And we have noticed again and again that when we begin asking for something, it appears. Sometimes we have to give it time, and sometimes we find that we really want something else instead. An answer, though, invariably comes through.

My parents were out to dinner with friends of theirs, Bryan and Susan Davis. When the Davises found that we were beginning to explore the idea of homeschool, they revealed that they were homeschooling their five children. They gave us a book to read and some solid information. Mother quickly found Nancy Wallace's book *Better Than School* and followed it with the Colfaxes' *Homeschooling for Excellence*. She made many phone calls and talked to many people. Eventually she had enough confidence to discuss the idea seriously with my father. All three of us decided that I would be homeschooled for the eighth grade.

My father, a conservative at heart, had been schooled in the good-old-fashioned way: a proper upper-class education at a private academy, then prep school, etc. Needless to say, he was less than thrilled with my decision. But he had seen how much I had suffered and knew that something had to be done. So he agreed.

We discovered that there are many ways to approach homeschooling. Some people get together in groups and share projects loosely. Others set up a daily schedule and have detailed lesson plans—in effect, mimicking institutional learning. One may also simply devise a loose curriculum and follow it leisurely, making adjustments as they deem necessary. That last plan sounded good to us.

In Florida there are different specific requirements depending upon which county is calling the shots. In Orange County we would be required to write a letter to the school superintendent simply telling him that we were going to homeschool. At the end of the year we would submit a portfolio with examples of my work, the names of the texts we used, and any information regarding tests I'd been given. We could also make any comments we cared to with regard to my progress and future plans. (In these portfolios, we have always chosen to explain our choices in depth. So far, these reports have been well received and no remediation has been suggested. They cannot make us remediate; they may only suggest it.)

During each year, the school administrators would let us know about any tests available and we would be able to use them if we cared to. (My first homeschooling year I did take several tests, but since then I have not bothered. They would only show what we already know: I'll ace the verbal and show weakness in the math application.)

Many families who elect to homeschool do so only through the eighth grade, and then place their children in the regular system beginning with the ninth grade. This is so that they can get a high school diploma, garner a Grade Point Average (GPA) and, you might say, play the game for college entry. In Orange County, one may not enter school after homeschooling past the eighth grade, unless one agrees to begin at the ninth grade. In other words, one may not start as a tenth or eleventh grader. This is because the school system must guarantee that graduating students have completed the prescribed curriculum and attended a certain number of minimum days. They feel that they cannot guarantee the quality of what has been taught at home.*

With this in mind, I knew that I could homeschool with impunity for one year. I knew that the bulk of the eighth grade curriculum would be quite easy to complete at home (or with a tutor); from that angle we had no fears. I could experiment and if we did not like homeschooling I could then return to school.

But could we keep this up through high school—when there would be no going back? How hard would it be to learn biology, chemistry, physics, higher math...*that* uncertainty was scary.

And what if I really did need the constant contact of lots of peers (even if that contact was negative) as suggested by so many people? Schooling is stifling enough, but would my intellectual development suffer even more without the few benefits that the system offers? What about exposure to things like debate teams, drama classes, physical education, parties, homecoming proms? Can there be life without participation in established traditions?

If I elected to return to the fold after the eighth grade I would lose nothing. On the other hand, if I stayed out after that, I would enter a kind of no-man's

---

* I understand, by the way, that other counties in Florida are much more cooperative with homeschool families. They do what they can to allow students as much access to their schools as possible and appear to want to keep a friendly relationship.

land of educational purgatory. I'd be a person with no credentials, no number. A kind of blank, not exactly a dropout, but without certification. But what choice did I really have? It was either that or my sanity. After all, at that point I was either already a "blank" or well on my way to becoming one.

At the time, though, none of this really held my attention. The truth of the matter was that I was ready to do *anything*. And when I got out, I had no intention of going back.

Ascent: Reality

The first year—"eighth grade"—1989-90

Thank God no one forced me to stay in school! When people lose sight of their hopes and can see no way out of a hellish existence, they lose their will to live. And when that happens, nothing can stop them from playing out their final struggle, be it suicide, crime, or whatever. And, of course, drugs are always a way out, perhaps permanently.

I made an agreement with my mother that she would need time to do her own things occasionally. Sure, Mom. You let me sleep and you can do whatever you want. Yes, I had my plans, but in the beginning all I wanted to do was to sleep. I also needed a good solid year of looking out the window, to make up for all the times in school when that wasn't allowed.

Actually, this worked out pretty well for both of us. When she wanted to, Mom had lunch with friends, shopped alone, or did whatever she liked without me. Mutual stifling was kept to a minimum, although we certainly had our moments. But, for the confusing daze that the first year was, I think that our relationship didn't suffer.

That first year, my parents also insisted that I study some of the traditional subjects with a cooperative spirit. No grousing. No griping. Not a dirty look from me or back to school it was. Mom would teach me English, history, and "life skills" (how to get around in this world on my own).

We would also select video documentaries which would augment the other studies and which were fun for us both. We saw some great ones, too. Probably my favorite of the many we saw was *Connections*, James Burke's excellent BBC series which deals with the "spark" of progress, starting with the simple invention of a primitive plow, and then following the progression through to our own modern times.

As the year went on, we began to realize that the books I read and the movies I watched were major contributors to my education. So we listed them, too, in our year-end report.

Tutors came to the rescue in areas where my Mother did not feel competent, or simply did not have time. For example, I studied algebra (using the Saxon method, which I detested) and computer literacy with a gifted teacher who was himself an engineering student at the time.

Another important area for me was *basic* math skills. As I've said before, the various standardized tests showed a definite weakness. The school system had ignored this when my mother brought it to their attention because my overall skills were very high. They said it "would straighten itself out eventually."

But I realized that I had to do something about it. We were lucky enough to find George Rule. He is retired now, but his specialty when he taught professionally was working with students like me who needed math remediation. He told us that he had had many students over the years, quite a few of whom had been in a predicament similar to mine; they were not at all "slow," but had received inept math instruction and thus been crippled. I think that once such a hole in the learning progression materializes, it is like a black hole. It attracts and devours everything else one tries to learn in that area. When I tried to learn math, the new material kept falling into the abyss and disappearing.

Mr. Rule worked with me until he was satisfied that I had learned and understood all that he could teach me. He refused to take any money for his work. We offered, but now that he was retired, he thought it would be wrong to ask for payment. Yet, he felt that since he had been given a gift for teaching he should continue to use it. He has my thanks and respect. You don't meet many people like him.

I studied music composition and theory privately—but that would have happened even if I had stayed in school. I found immediately that I liked music and wanted to spend more time on it. If we had been more able financially, I would have been glad to spend a good hour each day in music class. The most we could afford, though, was one two-hour session a week.

Music seems so bizarre when compared to arts like painting or drawing. Composing music is not the literal creation of art, per se. Rather, it is the exact description of art—frozen movement. It's like writing detailed instructions for a painter, using a very exact code.

Luckily my teacher, Jamie Sterret, is very flexible, and we attacked the subject from an unusual angle. The first few months, actually, he tried to use his standard teaching method, and I tried to follow it, although I found our working style to be rather cramped. Soon, though, as the atmosphere became more relaxed, the lesson turned into more of a discussion. This is a very interesting approach to teaching and learning in general. It not only puts the teacher and student at more of an equal status, but it also provides a sort of circular style of learning where the teacher is simply there to support the pupil, and that pupil, rather than having the information crammed down his or her throat, is free to discover jewels from the teacher and make the resulting connections on his or her own.

Over the months, I developed quite a friendship with Jamie and it has occurred to me that this, too, would not likely have happened in a regular school class. He and I have so much more than music in common. We have a very similar philosophy of life, and enjoy talking together about things other than music. Being a friend with my teacher makes learning from him so much easier.

Trips were also a significant part of my first year of homeschooling. Two of them were just for fun and education—basic exploration. The other was our trip to Houston, Texas, for my oldest brother's wedding. While in Houston, we took advantage of the chance to see some of the art galleries and museums. But the wedding itself was interesting too, one of those bits of our culture that I had never really been in on before. I had previously attended a wedding or two, but I have a quite different view of the whole affair now. There is so much preparation and ritualistic action beforehand. No wonder that so many couples complain that their relationships change after the wedding. With such an elaborate send-off, what can you do to live up to it?

The first "education" trip was in October. We hopped in our car and headed up the East Coast, planning to be gone for about two weeks. Quite a bit of this trip was spent at some of the famous battlegrounds. Personally, I have never been intrigued by such things, and it looked like more of the same to me. Perhaps if there had been piles of charred bones here and there I would have perked up, but it seemed mostly like just another nature hike to me, sometimes not even that.

The trip did have its moments. The museums were top notch, and I enjoyed visiting the homes of George Washington and Robert E. Lee. We also saw many caves, including Luray Caverns. Caves have always held a special fascination for me and I never grow tired of visiting them.

The next big trip was in March. We flew to Arizona, one of my favorite places, and rented a car. We drove up from Phoenix to the Grand Canyon (seeing everything on the way), and then up into Utah. During the trip we visited, among other places, Zion and Arches National Parks, Flagstaff, the Apache reservation, and, to my special delight, Sedona, which is a small haven for art.

Travel is always exciting. It broadens one's self-confidence, in that one realizes that one can leave home and still exist. Something about a change of scenery and climate seems intrinsic to the essential creative process, from many standpoints. Being away from home gives me time to think, and being in a new locale reminds me that there is so much more in my life than the petty everyday worries. It's hard to put my finger on it, but sometimes just hopping in the car and going to the next neighborhood, or across the country, can provide a catharsis and put me in touch with the fact that I can actively control my own destiny.

I continued to work independently on my art right along with the more structured educational pursuits, and grew more and more intrigued by video games, which continue to play a very big part in my life. The modern video game is, in my experience, the only art form that makes use of architecture, graphic design, music, animation, and storyline, yet remains *interactive* and is therefore an exercise of both the player's coordination and mental ability. In other words, it incorporates many art forms (especially now that CD-Rom is a reality) and it won't turn your brain into jelly the way that television will.

Just before we began homeschooling, we had purchased an Amiga 2000 computer, which we chose because it is one of the only computers available with the necessary hardware and software that would allow me to create high-end graphics and to animate them. Yet, later that year I moved away from animation. The computer's memory limitations and the lack of a hard drive prevented me from creating animations longer than a few hundred frames.

But as my specific interest in animation faded, my fascination with video games grew. Because I knew almost nothing about the technical side of video games, which were little eight-bit jobs at that time, my imagination was not limited by technical concerns. I was able to see far ahead into the future of what the home video market would become: boxed realities to be enjoyed at leisure; interactive fugues of art, music, and story. Indeed, I glimpsed in home video games, primitive as they were at the time, a high potential to express my art.

So I moved quickly toward finding software that would allow me to set up little simulation games. I was disappointed regularly. It's a pity. Such a construction set would really not be that tough to create; I've dabbled enough in programming to know that. But everything I found in the way of software had problems that rendered it useless. (I've found this to be true with a lot of software: Capabilities are grossly exaggerated. What I end up getting is nowhere near what I've been led to expect.) Eventually I gave up that quest in disgust, wanting a way to test out some of my plans, but not ready to learn full programming at the time.

But my interest in game design did not die out. That first year, I assembled a small portfolio of my computer graphics and sent it with a cover letter to one of the American-based Nintendo stragglers. After a few weeks I phoned the person at that company I assumed was their director. His description of my work was, "Cool, but not killer." And I can't argue. I was, after all, just thirteen.

After a few encouraging words he bade me farewell, and that was the end of my relationship with that company.

This did not discourage me, though. I continued to work on my art and a few months later saw an ad in the back of a recent issue of *Amiga World* magazine. A quickly growing subsidiary of one of the video game giants was seeking programmers and game designers.

I used a similar format for my second portfolio that year: a red binder with page covers on the inside and a (way too lengthy) cover letter. The inside of the binder was filled with a sort of story that I had edited together via photocopier with a large number of my drawings and quite a bit of text too. The whole thing seemed pretty tolerable at the time; I can't even stand to look at it now. Let's just say that my art and writing skills have come a long way since then.

With high hopes I Federal-Expressed my little abomination to the unsuspecting company. Of course they probably get so much stuff from thirteen-year-old would-be game designers that my contribution could have gone unnoticed. However, I eventually did pin them down and learned that they had found my first attempt "interesting," which was very diplomatic of them because it *did* suck. But I got some good feedback and set about improving my art. If at first you don't succeed...

That first year we did struggle with certain aspects of homeschooling. For a while, Mom had a problem with my attitude regarding English. The English book was quite dated, and I would interrupt her often during our lesson to argue some obscure point in a sentence being diagrammed, which would often send us off on wild tangents. Eventually she would get fed up and insist that I forget whatever intrigued me or enraged me about the content of the sentences, and just diagram them. After all, the subject matter was hardly of concern to the essential grammatical quality of the sentence.

It all worked out, though, to illustrate an important education theme. I got angry once and told her that her approach was one of the things I hated most about traditional schooling: the shut-up-and-do-the-work attitude—"This is an English class. It is *not* philosophy or social science!" Of course I understand that this is a necessity in a normal classroom situation; the teacher cannot take time to explore how everyone feels about the content of every sentence they are parsing. But we were not in that sort of classroom.

After a bit of debate, we finally decided that if a piece of obscure information or some such aroused my curiosity, then rather than interrupt the lesson, we would simply write down the sentence and discuss it at dinner. This way we could include my father too. So the dictionary and often several volumes of the encyclopedia joined us at many meals. It turned out to be a lot of fun.

Another thing that bugged my mother was that I'd sometimes sit around and look off into space for what seemed hours on end. She would accuse me of wasting time.

But I was not wasting time. No. There is no such thing as wasting time. Whether in art or math or philosophy, important thoughts do not pop, fully formed, into one's mind. One must develop them bit by bit. I'm sure all the great thinkers have appeared to others to be wasting time.

That first year my life had transformed completely and I was reeling, trying to put it all in order. The first year out of the oppression of school is a shock to one's system. I suppose I can understand why it was alarming to Mom that I was spending so much time woolgathering and sleeping. But when you think about it, I had never before had such a block of time to call my own. There had been sinister "responsibilities" hanging over my head—always homework to be done, etc.

I was truly relishing my new-found opportunity to use my own mind one hundred percent of the time. I was not quite used to the idea of not doing something measurably valuable at all times, and I did suffer a bit of guilt. But I would say to any prospective homeschooler: Don't let such pressures bother you. Woolgather with impunity. (Grace describes this phenomenon accurately in *The Teenage Liberation Handbook*. Reading what she said made my mother and me feel considerably better.)

By that summer, my "dreamy" phase was almost over. Natural talents and resources had come back to me, much in the way energy returns to a person after a long, restful sleep. I was on fire with new ideas, proof that my woolgathering had not been wasted time. I had simply been learning how to use my freedom—sort of like hostages must have to do when they are released.

That was also the summer that my mom finally found the time to sit down and really read through all of the back issues of *Growing Without Schooling* (*GWS*) that she had acquired, as well as through the stacks of books and articles on the subject of homeschooling. (Our thanks to Susannah Sheffer, the editor of *GWS*, for helping us find articles relating to older homeschoolers.) Apparently my circumstances were somewhat unusual: Many homeschoolers have been homeschooled since an early age, untainted by the ill effects of the school system. Consequently, there is a lot of information for homeschooling younger children, and not so much about starting later.

It was a very relaxed summer, perfect for contemplation of the upcoming year. We had to make quite a decision, having completed eighth grade and facing the ninth. If I stayed out of school now, I would never be allowed to come back in, and it seemed I could very well end up locked out completely when it came to finding a job, college, etc.

Then again, I wasn't going to go back into what I had just escaped. I did not want to conform again to that diminished self. This is where *GWS* was most helpful. Several homeschoolers described what happened to them when they approached higher education. It was consoling to know that they were finding their way into the most prestigious colleges in the U.S...in fact, probably the most prestigious colleges in the world. And it was especially nice to know that universities were contacting Holt Associates (the publishers of *Growing Without Schooling*) asking how they could attract qualified homeschoolers. The numerous success stories were encouraging.

By the end of the summer we had come to our conclusion. Success or failure, I would be allowed to continue to homeschool. We all agreed that it would be better to take this chance rather than to plunge me back into almost assured doom.

The second year—"ninth grade"—1990-91

At this point, my parents had the courage to hand me the reins of my own education. We shared the understanding that if what I was doing with my time didn't satisfy them, then we could fall back to using a tutor or at least a daily schedule. So with this security I was allowed to control my own life even more fully than in my first year of homeschooling.

I think the decision was wise. In addition to making my life a lot easier, it freed me to use giant blocks of my time for immersion in whatever subject seemed appropriate. It is much easier to lever knowledge or skill acquisition around when there are months available rather than hours. Having six or seven little periods every day, each focusing on a completely different subject, and often seeming at the time abstract and useless to the student, is like trying to roll around a boulder with hundreds of little toothpicks—some of which are only theoretical anyway. At the other extreme, where there is a *whole year* available for learning a *single* chosen subject, exceptional progress can be made. At least that has been true for me and for others who have commented on their self-education.

So school was out of the way permanently and, furthermore, I was in control of my own education. My parents had gone from "teachers" to "facilitators." Now the fun part: Reach my goals!

My major goal was (and is) to get a job in video game design, specifically at the second of the two companies to which I had already sent my work samples.

I have never seen game design merely as a "trade," something about which I would read books and study specific information, and "learn." Rather, I think of it as an art form. Even the first year I could see that to be truly proficient in any field of design, I would need to incorporate into my thinking as much creative, useful knowledge as possible from many fields. There is no one tried-and-true method of being innovative.

The need to be as well-rounded as possible became apparent immediately when I took a closer look at some of the background graphics in a favorite video game of mine. One of the most important elements in a game is location. Unless the gameplay itself is truly captivating, and sometimes not even then, a game will just fall flat without a supporting environment for the various characters to inhabit. One might argue that it really wouldn't matter what the backgrounds look like as long as they get the point across (rock, ladder, stairway, water, door). But quite the opposite is true, and the broader the knowledge of the designer, the more challenging and exciting the game can become.

My computer had played an important part in my artwork, but the main problem with trying to develop artistically with a computer as the medium is that there is no program which can really sketch. I have found that to be able to approach professional-level computer graphics, one must already be able to draw. The machine is no substitute for that.

So I decided to take a break from the Amiga and go on a sort of art quest, looking for books of artwork that would inspire me. As a result, I developed a nice collection of relatively obscure volumes. I have never plagiarized, and I never will knowingly, but there is something inspiring about looking at good artwork. Observation refines one's style, though not necessarily one's technique.

The biggest artistic mistake that I had made during my first year of homeschooling concerned the exhaustive preparation of full, finished portfolios, which I then submitted to companies I hoped would employ me—at age thirteen! These portfolios were premature and took a great deal of time to produce. I should have been using that time to develop basic artistic skills. But that is what this kind of schooling is about for me: I make my own mistakes and I learn my own lessons.

As the second year progressed, though, my art abilities developed more and more. I also found time to expand my interest in architecture, something that has helped greatly with computer graphics.

So finally I again took a large number of my sketches and photocopy-edited them into a sort of booklet, which, with a cover letter, became my new portfolio to send to the game company. A good response came back. They said that they had no opening at that time but would like to consider me again after the first of the year.

As far as my formal, academic education went in my second year: I pretty much dropped everything, including math. Looking back now, at the start of my fourth year of homeschooling, I sort of regret this, but, then again, I doubt I would be able to draw as well as I can now, had I spread myself thin trying to do too much. Anyway, now that the art is under control, I intend to put all of my time into learning higher math. It might be better this way, since a real need for that subject has developed out of my life.

That second year I did stay with music composition. I was not making the progress that I would have liked, but I was acquiring a good familiarity with the subject. Perhaps the way I was studying was causing me to jump ahead of myself. (With Jamie, I continued to ask lots of questions and range far afield of the more normal learning progression.) I was never really satisfied to compose simple little pieces when my head was filled with more complex ideas. The baby steps were frustrating.

I was not taking piano usage at the time; I was simply working with the piano as a tool for composition. As a result, it was difficult to perform my own creations! If I ever have the opportunity, I would like to become a proficient player, as I have discovered that the most dramatic improvements in my compositional skills happen when I can sit down and play work that I admire. Something like counterpoint really has to be played to be appreciated, although its beauty lies in the cerebral activity of spacing the notes in correct relation to one another.

That was also my Year of the Book. I spent hours each day reading (and still do). Since then I have plowed through shelves of books. I started out with fantasy. I liked Piers Anthony's work but grew tired of it because Piers himself seems to lose interest in the concepts he starts with. His novels tend to descend into silliness.

From Piers Anthony, I moved briefly into Stephen King territory, and stayed there long enough to complete *It*, *The Eyes of the Dragon*, and *The Stand*. Plenty long enough. Among other things I really like King's characterization.

From there I went on to read Mervyn Peake's *Gormenghast* trilogy, an epic bit of Gothic writing, now a classic. (I highly recommend the first two volumes; ignore the third.) I continued with short stories by Franz Kafka and H.P. Lovecraft, as well as the *Dune* saga by Frank Herbert.

Of course the years' reading material has been peppered with the usual assortment of bizarre books. I have books whose topics range from musical anecdotes to *feng shui* to the study of unmentionable language. I have art books, math books, physics books, books on war strategy and philosophy. I sometimes joke that in lieu of a resume, I should photograph my bookshelves.

The first year I had been pretty much a hermit...by choice. The second year offered me much more in the way of a social life. I met several people through Justin Page, the one person with whom I kept in touch after my escape from school.

However, one of the most nagging problems (understatement) was the condition of my health. I was almost never sick, but my body was definitely in need of work. During the years of school I had put on quite a bit of weight. I spent so much time sitting around that I was not exactly a wellspring of strength and energy and I was very much aware of this.

Probably the main reason for my phlegmatic condition is that I never got into sports, for many reasons. First and foremost: Most of the prominent sports (football and baseball, etc.) are competitive. Naturally, a team captain is not going to allow an inferior or inexperienced player onto the team. For this reason, I used to never be chosen unless it had been mandatory that everyone be chosen (a great ego-builder). Another problem was that the coaches assumed that when we entered the first grade we already had a complete knowledge of how to play these games. This just wasn't true. All in all, these activities seemed pointless.

I did attempt to get into games with some of the neighborhood children, but the other players did not want to take time to teach someone like me who did not have natural talent.

As a result of all this, I detest being forced to play sports. But I must keep in shape somehow. For a while, I considered aerobics, but had been turned off by the whole atmosphere (middle-aged women sweating away; no one my age to be seen). My mother taught yoga several years ago, but spending a few hours each day doing yoga in the living room with my mother wasn't exactly my idea of fun.

Eventually I asked my doctor if he knew of a good personal fitness trainer. Working out with free weights and the Nautilus equipment had appeal, but the danger is that until one is eighteen or so, the ends of the bones are still soft and can be bent out of shape. As a result, while one may have a perfect *looking* body, if the early training is wrong serious problems may appear later. What I was looking for was a good trainer who would show me the different exercises, explain their benefits, and work right with me to be sure I did them correctly.

Through our doctor we found a very good trainer, Dennis Delos-Reyes. I was a bit unsteady at first. I was overweight and I don't think that anyone really thought that I would stick with my exercise for any length of time. But, as I got deeper into it, I found that I really enjoyed that particular form of personal fitness because it is exactly that: *personal*. It is not something done as a group or a team, and the only person that one has to compete against is oneself.

Over the past year and a half of training, I have reduced the weight that I had been carrying around with me. As far as musculature goes, I am still relatively weak, but much better off than when I started.

Now that I am somewhat in shape I intend to go into a much more rigorous program. Once again, I don't know how much progress I will make with the weights, because I am not yet eighteen. Therefore, I plan to switch to tae kwon do for a while. We've found a teacher who is well-recommended. I'm not sure how deeply he is able to get into the real philosophy of the method, but should I find myself on fire to learn the martial arts more fully, I understand that there are plenty of fine instructors in California (where the companies are located that might hire me as a game designer someday).

Acting, too, came into my life that second year. A friend of mine had also chosen to homeschool, but for different reasons. He was hoping to get a lead part in one of Nickelodeon's teen comedies (which he did, and still has the part, I think). Essentially, he was doing what I had been doing: freeing himself in every way he could so that he could concentrate completely on his career. (Incidentally, he chose a correspondence course to satisfy his need for schooling. As a young actor, it is very difficult to juggle school with casting calls. Then, if you actually get an ongoing part, you find your hands are pretty full. Generally the studio provides schooling for cast members.)

He had been taking acting classes at a local acting school and eventually convinced me to come to some classes with him. The instructor, always eager to find new talent (*paying* talent, of course) said that I could participate in a few classes before signing up as a customer.

The class was a lot of fun. The other students were all very professional. They really loved acting and were serious about their careers. They didn't spend much time messing around, and they all had agents and head shots (professional glamour photos).

The third year—"tenth grade"—1991-92

My art was developing well, but I began to feel the need to get into a formal class. I was hoping to have some real, ongoing instruction while I worked. I also thought that it would be much more inspirational having other artists working around me. Feedback is excellent nutrition for the imagination. Justin and I had collaborated on several projects, and I had really enjoyed the team effort. In short, I definitely could see the advantages of working with another creative person, or a team of them.

My first thought was that I might be able to get into a community college, not necessarily with the idea of earning credits, but rather with the goal of consuming whatever knowledge was being offered. I met first with the head of the art department at the college to show her my work and see if she thought I would fit in and if my work was enough advanced to benefit. She said that I would be welcome in her class if the administration would allow the entry of a student under sixteen. I found it particularly satisfying that she thought from my work that I had taken life drawing classes. I had only recently started studying books on the subject and was pleased that it was noticeable that I was getting into shape.

So, we started confidently up the chain of command at the college seeking approval of my entry into art class. We thought there should be little trouble, since the teacher approved. But the whole process turned out to be very ugly, and the results did little for my respect for the "educators" at that school. Their answer to our request was an emphatic and resounding NO!

First, we were told that it was illegal for me to attend classes at a community college if I was under sixteen. But we did not give up. We investigated the truth of this statement through the executive director of the legislature's committee on post-secondary education. It was a lie. We found out that each county made its own rules—which meant that each county could adjust those rules without breaking any laws.

We went through several other exercises, including asking the Superintendent for Instruction for Orange County Public Schools to call the president of the college and try to work things out, but it was all useless. Calcified thinking stopped our progress.

Now, correct me if I'm wrong, but isn't the entire point of having schools so that people may be *educated*? When did this change? Why can't an intelligent, dedicated, and, most important, *interested* student be accepted? I offered to take the class without receiving credit. I was even willing to pay extra if necessary. But the damned bureaucracy, which doesn't even appreciate the importance of art, stood in my way.

In the meantime, my friend Justin suggested that I try to get into his public high school (he was no longer at Prep H). According to him, this school had an excellent art program, and he even recommended a specific teacher, Ms. Ramona Pelley.

Ms. Pelley was kind enough to come to my home to meet me and see my work (in the *summer*, no less). She said that she'd be glad to have me in her class, in whatever status I could manage. Again we tried a "front door" approach, with no luck. The administrators told us that there was no place in the budget for homeschoolers, and, of course, it would be impossible to *enroll* in any way at all. There was just no mechanism in place for students to take a single class. (Actually, I intended to stay all day and take *all* the classes Ms. Pelley taught.) If a student is not enrolled as a full-time, grades nine-through-twelve participant, he has no place; there is no room for deviation.

But genius struck. I remembered that in grade school there had sometimes been people in the classrooms who were not teachers but helped the teachers. These were ordinary people, either adults or sometimes high school students, who had free time or who wanted to work with children as a part of a high school project. The program through which they worked was called Orange County ADDitions volunteers. Maybe I could get in that way if an age limit didn't keep me out.

Success! That was it! There was no age limit. Of course, when we called for information we didn't tell them that I intended to be a clandestine student, bootlegging learning through the back door. We held our breath for months, but no one challenged me at the school and I deliberately kept a very low profile.

My plan was to go to school every day but Wednesday. (Wednesday was a short day at school, and the teacher always showed a video tape throughout the day. Same tape all day to every class—I obviously didn't need that.) I would participate in every class the teacher taught, except her free period. That hour I would go to the library, or read quietly somewhere else.

This schedule did not interfere with the other classes I was taking—music and personal fitness—nor with my normal habit of reading and drawing and such. I planned to follow wholeheartedly all the assignments that Ms. Pelley gave the class.

It turned out that Ms. Pelley is a truly inspired teacher. She is always on the go, even on a down day. It's really great to watch her work. She is always enthusiastic about whatever project the class is working on, and she participates herself. She really gets into it, sometimes taking entire class periods to explain an assignment, or to sort through piles of clippings and old books with the students.

One of the things that I like most about Ms. Pelley is that she never would favor one student over another. She could see the underlying force behind the most primitive work, and would never let appearances fool her. Sometimes she would pass over a perfectly rendered piece in favor of a wildly arranged stick figure, commenting on the mood and undertones behind the work.

She admired everyone's creative expression, from the photo-realistic to the avant garde to the childishly basic. It was very difficult to do wrong in her class, and yet she somehow kept the feeling of intensity going. It was never an easy grade to get or to maintain.

In fact, my only complaint about Ms. Pelley herself is that she would not, *not,* allow talking. To me this was quite sad, although perhaps necessary. (Maybe other teachers in nearby classrooms would misinterpret the noise as lack of control on Ms. Pelley's part.) Talking can be instructive to an artistic class-room environment.

An example: I sometimes like to use a non-photo blue pencil in lieu of a graphite lead on a work before inking. The guy sitting next to me noticed this and asked me about it, but Ms. Pelley cut me off. It was a rough day and she did not want talking.

I found it a bit ironic that a guest artist later that same day would end up explaining the non-photo blue method to the entire class, but that was just a coincidence. My point is that the student next to me could have missed out on a valuable bit of technical information. And, of course, the case could be reversed had I wanted to learn something from him.

In creative development, sometimes it can be incredibly helpful to be able to talk with someone as ideas are occurring. It is also stimulating to just be relaxed and working surrounded by a group of friends even if conversation is not taking place that concerns work in progress. Pleasant talk, in itself, is enabling.

Art class and Ms. Pelley's able instruction were not the only experiences I had at that school. My unique situation gave me the opportunity to do pretty much whatever I pleased. And so, whenever the class would get boring, or I'd start feeling "school paranoia," or my attitude would drag, I'd leave and wander about the school—and occasionally even leave early. It was in this way that I had my first run-in with one of the many school "ladies" (you know, the library ladies, discipline ladies, lunch ladies) in the administration office.

I went in with the intention of using the phone and was confronted with not one phone, but what must have been Phone Heaven. All of these phones were presided over by someone I'll call the "Phone Lady." Naturally I assumed that I should be allowed to use one of the devices, so I asked her nicely enough if I could make a call.

She seemed quite put out suddenly. "No. Students may *not* use the phones. I don't know who sent you but you may *not* use any of my phones."

Okay. I showed her my ADDitions Volunteer badge. (I kept it in my pocket so as not to cause a fuss during class.) She seemed quite suspicious. How could she risk allowing one of the unwashed to use one of her phones?

I finally convinced her that I wasn't a student, and had to work hard to convince her that I was not some "dropout from another school." Then she quite graciously allowed me to use one of her phones ("One," as if I wanted to use all six, maybe). I picked up and began to dial when she added, *"and no 900 numbers!"*

Then there were the "library ladies." These are people who apparently have no lives. They are suspicious of everyone and everything. I have actually had them follow me around the library. After a while I would tire of the sport and leave them confused in the Reference section. They act as if the books are their personal property and they must do everything to discourage the students from using them.

In general, it was like being in a very bad restaurant most clients couldn't leave—except that I was an exception. I could, and did, leave whenever I felt like it. In my position of freedom, yet giving the impression that I was just another student, I was able to see how disrespectfully the students in this school were treated. I saw many instances of gratuitous hostility on the part of a faculty member or administrator to a student. These people serve as examples of how adults behave. Is what we see what they really want us to copy?

The bottom line: I was there to learn. I was learning voluntarily. I was not a prisoner like the rest. I anticipated formal art training, and had in mind learning things like exercises in oil and watercolor usage, with real focus on the science behind mastering art, since I hope to become a truly fine artist one day.

Even here, though, I was disappointed. What I expected from the class and what it turned out to be were quite different. Don't get me wrong. I have utmost respect for the teacher, but the curriculum was simply not fine arts. It focused more on graphic design. I was pleased that Ms. Pelley was trying to prepare the students in case they wanted to study fine art in art school or college, but the real goal of the class was overall personal *style*, not the specifics on *technique* that I had wanted.

Thus, increasingly, I found myself just hanging out in art class as much as actually learning. It was fun, though, and educational in some ways. Probably the most useful artistic technique I learned was the creative use of line (line quality). And I helped to develop two of the year's assignments. Most of the curriculum, though, was redundant for me.

Furthermore, the school system doesn't take art seriously, even though their enormous office building downtown pretentiously displays student art, framed expensively. Ms. Pelley was forced either to buy the necessary supplies herself, or just use the meager tools supplied by the school. She's too dedicated for that nonsense, so she, *personally*, bought the paper, pencils, etc.

(In general, when I see how high school art classes are taught, it's no wonder that no one in them really progresses the way they might if they were working from a different approach. Consider: The focus of most high school art classes is to turn out finished pieces. Even the worksheets have to be "finished." In other words, rather than concentrating on rudimentary skills like depth, perspective, anatomy, motion, proportion, balance and color scheme, the real effort is put into *finishing* techniques like shading.

I can't tell you the number of times I've seen poorly drawn images, mostly of floating eyes and thorny roses, which have no picture quality about them other than the fact that they are shaded with utmost delicacy in hundreds of shades of pencil gray...in all the wrong places. Carefully, carefully crafting something that should have been discarded early in its development.

But why, really, are so many of the basic skills missing? It seems a complete mystery until you look at it through numbers: using the high school method, the average art student produces about twenty-six drawings in a school year, whereas a free art student, not being pressured into chugging out finished work, has the time and confidence to practice the basics. For example, I sometimes sit with my drawing board doing sketch after sketch...and tossing them all into the trash. In the school environment I could do no such thing. My work would linger in a sketchbook, and poor art work is *not* something that should linger.

Only by evolving a picture in my mind can I develop it into something with real depth and style. When working on a new character, for example, I'll start out with the basic shape, then work each part in a separate little image until I get it just right for the personality that I'm trying to put onto paper. Is the character good? Evil? Maniacal? Will it wear mirrored glasses? A hat? Contact lenses?

In a quick sketch, I can easily picture all of these options at blinding speed, something that not even the finest artist could accomplish if required to work each sketch into a finished product.

In the course of one school year, the art student may do 26 drawings. And I will do 226!)

What really kept me going back to school, though, was the socialization, both positive and negative. This was the first time I had ever been in control of the situation. My previous socialization in school had been as a victim. Then I spent two years of homeschool choosing to limit my contacts. (The vital word here is "choose." I was not limited because of the homeschool mode; I used it as an *opportunity* to heal myself and control my exposure. There is quite a difference.)

In order to get along in my new-found situation in high school, I borrowed a technique from Justin. I took the chip off my shoulder, and treated everyone I met essentially with firm, indifferent respect. In other words, if you want to talk with me, fine. I'll talk to you. If you want to attack me, fine. I'll attack you back. To my surprise, I formed no enemies that year.

Now that the year is over, Ms. Pelley says that she was amazed how well I got along with everyone. I sort of moved *through* the social crowd, rather than attempting to stand in it, or section off a part of it for myself.

The lunch group was an interesting development that year. Most groups in the school consisted of only a certain type of person, i.e. Progressive, Metalhead, Preppy, etc. But our group, as Justin often commented, was probably the most politically correct in the school. We had at least one of everything. Sometimes whole bands of Progressives would show up to eat with us; sometimes the Metalheads would join in. It was all very informal. We were more like a gathering of representatives than a group.

You know, it always strikes me as ironic how some people strive for identity as *individuals* by joining a *group*. They assert that "We are individuals," promptly neutralizing that by clinging slavishly to each other. You would have great difficulty finding a more introverted, conservative group of individuals than the students at this school. They scream and cry for acceptance, but only for themselves.

(I think of introversion as being almost a defense mechanism, holding onto the only core of reality in an utterly confusing and threatening existence. Introversion is when a human being is *forced* to turn inward for help and guidance because the outside world has failed him. Yet, surprisingly enough, after my childhood years of unpopularity, I am now anything but introverted. My three years of rest have provided me with the vital confidence and self-esteem that school had stripped from me.)

It was incredible how near to violence the student body was most of the time. Often, a minor disagreement over music provoked a fight. You'd really think that the school's environment should provide a melting pot of cultures and beliefs that would tolerate each other. But nothing could be further from the truth—people mixed with one another like oil and water. People inevitably found some way to isolate themselves in their own, private little universes.

That Christmas, Christy Beckert, now a good friend who has also left school, brought gifts for everyone in the lunch group and for other friends too. We were all quite surprised as we hadn't planned to exchange gifts—and we were startled by the nature of the assorted presents.

That day was one of the best at the school. I found a deep respect for Christy. She had brought us all carefully selected and wrapped vegetables. Tooth Fairy (one of the most intriguing people I know) and I received large, purple, sinister-looking vegetables. Justin got a rather surreal orange, spiky thing. Ms. Pelley was given a beautiful bell pepper. Each selection seemed to be perfectly suited to its recipient's personality.

I was really struck by these gifts. They were so appropriate and probably the only thing that could really embody for me the concept of giving gifts. They were personal, functional, and irrelevant. There was no concern about what they may have cost, and no guilt experienced because we had no countergifts. Solid, yet temporary, Christy's gifts said so much more than most.

It was not until the end of the year that I fully realized that my persona, my "mask," had finally fallen away and that I was being myself without artifice. I had been accepted without having made any effort in that direction. This was the first time that I had really not cared what people thought of me and, ironically, this was the first time that I had found a real niche in a social group.

Speaking of acceptance, I had been a bit worried at the beginning of the year about going into a regular school. Who knew how students were going to react when they found out from me that none of us really had to go to school at all? I was disappointed with what I found. Most people who noticed and then cared enough to ask me about my unusual situation (they could see that I only came to school sporadically and left when I felt like it) couldn't really fathom the concept of "homeschooling." They were confused, especially by the way that I am doing it: completely free form. Eventually, most assumed that I was some sort of genius who was in a special program. That is a concept they understand readily, because they are used to people in special programs receiving special treatment. Everyone else seemed to just accept whatever I was and asked no more. They lacked curiosity.

Some of the attitudes that I encountered were pathetic. Most of the students I talked to didn't know or care about anything. There are exceptions, of course. But most of them are just marking time until they are out. They have long since resigned themselves to the inevitability of their prison sentence and that is what it has become: a sentence.

Like other schools, this school didn't seem to emphasize what is really important: the ability to think, for instance, or how to get along in the real world. It is all so false. The school even had its own expensive TV production lab and every day a news show was broadcast. It was pathetic. The principal would use it to curry favor from his superiors by having them interviewed on the school news. Who cared. There seemed never to be any real use of *student* ideas or talent.

Toward the end of the year, when massive budget cuts were threatened here in Florida, the school administration made it mandatory for every student to write to the legislative representative. Using students as forced lobbyists was bad enough, but I could hardly believe my eyes when they actually showed an example of a "correct" letter on the school news! I mean: a) half the students probably just copied it down because it was a requirement, b) those intelligent enough not to copy it were insulted by it, and c) this is a *high* school, please, not *low* school, not *idiot* school. (And these administrators certify at the end of four years that their students are functional.)

Several days later, the students were encouraged to demonstrate. This was to be a "spontaneous demonstration" by the poor students who, with tears in their little eyes, were protesting budget cuts in education by the State of Florida. The principal and his cronies thought they would have a nice little protest. They had the students make signs and "riot" in the halls (all strictly controlled, they thought) long enough for the principal to get in a good show for the media. Then they blew their whistles and told the students to go back into their cages. Right. That's when the real riot started. The students used this opportunity to continue to riot and vandalize the school. I don't believe, somehow, that it had anything to do with budget cuts, although of course it was portrayed that way.

In addition to going to that regular high school as a "volunteer," I also did some other things. During the year I took some very educational private lessons in oil painting with a local artist.

(This artist was a bit surprised by how quickly and easily I took to the medium—but I wasn't. It had been the same with all of the mediums I had tried. While one can never *master* a medium simply by thinking about it, one can gain an advantage by having a very strong imagination. For example, as my drawing improves, I'm not sure whether I'm getting better at the drawing per se, or simply better at the visualization supporting it.

Before I even begin a painting or a drawing, I take a few minutes to imagine what it will feel like to apply each brushstroke, and how the paint will react with the underpainting. I visualize the object that I am drawing as three-dimensional, and then drawing it is simply the act of caressing its outlines with a pencil or pen.

From a technical standpoint alone, during the three years that I had no formal art training, my talent for it increased unbelievably, something which perplexed me until recently when I realized this visualization connection.)

Regarding my ongoing interest in becoming a game designer: I talked to the manager of the company in California who had said that they wanted to reconsider me for possible employment in 1992. She gave me a good idea of what to submit.

I hurriedly put together an elaborate two-booklet portfolio of samples of the year's work. The first booklet focused on a special set of characters that I was, and still am, developing. The second was simply a compilation of drawings and paintings from my sketch collection (all with copyright protection, of course).

Several weeks passed. I got nervous and called several times. They said that my work was still being looked over and not to worry about it. They were interested, I was told, or they would have mailed me a rejection letter.

Sure enough, for the first time my work was actually returned to me with a very nice letter. They weren't ready to offer me a position yet, but they encouraged me to come see them the next time that I was in California.

I am a very determined person. The "next time" that I was going to be in California was right away. I arranged a meeting with them in late June, 1992. It turned out pretty well considering that by the time the hellish six-hour flight was over (I had been unable to sleep well for days prior to leaving, as well), I was so mellow that I could barely speak. My brother met me at the airport and I went to his home where I managed to eat a bowl of soup. I was feeling a bit ill.

My brother then called the company and got directions. On the way, he pulled the car part way into the parking lot of a dilapidated building that had half of a fiberglass rhinoceros sticking out of it and said, "Well, here we are." I am used to his jokes and that helped lighten me up a little. We drove on.

I had read an article about game design in a magazine a week prior to my trip, and was a bit apprehensive. There was that subtle feeling also of "Dear God, what have I gotten myself into?"

But when we got there my fears evaporated. I honestly can't think of one thing I didn't like. Not only was the company and the job ideal, but the location was excellent and the offices turned out to be very nice.

I was a bit too dazed, though, to really appreciate all this fully. In a way my lack of sleep helped, as I wasn't as nervous as I think I might have been otherwise. In fact, quite the opposite, I felt near comatose. I only wish that I had been more alert to answer their questions. I was so spaced-out that I probably couldn't have told them my last name without thinking about it.

Maybe it was a surprise for them to find out that I was fifteen years old. Maybe not. But they did not seem at all condescending. The "meeting" (I have yet to figure out whether it was actually a job interview) went on for about two hours. This was encouraging because they weren't required to spend that much time with me. They could have cut it short easily. I would have understood. They are business people and their time is valuable.

I flew home the next day in a kind of stupor. I don't know whether it was the jet lag, the excitement, the loss of sleep, or all three, but the whole stay in California had a sort of dreamlike quality about it.

As soon as I got off the plane I set about writing the paragraphs that they had asked me to prepare (I hadn't thought to bring any of my writing samples on the trip) and some notes of general thanks. I was, and continue to be, very grateful to them for taking their time to meet with me, and for their advice.

A few weeks later I received a letter declining to offer me a job but giving some good guidelines to follow and expressing interest in me for the future when I have completed art school. I really hadn't expected anything more.

The trip was mostly for education's sake. Of course, I figured that if I could get a job in the process, great.

Into the fourth year—"eleventh grade"—1992-93

I was very pleased that the company said nothing about my art or writing being deficient when they wrote to me. I don't feel as though I am behind in those areas, though they are skills that can never be improved enough. I'm sure the company knows that my work will continue to progress naturally since I am always practicing.

What they mainly wanted me to learn thoroughly was math, something I had neglected until recently. I have always seen the value of it, but believed that a knowledge of higher math would not be necessary in my life, as I can communicate proficiently in English and saw that a game design job would not require me to do any actual programming.

But as I gradually recovered from my trip and the company's following letter, I realized that since I still wanted to design games, I would pretty much have to dedicate myself to learning math, however long the process took. And so, that being the top priority, I have begun.

As I type this, I am already several chapters past the first "semester" of algebra 1, with less than half of the book to complete. I have been studying the subject for a month under a tutor who is qualified to take me all the way to the other side of calculus. We meet for one-hour sessions five times a week, Monday through Friday.

Seeing the progress I have made, I look forward to keeping up a similar pace throughout the upcoming years. The experience so far has also given me some excellent insights into the faults intrinsic to the grading system—a system which provides a grossly distorted measure of a student's comprehension.

The concept of grading is erroneous because it judges a student not by how much he or she comprehends, but by how many mistakes that person makes on the way to learning, thereby focusing on a person's faults. Of course, we learn through our mistakes; making them is not an indication that a student is weak.

Also, grades frequently place the responsibility for evaluating students on a rather mechanical system. Teachers often say, "I know you are a much better student than this, but we have to go by your test results. Better luck next time."

I look forward to a very free year on several levels. My career goal is in sharp focus now, and I can see how everything that I am working on has a bearing on what I want to be doing in the future; there is no nagging worry that I am in some way not doing as much as I could.

My weekends are spent with friends—most of whom are still in school. Generally we go to see a movie. Sometimes, though, we turn our mutual creativity toward a project of some sort. Last year, for instance, Justin and I wrote and illustrated a comic book. It didn't turn out too well, but it had some nice art in it.

I'll leave my little story here. I hope that in a few years I'll be able to come back and write a happy ending for this one, and a promising beginning for the next.

Gwen Meehan, Patrick's mother
Orlando, Florida

A Parent's Perspective

In looking back at the emotional roller coaster we found ourselves riding that first year, I realize that much of the unhappiness and confusion was the result of my own inept expectations.

I found it hard to push aside the responsibility that I allowed to burden me unnecessarily. Could *I* give Patrick a proper education? Would it be my fault if he couldn't keep up in the world when he reentered school (at either ninth grade, if we had given up after the first year, or at college level) or went out on his own later? What would people think? If I were proved wrong about this form of education, how would my husband feel? And would there be any time at all left for *me*? (The fact that I would even consider my own feelings in the face of Pat's tribulations produced a guilt that was almost overpowering.)

The question of what constitutes a "good student" also haunted me. You can see by what Patrick has said that I was distraught when I couldn't immediately identify whatever he was doing with "learning." I had had visions of Pat, unrealistically acquiescent, hanging on my every word as we sat at our idyllic kitchen table studying. We had some real arguments over all this with me threatening to send him back to school. Fear loomed out of the shadows at me any way I turned.

But all that is behind us now. I realize that I had been undermined by my awe of authority. I had been coerced into abdicating confidence in my own ability to know what is best, and I had given my confidence to "teachers" instead. My own role had been confused and therefore my expectations were invalid.

My concern about how other people would react has also been resolved. At first, we tiptoed into the world fearing the day when we would have to answer questions from the inquisitors. Poof! No problem. I have been astounded at how few have disagreed with our daring to homeschool. Before we discovered this alternative, I spent *years* agonizing over Pat's pain. You would think that friends would be thrilled that we solved the problem. Most were, but we did lose several who, I suspect, were afraid their own children might want out when they saw Pat's transformation.

Most strangers we meet are surprised that homeschooling is possible. Most acknowledge that the education system is unsatisfactory. Most have said that they wish they had the courage to homeschool. Some have even suggested that I must be a saint! Ha! They simply do not visualize themselves as being able to be part of a change. (Could they be reflecting their own education?)

The first question we are always asked is about Pat's "socialization." I respond by asking them to go back to their own schooling and see if they really were happy with their own socialization. I suggest that even if they were the most popular person in the school, if they will look at that experience honestly, they'll recognize that it was not a wholly positive experience. (The most popular/beautiful/talented person in the school is hated behind their back and they know it surely.) No one has ever disagreed with me. Rather, people are most often shocked that they had never stopped to look at that part of their life realistically before.

Sometimes I wonder if our halcyon memories of school are distorted within us—the same way abused children "forget" their abuse. Since we are told that the schooling we are getting is good for us (even though we *feel* it is wrong), we convince ourselves that we are...we *must* be...having fun. Aren't we?

Naturally, I expect sometime to meet people who claim that their school experience was totally delightful. But the people to whom I have spoken have admitted that they were really unhappy and insecure and that they had taught themselves to project a happy face because that was what was expected of them.

I'll never forget a boy who attended prep school with Pat and professed to be Pat's very, very best friend. He wept remorsefully as he admitted to us both that he had deliberately abused Patrick—because otherwise he would have jeopardized his own prestigious and hard-won position in the peer pecking order. He knew he was being hateful. He himself had been a victim before his acceptance into the group. Privately he acknowledged to us how much pain he had suffered. But this did not stop him from wounding his "friend." He is still at that school. He is popular. I often wonder at whose expense and of what value that kind of popularity can be.

At the beginning of our fourth year of homeschooling, I am completely relaxed. I have plenty of time to do what I want to for myself. My husband has been very supportive all along, even though the entire idea has been contrary to his up-bringing and his schooling. We are confident that Patrick is getting the very best education we can provide for him in Orlando, Florida. We have not had to endure the terrible teenage rebellion period which everyone dreads; Patrick has nothing against which to rebel except his own decisions. (We are not naive about what it's like to have a rebellious teenager. We have raised two other boys very successfully and I could tell you some stories!)

All of the problems resolved after the first year when I relaxed into the idea that Pat is capable, worthy of respect at any age, and that I would trust him completely. He is open to our guidance, and he has not let us down. Together we—Pat, his father, and I—can find answers to our questions. It has worked splendidly. I feel better than I have in years. We are seeing our son mature tranquilly. The pain and fear have evaporated.

What about the future? When I look at and talk to the pitiful specimens emerging from high school incarceration, with no feeling of accomplishment or preparation, I know that Patrick has gotten a better start. We realize that there are shining examples of wonderful young people in school who *do* feel good about what they have done—the Bell Curve is alive after all! But my concern is for the majority. Although well-publicized, superstars are rare.

Incidentally, we are proud to have been involved in the freeing of five other students. One, Jay Graham, was already thinking of homeschooling and his mother, Rita, called us for support. They are doing well and have changed their conception of education completely (Rita has a Ph.D. in education) even though they have another child who has elected to stay in traditional school. Christy Beckert, whom Patrick mentions in his essay, has left school also. She has been busy taking courses relevant to her interest in photography and art. In addition, three others are now homeschoolers. They are the elementary school age children of one of my husband's business associates. They have been out only a few weeks and they feel so much happier already. The night before they started, one of the girls said, "I can't wait until my first day of homeschool tomorrow!" The whole family is enthusiastic about the possibilities.

Patrick Meehan
Seattle, Washington

Further Scents from Subsequent Nightmares

F or me, homeschooling was the only choice that made sense. I have zero patience, am a hands-on learner, like to be in control over how and when information is presented to me, and want to be able to ask questions, go off on tangents and demand multiple perspectives. When I'm forced to move through a subject without understanding every aspect as I go and also understanding where I'm headed, I become confused and irritated. Any style of education where subjects are served up like parts off an assembly line is anathema to the way I learn. The choice I made was

Photo by Benny Tsai

between assured failure in high school and possible failure at home.

My perspective now concerning elementary and middle school is that I was a sensitive child, quick to take affront and escalate problems, so a lot of the problems I had or thought I had were my own doing. That's not to say that I didn't also find the curriculum tedious, boring and irrelevant to anything that interested me.

All signs would indicate now that my decision to homeschool and pursue my own interests turned out to be good for me.

Shortly after completing my essay for *Real Lives*, I had the opportunity to intern at SEGA, working as a grunt on a *Sonic the Hedgehog* spin-off.

It was a mixed experience, but enough to solidify my interest in video game development.

In 1994, at the age of eighteen, I enrolled at the DigiPen School of Applied Computer Graphics in Vancouver, British Columbia, the only school then (and now) in North America endorsed by Nintendo to teach computer science and programming as it pertains to video game development. When I attended, they offered only a two-year diploma but have since relocated to Redmond, Washington and expanded their courses to offer a four-year Bachelor of Science. For the electronic entertainment industry, a school like DigiPen, which produces computer programmers, is analogous to a specialized institute like the Rhode Island School of Design that produces artists, illustrators and industrial or graphic designers.

When I graduated in 1996 I was immediately hired as a Software Architect by Nintendo Technical Development to join the R&D team working on what would later become the GameCube (Nintendo's newest game system). I've worked in the industry since for both large companies (Nintendo) and start-ups (Interactive Imagination). To date I've been a software architect, a lead programmer, a technical director, and a game producer and director. I've never wanted for employment and have consistently been well paid.

I should point out that although I was miserable in middle school, my present career path is more a function of my choice of technical school and personal dedication than of my decision to eschew high school. I chose my professional goals before homeschooling, so my time out of high school served me as a means to an end.

As far as the debate over the best flavor of education goes, I remain agnostic in spite of my own experiences. I don't have children of my own with whom to compare experiences, don't know anyone who has children of middle-school age and am not in contact with other homeschoolers. That said, I'll touch on two features of homeschooling that have become more apparent to me in retrospect.

Perspective on College

Although it might seem counterintuitive, skipping high school allowed me to gain perspective on college. When I entered DigiPen after homeschooling I did so with a sense of purpose because I was there of my own accord, understood the context of what I was learning, and could clearly see how the education I was receiving would further my goals. I was genuinely interested in the curriculum and had made up my mind to stick it out and learn the material no matter what. Of course I don't mean to imply that ambitious students who finish high school wouldn't share the same advantage.

Had I not left high school, I would have probably continued to sink into apathy. My grades could have slipped to the point where I would not have been accepted at DigiPen. Homeschooling gave me the freedom to pursue and refine my interests, to develop confidence and capacity for achieving goals on my own, to explore the implications of the career path I desired, to ponder the life I wanted to lead, to get hands-on experience in my field of interest, and to focus on improving the skills I would need to be accepted at the school of my choice.

Choice of Teachers

A truly gifted teacher is a rare and precious person. When I think about any educational scenario that has worked for me, a marvelous teacher has always been the defining factor. This was a key benefit of homeschooling. If a teacher was required for a subject, my parents could afford to seek out the best. I did not have to give up enjoyment of a subject (math, for example) because of inadequate teachers.

I was not bound to a single school's selection of teachers. And had my parents not been able to afford private tutors, I could have attended more affordable group tutoring sessions, and so would still have had more options than high school students. Homeschoolers have the option to pick and choose tutors in a free market driven by quality.

Before moving on, I'd like to mention the importance of two extraordinary teachers I've been lucky to have: Penny Parrish and Claude Comair.

Penny was my math tutor in preparation for my internship at SEGA and then again in preparation for my application to DigiPen. I would spend several evenings a week with her (and her memorable cats) to work through the curriculum at my own speed asking questions that she always answered with great clarity, insight and humor. Penny is an excellent teacher and without her help I would not have succeeded.

Claude is, of course, the famous founder of DigiPen (and now the Chairman of Nintendo Software Technology). The school is his passion; he personally taught several of the classes while I was a student. Claude has a way of presenting even the most technical subject in such a thorough, emphatic and human way that his lectures are spellbinding. He's one of the very best in his field, and his lectures on everything from microprocessors to the golden mean (performed impromptu, no less) inform me still.

Parting Advice

For parents, I think the best way to approach the decision whether to allow a teen to leave school is to simply be aware of the options and allow the teen to decide for him or her self. Remember, you do not have to spend your days tutoring or even hire a tutor. Your teens will succeed or fail on their own terms regardless of what you do; you can only stack the deck against them by forcing them into a situation that makes them miserable. When I have children of my own I will allow them to attend school or not as they see fit and hope that I will be able to afford the full spectrum of options for them.

For teens, whether you enjoy school or are frustrated and bored by it, the choice to stay or leave should be made thoughtfully. Just remember that the college and university experience can be completely different from what you are experiencing now. Before making a decision, tour universities or visit technical and art schools that have accepted homeschoolers. Consider for yourself what your options in life might be should you decide to quit high school.

Tabitha Mountjoy, 16
Harrisonville, Missouri

Make Me Wild

*This story of my life is dedicated to everyone who finds
in reading it a portion of what I have found in living it.*

"**C**ome on, Tabitha!" shouts Amory, my eleven-year-old sister. It is springtime in Missouri. I tug a ladder along, following Amory as she scouts for birds' nests. Bird watching is not really my thing, but if I want to spend time with Amory, this rickety brown ladder must also be my companion. Not that I don't like the little thrills you get as you watch parents build a nest, eggs appear, baby birds replace the eggs (looking so naked with their featherless bodies and big eyes), and these little birds finally take flight. It seems an unbelievable miracle. Rather, I seem to lack enough patience for the endless wait that goes on *between* these events.

Photo by Amory Mountjoy

I have reached Amory now and put the ladder in place. As we look into the nest, we notice one less egg than there was this morning. Amory fumes as she rattles off the numerous fates that could have come to the unfortunate egg. She considers the different predators—snakes, owls, and other birds—that might have eaten it.

I have had enough bird watching for now and offer to carry the ladder back to the garage for Amory if she is done with her rounds. She accepts the offer and no doubt appreciates it greatly as she usually has to lug the ladder herself. She is not done bird watching, however; she is only finished with the front yard. The trees behind our house are much bigger and she can climb them, without the ladder.

I head off for the barn where I spend most of my time. I sense the sweet smell of hay and the feeling of hard work and trust floating in the air. Since I was six I have had at least one horse. My horses have taught me some of the most important lessons I have learned—like responsibility, respect, and commitment. In fact, they have taught me more than anyone else in my life. I think being responsible for a living creature was very important in my growing up. Going outside in the middle of winter before I had breakfast to break the ice covering my horses' water so they could drink taught me to put myself in somebody else's place. Knowing that the horses depended on me also strengthened my devotion.

I call out for Shari, my beautiful Arabian mare with her sweetly dished face. After I work her out—a process which includes lunging her on a lead line, riding her at a walk-trot, and then cantering inside the arena—I ride her in the pasture. Last year I boarded her at a training barn for about six months and worked with her trainer so that Shari and I could work together better as a team. We learned leg and voice commands, a more subtle form of training than rein commands.

I have been working with Shari for about two hours now and as we tune up, we turn to more advanced communication. Eventually, I will use only mind signals, something I discovered on my own. (It usually takes about thirty minutes for us to start communicating really well, but this fluctuates depending on the mood we are in.) It is difficult to explain the way I use mind signals, but if you imagine along with me I will do my best. I am astride Shari, her head is directly in front of me, and everything is very peaceful. I turn my head a little to the left of hers and open my mind. Horses think very differently from humans. Instead of thinking, they *feel* that, for instance, the place under the trees would be cool. They use instincts and some sort of sixth sense to determine which way they wish to turn.

My mind is open. I always visualize a yellow beam to see and feel if I am connected to Shari. (I use yellow because it is my favorite color.) I send out vibrations to her mind as I slowly turn my head until it lines up with hers. If I can find her mind, I can link my mind with hers and *ask* her to turn. When I do find her mind, the yellow beam becomes thicker and more stable because there is a mind on each end. When I ask Shari to turn, I ask with my heart, making it feel as much like the way her instincts work for her as I can. If she does not mind going in the direction I suggest, we go that way. If she does not want to go in that direction, Shari will get very irritated and shake her head. She also acts like she is pulling on the reins, even though she does not wear a bridle. She acts as if I were using the bridle to force her to go in a direction in which she did not wish to go. The way Shari responds to my signals is the way I know that we are communicating.

These types of wonderful experiences, adventures, and experiments have filled my youth with lots of fun times, laughter, and learning. I have been home educated all my life. During the earlier years the decision for me to learn at home was my parents'. Later, it was totally my own choice. I enjoy being different. Most people think the things I do are fascinating, and they seem even more interested in the way I think. I have never been programmed, so I do not usually have programmed answers. My answers are my own.

Some adults, of course, are skeptical and ask a lot of test-like questions: "What grade are you going into?" "How do you study math?" And of course, "Don't you think you are being socially deprived?" I usually respond to these types of people with answers much like their questions—that I finished my high school studies last fall, that my parents taught me math, and that I feel that I do just fine socially. These adults do not care about what I have learned, or the way I handle life. What they are thinking is one of three things; either, "I might start homeschooling with my son," or "She must be some kind of genius," or "Poor girl, she has never been to school. She doesn't know what she is missing." Any of these responses, going through their minds, is a comparison to their children or the children around them. They never look at *me* and say, How interesting, what do you feel about abortion, or the school system, or national healthcare— or anything else I think is important. These people are not my favorites.

However, most adults treat me equally. A good example of this is my volunteer job with the K.C. Mental Health Association. I work the crisis line and handle calls from people who are attempting suicide, who have just been raped, and who have other problems of a less emergency-oriented nature. I work fifteen hours a month, three five-hour shifts. The position is not easy but the director never questions my age. I am treated equally, even though I am the youngest volunteer in the history of their association.

One day when my mother and I were at the office, one of the workers passed out. Fortunately mother and I had taken CPR courses, and we were able to save the worker's life—or at least keep her going until the paramedics arrived. It was just like in the movies, as odd as that may sound. Mother and I were talking in a hallway. Mother could see around the corner, but I could not. I was talking along and beginning to wonder why she was not looking at me, when she touched my arm and asked me to look around the corner. Three women were on top of a lady lying on the floor. Mother and I quickly moved in and asked if they knew rescue techniques. We let them know that we did know CPR. As we knelt over the woman I found that she was not breathing, while Mother checked her pulse. The woman didn't have one.

The first time I tried to give her air, I didn't make a correct seal. But the next two breaths got to her, and thank God, her heart started beating again. If it had not started beating, I do not know if we could have saved her—she was twice as big as we were put together. Once the paramedics got to the office our job was over. I was fifteen at the time, and it was nice that the other workers did not make a big deal about my age. I was not treated as inferior or superior be-cause of my age; it was simply accepted that Mother and I had helped a lady live. We passed hugs around and then everyone went back to their work. Just because

I was younger did not make what I had done any more amazing.

I enjoy being around adults who are open minded. I am as big as they are physically and have the same mental ability. The only difference between teenagers and adults is the simple fact that adults have more life experience. Something I get put in my face a lot is how I am so idealistic. I believe that everything works for good and I also feel that if something needs to be changed for an individual, it should be changed. (I suppose I am talking mainly about school and the work of teachers, principals, and counselors. They seem to be geared for the *group*, not for the individual. I think that is wrong.)

Whatever their values, young people seem more likely to just jump into something without sitting back and looking at the hurdles. Young people tend to start racing and assume that they will give the jumps their best shot. Well, the truth is, there is something to be gained from idealists, as well as from older, more practical people. The practical outlook gives you a much more secure feeling in life. Idealists tend to take the more uncertain path and sometimes they crash. Other times (I like to think more often than not) they fly! A favorite quote of mine is, "According to aerodynamics the bumble bee cannot fly; I guess no one offered to tell the bee."

The thing I enjoy most about not being institutionalized is the way I can do things that interest me. Not only can I do things that I find fascinating, but also I can study them at my own pace. I do not have to keep up with or wait for a class. In fact, I rarely think of the things I do as something that I should do for school. A lot of people tend to think that kids will not learn unless they are in school. I suppose that is something that unschooled people are here to show, that that is not true. Just by living, you learn. Life does not have to be structured or

boringly repetitive in order for one to be smart or learn a skill.

In the next sections, I will group my activities as though I were in school, so that you can understand how the things I do cover academic ground. But I do not do the things listed below in order to fill academic requirements, and I do not do them in any kind of order at all and certainly not the order in which they appear here. I do the things I do because they are what I enjoy doing, not for any other reasons.

Also, I do not keep projects in narrowly designated subject groups. My projects quickly change into ideas, and ideas are not stagnant or scheduled—they grow and expand.

Biology

This last fall I have been putting a cat skeleton together. It has been fascinating and very enlightening. I found the skeleton in some tall weeds about two months after the cat died. (She had been a barn cat.) Because the cat was in the weeds and it had just rained, I could not find all of the bones. The bones I was missing were long thin bones, like ribs, or thin leg bones. Before I had started this project of assembling the bones into a skeleton, I had had no idea how many different parts there are to a single bone. For example, I had always thought that the leg bone was just a bone. Inside the bone, however, is marrow, and outside the bone is parieostum.

Since I found the cat, and no one else had touched her, it was sort of like an archaeologist's find. It was a strange feeling to be digging for remains in the mud because previously, I would never have picked myself out to be the type to do something with dead animal parts. However, when Amory held the skull in her hand and remarked that this pile of skin, fur, and bones was all that was left of our cat, I became intrigued. Bending down, I found the lower jaw and fitted the pieces together. It looked so mystical. I held the jaw open and the teeth were jagged. They looked like they could come alive. The soul of the animal had really left its mark.

Photo by Amory Mountjoy

After I found as many bones as I could, and I had separated the skin and fur from them, I began to put the pieces together. It was exactly like putting together a puzzle, a skill I had started before I was able to talk. I put the head, backbone, and tail together with glue.

However, ever since I first picked up the head, the bones had had a mystical meaning for me. By the time I had finished putting the backbone together, I was looking for a way to give the whole thing more meaning than just a "skeleton." So when I found a white feather, I knew that the skeleton needed to become a spirit symbol. I made a cross stand out of leg bones and put the feather on the head. I am still looking for flowers to go in the eyes and mouth.

Making this spirit symbol has been a great creative release for me. I have never been in a classroom with a dissection going on, but I do have friends who are in high school and dissect frogs, mice, and other animals. Even though my project with the cat and dissections in a classroom both have to do with anatomy, it is hard for me to see them as the same type of things. I think that it is sad that so many kids are forced to do dissections without being able to use their imagination because there is so much *room* for imagination with an animal. It would be interesting to see what different kids would come up with other than merely putting the animal together or taking it apart exactly like it was.

For example, this last month I carved a miniature arrow out of wood and made a stand for it out of the cat's rib bones. Also, I started making a necklace for a friend out of one of the leg bones made into long beads. Mother and I had been in an ethnic shop downtown and we had seen old bones with the marrow taken out of them and that had been dyed with natural materials. I asked an employee how they had gotten the bones to look the way they did. She said they had cut off the ends of the bones and boiled them in water to remove the marrow. Then they had dyed the bones with bark or berries. I went home and began this process using one of the cat bones. So far, it has worked really well. All I have to do now is dye the bone and put it on a string. The possibilities of things you can make from bones are endless.

Recently, my two younger sisters and I have been going to a park near our home and looking for snakes. I love snakes. My extended family has kept them as pets for a long time—from little snakes to twenty-foot Boa Constrictors.

The first time I came in close contact with a wild snake was a little over a year ago. My family and some friends were on vacation in the Ozarks around March. One night, everyone was sitting around a campfire, and I went to get something to eat. There was a pile of sticks right in front of the cooler, and it was far enough away from the fire to be quite dark. I was walking on some of the sticks that had strayed from the pile, when all of a sudden, I stepped on something like rubber. A loud hiss came from the ground, a lot like a cat's hiss.

I became concerned as I realized what I stepped on was a snake and not a stick. I was so much bigger than the snake—had I hurt him? Had he already been hurt and had I added to his pain? As these thoughts went through my mind, the snake tightened his muscles and I was almost propelled off of him. One of my parents' friends helped me get him back into the forest by nudging him that direction with a stick. Later we found out that the snake was a copperhead and the only reason I was not bitten was probably because he was not totally out of hibernation yet.

I had never caught wild snakes until a wonderful experience about a month ago. A friend, my two sisters, and I were out in the park, just taking a walk, not looking for anything in particular, when we heard a snake moving through the grass. I quickly told everyone of a lady I had met who had told me how to catch a snake by putting a forked stick over its head and then being able to easily reach down and lift it up. So after chasing the snake through the bushes for a while we caught her and I lifted her up. We kept her for about ten minutes before letting her go.

Snakes are one of a kind; there are no other animals or reptiles quite like them. When I catch a snake and it twists around my arm and intertwines through my fingers, it feels wild. They are so coordinated. When a snake moves, each piece of its body takes the exact place of the piece before it; you hardly notice it is moving until it is gone. Snakes seem to be a single muscle with tremendous strength, flexible beyond belief. To watch their bodies expand and contract as they breathe—to watch them go from being plump and round to incredibly thin—is breathtaking. When I pick up one of these wild creatures it feels like I am touching on a different culture.

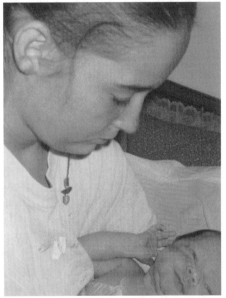

Photo by Denise Gay Thate

I am interested in midwifery, probably because my mother is a midwife. I am extremely grateful for that, because it is exciting to help out with making an old profession come alive again. Midwifery is accepted through most of Europe and Asia as excellent care for pregnant and birthing women, and I am very honored that I have been asked to attend about fifteen of these miraculous births. I am not what you could call an apprentice but I do have a very active role in the births. And just being *around* someone (like my mother) who is so interested in the subject would make it impossible not to learn quite a lot. I learn anatomy naturally, as that is one of the most important parts of a birth. There is nothing as amazing to me as watching a new human come into this world.

Recently I attended a birth as an assistant. One of Mother's clients was here having a prenatal checkup and she unexpectedly went into labor. Mother couldn't find any of her normal assistants, so I helped more than I do when I just go to observe. I helped rearrange the house, brought instruments upstairs, and laid out oils and warm and cold compresses. After the mother started pushing, I helped make teas and I warmed baby blankets. I am grateful that birth is a normal part of my life.

Social sciences

I read psychology and sociology college texts. I am seriously thinking of going into the psychology field so I have many books that were written by psychologists. One of my favorites is *The Pathwork of Self Transformation*, by Eva Pierrakos.

I have several psychologist friends. I met Cindy because she is one of Mother's friends who had her baby at home. I met Jane and Mike through their daughter Soni, whom I met when I was at my cousin's baseball game in St. Louis. (Soni played on his team and is my age. She invited me to her house to spend the night after the game. I did and it was the beginning of a great friendship with the entire family.) My psychology friends help me out with different things that will be important later. They tell me what it is like to be a psychologist: the rewards, and also the times when things fly out the window—when they have no control over the way something turns out. Jane and the rest of her family have invited me to go on their family vacation which will include a psychology conference. So Soni and I will be able to attend a conference for licensed psychologists. And afterward Soni and I are going to Virginia to the Seven Oaks School for an intensive week of pathwork training; pathwork is the specific kind of psychology I might want to go into.

I like pathwork psychology because of its unique approach to mental, emotional, and spiritual healing. It employs an awareness of metaphysics, of the continuation of the life stream of the soul (i.e. reincarnation), and of individual and group dynamics.

Working on the Kansas City Mental Health crisis hotline has been very helpful in broadening my outlook on the human mind, and thus an uncompromising contributor to my inextinguishable curiosity on the subject of psychology. Once a little old lady called me wanting to know if she should commit herself to "one of those places" because she thought and lived very differently than her family. After telling her that in my unprofessional opinion she did not seem crazy, she was so relieved that she offered to buy me anything that her purse would allow. I refused, but she continued to offer—"flowers? a hot meal? perhaps company?" I assured her that I was really very content at the moment but that I greatly appreciated her generosity. She concluded that I had helped her immensely, that I was the nicest person she had talked to in a long time, and that if I ever needed someone to talk to, I had a friend in her. We hung up on the best of terms.

Then there's the other side of the coin: the drunken man calling from the pay phone outside of the bar from which he has been kicked out. He tells me that his wife has ordered him to leave. I suggest seeking help from his family, but he does not know how to reach them. (The way he puts it, actually, is that they have lost track of him.) I am sure by this time that if he had a dog it would run away from him. I tell him about the homeless shelters. He explodes with wrath. "I've been to them before," he bellows into the phone, "They are degrading!" After a long line of obscene language he decides to cooperate. He states that as degrading as the shelters may be, he will consent to going there—*if* I can guarantee that there will be a bed waiting for him when he arrives. I inform him that on the contrary, there probably are waiting lists, and the sooner he enrolls the sooner he will be admitted. He screams at me that this is like all the other hotlines and that they never help. Also he tells me that I am worthless and that if I cannot help people I should be fired from my job. Then he hangs up. As I lower the receiver, I silently remind myself that I volunteer for this job for the people who *want* help.

My mother is working for the legalization of midwives. In Missouri, midwifery is illegal so I have grown up in a family where you fight for what you know is right. I will cherish that forever, because I have learned that if you know something is wrong, you can work to make it right. At present the midwives have a bill at the capitol which legalizes both midwifery and a training program for midwives. The bill has passed out of the house and is in the senate. Legalization takes a lot of work both at home and at the capitol, which for us is about three and a half hours away.

I have probably spent more time at the capitol here than any other person my age. I have sat in on meetings on how to get the bill through legislature; I have wandered around the capitol for hours looking at statues and reading inscriptions. I have gone around with Mother while she lobbies, which generally includes talking to representatives and senators, explaining our bill, and explaining why we are trying to get it passed. I have sat in on discussions with our sponsor, Representative Carol Jean Mays, which are usually hodgepodges of ideas. And I have also gone to public hearings where the committee members in our little group of representatives or senators vote on whether to send the bill on to the floor or to kill it. Speakers range from elderly men and women to nine-year-old girls, from rich doctors to Amish couples. It is pretty hard to be around people who constantly talk about the judicial and legislative systems without learning all about it.

English

This area is too expansive for me to include all of the things that I read, write, and in other ways express myself through the English language. Here, however, are some of the things that are my favorites.

I love to read; I read just about anything I can get my hands on. My favorite classics are *Les Miserables* by Victor Hugo, and the *Odyssey* and the

Iliad by Homer, as well as the works of Tolkien, Twain, Longfellow, and other great inspirers of the imagination. Another favorite book is *The Education of Little Tree*, by Forrest Carter. I love books about Native Americans, but usually only when they are written *by* Native Americans.

I also write all kinds of things from poetry and adventure stories to writing for this book—and most important, corresponding with friends far away. I have also been a writing apprentice to Susannah Sheffer, the editor of *Growing Without Schooling* (a magazine for homeschoolers). The apprenticeship consists mostly of me sending her my work and her sending back her reflections, questions, and suggestions, etc.—a process which works really well.[*]

* * *

I think that being home-educated has given me a much different outlook toward life. For example, we live in a rural Missouri town that is somewhat narrow-minded. If I stayed here all of the time I would be a very different person than I am now. However, we go up to the city quite often. (Because we are home-educated we can go up anytime—not just on weekends and holidays, but also during the week.) Downtown in Westport, I eat ethnic food, buy ethnic clothing, and see people who make us look conservative. I feel that it is very important to see and be around people who do things very differently than the way I do them.

Being home-educated also lets me do different kinds of things because I have more time in which to do them. One day a friend and I went to see an absolutely fabulous daytime concert by African dancers, singers, and storytellers. The dancers and the music were wild! The room came alive with the audience clapping and chanting simple African chants. The audience was not there merely to watch; it was there to encourage. The louder we chanted and the faster we clapped, the higher and more frantically the dancers leaped, spun, and seemed to fly through the air. A concert like this one would change thousands of people's attitudes toward life, and because I did not have to be in school I got to be there, in the middle of the weekday, seeing all that positive energy flow through the room, through the people, carried by the music and by my heart, each person's heart, always to be remembered. This is the most important thing that home education has given me: the ability to experiment and to look at things in a new way. To seize the day!

Another thing that our family did recently was to go to one of the social events held for the peace and dignity runners. The Peace and Dignity Run was planned three years ago by Native Americans. Groups of people started out from the four corners of where their nations' boundaries had been—one group from

---

[*] See Susannah's book on her work with Tabitha and other young writers: *Writing Because We Love To: Homeschoolers at Work* (Heinemann-Boynton/Cook, 1992).

Alaska, one from Guatemala, one from the east coast, and one from the west coast. The groups from Alaska and the two coasts met here in Kansas City this weekend. Now these groups will run down together to Mexico and meet the runners from Guatemala. They should get there around October of 1992.

One of the festivities for the North, East, and West meeting this weekend was a youth dance which we attended. We met several people there, one of the most interesting being Denty, a Native American from Alaska, a drummer and a chanter. Denty had so much spirit; he was truly alive, his eyes shone and he beat his drum loudly and moved his body with the rhythm of the drum, of the night, creating the feeling in the room.

Denty also spoke of the vision of the runners, explaining that they were running to reunite the nation, bringing a message of brotherhood and sisterhood to the people. He said that since the European invasion there had been hard times and suffering among the Native Americans, but that they were not the only ones who suffered. *Everyone* had suffered, because we are all separated from each other. The runners feel that we should put the past behind us and be brothers and sisters, one people. He pointed out that we have much more in common with each other than we have differences: We walk on the same earth, drink the same water, and breathe the same air. I could not have agreed more. The peace and justice runners were honoring the young people who are the ones that they feel can bring about this change.

(I do believe all people should work together, whether they are of different ethnic groups or different age groups. I feel that people should have a strong sense of brotherhood and sisterhood, that churches and religions should be very cooperative. Mostly, I feel that people of the United States should be called Americans. I think that if you are proud of where you originally come from then that is great. But I do not like it when someone says, "The black population is doing this," or "Mexicans are up to that." We are all Americans. Rarely does one ethnic group function in isolation in our society. The Amish are an obvious exception; they do function primarily on their own.)

Another person we got to meet there was Nathan Chasing Horse, who played Smiles A Lot in the movie *Dances With Wolves*. We got to not only meet him but also dance with him. Nathan is a beautiful dancer; he danced some of his Native American dances which are so full of spirit and high energy. If you have ever seen Native Americans dance then you probably remember it; if you have not, try to imagine every part of the body moving in perfect rhythm. Nathan's hair was below his waist and braided in three braids. He was dancing about two inches away from my face with his arms and hair swinging in wild rhythms that seemed to be out of control, yet, not one arm or braid ever hit me—so he obviously knew exactly where every piece of him was at any one time. The beauty and rhythm of his dancing was breathtakingly wild.

I loved the spirit Denty and Nathan had around them, and I would very much like to go and see the runners again. Seeing them, I got the same sort of feeling that I got when I watched the African dancers—a feeling of peace, harmony, and rhythm. I will never forget them.

Among my friends are adults, peers, and babies. I adore my baby friends. Tae's one of the cutest little two-year-olds I have seen in my life; she is Shirley Temple all over again. Her curls are as appealing to the eyes as her personality is to the spirit. She is more animated than her peers and more agreeable than you can imagine possible! I tend to be able to talk to adults and little children whom I don't know more easily than to teenagers whom I don't know, simply because I have had more experience at that. I have several teenage friends but most of them live at least five hours away so I don't see them often. Now that we live in town I am finding more friends my age, but it is difficult to meet them because they are in school. The only way I can meet teenagers is after school or in the summer, although usually they have something to do with the people they already know so it is still difficult.

Amory, Kalista, and Tabitha Mountjoy

Some teens seem to think that I am very different, that my life is perfect. I might say to all of the people reading this book (especially the teens) that kids who don't go to school are just like everyone else in many ways. We have problems and have fun just like you. My parents have split up like some of yours have, I have my own deadlines to meet (such as this essay), and a list of movies I want to see.

One of the most wonderful things about my family and our friends is the way we all get along so well. We all love each other and even though there are misunderstandings, I can't ever forget that everyone loves me; it is so obvious. Though some of our family's close friends are all over the world, we never lose touch. Most of the time we just write but sometimes we talk by phone. Summer will be filled with social activities. Soni is coming to visit and we are all going to drive to Colorado and Montana to visit some old friends who now live there. In July my two sisters and I are going to a diabetic camp (Amory has diabetes). And of course in August I am going with Soni and her family on their summer vacation.

Because other kids are in school, summer is when we see the most people. Other than the trips I mentioned, we go to the pool almost every day. I love to dive and am on the local swim team. Outdoor activities are what I enjoy most: camping, hiking, horseback riding, tree climbing, and swimming.

Ever since I can remember, I have had a wild imagination. Sometimes my wildness comes out in the things I do—like galloping my horse bareback through the woods, pretending I am in a different space and time. Other times, it finds its way into my writing. Like now.

Forest Song

Wild—Please make me wild.
Free—Yes set me free.
Let me know what I can do.
Remind me how my body moves.
Tell me everything's in my reach
That all I have to do is need it.
Show me how to laugh again,
How to dance and how to sing.
Help me see life at its best
Without stress—just peaceful rest.
Everything in harmony
Working for some magic thing.
Beyond my mortal mind's process,
With my soul it passed the test.
Something sure and strong and true
One thing that helps both me and you.
Cause and effect work instantly.
Acceptance—I feel inside of me.
All life's a purpose
And all purpose life.
Some place where time is not a master
My heart and spirit swell much faster.

Tabitha Mountjoy Hall
Eugene, Oregon

Creating and Recreating my Life

Looking back at all that I was doing ten years ago when I wrote my first autobiography—I was busy! Time has continued to fly right along and although I have chosen more focused directions since then, my life still carries the same enthusiasm and joy of discovery that I find when I go back and read the words of my younger self.

Tabitha, Steve, and Ariel

When I was about eighteen I was in the middle of trying to find what I wanted to do with my life as a career, and I stumbled across Structural Integration. Better known as Rolfing, Structural Integration is a form of somatic education and bodywork that works with the repetitive motions of the body. It looks at why we stand or sit the way we do, what makes one person slouch while another is hyper erect, and works to bring more balance to the individual. After deciding to pursue this line of work I began a deep and extensive exploration of my own body's habits and patterns, and found ways to move through and improve them. And I enrolled in the Rolf Institute in Boulder, Colorado, where I completed an intensive training process with inspiring teachers and fabulous student peers.

Rolfing has been a way for me to combine my love of movement and my interest in the inner workings of the mind. Although Rolfing is not a form of psychology, it is a holistic approach to the body, and in my professional opinion the mind and the body are so closely related that they cannot be dissected one from the other.

When I was twenty-two, and nearing the end of my Rolfing training, a friend wrote that she was planning a trip around Mexico and looking for a companion. So after I graduated, I spent the spring working at a spa doing bodywork. (While at the Rolf Institute I had learned "skillful touch" massage, and then this work had helped put me through the rest of my training.) Then that summer, with virtually no Spanish speaking skills, but with a bilingual companion who had grown up in Mexico, I set out on another of life's adventures.

Our trip was amazing. We spent two and a half months riding buses from town to town around the Mayan and Aztec ruins, and then backpacking around each town. It turned out that we were fabulous companions—we were compatible about how much money to spend and on what, we could both hike about the same distance before needing a break, and we both agreed on one solid rule: Once we had gone past our limits and were dead tired but had to keep going, we would not say one more word to each other unless absolutely necessary before a shower, food, and sleep, in that order. It saved our friendship. And I will say this: I could do the exact same trip, see the exact same things, eat the exact same things (usually tortillas and cold beans out of a can; they travel well in a backpack, it's hard to catch amoebas from a can, it's protein, and it's cheap!) and I would not only have a great time, but there would be new things to see, do, hear, and experience that would make it a completely fresh adventure.

After I returned from Mexico I decided it was time to start my Rolfing practice, but I still wanted to travel and experience new places. I decided to move to Charleston, South Carolina, since it is one of the closest coastal cities to Missouri. So I loaded everything I owned into my little Escort and headed south with a thousand dollars. Within a couple of weeks I found office space and a place to live. Somehow as soon as I saw this place I knew that I needed to live there, and within about a month I found out why: I met my neighbor Steve Hall.

I had actually noticed him as soon as I moved in, but I was so attracted that I was too shy to make the first move. But once we did meet, we were inseparable. Our days were filled with taking our dogs to the park, baseball games, motorcycle rides, and laughter. I was building my practice and Steve was in school full-time studying criminal justice; we were also both working a couple of side jobs, but in the midst of all this activity our relationship grew. We were married a couple of years later in a beautiful ceremony that we wrote from scratch uniquely to fit us.

As for my practice, working with people one-on-one was easy for me and Rolfing was something I knew and enjoyed. The harder things were selling—going door to door and introducing myself, and of course public speaking. But one by one I looked my fears in the face and found ways to overcome them. My practice was successful and supported me comfortably. As I found ways to grow and strengthen myself, my business grew, and my biggest reward was helping people feel more comfortable in their bodies.

After about four years of living in Charleston, Steve and I decided it was time for a change of scenery and pace. He received a job offer to work for the sheriff's office in Eugene, Oregon, and we accepted it. I spent time closing my practice and wrapping up with my clients, which was sad and challenging, as I had worked with these people quite intensely. And then I packed up and drove across the country to join my husband.

Once in Oregon, and with lots of time to think through what I wanted to do with my life, I decided not to open another practice right away. Feeling closer to being ready to start a family I wanted to find a career that would not require my every waking moment. I decided to study everything I could get my hands on involving real estate. I have read several books and met other people who do real estate investing, which is what I am interested in now. Currently I am studying for my Realtors license so that I can have more access into the market.

I am also very involved with an organization that my mother started, called MorningStar Community—Spiritual Center for Instinctual Living. Our main objective is to honor the simple and sacred. We promote living closer to nature and in tune with ancient wisdom—home birth, home education, home health, and home death. The center is located on beautiful Ozark land. It has a Spiritual Retreat Center, offers Wellness Education (this usually involves one-on-one consultations that help people learn how to stay well and healthy instead of what to do once they are ill), and is the headquarters for MorningStar Yoga (a type of yoga that my mother has developed, which builds on her Vinyasa Yoga training and also incorporates spiritual practices and instinctual living). It also has a fabulous Mission Outreach Program, whose focus is CASA, located in Mexico. CASA is a huge project designed to help the poor, primarily women and children. It includes a hospital run primarily by midwives, a midwifery school, and outreach health and education programs. My mother has volunteered there extensively over the last ten years, usually for several months out of the year, sometimes for the entire year, and many other Community members have also volunteered there. We also send funds and supplies.

As the president and a member of the board I have been working in very close contact with my mother, Sandra MorningStar. Lately, I've mainly been working on legal documentation—our organization has been active for over twenty years, but we are only now putting together the documents to make it a not-for-profit organization, and therefore able to operate under tax-exempt status, which will allow for much greater growth and expansion. I am truly honored to be a part of this organization that has such peace at its core and is able and willing to share a beautiful way of life with others. We have put together a web site with tons of pictures and information, at www.morningstarcommunity.org.

I am also beginning a big new adventure and the grandest journey of my life; Steve and I are expecting our first child in October! I am looking so forward to this new addition to our family! (We already have three dogs.) Being pregnant has been amazing so far. Steve and I are planning a home water birth, and my mother will be our midwife. It is amazing how life works, one little miraculous moment after another.

Looking back on my homeschooling years, what advice do I have for teenagers on a similar path? It is *your* life and future; live it consciously. Study what you love; that is one of the real benefits of unschooling. I believe that we homeschoolers have an advantage in that our minds have been allowed more freedom, and tend more naturally to think outside the box. However, I would also advise seeing if you can spark within yourself a desire to study personal finance. It can help you no matter what your other interests are, and it can enable you to do more of what you dream of. Personal finance does not have to be the drab subject that it often gets made out to be; I have found it quite fascinating and only wish that I would have started learning about it sooner.

For parents, I'd say this: One of the best things that I feel my own parents did, that made me want to study and learn, is that *they* were always studying and learning something that interested them. They did not shove the idea of learning down my throat; in fact, growing up I am not sure I ever even thought about it. I just knew that in my family, whatever you were interested in, you studied to find out more about it and this process added to your fascination. Children learn by example, so find something that you love and start learning about it. *Show* them how to create an exciting and fulfilling life.

Will Steve and I homeschool our own children? As of right now we are undecided. We strongly support home education; however, I think our choice will depend largely on our child's personality. Ideally, I would love to find a specialized alternative school that would fill our children's needs for freedom and self-expression as well as for social interaction and group activity.

But for me, unschooling was an extremely rewarding experience. I have been able to do so many things as a student and as an adult that have been made possible by unschooling. And today, at almost twenty-eight, I feel as much as ever that I am creating my life as I want it to be. In the last few years alone I have traveled to Mexico several times, studied aviation and flown small aircraft, found my husband, and am starting a family. I ran one business successfully and am now starting a second. Studying and learning should not be activities that we do joylessly for twelve years in order to go to college and get a good job and then not have to do anymore. They are processes we can benefit from throughout our whole lives, continually creating and recreating our lives as we want them to be.

Kevin Sellstrom, 16
Wilton, California

What Radios and Bicycles (and everything else) Have to do with my Education

Someone once asked me, "Don't you feel left out by not being in school?" I said to them, "I would feel left out of the world if I were *in* school." In school, I would go crazy being locked inside a building for five days out of every week, having to spend every waking hour thinking about school or doing homework. I couldn't appreciate being told what I had to learn, not to follow my own interests, and that everyone else knew what was best for me.

Because I am homeschooled, I can ride bicycles, talk on ham radio, work on electronics, read books, play the piano, conduct business, and meet other children, teenagers, and adults who have more in common with me than just going to the same school. I can get lost in a science museum for a day, stick my nose in a history book for two days, or spend a week designing experimental antennas for ham radio or learning how to program my computer. I can't justify giving up all of the world's offerings only to let someone else control my life and tell me that it is best for me to sit in a chair for six hours a day while they feed me what they think I should know and divert me away from what they think I shouldn't know. In short, I would feel left out of the gigantic picture of life if I were in school.

Photo by Gary Sellstrom

No recession here

I have my own tractor business, which is a small branch of our family business. With a five-foot mower on our small Massey-Ferguson diesel tractor, I do large mowing jobs for customers in our area. Also, I do a lot of other work such as rototilling, weed-eating, plumbing and irrigation installation and repair, and residential lawn care. Because we live in a rural area, there are a lot of uses for tractors, and I have gotten pretty good at operating them. I charge about twenty dollars per hour for mowing—which seems like a lot, but this cost includes rent, wear and tear on the tractor, and replacement parts. Still, I get a good profit from my jobs, and my customers get a good deal too—most of the adults providing the same service in our area charge about 50 to 150 percent more than I do!

If you have a marketable skill, and have the time and ambition to run a business, then go for it. My claim to fame, and best suggestion on how to start and run a successful business, is to do a good job at a reasonable price, and to be personal. Care about your prospective and current customers; a smile and a little friendly conversation go a long way. My business is not a get-rich-quick scheme. I do this work because I enjoy it; the money is an added benefit.

Another thing that I do both for a little bit of money and for fun is to work as a trap boy at the local gun club. The gun club our family belongs to has an indoor shooting range for practice, and an outdoor trap shooting range. I don't shoot often, and when I do it is usually only rifle and pistol at the indoor range. Most of the time I work the trap machine or run the shooting events the club has every month.

Trap shooting is shooting at moving round clay targets that are thrown up into the air by a trap machine. The trap machine is in a building that is about six feet square, and about three feet tall. Sometimes the buildings are partially underground, and usually they are made of concrete or brick. As a trap boy, my job is to sit in the little building and load the targets, one at a time, onto the machine. When the shooter is ready to shoot, he calls out and another person pushes a button which causes the machine to fire the target. I then load another target. I have been working for the club for about two years, and I am in charge of setting up schedules for the other three trap boys as well.

Also, I have recently been appointed the public relations officer for the club. My duties are to let the public know about the club and what we are doing. I put notices on bulletin boards, send information to other shooting clubs in the valley, and get information to other public places where people will see it. I also write press releases and send them to newspapers, radio stations, and television stations.

In addition to my tractor business and gun club work, I have been offered positions at a Boy Scout summer camp for the third year in a row, as a tractor operator for a farmer, at the local hardware store, and at a bicycle shop. No recession here.

I volunteer all day every Thursday at the school in town for mentally handicapped children. I do this just for the fun of helping out and the reward of seeing them gain something from my work. The whole school has about forty-five students and the class that I work in has about twelve students.

My work generally consists of helping the teachers when the class breaks up into small groups to work on reading, math, handwriting skills, etc. I also work with one or two kids at a time on the computers, helping them with learning games and a few other programs. Many of the kids are very good at running the computers—some of them are better than I am with the Apple computers they use. Another thing I do is work with the kids using hammers and nails to practice pounding nails into wood, and building simple forms.

The biggest thing I do there, next to helping the teachers, is to be a friend or "buddy" to the kids, most of whom are between ten and thirteen years old. The first thing several kids do when they get to school on Thursday mornings is to make sure that I am there. With the kids, I eat lunch, play basketball, ride bicycles, do chalk drawings on the sidewalks, and play other games at recess. I also help with the school swimming program in the spring, summer, and fall. I enjoy working with both the kids and teachers. The friendships I have with all of them, and seeing the kids learn something valuable, make it worthwhile.

Photo by Twyla Rowe

Through my work at the school, I have become friends with many of the teachers, some of whom also tutor students who have been expelled from regular school or who have problems and can't go to school. I am encouraged and supported by the teachers one hundred percent in my homeschooling adventures. I have also met several other teenagers, both homeschooled and from the local high school, who work there once in a while. The high school has a program for students interested in teaching—they can spend a half day at the school and see what goes on (one time, not every week). I have been volunteering there for about three years now. If I went to a public school I would not be able to spend so much time there because it would "take away from my education."

Homeschoolers have many advantages when it comes to finding a job and fitting into society and the real world. Because they have such freedoms in choosing what they want to learn, they can start early to develop skills that will help them get work when they are ready. Through working and volunteering at different jobs, homeschoolers can learn a lot about finding jobs and they can determine what kind of work they want to do. For instance, I worked as an assistant for a local farmer for about two years. The farmer produced organically grown fruits and vegetables and freshwater fish and sold them directly to the public. I did many jobs on the farm, including picking produce, helping seine fish, and irrigating fields. I was also involved in direct relations with the customers including sales and answering the phone. From this work, I learned a lot about organic farming, crop management, and the use of different farm utensils. So, homeschoolers have a big advantage when it comes to finding work because they often have prior experience in the field. Homeschoolers are also more interested in what they are doing because they have had a chance to explore and knowledgeably choose what they want to do.

Many employers realize that homeschoolers, because of their diverse backgrounds, have a superior education to some publicly schooled job applicants. Homeschoolers also have the resourcefulness and creativity to make uncommon ideas work to make money, either for their employers or directly for themselves. Finally, homeschoolers are more likely to have the initiative to start their own businesses or to find a way to make a living without relying on employers.

School, homeschool, and beyond

When I was in kindergarten, I put up with the program. When I was in first grade, I had a good teacher and enjoyed school most of the time. Then we moved and I was put into a second grade class at a public school that, at the time, happened to be rated one of the top schools in California. I had a good teacher who nevertheless was restrained by having to teach a class of thirty-five children everything the state prescribed, nothing more, nothing less: basic math and reading, the four food groups, and Columbus.

In third grade I was bored to death in the same top-of-the-line school. My class covered only twelve pages of our English textbooks, and we did nothing else to compensate for what we didn't know or hadn't learned (although this may have been more good than bad). By mid-year, working at my own pace, I had completed most of the math tests. And I had read most of the little sixty-page books in our fancy reading set (we were given fifteen minutes per day for this).

I was also regularly picked by our two teachers as one of the "secret three" students. The teachers picked three students each week who had turned in their homework and best put up with the boredom of school, and these students were rewarded for their tolerance. (The class was not told who the secret three were until the end of the week, hence the term "secret.") Getting picked got us privileges to a cup of popcorn, listening to a song on the record player, ten minutes of "instructional" time using the Big Track toy during class, or other items of that sort. I redeemed very few of these privileges because most of them were just as boring and unappealing as the rest of school.

Despite all of my school-induced qualities, I was not in the GATE (Gifted and Talented Education) program. At the end of the year I passed the state tests well but had not learned much that I wanted to learn. My parents were very displeased with school, and so was I. So we decided to quit. That fall I got involved in our school district's Independent Study Program, which was called Community School, and that was the start of my homeschooling life.

In the Independent Study Program (ISP) we were allowed a lot of freedom to do as we pleased. Also, we were allowed and encouraged to participate in any school district functions we wanted to. We met with a para-professional once a week who helped us if we had questions and to whom we turned in our weekly time sheets. These time sheets were an estimate of how we used the twenty hours per week of "learning time" that the state required. We were also given the opportunity to use *any* of the district's textbooks that we wanted to, based not on age but on what we knew and what we wanted to learn. For example, my brother used math books several grade levels above his age group. However, we were not forced to use any of these books if we didn't want to. For example, we were free to use a math, history, science and handwriting book— but also free to say no to the spelling, English, or reading book.

It was also from the director of this program that I learned a very important truth about public school textbooks: They all provide essentially the same information. The biggest difference between a second grade and a sixth grade science book is that each year they add more words and make some of the words longer to make you think that what you are reading is in some way better or more complicated than what you read last year.

While we were in the ISP we also began to get involved in a cornucopia of other activities unique to homeschooling. When I was in school, field trips tended to be generally boring and uninteresting—and when we did go on a trip that had the potential to be interesting, we were usually so rushed for time that we didn't see or accomplish much at all. For example, on a trip to the state Indian museum we would be given ten minutes and then we would hear, "Okay, kids, time's up—It's time to hurry up and get back on the bus so we can get back to school," and so it would become just as boring as any other field trip.

In the ISP, we didn't limit ourselves to the usual places public school kids went. (And we still don't.) We went on field trips to both of the local airports, banks, libraries, the sheriff's office, television stations, the power company, and the County Office of Education. We took a tour through the Folsom Dam and power generating station. We visited the nearby nuclear power plant

(Rancho Seco) when it was still generating electricity.

When I say "field trip," I am generally talking about a much different type of trip than school kids are accustomed to. When we go on field trips, we are not a large group of kids. Rather, there are usually about ten or fifteen kids in a group and it is not uncommon for just our family or just two or three homeschool/unschool families to go on a trip together. This way, we get a more personalized tour and it makes it easier for the tour guide to tell us what we are interested in hearing about. We also can get to know the guide better. And we are not as pushed for time because there are so few people and we can stay until we are ready to go, instead of until the *teachers* are ready to go.

When we started homeschooling, we went on trips because we *wanted* to go and were interested in what we were going to be seeing. We weren't there because some teacher thought we would all enjoy seeing an exhibit displaying art by some unknown artist who had died two years ago. Because we wanted to be there, our attitudes and behavior were very different from those of public school kids. We weren't just a bunch of kids chattering to each other and not listening to the leader. We got to see a lot more on field trips than the average school kid does.

After we had been in the ISP for about a year, we moved from one county to another. Because the county we moved to would not transfer their ADA money (the money the school district gets from the state for having a student in its district) back to our old district, we had no option but to quit our old ISP. Our new district didn't have an Independent Study Program, but we were able to get a transfer to another local district, in the same county, that did. In this ISP, they handed out regular school textbooks and lots of ditto sheets, based on how old we were. It was boring and wasn't working well, so we quit. That was when we began the excitement of homeschooling entirely on our own.

(You can see from my experiences that some California school districts' ISP's are better than others. Of the two programs I just mentioned, the better one was in a relatively small district with fewer students and staff and presumably less money. The other district had a lot of students, a lot of staff, and much more money. The only significant difference between one ISP and another is the administration. Some ISP administrators and their staff believe that a good job can be done if the students are allowed to join in the planning and steering of their own educations and that the students need only someone to oversee them and to be available to provide information or assistance when students ask for it. Meanwhile, other ISP authorities believe that their students should use regular public school curriculum and lesson plans in a schoollike environment to learn "properly."

If a person wants to work through an ISP and all that is available is the latter kind, I certainly wouldn't recommend it. If, on the other hand, a student has access to a less structured, more independent ISP, it certainly is a good place to start homeschooling. Some ISP's give a lot of freedom for people to do what they want to and for most people this is certainly better than normal public schools.)

Many homeschoolers in California get by without doing *anything* to let the state know what they are doing, but many others do like we do now, determining that their home will be a private school and filing a private school affidavit. Our school's name is Kevin Lawrence Union School. (We combined my name with my brother's middle name and added "Union School.") In our "school," my dad is the principal (in addition to his regular job working on radio and communications equipment for a local power company). My mom is the "teacher," and we have two students, my younger brother and myself. These positions as "teacher" and "principal" are more to please the state than anything else and are not "principal" and "teacher" in the traditional school sense of the word. My parents actually do little as far as teaching me goes, although along with many other people, they are quite involved in my education.

Most of what my parents (and other people) do toward my education is to help me gain information in any area that interests me and in which they can help. My parents help me by transporting me places, directing me to where I can find answers to my questions, and discussing or answering my questions. Other people in the community help me, too, by giving me information or just showing me a new way to do something. You can learn a great deal from people who aren't necessarily teachers. I learn from radio operators, neighbors, the people I work with at the school for handicapped students, my employers, and many other people I meet.

As far as the law is concerned, a private school in California is not required to have certified teachers as in a public school, but if the school wants teachers to be certified that is their option. (My mom is not a certified teacher.) The law also does not require us to take tests or to have strict class schedules. Private schools can do just about whatever they want to when it comes to class schedules and most other things.

Essentially, all the California state law requires is three things. We have to keep a record of all students attending the school (my brother and myself) and days that they are present (every school day that we decide is a school day). We have to keep a record of the courses offered by the school (English, math, science, social science, arts, health, P.E., other language, vocational ed, and driver's ed). The last requirement is that a record of the names, addresses, and qualifications of all the faculty members be kept and that all of these records be accessible to applicable officials should they happen to ask (which is rare in California since the officials have better things to do). The law also says that you have to be in school at least four hours per school day, but it doesn't say that you can't spend that time visiting the library or going on a nature walk, or that it has to be in a school building. In other words they don't care how or where you spend your time just as long as you spend it learning something.

As far as courses go, they don't say what a course consists of, so this is left up to our imagination. For example, if you go to the library twice a week, get a stack of classic novels, and read them, you have a literature class. When they say "course," they mean a general area that fits under a certain title, such as English, math, or science. These are some of the ways that we handle the not-so-difficult, but intimidating, legal aspect of homeschooling.

For a few years after we started homeschooling by ourselves, I took the Stanford Achievement Tests, but all they told us was that I had the academic knowledge equal to someone who had graduated from high school. At that time, I would have been in sixth or seventh grade in a public school. Not very helpful. The last standardized test I took was the California High School Proficiency Exam (CHSPE). I took this a year ago and passed easily.

The CHSPE is a test given by the State of California for high school students in or above the second semester of tenth grade, as a way to get out of high school before you are eighteen. The certificate received for passing the CHSPE is the legal equivalent of a high school diploma and all businesses, schools, etc. subject to California law must accept it. The exam consists of two short essays (about one or two paragraphs each) and two hundred multiple choice questions covering math, reading comprehension, and writing. You are given twenty minutes apiece to write the essays and three hours and twenty minutes to do the multiple choice questions. Passing the CHSPE exam gives school students a legal way to get out of school with the equivalent of a high school diploma at age sixteen. But I took the exam when I was fourteen, by filling the grade requirement instead of the age requirement. Often, school kids use this exam as a way to get a job or do other worthwhile things instead of going to school. The CHSPE also makes it easier to get into college at a younger age. When people ask you what you are doing out of school you can simply tell them that you have graduated.

I found out about this exam a week and a half before it was given, and I had very little time to prepare. But the preparation was not difficult. All I did was get study guides from the library (Barron's and Arco publish them and they are very helpful). I tried the practice tests in them to get an idea of what kind of answers they were looking for in the exam. The biggest difficulty I had with the exam was not choosing the correct answer but choosing *which* of the correct answers they wanted.

(One thing I don't like about standardized tests, as well as tests in general, is that you have to give the answer that the test writer is looking for, even though there may be more than one applicable answer or solution. I think tests are not necessarily as good a representation of academic knowledge as they are of judgment—not of what answer is best, but of what answer the test writer is looking for.)

Academics at Kevin Lawrence Union School

Now I'll try to tell you about my life as a homeschooler and some of the ways that I spend my four hours per day of "learning time." As far as academics go, I spend at least five hours per week reading, working on math, and doing other traditional academic subjects. However, I have sometimes been known to spend upwards of five hours per day studying these things, which translates into about twenty-five hours per week.

The same freedoms that I have in many other areas, I also have in deciding what I want to study. I don't have a "lesson plan." When I see a book lying on a table or I hear of a subject that strikes me as interesting, I pick up a book and read about that subject until I am satisfied. For instance, the other day, I was looking at a series called the *Wonder Books*. I saw one book that looked interesting, entitled *Great Inventors and Their Inventions*. This book and most of its series were published in the 1930s and 40s but the information is still good, just not up to date. (They make great history books.)

Anyway, this book talked about some of the great inventions from the safety pin of old, to the "recently developed" zipper. It was very interesting, since it talked about things that, at the time, were just being developed, but that we now either take for granted or that never were appreciated by the public and therefore never developed further. I sat down and read until lunch. One thing I read about, for instance, was Polaroid glass. Polaroid glass was developed in the 1930s and consists of spreading microscopic, organic, polarizing crystals on a very thin layer of plastic, and sandwiching this layer of plastic and crystals between two layers of glass. Polarizing glass allows some light to go through but other light can't. This technology is currently used in sunglasses, in photographic lenses, and for many other purposes.

I read both fiction and non-fiction. In fiction I like to read survival stories, especially those based in the outdoors, some mystery stories, and some novels (but I don't read gory grocery store novels). I also like to read classical literature including work by Charles Dickens, Samuel Clemens (Mark Twain), and Jonathan Swift. I do have a literature textbook, but I read it only for the literature contained in it; I don't answer the questions or write the poems that they want unless I choose to.

I read non-fiction about the outdoors, camping, and bicycling, and I also read about more "academic" subjects such as Native Americans, U.S. history, world history, and modern history. I read my dad's college geology books because I am interested in geology. I use the encyclopedia to get information on a particular subject. And I am currently reading an unabridged copy of Charles Darwin's *Origin of Species* that I got from my aunt.

I also use library books to learn about things. If I want to know why something did or did not work, or how to revive plants and trees after they have been burned by a grass fire, the library has something to help answer my questions. To name an example, when my dad, brother, and I were building the stainless steel racks for our bikes, we needed to know if stainless could be welded with our equipment. I went to the library and got a book on welding (this was before I took a welding class at the community college) and looked it up. I determined that it couldn't be welded, but it could be bonded with brass, which is called brazing.

Another example: After our family's recent trip to the Grand Canyon, Zion Canyon, and surrounding area, including hikes into Anasazi cliff dwellings, we went to the library. I wanted to know more about the Anasazi, Hopi, and Navajo groups of Native Americans that lived in the area, and I found several books that told me more than I could learn in the few days I was actually there. I wanted to know this information for no particular reason other than to satisfy my interest.

If the card catalog or computer reference doesn't have what I need, I ask the reference librarian. Easy enough. For example, when I was looking for a series of fictional mystery books written by a ham radio operator and involving ham radio, I didn't know the titles or author so I asked the librarian for help. The librarian directed me to the ham magazines, where I found an advertisement for the books. I didn't find the books themselves at that library, but I did find enough information to look them up at another library that did have one of them.

There are many other good sources for learning materials that are too good to be passed up—like TV. For instance, I just watched a great series on the history of computers, entitled *The Machine that Changed the World*. This and many other fine programs are available free for the watching on public television. Other networks and independent stations shouldn't be forgotten, though. On a local independent station, I recently saw a program about the life of the man who pioneered moving photography, otherwise known as "movies." It was well written and seemed to reasonably and accurately portray his life.

The main textbook I use regularly is a Saxon *Algebra 1* book. This book happens to be a teacher's book, but the only difference between it and the regular student book is that they add a supplement in the back with most of the answers. If you think that this would make it easy to "cheat," you are right. School teaches kids that the answers to questions are supposed to be "Top Secret." They aren't. I look at the answers often when I am having trouble or if I am unsure about what I am doing. It helps me to know the answer right away instead of when the teacher can check it. If I am unsure, I often do a problem and then look at the correct answer to check myself. If my answer is right, then I know how to do the next one. If it is wrong, I try to figure out how they came up with the correct answer. In homeschool/unschool, there is not a need to cheat—nothing is proven by it, and you don't have to pass a test or earn a grade. Instead, the object is to learn what's important, and retain this knowledge. Sometimes, you gain more understanding by looking at the answers while you are studying.

I probably don't do as much math in the traditional sense of the word as a public school student, but what I do has more meaning. I am studying algebra, and I consistently use all kinds of math in many applications. Because I can extend my interests into many areas and go as far as I want to with them, I get into areas that rely heavily on math. Consequently, I use math a lot. I use math and algebra for finding lengths and specifications for the design and construction of radio antennas. I use math to establish prices and determine how much to charge customers for the services rendered in my tractor business. While earning the surveying merit badge in Boy Scouts, I used trigonometry to determine distances. What I know, I use. Because I use what I learn and I determine what I need to learn in the first place, I feel that my knowledge of math is superior to what kids learn in the time they spend in a math classroom each day at school.

College

Burning steel with an oxyacetylene cutting torch   *Photo by Gary Sellstrom*

The CHSPE helped me get into a local community college (Cosumnes River College) where I am taking a course in welding on Tuesday nights and totally enjoying it. I chose welding both because it was something I was interested in and because it was something I could relate to since we have an oxyacetylene welding set at home. I have used skills I learned in the class to build a bicycle work-stand and to make and repair many things, from car and bike parts to amateur radio antenna mounts.

I started college because it happens to be close to where I live, and it has a lot of good courses on many subjects (as do many other community colleges) for a reasonable price. (CRC is six dollars per credit and most courses are two to four credits.) It is not as hard as you may think to get into college; some are easier than others to get into, but all CRC asked for was a high school transcript. We made a transcript on the computer that consisted of a chart with all of the "courses" that I took in high school and a grade representing how I thought I did in each area. I chose the grades myself (and I didn't give myself all A's). We made an appointment to see a counselor and they didn't even look at the transcript.

Another thing I found that helps get you enrolled more easily is to look through their catalog and find a class that you are interested in that is not likely to be very full. The college will be more concerned about filling the class than with doubting your qualifications. Once you have been there for one semester it is easier to get back in for the next semester. It is also worth the money to buy a catalog when you anticipate starting, not only for the class information in it, but also for the massive amounts of other very helpful general information.

One other bit of information for anyone trying to get started in college is that the counselors and much of the college's printed information make it seem imperative that you take their assessment tests in math and English. But this is not the case. My welding teacher brought up a good point: The counselors "forget" to tell you that these tests are not required for all classes (as they imply) but only if you intend to enter a math or English class. Even then, they often don't care unless you have done poorly in past classes.

Another way to get into a community college is by concurrent enrollment. Concurrent enrollment is a term for going to high school (or homeschooling) and attending college at the same time. This is also a way to take classes at a community college and get credits when you have not yet legally graduated from high school. I did this my first semester at CRC because I was not old enough to have legally graduated from high school, even though I had passed the CHSPE.

If you are as apprehensive as I was when I started college, it might help to start with only one class for the first semester and to find someone else who has been through that class and talk to them about what to expect. Once you get started it won't be hard. I talked to a friend who had taken the welding class the semester before I did and he said that it was not a hard class and that the instructor was easy to work with. He was right. Also, if you have a friend who is enrolled in a class that you are interested in, it might help to sign up for that class and make arrangements to study or practice together. I had several friends whom I met after the class had started who were having difficulties and triumphs similar to my own. We talked often and compared notes on our projects. College is not really worth wasting much nervousness on, and it can actually be fun.

Living is learning

One thing that is drastically different between homeschool and public school is that in homeschool you have the time to follow your interests. You aren't limited by class schedules or what the teacher wants you to learn. The way we homeschool, what is traditionally thought of as "life" and what is commonly considered "education" or "learning" are tightly interlaced. Homeschoolers learn (sometimes unconsciously) from everything they do, from employment opportunities to conversations. For example, one day I met some people who have lived in our neighborhood for a long time, and I talked with them about what it used to be like twenty years ago when there were not any roads or schools around. I learned a lot about our local history from this friendly conversation.

I don't think homeschoolers are unique; all people have this ability to learn while living. But because of the many freedoms and possibilities that homeschooling offers, it is much easier for widespread learning to happen in a homeschool environment. Homeschoolers have the time and energy to expand their interests so that they naturally become academically fulfilling. Some of the ongoing "non-academic" things I learn from—besides my jobs—are playing the piano, photography, Boy Scouts, ham radio, computers, bicycling, and beginning to drive.

I enjoy playing the piano and I have been taking lessons for about three years. I have played at several recitals and church services, and twice in piano festivals put on by a local church. Each festival had around twenty pianos and over thirty players who all worked together to put on a one-hour program. I practice from one to two hours a day, and I have a half hour lesson each week.

Another of my hobbies is photography. I take a lot of slides of the places we go and I've put together slide shows of several trips including Death Valley, the Grand Canyon, Great Basin National Park, Zion National Park, and numerous Boy Scout excursions. I would like to get the facilities and learn how to develop my own film at home but I don't have the space or the supplies required to do this—so I hope to take a class at the community college that will cover this material. I once used my dad's camera with a telephoto lens to take a series of prints of a baby gosling from the time it poked through its egg until it climbed completely out of its shell.

I am the Senior Patrol Leader of our small Boy Scout troop in the country. We have scouts from ages eleven to sixteen, and do many different activities from camping and backpacking to bicycling and being the colorguard in local parades. Scouting is one way for kids (especially homeschoolers) to meet and do things with other people. Even if you are not worried about that, it is still a fun way to learn new things.

Photo by Gary Sellstrom

Ham Radio

I am a licensed Amateur Radio Operator and actively involved in our local ham radio club. Ham radio operators are basically hobbyists who experiment with radio equipment and have fun with it. When they are needed, however, they volunteer their services willingly for emergencies, natural disasters, and public service. They are not allowed and do not expect any reimbursement. I got started in ham radio because my dad has had his license for over thirty-five years and I used to go to a lot of ham radio functions with him. (My grandfather had an Amateur Radio License for many years as well.) When I was twelve, we went to a ham swap meet. I saw the table of a local club that was offering classes for people to get a ham license. I signed up along with my mom and we took the class together. I passed and got my license, but my mom didn't so she took it again later with my brother and they both passed. Now our whole family uses ham radio to keep in touch with each other since we all have licenses.

I have used ham radio to provide communications for local marathons and other events. I also run our radio club's Thursday night net (short for network) on a regular basis. This consists of calling off the list of people who regularly check into the net (roll call, more or less), and directing the activity on the frequency for approximately forty-five minutes. (The main purpose of this net is to provide a meeting place on the air for local amateurs, and a place to ask or answer questions about amateur radio. The net is also a way for club members to gain experience in operating as net control in public service and emergency situations. I also answer questions on many aspects of ham radio. I have put on demonstrations at several homeschooling conferences and met many new people that way.)

One event I helped with was a local charity marathon in nearby Clarksburg, where I provided communications from a refreshments station for the runners. I relayed information such as when the first runner passed our station and when we needed more water, and I called in for a van when a runner collapsed near our station. I also helped to provide communication for another local race that is billed as "the world's oldest triathlon."

Most of the time, though, I just talk to other people for the fun of chit-chatting with new people and old friends. I have become acquainted with many friends on the radio and now I know them by voice—so that when I turn my radio on and hear someone talking, I often know immediately who it is. I have also met many of my radio friends in person. One interesting person that I met after talking to him on the air is an old man named Joe. I had heard him on the air and talked to him several times in the past two years—about many things such as education, airplanes, how his new radio works, and how he is replacing his burned areas of lawn that didn't get enough

Photo by Robert Menzies

Kevin provides radio communication for Eppie's Great Race

water—but I didn't get to see him in person until about six months ago. Joe is legally blind and walks with a cane, but he gets around very well. When I was talking to him the other day he mentioned that he has been involved in Amateur Radio since 1920 and that he got his license when he was ten years old!

Ham radio is also a great way to learn about geography, especially that of unknown, hard-to-reach areas of the earth. I have talked to people in many parts of the world that aren't even mentioned in most school geography classes. Sometimes our conversations last a long time, and sometimes atmospheric conditions cause our contacts to be cut short. Whatever the case may be, after a conversation it is always interesting to look at the world map and understand exactly where that person is in relation to other parts of the world and in relation to me.

I have talked to Hiro in Japan several times, about all kinds of things from weather to radio phenomenon and more. Hiro lives in Fukui City, a small city on the coast of the Japan Sea. I talked to him at eight o'clock at night and he was on a break for lunch, eating while he talked!

Another interesting conversation I had one afternoon was with a man named Ken on Kwajalein Island (pronounced Qua-ja-lean) in the Western Pacific Ocean. Ken was also on a lunch break while I talked to him in my early afternoon. He had walked over to his club's radio station for a short conversation on the radio and I happened to catch him. In talking to him I found out that he walked to work every day, that he had a bicycle, and that his bicycle was his primary means of transportation other than walking. We also talked about the weather and the address to send a QSL card (confirming contact between two stations). He said that his island is about three and a half miles long and about half a mile wide. I found out later from his QSL card that the average elevation on the island is about six feet and the average temperature is about eighty-two degrees Fahrenheit—and varies only by about two degrees year-round! They get about 105 inches of precipitation per year. The total area of the island is less than two square miles, and the only automobiles allowed are a handful of U.S. military vehicles.

I have talked to many other rare parts of the world too. Following is just a short list of some of my favorite contacts. I have talked to hams in:

- Russia, including the New Siberian Islands, and Sakhalin Island
- many islands and countries in the South-Western Pacific, including the Cook Islands, and several of the islands that surround New Zealand
- the Marshall Islands, including Raratonga Atoll and Kwajalein Atoll
- Australia and New Zealand
- China and Japan
- Canada and all over the USA.

As I hope you can see, ham radio is more than just a hobby; it is a valuable part of my education. And it is another place where a non-academic interest has crossed over to become an integral part of my education. Numerous educational facilities across the country are now realizing the possibilities of ham radio and are setting up ham radio classes and stations on their campuses.

Also, ham radio is another part of my life that is improved by homeschooling because I can get on and talk to people during the day, not just in the evenings after school. The best way for someone to find out about ham radio and get a license is to find another operator and talk to them, or call a local radio shop. Or, you can write to the American Radio Relay League at 225 Main Street, Newington, Connecticut, 06111.

I am also entering into a new and exciting combination of interests, Packet Radio. Packet radio is a combination of computers and Amateur Radio, similar to modem operation. It involves the use of a terminal—or computer emulating a terminal—and a Terminal Node Controller. The TNC does much the same thing that a modem does but it transmits data over the radio instead of telephone lines. Users can store and retrieve messages in Packet Bulletin Board Systems (PBBS) and in packet mailboxes, and they can talk directly through computers to other people across the county or across the country. You can find out about Packet Radio opportunities near you by contacting the American Radio Relay League, address above.

Computer

Computers are a great invention because you can always learn something new about them. I typed this essay on a word processor on our Amiga computer, and I have learned enough to type our homeschool support group's newsletter—but that is barely the tip of the proverbial iceberg of what there is to know. I am a member of the local Amiga computer club, and in times of severe catastrophe I have talked to many people from the club in an effort to solve problems.

For example, when I was cleaning up and organizing the display and installing programs on our new hard disk, something else apparently got moved accidentally, and when we went to start up the computer next time, it wouldn't work. By talking to another member of the club over the phone, I was able to get an idea of what I had done and to boot the Workbench program and reformat and install the hard disk so that it would run again. The person I talked to gave me some tips on how to avoid this problem and what to do if it occurred again. (It did recur, once, and I solved it without a hitch.) This is an example of how one person can learn from another without having to go to school or involve a special teacher. I've learned a lot about our computer by reading books and talking to other users; I didn't learn any of my computer knowledge from a "computer teacher."

I am so busy with other things that I don't have time to get deeply involved in the computer club, but even so I have met helpful people. The computer is an important part of my life especially because I am the only one in the family who has a working knowledge of this particular computer. My mom is good with the older C128 that we got several years ago, and now I am teaching her what she needs to know to be familiar with this new computer so that eventually she will be able to do what she wants without help from me.

Bicycling

Bicycling is another of my favorite hobbies. I have a mountain bike and a road bike and I am very involved in keeping them maintained. I also enjoy riding them. Because I am homeschooled I have time to work on my bike during the day, and to ride in the early morning and afternoon. Instead of riding to school I regularly ride to Scout meetings and to get the mail at the post office (I take an off-road shortcut). Bicycle riding—one of the best sports for endurance and general fitness—tends to be much of my exercise as I obviously don't have a "P.E." class.

It is difficult for homeschoolers to get into some competitive sports. I say *difficult* because it is not *impossible*. If it is really imperative that you get into school-type competitive sports, there are ways to get into regular school programs. Also, community or local teams can fulfill your sports craving. Like I said, I prefer bicycling to sports, but I don't speak for everyone.

Maintenance—Bikes, Tractors, Cars

I taught myself bicycle repair; I have totally rebuilt several bikes and do my own twice a year. I can patch tires relatively fast, and taught myself how to true wheels to near-perfection. I have never taken my bike to a shop to have it serviced and when I worked at Boy Scout summer camp last year, I was asked to maintain the mountain bikes and gear that were borrowed for a week-long bike trek.

The trick to bike maintenance is to remember that everything on a bike does something important (if it doesn't then it doesn't need to be there), and once you determine *what* a part does, you can determine *how* it does it. Instruction manuals and books from the library are good for learning bike repair; some are better than others.* I would like to get into bicycle touring but it is expensive to buy the gear required for this hobby if you buy it commercially. I can make most of the necessary gear, though. For instance, we made a pair of racks from

---

* An excellent resource is *Anybody's Bike Book*, by Tom Cuthbertson (Ten Speed Press, frequently updated). The theory behind this book is "If you can ride it you can fix it," and it lives up to that by giving very clear and thorough information.

stainless steel tubing and aluminum plate that are just as strong and stiff as any commercial rack and nearly as light.

I am actively involved in maintaining our cars, tractor and equipment as well my bicycles. I help friends in the care and repair of their bikes as well. And I spend time on other, less complicated maintenance projects. For instance, I spent a total of about two work days over a three week period, contacting people to try to find fuel filters for our thirty-year-old tractor. Many people who were supposed to know about tractor parts knew less about this tractor and these common filters than I did. So I found out that I needed standard filters and I ended up cross referencing them in a filter book and ordering them from a local automotive parts store. I also spend time trying to find parts for bicycles, cars, radios, computers, miscellaneous electronic equipment, and a whole slew of other things.

Driver's Training and the Homeschooler

I have a student driver's license and I'm practicing to get my regular license. A homeschooler has the same driving privileges as any other person the same age. It just might mean that you have to get the forms and fill them out yourself instead of the school doing everything for you. In California you can get the forms and sample tests the same way any other private school would—by ordering them through the Department of Motor Vehicles. You can ask your parents or other reliable adult(s) to be your driver's ed teacher(s), or go to a private driving school. In many of our local school districts the schools are not providing driver's training (behind the wheel) anymore so public school students are having to go to private sources to get their licenses anyway.

The only disadvantage of not being in a school is that you have to call the DMV yourself. Tell them that you are with a private school and that you want the forms and information needed to provide driver's training to your students. They will probably ask how many students you expect to take driver's ed this school year. If you are the only one, then you will obviously only need materials for one or two students—perhaps several homeschooled/unschooled students can study together. The forms are easy to fill out, and as soon as that's done you can start driving with your "instructor."

In addition to driver's ed books put out by the state, you can order books from many curriculum companies. We ordered used public-school-type books, and in some cases they were more helpful than the state books. The state book, though, is much shorter and to the point. Either one will help a lot. As it says in the *California Driver Handbook*, "You may be a little nervous about getting your license. Relax, you have a lot going for you."

Friends: quality, not quantity

The next thing that I have to say is in response to the always-asked question, "But how do you get a social life without school?" I get along just fine without school. I have friends in my welding class, at the school where I work, in Scouts, from the school that I used to go to, and more. Too many to count. School doesn't make friends *for* you or provide you with a social life. All it does is to surround you with several hundred to several thousand people who are the same age as you. With this many people, it is very likely that you will meet a few who share something in common with you, but real friends are more than just people who have lockers next to each other. A good social life requires more than knowing the names of a few hundred people that you pass in the halls each day while rushing to your next class. As they say, quality is better than quantity; a few really good friends are better than a lot of friends who will forget about you a few minutes after they have talked to you. And school teaches you that it is best to associate only with people your own age. Is this the case in the real world, among real people? A friend of mine said, when she was interviewed on the subject of homeschooling by a newspaper, "How often do you go up to a person and say, 'I am forty-two, are you forty-two? If you aren't then I can't talk to you'?"

I have many friends in our ham radio club and recently I was asked if I wanted to be nominated for the board of directors to fill a vacated position. (I had to say no because I am too busy with all of my other activities.) There are many homeschool kids that I am friends with, some of whom I see regularly. I am also involved in our church youth group and have many friends there as well. Many of my friends happen to go to public school, but this isn't a problem. Many of them wish they could do what I do instead of school.

One problem I do have is that I live in the country. Wilton is about fifteen miles from the town of Elk Grove, and about thirty-five miles from the city of Sacramento. This makes it a little bit difficult to see a lot of people regularly but I do nevertheless manage to meet plenty of people from all sorts of different lifestyles. Unfortunately there are not a lot of other teenagers living in this area (at the moment, I can only think of five teenagers that live within a four mile radius of me).

About dances and proms, I wouldn't go to dances even if I was in school! Some homeschoolers may miss dances and parties, but it isn't hard to get into school dances or community dances. On the same order, nobody says that you can't have a party or go to parties with your friends and do the same things as any public school kids would do at parties. I am not the type that needs to dance or attend rowdy parties, but like I said earlier, I don't speak for everyone, and if you want to dance and party, go right ahead.

People seem to put more emphasis on the socialization part of school than on the learning part of school. I thought the main purpose of school was for you to learn how to survive in the big world. If school is mainly for kids to get along and make friends with everyone else their age, then they would be better off to make school a year-long party with no curriculum and no requirements to learn anything. When that's over, let kids get out and get involved in the world and learn what they need to know without everyone else butting in. This may not be the best alternative to our current dilemma but is it the worst? It would sure save the government a lot of money that could be better used to solve our environmental problems, or pay off our national debt, or both.

***

I believe that the early settlers of America had a good program without compulsory schooling. People did work they enjoyed doing and made a good living and if they needed to know math or reading then they learned what they needed. Their minds weren't cluttered by things that they didn't need to know and they put what they did know to good use. In those days kids weren't stuck in a building for twelve or more years of their lives to make them "smart." Instead they were out getting along with real people of all ages, and learning what *they* needed to know. Kids were apprentices to blacksmiths, or sewed dresses for a seamstress, or sold supplies at the general store, or whatever the case might have been. They didn't need school to learn how to live and they weren't all poor farm people, either. Abraham Lincoln didn't go to school and yet he was elected to the highest office in the United States Government.

In case you already knew that, here are some other people who got along just fine without traditional school: Thomas Edison was only in school for about three months. Orville and Wilbur Wright never got far in high school because they were more interested in working on other things; they changed the world forever with their work on bicycles and powered airplane flight. Benjamin Franklin had only six months of formal schooling but if it weren't for him the United States probably wouldn't be the same. Brigham Young was in school for only eleven days. Later he led the Mormons west, and formed over two hundred towns, cities, and villages on the way. The list goes on and on and on. Chances are you, too, know of someone who didn't go to school but turned out fine.

Photo by Chris McParland

Kevin volunteers with Project RIDE, which seeks to improve the physical, emotional, and social well-being of special needs kids through horseback riding.

Kevin Sellstrom
Elk Grove, California

Things Change

Wow, here I sit in the midst of Montana, enjoying a brief vacation and attempting to recount nearly twelve years of change, consistency, experiences, and opportunities. I've been offered many jobs, taken a few, made many mistakes, learned more than I thought I ever would, learned that I will never know everything, become an Eagle Scout, got married, bought a house, and frequently questioned "why." I am now a school bus driver, and still attending college, but this time in the quest for a teaching credential in special education. My wife, Liz, is a recently graduated anthropologist, searching for the perfect job in a field she loves. We live with two orange cats in a small cottage built in 1940 in the historic section of Elk Grove, California. Life is hectic but good.

If you've read our previous essays already, you are probably expecting to find a group of young CEO's, leading scientists, and wildly successful entrepreneurs. I am not quite there yet...but life is pretty nice anyway.

Things Change

Shortly after writing for *Real Lives*, I was offered a part-time job by a friend of a friend in the school district—it seems that the news of my work with the kids at Jessie Baker School had preceded me. I was asked to coach high-school-aged special needs students on job skills. Soon after I began, I was hired to work full-time at Jessie Baker with the students I'd been volunteering with—and thus at seventeen I became the school district's young-est regular employee. I spent almost seven years there, during which time I decided that helping others to learn and grow was my desire, and that I espe-cially enjoyed working with developmentally delayed kids. I had begun a path toward a welding and industrial technology degree, but changed course, and am now working toward a teaching credential.

During the time I worked at Jessie Baker, I also became more deeply involved as a volunteer with Project RIDE, a therapeutic horseback riding pro-gram I got involved with around the time I wrote my first essay. As the program grew I was asked to fill a seat on the Board of Directors. I was eighteen and had very little experience in the management end of things but with a homeschooler's background in problem solving and learning-as-needed, I quickly acquired the skills and information necessary to help oversee the operation of this rapidly growing non-profit corporation.

When Project RIDE built a huge indoor riding facility and began sta-bling animals overnight during the winter of 1994-1995, I was again asked to help out by keeping an eye on the animals and facility.

Jumping at the opportunity to move out on my own and try something new, I moved into town and into a new turn in life. As we learned of the incred-ible demands of operating and maintaining a 34,000 square foot facility, we began to formalize the corporation and its needs. As these needs grew, I often stepped in to fill them, eventually defining and then filling the position of Facil-ity Manager as well as Caretaker. In these volunteer positions I spent less time walking in lessons, and more time (thirty to forty hours per week) cleaning, caring for horses, managing the facility use by RIDE and outside groups, and coordinating the continued construction and maintenance of the entire facility. Additionally, my "Other Duties" included balancing the $150,000 budget, coor-dinating fundraising events, making sure that every single use of the facilities fell within the many legal, school district, and philosophical guidelines govern-ing the program's operation—and more! The necessary politicking required of me as a board member was less than enjoyable, but the overall experience was positive and provided five years' worth of enjoyment and opportunities for growth.

Through my connections in Scouting, I began working at a Boy Scout summer camp in the Sierra Nevada Mountains. Initially, I taught basic camping skills to Scouts of all ages. As the camp grew I found a niche in sharing my love of biking and boating. This eventually grew into a year-round passion for teach-ing boating safety and appreciation of the water. Having sought out the necessary information and continually learning new techniques, I found myself teaching water-skiing, sailing, windsurfing, and all of the basic water safety skills. While the Scouts paid a bare minimum in salary, the summer camp staff opportunity paid top dollar in experience. We lived and worked for two and a half months each year in one of the world's most beautiful environments, at no cost, while sharing our favorite outdoor skills with young people who truly wanted to be there. For nine years I spent summers leading backcountry mountain bike trips, swimming and teaching boating in crystal clear mountain lakes, backpacking into the Sierra wilderness, and enjoying starry nights around the campfire. It was at summer camp, too, that I met Liz. Having also grown up in a Scouting family, she was as excited as I by the opportunity to teach nature and Scouting skills. I spent most of my summers there between 1990 and 1999, until my job change eliminated those long summer vacations.

So, at the age of eighteen I was working full time at the school, volunteering at RIDE, attending evening college classes, advising a Boy Scout high adventure Exploring/Venturing group, and spending summers teaching at Boy Scout camp...what more could there be?

Little did I know, there was going to be more—much more! In 2000 it must have been time for a change. In a year's time I got married and bought a house. Amidst those personal changes, I also became a school bus driver, mostly to allow me to both continue college and keep paying the bills. I drive a wheelchair bus transporting children with special needs—I have an early morning route and an afternoon route, and between routes I go to my own classes. In addition to accommodating my schedule, my job lets me continue working with the young people I enjoy helping, and keeps my foot in the door of special needs education. I have really enjoyed this career—I've developed an excellent rapport with each of the students I transport as well as with their families and teachers. All of the personal interaction allows me to get to know the students, gain insight as to their abilities, and have a significant impact on their lives and learning.

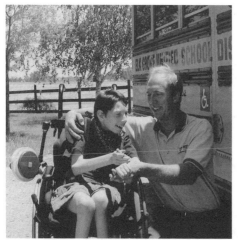

Photo by Sarah Riegelsberger

Between my new job, an increased focus on school, a new home to enjoy, and a general frustration with the level of politics I was forced to tolerate, my time was too short to continue the many hours I dedicated both to RIDE and to Scouting. Instead, these changes provided a good excuse to let those go and make room for other pursuits.

I have found time to get back into Ham Radio, after a long absence due to lack of time. When I changed jobs, I took a job at a bicycle shop to pay the bills during the lengthy training period to become a school bus driver. I have since continued to work there part-time as a hobby of sorts. Owning an old house also requires a certain dedication of time and skill to keep up! We have made a commitment to attempt to restore it to its original splendor—causing us to become very friendly with the staff of the local hardware store.

Basically, things have changed!

Not everything changes, though—the larger learning patterns and skills that we all wrote about as teenagers have not only stayed with me, but actually grown with each new experience. My experiences in learning how to restore an old home have exemplified for me the one thing I appreciate most about homeschooling—the way it encourages us to draw on both our intuition and our common sense to learn what we need for any task, when it is needed. In my own life, this intuitiveness has shown up in many ways, including my adaptation to the college learning environment, learning to fix and restore cars, and of course home repair. As with my recent project of repairing and fine-tuning our back-yard fish pond—I pressed these skills into service as I researched the natural environmental controls that go into such a pond, the physical building and circulation requirements, and the flora and fauna mix that best leads to natural pond health.

Way Back Then...

When I wrote the first time I was just getting into the college swing. When industrial technology interested me, it was a simple trail to a degree and beyond. After some time working with kids though, my motivation changed. So, with a certificate in Welding and just a few classes short of an A.S. in Industrial Technology, I made the decision to try teaching, promptly changed majors, and began a whole new course of study. Although early on I took a lot of courses that will not directly apply to my current goal of getting a teaching credential, I don't regret a single one. Will teaching be my final answer? Not likely, things change. Will I benefit from the knowledge I gained in those "excess" courses? Absolutely! I have learned from and enjoyed most of my courses and found that there truly are many good teachers out there, relaxing my take on education a little as a result.

Back then I was pretty staunch in my opinion that public schools of any sort were less than productive. While they may still be far from ideal in most cases, there are a lot of success stories among public school students. I believe there is room for success in any environment, including public schools. However, the bulk of these schools and the system at large lack the flexibility and trust to lead every student to an ideal education.

I do find it ironic that I feel the desire to teach school, given my homeschooling background. I have found a niche, however, where my philosophy and background can be advantageous. In the realm of special needs education it is accepted that while some children may not have the same abilities as their peers, they nevertheless possess a tremendous capacity to learn and to experience their world. Those of us interested in teaching them attempt to help them to achieve all that they can—to *reach their fullest potential*, whatever that may be. There is no reason that the logic in this philosophy could not apply to other realms of the education industry, just as it presently does to most who homeschool. Really, there is no better, nor more individual, goal in learning than to acquire the skills and knowledge that will lead us to our highest potential. Unfortunately, the industry has yet to learn that we *all* have special needs and that *everyone* will reach a different potential, in a different direction, requiring a different approach to learning as we grow. While individuality is often suppressed in most domains of the standard public school system, special needs teachers are not only encouraged to honor individuality, they are *required* to. This freedom is what draws me to teaching those with special needs and overcomes my disappointment with the general concept of public education. Additionally, my experiences working with a small cadre of exceptional teachers, who truly are able to encourage individuality and success on a small scale, give me hope for those students and teachers who are and will always be involved with public schools.

Would I do it again?

In hindsight there are always things we would like to have done differently. Is homeschooling one of those? Not for me. I am satisfied with the outcome of my "educational years" and find no reason to have done anything dramatically different. Will my kids follow my lead? We'll see. That's a bridge yet to be crossed, but I imagine that they will.

Given the opportunity, I would absolutely encourage others to skip the traditional school experience as I did, and find an option that better suits them. I recognize that there are those for whom the standard school pattern seems to work, but I still believe that homeschooling of some sort provides far more opportunity to succeed. Whatever your choices, I hope this encourages you to find the path that best suits you!

Amanda Bergson-Shilcock, 16
Bryn Mawr, Pennsylvania

Homeschooling is another word for "living"

for Susannah Sheffer, mentor and dear friend

When I was eleven years old, I became tired of people asking me the same questions about homeschooling over and over again. So I put together a pamphlet that answered those questions once and for all. Part of it went like this:

Photo by Susan Shilcock

Q. What's the best thing about homeschooling for you?

A. Two things. Being able to have lots of freedom and liking to read. Most kids I know who go to school hate reading.

Q. What's the worst thing?

A. The worst thing is when I feel like playing with a friend and my sisters aren't home and my brother's asleep and my homeschooling friends are busy and all my other friends are at school, then I really feel like if I had been going to school I wouldn't be sitting at home not having anybody to play with.

Q. Do you have a regular schedule for doing your work?

A. If you mean, do I have Math at 9:00, English at 11:00, Lunch at 12:00, no. If you mean, do I have to do certain work every day (or every week), yes. For example, Mom says, "Amanda, I want you to practice your violin for fifteen minutes before noon." If it is 9:00, I know I can start anywhere between 9:00 and 11:45.

Even though one of the best things about homeschooling is that you can be relaxed about your schedule, there are lots of times when I do have to schedule. Both my parents and my brother and sisters lead busy lives, so if I want time with them, I usually have to schedule it ahead of time, such as this: Early one morning I go to [my younger sister] Emily, who is working in her office, and say, "Em, want to come play dolls with me now?" She says, "Well, I have a violin lesson soon, then later I go over to Gabriella's house, so I'll play dolls in between." Or, maybe, I'm working on the computer, and my Dad comes up to me and says, "Amanda, will you help me take apart the treehouse?" I say, "Sure, but first I have a phone call I have to make, and then I have to empty the dishwasher." Dad says, "Okay, see you in about fifteen minutes."

Q. What do you do when you want to know something and your parents don't know the answer?

A. There are several things that I can do. One is we have a fairly large library in our house, so I could go there and look it up in the encyclopedia, or in some sort of book which I think might hold the answer. Another option is to ask a family friend who I think might have the answer. Another thing I can do is ask one of my siblings.

Q. Would your parents let you go to school if you wanted to?

A. Yes, I've always had that option and about once a year my mom or dad asks me, usually in September, "Do you want to go to school this year?" I usually say, "Not this year." Sometimes I say I'll think about it, because right then I'm thinking, "Boy, I would have some really neat classes if I went to school." Then I think, "But what about always being on the teacher's schedule...," and I say no.

Q. Do you consider yourself a social outcast?

A. No. My view is that I have plenty of friends my own age, and also many younger friends. I also feel that I have some friends other kids don't have—adult friends.

Q. Do you ever go anyplace outside your home?

A. This definitely has something to do with the question, "Do you consider yourself a social outcast?" but it also evokes a different answer. The answer, of course, is yes, I go lots of places outside our home. I do a slide presentation with my dad when we go to conferences and I have several slides of gatherings of homeschoolers and school kids alike doing fun stuff—taking sleigh rides in the snow, making apple cider, going on a long nature hike, camping out—lots of fun things. I go lots of places. One thing that really helps me be able to do that is my volunteer work at St. Edmonds Home for Crippled Children with my sisters Emily and Julia and my mom, Susan, and my volunteer work at the Lower Merion-Naberth Watershed Association with my sister Emily. I also volunteer at the Schuylkill Valley Nature Center. I'm what they call a teaching volunteer. On Wednesday mornings I go out there and teach a bunch of school kids. What we do is we go on a trail and answer their questions as they go along and stop once in a while for a game or an explanation or something like that.

I wrote that pamphlet five years ago. I am now sixteen, and still homeschooling. Some of the questions people ask have remained the same over the years, and some have changed. I want to highlight four misconceptions which crop up quite often these days:

1. That all homeschoolers homeschool for religious reasons. This is not true. Many homeschoolers do, but the number is far from being the whole of the homeschooling community. My family does not homeschool for religious reasons.

2. That the only teachers homeschoolers have are their parents (or parent). This, again, is not true. Especially after one reaches high school age, there are many subjects the parent may not feel comfortable teaching. For example:

Last year, when I was a high school "freshman" (I put this term in quotes because I try not to place myself in a specific grade level), I discovered that the vast majority of people my age were receiving exposure to biology. Well, my parents were no more prepared to teach me biology than to fly to the moon! So, Mom swapped services with another homeschooling family we know. She worked with their ten-year-old son on English and math, and the mom, a former high school biology and college nutrition teacher, taught my sister and me biology and beginning chemistry. There are countless other examples of this kind of process throughout many homeschoolers' lives.

In addition, many homeschoolers, including myself, often work independently, without any need or desire for formal or even informal teachers. For instance, last fall I decided to teach myself to touch-type. This was not an out-of-the-blue decision; Dad had been telling me for years what a difference it would make in my work. (Before, I did one of three things: 1) I typed my stories out myself with two fingers before I sent them on to Susannah, my writing mentor, 2) I wrote them out by hand and trusted Susannah to understand, or 3) I sent her a dictated tape, which she would then transcribe.)

Anyway, I was full of excitement but had no place to start. I finally remembered an instruction book a friend had given me, and I dug it out. It was pretty old; it talked about returning the carriage at the end of each line, and about good erasers—the rubber kind! But the keyboard is one thing that hasn't changed, so the book still worked for me. I spent several late nights resisting the ever-present urge to look down while I learned the keyboard, and then continued on with some very tedious exercises. (If you don't believe me, try typing "Sue was a sure bet to see the silly seed setting races" over a whole page!) Finally, I had had enough. I decided the rest of the exercises were good for hopeful secretaries, not me, and spent the rest of my practicing time on real things like writing letters. Of course, I did some backsliding—no method is foolproof, and at times it was so much easier to slip into my old, comfortable system that I succumbed.

I'm still not the fastest or most accurate of typists, but in my humble opinion I'm not so bad.

3. That a homeschooler goes to "school at home" (and therefore never gets out of the house), complete with a school desk, the Pledge of Allegiance, countless worksheets, and a rigid schedule. Well, this is certainly true for some homeschoolers, but my gosh! If you showed this to many of my homeschooling friends, they'd cringe and say, "This is why I *left* school!" Needless to say, that is not at all how my family homeschools, and I'll show you examples a little later on of just how we do homeschool.

4. THE MOST WIDELY HELD HOMESCHOOLING MISCONCEPTION OF ALL TIME: That homeschoolers will never become "socialized." I would say that one hundred out of every hundred people who ever found out I was homeschooling asked me this question in one form or another. This is what I usually say to them:

"Well, you know, a lot of people ask that question. I actually think homeschooling offers better options in some cases than schools. For instance, in a school setting, one is likely to find many people of one's *own* age range (say, within two to three years), but with middle schools and high schools in separate buildings most of the time you never even *see* people significantly older or younger than you. I count myself very lucky to have, in addition to friends my own age, many close adult friends, and a good number of younger friends."

I also want to point out that a lot of my schooled friends have difficulty relating to their younger siblings. They don't usually ask questions about their days, attend their sports events, or just generally spend time with them. Why? First of all, they are separated from them for seven hours a day, five days a week. Second, they are taught by their friends that it is uncool to be close to their sisters or brothers. (However, I do not mean to generalize here. Many young people have perfectly good relationships with their siblings.)

A Bergson-Shilcock jam session   *Photo by Susan Shilcock*

Now I'd like to give you a little background on myself and my family. My sisters, Emily and Julia, are ages fourteen and eleven, respectively, and Nicholas, my brother, is eight. We live in a big stone house in a suburb of Philadelphia, and we have a golden retriever named Biscuit.

My parents say that they didn't make a conscious decision about my education—i.e. "Let's homeschool our daughter Amanda all the way through high school." Rather, they almost fell into it. They claim they looked at me when I was about seven (Pennsylvania doesn't require school attendance until age eight). They considered what I was doing (astronomy: studying the night sky with my uncle, staying up late to watch shooting stars in August; nature and biology: exploring a local nature center, dissecting crayfish, studying pond life; reading: three hours a day). Then they considered the things I would be doing in school—like learning my ABC's. So, one reason my parents didn't send me to school was that it seemed sort of pointless for me to go sit for five or six hours a day in first grade while the teacher taught me what I knew all over again.

Also, my parents and I were very close, and we enjoyed spending time together. Going to school full-time would have not only cut into our weekday time, but also into our nighttime hours, what with homework and going to bed early so I could catch the bus in the morning. I was very much a homebody, in the sense that I loved being around my family and it would have been quite a wrench to go off and leave them. So I think going to school would have been not only pointless but even hurtful to me.

So Mom and Dad said to themselves, "What can school give her that we can't?" And the answer was, "Nothing." In the years after that, my parents and I continued to ask ourselves this question, and the answer was always, for me and I assume for my parents, "Nothing."

A lot of people seem to have the idea that my parents have brainwashed me or something, that it's not natural for a teenager to spend—and *enjoy* spending—so much time with her parents. This is a very scary misconception to me, because people can so easily be persuaded into believing it. As you will see, I actually spend quite a bit of time outside the home, perhaps more than a "normal" teenager. But also, my parents do not stand over me with a stick and force me to sit hunched over a tiny desk, doing worksheets and assignments. I actually think that I have a healthier relationship with my parents than do many of my friends. I know my parents' feelings on certain issues, and I know the few rules they expect me to absolutely obey, but they also know and respect *my* feelings, and don't play the "heavy parent."

In the early eighties, when my parents were deciding not to send me to school, "homeschooling" was neither a well-known term nor a very well known process. (It still isn't, actually, but it's better now than it was then.) This was due, in part, to the fact that laws about schooling in many states were extremely vague and unclear, or else blatantly unfair to homeschoolers. It was also due to the fact that widespread homeschooling, though it existed, had not yet been publicized very much by the media.

John Holt's books (*How Children Fail*, *How Children Learn*, etc.), and his magazine (*Growing Without Schooling*, which is still published bimonthly) were of great help to my parents. Alternative education was very big in the 1960s and 70s, but homeschooling was not nearly so well known. By "alternative education," I mean schools that, for one reason or another, may be extremely open-ended, but are still in most senses of the word, schools. Usually, you still get grades and you still sit at a desk at least part of the day. Also, you usually continue (like in regular school) to be mainly supervised by adults, and you often continue to be confined in one building or even just one room. I don't mean to put down or criticize alternative schools in any way, but I do want to erase any confusion about homeschoolers versus alternative schools.

Now that I've gotten the misconceptions out of the way, and given you a little information about my family, I'd like to tell you about just what it is that I do. People often say, "But can't you just tell me what a typical day is like?" Well, the answer to that, in my family at least, is that there is no typical day. Each of the four children in my family has different jobs, activities and events to attend, and they vary from day to day. I am, naturally, going to focus on my own life.

Working at the Library

One rainy Monday morning, I was sitting behind a large desk. A young girl came up with her mother. "Can I check out these books?" she asked me politely. "Of course," I answered. I took the books from her, opened them up, and began to scan their barcodes with the laser gun we use. As I did so, I realized that the girl was not watching me, as young children usually do. (They're fascinated by the gun.) Instead, she was standing on her tiptoes to see over the desk. Her attention was caught by something on a shelf under the desk. "Who's Ruth?" she asked abruptly, turning to me. I was taken aback until I realized that what she was looking at was a box on which was printed, "Ruth's Problems."

"Ruth is the librarian in charge of video and audio tapes," I replied. The box she was referring to is where Ruth keeps all of the tapes she's had complaints about—i.e. fuzzy sound, etc.

The little girl turned to her mother. "Boy," she said solemnly, "Ruth must really like problems—she has so many of them."

I work three or four days per week for a total of ten to twelve hours at our large local library. I work in the children's room, and, contrary to popular opinions about libraries, it is not quiet up there! I have worked there for two and a half years, so I'm pretty used to it by now. I began as a volunteer, which came about because Mom and I were keeping an eye out for volunteer opportunities since two of mine had recently come to an end. We were at the library one day, looking at books, and all of a sudden, Mom said, "Amanda! I know where you can work!" I immediately realized what she was thinking, and jumped in: "Here? Mom, this would be a great place to work!"

I don't know why we hadn't thought of this before—the only reason I can imagine is that, having seen "Help Wanted" signs for paid pages (who have to be at least fourteen) around the library for so many years, it never occurred to us that they might have a volunteer program too. Anyway, we filled out the necessary forms, and I became a volunteer, working two hours a week, which was not nearly enough for me!

When I turned fourteen, I became a page. Now I do just about everything: I check books, tapes, and videos in and out, I repair books (give them new covers, etc.), I put books away, I answer the phone, I (try to!) find answers to reference questions, I put up and take down displays, I accept fines from patrons for overdue materials, I process new books, and I do many of the above using our new computer system. I also place calls to other libraries to try to get books, send books back to other libraries (we have a program called Access Pennsylvania which enables patrons to take books out from and/or return books to any library in the state), and once I even did a storytime with songs for young children.

My family teases me that I fit the stereotypical image of a librarian, with my bifocal glasses and my nose always in a book. Of course, I don't read on the job! However, I have burned the midnight oil on many occasions, since one of the perks of working at the library is being able to read any of the new books which pass through the office before the patrons even know they're there!

Ballet

One very hot summer afternoon, I was working in a school as other children looked on. No, I wasn't in summer school! The other kids were taking part in a summer program, and I was working—that is, preparing for a ballet performance by warming up my muscles with stretches and exercises. After the rest of the company and I were ready, the performance started.

"Good afternoon," said Jeannie, the artistic director of our company, "I'd like to tell you a little about ballet before we begin to dance." She spoke for a few minutes about the history of ballet and about our company, then introduced us and had us each demonstrate a simple step. Next, she asked if anyone would like to try some dance. The audience of middle-schoolers laughed, thinking she was joking. She wasn't.

Eventually, we got four volunteers. Holding her microphone in one hand, Jeannie helped the girls (no boys would volunteer!) into a reasonable imitation of the position four of us were in: ballet first position, standing with feet turned out and heels touching each other. Then she asked us to demonstrate the beginning of the dance we'd be doing. Wearing white leotards and funny-looking white bows on our hair, we started dancing *Les Danse de Petits Cygnets*—The Dance of the Little Swans. This dance is done entirely with linked arms—there are no steps done individually, so you have to be perfectly in unison.

Well, we did the beginning of the dance. Then the volunteers tried it. It was a sight to behold—four girls of different heights, wearing street clothes, trying to do steps that were totally unfamiliar to them! However, everyone had lots of fun, and, I think, gained new understanding of just how hard dancing really is.

I am a Senior member of the Devon Festival Ballet Company. I take five to seven ballet classes per week. I've studied ballet since I was seven, with a two-year break while I was more interested in gymnastics. I've been a Senior member for a year, and before that I was a Senior apprentice for a year, and before that I was a Junior member for three years.

The company is made up of from fifteen to thirty members. (The number varies because people, especially Junior members, become disillusioned and quit the company, or just quit ballet altogether. Older members leave for more diverse reasons—they get accepted into a bigger company, they go to college, they can't afford it, or—for some teenaged members—their parents don't like it.) The Junior Company members are ages ten to thirteen. When you're fourteen, you can be accepted as an apprentice, but that doesn't happen automatically. Senior Company members range in age from fifteen to forty, with a large chunk being fifteen- to twenty-year-olds.

With the company, I have performed at a local outdoor theater; in Cape May, New Jersey, at Convention Hall on the boardwalk; and at several local schools. One memorable summer, we did six performances in four days for a community service program. This last was especially fun because we felt like a "real" company on tour, since we would walk into a place at 1:00 P.M. and perform at 2:00. Just like large companies that tour for months, we had to get used to lots of new situations in a very short amount of time—carpeted "stages," huge auditoriums, noisy (young) audiences, and music and costume problems.

The Pastel Quintet

One chilly day last December, I stood on a slippery sidewalk, waiting as uniformed men searched members of my family. We weren't being arrested; we were simply entering the White House, in Washington, D.C.

Finally, the men let us pass through. We waited on the other side of the gatehouse for our violins to come through. And we waited. And waited. And waited. At last a voice called sheepishly, "Could one of you come back for a second, please? We can't seem to get the violin cases open."

Photo by Susan Shilcock

I am a member of a violin quintet, called The Pastel Quintet because of the colors of our concert dresses. The other members are: Sarah (age thirteen) and Andrea (ten) Kaplan, and my sisters Emily (fourteen) and Julia (eleven). We have been together for four years and more than 130 concerts. We play mostly at area nursing and retirement homes, but also for many women's groups (particularly women's church groups), and for several local public schools. (Andrea and Sarah attend public school.)

The high point of our careers so far was our White House concert for private tour groups during this past Christmas season. We were featured in several local newspapers, including the Philadelphia *Inquirer*, before we went. It was fun to be recognized as I was working at the library, or shopping at the grocery store. When the day came, we all drove down to Washington on a Monday morning—the five of us, our four parents, and my brother Nicholas. We arrived about one p.m. We weren't scheduled to play till four, and they weren't expecting us till three, but it took us forever to find the entrance, and then we took thousands of photographs outside the gates. Some tourists even came up and had my dad take a picture, with their cameras, as they posed with us!

Then we had to go through a million checkpoints, and my mom almost didn't get in because she had thought she'd travel light and not bring her purse, which had all of her ID, including her drivers' license, in it. I guess the Secret Service people decided she didn't look like a terrorist, though, because they let her in.

Once we got inside, we walked down a long hall, and went into a private room where we left our stuff. It was the first day the White House was open after being decorated for the holidays, so we were the first outsiders to see it. But by that time it was pretty late, so we just had time for a quick tour. Then we took up our positions at the end of the entrance hall, and began to play. There were several groups of musicians there, but we were the first one that people saw as they came in. Ironically enough, the private tours we played for were senior-citizen tours!

It was pouring rain, so the White House personnel (who incidentally couldn't have been nicer) told us there would "only" be seven to eight thousand tourists, instead of the nine thousand they had been expecting.

We played for an hour and a half, had a cookie break, and then played a half-hour more. We couldn't believe the sheer number of people that kept coming through! The line moved pretty continuously for the two hours we played, even though a lot of people wanted to stop and listen. Despite repeated warnings about no photography, hundreds of people took pictures. They photographed us, the eleven-foot wooden soldiers on either side of us, and the stunningly decorated trees around us. Some people sang along with us; some conversed loudly with their friends, ignoring us; some applauded. (I would estimate that only one or two people out of every ten were actually there at the finish of a song, but coming past in the middle of a song didn't stop people from clapping.) Some people asked who we were (so Mom gave them tiny flyers), and some actually started crying, I suppose because we were playing sentimental Christmas favorites. (Not to neglect the Kaplans, or others that celebrate Hanukkah, we included a few of those songs too.)

We were sad when it was over, but we all agreed that if we never played "Jolly Old St. Nicholas" again, it would be too soon!

The Pastel Quintet began when Julia, Emily, and I were Suzuki violin students. We had two group and two solo concerts per year, and we wanted to do more performances. Mom suggested that we go to a nearby nursing home and play. She suggested a particular home because she thought it would be neat for us to play for a woman who had been one of Mom's favorite baby-sitters when she, Mom, was a little girl. Perfectionists at heart, we decided we needed piano accompaniment. We decided to ask Patty Kaplan, whose children, Sarah and Andrea, had gone to my parents' family resource center (more on that later). Then we realized that it would be kind of rude to ask Patty but not Andrea and Sarah, because they were musicians too. So we talked it over and decided that we would invite them too. So, we invited the Kaplans, they said yes, Mom called the nursing home, they said yes, and we began to put together a program. All along, we were under the delusion that this would be a one-time thing.

On the appointed day, we went to the nursing home, played our program, and went to talk to Mom's friend before we left. Well, it took us forever to get to her! People kept coming up to us, most in wheelchairs. They told us how much they had enjoyed the performance, how we reminded them of their grandchildren, how they or their children or their grandchildren or their sister's husband's third cousin played the violin, how young we looked. (We were ages six to almost-twelve, which didn't seem young at the time but in retrospect seems infantile.) Even a couple of nurses came up to tell us how much they appreciated our coming. Anyway, we finally got out to the parking lot, and then, all at the same time, we looked at our moms and said, "Where do we play next?"

From there it snowballed. We had played the first concert for free, and also the next four or five, but then an activities director said to Mom, "You know, we do have budgets for these things. We'd be more than happy to pay you." Mom accepted, since costs for Xeroxing the programs were mounting. She also began to say, when we got what came to be known as a "PQ phone call," that our fee was from "zero to fifty dollars." The money initially went into a savings account, but we've since donated some to charity, spent some on matching dresses, and now pay ourselves a salary from time to time.

In the course of a concert, particularly one in which she has been introduced as the group's "leader," Mom usually talks a little about the real leaders of the group—us. I suppose the reason people seem to look to her as the leader is that she is an adult. However, we really do govern ourselves. This is how a typical rehearsal might go:

On an agreed-upon day, the Kaplans arrive at our house. We banish Patty to the dining room with Mom and retreat to the living room, which contains the piano. We unpack our instruments, and decide whether to have the business part of our meeting first, or begin by practicing. Usually, we have the meeting.

Julia, our treasurer, tells us how much money we have. She also tells us how much we'll have after our next set of concerts. (We try to schedule them in groups for convenience's sake.) Then I tell about the calls we've received since our last meeting. We decide whether to accept each invitation—does it conflict with Andrea's tap class, or do all of us have a ballet rehearsal, or does Julia have a special soccer clinic? If the schedule works out, Andrea, the secretary, writes down our acceptance. Unless, of course, the concert requires a drive of more than forty-five minutes! (We've found that a longer drive makes us cranky.)

After that, we usually debate (loudly) our next program, using our most recent program as a basis. Whatever we come up with at that meeting will be what we play for the next five to seven concerts, so we try to please everybody. Not easy, considering Sarah's views on "When the Saints Go Marching In" ("Bleetch, do we have to play that *again*?"), Emily's views on her harmony part in "Farandole" ("I can't stand that—*da da da da da da* the whole time!"), and my views on "Hunters' Chorus." ("If I hear that intro one more time, I'll scream!")

After we weed out every song someone doesn't like, every song we played the last time we were at the particular home (we get a lot of repeat business), and every song we're all bored to death with, we're left with one or two songs! Then, lolling on the sofa, doing ballet *barre* exercises, grumbling, smiling, giggling, we put pieces back in the program. We argue, browbeat, cajole, and persuade each other into doing the traditional songs "just one more time," and convince each other that we really can get that new minuet ready by concert-day (typically four to six days away).

Then we call for Patty, and explain to her what we've decided. She (often) agrees, and we settle down to work. A usual practice lasts two to two-and-a-half hours, but they have been known to run almost four. When we finish, the Kaplans depart, and the Bergson-Shilcocks collapse on the sofa, exhausted but exhilarated.

Academics

I do algebra with my aunt, English and history on my own, and I have studied various other subjects at other points in my life. I usually decide what I want to learn, how I want to learn it, and when and with whom I do it. I have always had a strong interest in reading and writing, so I have never, not once, been assigned a book to read or a composition to write. My parents and I have tried to keep fairly on top of what my "peers"[*] have been learning (actually, we use the phrase "being exposed to"). For instance, as I mentioned earlier, in ninth grade, we discovered that chemistry and/or biology is commonly taught, along with a foreign language. Sometimes I make an effort to do roughly the same thing as the schools, and sometimes I just choose to forget about it. I never work under deadlines or schedules except for those I set myself. My parents believe that, for example, knowing a smaller chunk of algebra well is better than memorizing the whole book, chapter by chapter, and having it all disappear come June.

One of Amanda's recent interests - sparked by a hearing-impaired friend in ballet - is sign language

Photo by Susan Shilcock

Math

I am not good at studying math on my own. I get stuck and frustrated and generally miserable. I don't know why this is—I seem to be good at teaching myself other things, and I am good at reading instruction manuals, but algebra escapes me. I did learn arithmetic by running a small bakery out of my home from when I was seven until I was ten, and later did double-entry bookkeeping for Open Connections, a resource center my family runs. But although I really have taught myself a lot of math, in the case of higher math it hasn't worked.

So, over the years I have worked with my mom and with a private tutor. I ended up working with the tutor because one year my mother said that she wanted to go over my textbook on her own, to refresh her memory a little before

---

[*] What an awful word—I always think of some nineteenth-century English earl or something!

she started to work with me. I was ready to keep moving, though, and she was so busy that I was afraid it would be a while before we got down to it. I suggested that maybe it would be easier if we found somebody else who was already involved in math. So, Mom being the very understanding person that she is, began asking around. She found a friend of a friend, whose name was Cheryl. Cheryl was a tutor for schoolkids who were having trouble with math, and when she heard about our situation, she was enthusiastic. She came to our house once and worked with me, and we were both happy with the way it went. We worked together for about a year, for one to two hours a week.

This year I am doing algebra with my Aunt Nancy, and we work together for one hour once a week. She gives me homework, which usually adds up to between ten and forty-five minutes a day. I especially like the word problems! I enjoy working with her because she explains things clearly and uses examples of how algebra is used in everyday life. (For example, to figure out how much paint is needed for a particular room.) She also is flexible and will stay with me on a specific section as long as I need or want to. We don't use a schedule or curriculum—for a section on permutations and combinations, we tossed coins and picked numbers out of a hat. We also jump around a lot; though we are using a high school textbook, we don't progress methodically from chapter to chapter.

Aunt Nancy also builds on a lot of the algebra. So far, we (or I, as homework) have looked at her college philosophy textbook, measured floor space in my house, and estimated the combinations one could make from our various last names (mine, of course, being Bergson-Shilcock, and her children's being Shilcock-Elliott). She's also taught me tips for college, such as when I'm hurriedly (and messily) copying down problems, not to write my Zs like this: Z, because then I'll be confused later—"Is this ZY or 2Y?" Instead, I should cross my Zs, like this: Ƶ. We have a lot of fun.

Chemistry/Biology

When I was in "ninth" grade, my sister Emily and I took a two-hour biology class once a week. We were the only students, and the teacher was a friend of Mom's who had taught high-school biology and college nutrition. We had been lucky enough to pick up a really good quality microscope at a half-off sale at a scientific supply store. We had also gotten two dissecting kits. That was the only formal equipment we had. Victoria, our teacher, brought a biology textbook with her, and we began our work from that, then branched out.

During the course of the year, because Victoria was very flexible about how to go about our learning, we did taste tests (which were inconclusive!); conducted blood tests; looked at cheek cells and blood cells and generally used the microscope a lot; dissected a starfish, a frog, and a fetal pig (not my idea—Emily's!); gathered water samples from ponds and streams and viewed them under the microscope; and took a low-key, multiple-choice test. (Victoria told us that we had scored at a college sophomore level, which proved to us both how much we had learned and how unreliable and silly most tests are.) We also did some beginning chemistry with Victoria.

One of the high points of the year was getting to tour the bio/chem lab at Rosemont College, a smallish Catholic liberal arts college near us. This came about because the Sister who is head of the department is a friend of Victoria's. We were hoping to be able to sit in on a class, but that didn't work out. The Sister was really nice and said we could borrow any equipment that we wanted.

History

I have always read a great deal of historical fiction and many biographies. In fact, one of the first series I read was the *Childhood of Famous Americans* biography series. A natural extension of this interest is what I began last fall. I am now the proud teacher of a three-person history class! The students are my sisters and our homeschooling friend Michael.

We meet once a week for an hour. We are focusing on the Civil War period (sparked in part by the recent PBS/Ken Burns nine-part series, *The Civil War*, which I saw and loved). But if any of them is interested in some particular area, we will detour to explore it. For instance, I did a section on Civil War spies. It was so well received that when we did women of the Civil War the next week, I made certain to put in some spy stories.

We usually meet in our family dining room. Right before spring vacation, my students politely demanded report cards. My policy was going to be no report cards, but they were insistent. (I think they liked having a tangible grade—so they could easily say to their friends, "Oh yes, I got all A's!") I ended up combining my views and their requests, and evaluated them using four ratings: O (for Outstanding), QG (Quite Good), F,G (Fine, Good), and NSH (Not So Hot). Each student earned his/her share of NSH's: Class is generally informal; often, we begin sitting around the table and end up cross-legged on the floor. The NSH's were for their sometimes-disruptive handstands and cartwheels during class!

We meet Wednesday afternoons for an hour, usually from one to two o'clock. I began the year in a fever of excitement, buying new materials and supplies, making up lots of lesson plans. As the year went on, though, I listened more to what the kids wanted. I found that I not only didn't have time to make up lesson plans (even informal ones), more importantly, I didn't need them.

We have worked on two main projects throughout the year: a timeline which we illustrated with magazine cutouts, and a blank calendar which they filled up with names and dates of people's birthdays as the year progressed and we learned about them. We almost never do worksheets! I learn at least as much as the kids, both as I read to them and along with them, and as we work together to find out when the typewriter was invented, or something like that. I'd guess that this learning along with students is something most school teachers miss, maybe because they're not interested, or maybe because they're not learning but *memorizing* along with the students.

English

As I stated before, I do English on my own. This includes writing and editing both fiction and non-fiction. I taught myself to touch-type earlier this year because my hand got too cramped from always writing, so now I use my old battered typewriter, my dad's Macintosh, or faithful pen and paper, depending on what time of night it is. My best work is done at 1:00 or 2:00 A.M., a time I could never stay up to if I had to be up by six to catch a bus for school!

Since I read very widely by choice, I have never had to read a book—in fact quite the opposite, my parents are continually dragging me away from my books! This is another area in which I feel closer to adults than my peers, since many of them seem as if they never want to (or have time to) crack a book. I always try to be sympathetic when I hear them say, "I have to read forty pages tonight!" but sometimes it's hard.

With my adult friends, in particular a former Head Children's Librarian, I often discuss the problem of not having enough time to read! Since Patti, the librarian, and I get together once a week to catalogue books for Open Connections, my parents' family resource center, we use the opportunity to gab about the newest books (children's, young adult, and adult) and the best authors, and to swap books.

(Open Connections is a one-room, one thousand square-foot building next to our house which has housed, over the last fourteen years, an ongoing morning program for children ages four to nine, various courses taught by my father and others on homeschooling and related subjects, and numerous homeschooling gatherings, programs, etc.)

This past year, Patti and I attended a two-week adult continuing education course at a community college near us. It was called "Writing for the Children's Market." This came about because Mom, who had been looking for a course of some sort I could take, sent away for a catalog of courses from a college. She looked through it, I looked through it, and both of us spotted the same course. It featured a "well-known children's author." Also, it was only two sessions long, which seemed good, because I thought, "If I hate it, I'll only have to go one more time!"

Anyway, it turned out to be an interesting experience. Vivian (the teacher) was a *semi*-well-known children's non-fiction writer. She knew a lot about agents, contracts, publishers, and how to get a book published. She also seemed to know a lot about how to sell a publisher on a particular book. However, she didn't seem to know much about what *children* want. She advised not stretching children's vocabulary, and made some large, sweeping statements having to do with what children liked to read. (She seemed to think she was referring to all of the readers in the world under age eighteen, while I am of the opinion that she was talking about her *perception* of those readers.)

I did get some ideas out of the course, but I was disappointed by the total lack of creativity shown by my fellow classmates. Some had brought manuscripts, and what they read aloud was boring, adult-oriented "children's" literature. I think that one of the reasons I was (am) so critical of the course is that my parents taught me never to believe that just because a person happens to be standing in front of other people and lecturing, that doesn't necessarily mean that she/he is an expert.

Another new area of my homeschooling has also developed from cataloging books with Patti. I am now accompanying Patti to local schools to do booktalks. This is when a school hires a bookstore owned by friends of Patti's to do a bookfair. The store tells the school that included in the cost of the bookfair is Patti (and now me), who will come to the school a day or two before the bookfair opens and review some of our favorite books for the students. Patti and I get together a week or so beforehand. We plan out which old favorites we're going to do, and which new books we must read before the bookfair, so we can decide which of them to use. We try to do books that kids are not familiar with, and also books with exciting plots, so that we can stop at a suspenseful point in a review, and say, "If you want to know what happens next, go to the bookfair and buy the book!"

We usually do elementary and middle school bookfairs, but now that I am part of the package, Patti's friends are sort of using me as bait for the high schools—i.e. if we do your bookfair, we'll have *the kid's point of view!* Some adults seem to have this notion that kids are another species, or are from another planet or something, and therefore they, the adults, couldn't possibly know what the kids will like. So these adults are very excited about having *the kid's point of view.* (Conversely, of course, there are those adults who think that kids are too stupid to choose their own books.)

Anyway, much as I enjoy doing these bookfairs, every time I leave the school building after I do one, I feel a gust of relief. I think part of it is sympathy for the kids still stuck in there, and part is relief that I'm not stuck in there, and another bit is that I am recovering from the teacher-y atmosphere: marching in a line down the hall, the teacher's pet going to get things for her, the chatter of some teachers while we're trying to work, the cute-talk: "Now, Johnny, sit down and the nice lady will explain it all to you."

The part that makes me the saddest is when, at the beginning of a booktalk, with dozens of enticing books on our display tables, the children sit quietly, as they've been told to do. Patti finishes her introduction, and tells them that they may pick any book they see and she or I will talk about it. But they usually continue to sit, until one brave soul raises a hand. Patti picks up the book, opens it, and begins to talk. When she finishes, a sort of pandemonium breaks loose, with almost every child in the room straining to raise her hand the highest, to yell his book's title the loudest.

The reason I find this initial passivity so sad is that I can see, with my own two eyes, how no choices ("Johnny, you have to stop reading NOW. It's time for music class.") and fake choices ("Would you rather have your science test before your math sheets, or after?") affect children. They begin to believe that they are incapable of making their own decisions, or that they're not old enough or whatever. I see that continuing right down the line until I get a tenth-grader at the library who can't decide which of two almost identical reference books she should xerox from. "Which is better?" she asks me.

"They have the same information," I answer, "They're both recent; they both have good pictures. They're very much the same."

"Yes, *but which should I copy?*"

You see? How I wish that every child could have the same freedom I've been lucky enough to have: reading, writing, playing, working—*when I want*, and yet retaining a sense of family duties and commitments.

Just one more note before we go on to something else: I am not maligning the teaching profession. There are a good number of smart, well-educated (notice I am not saying "well schooled") teachers out there who really try to help their students learn. Unfortunately, there are six times as many who are over-worked, underpaid, never-really-wanted-to-be-teachers-anyway, often-ill people out there whose last concern is to help children learn. It is those that I have trouble with.

I am also continuing my work with Susannah Sheffer, who is editor of John Holt's *Growing Without Schooling* magazine. Since I was ten, I have sent Susannah my writing and asked for her comments. Less frequently—since she's near Boston and I'm near Philadelphia—I've spoken to her over the phone. This all started when Susannah was attending college nearby and working at Open Connections. I saw Susannah taking down some dictation for a little girl attending the morning program and, since I already thought of myself as a writer, I asked her if she would take down some dictation from me too. She agreed.

Susannah had already been around our house for quite a while, helping my dad with the homeschooling newsletter he was putting out, and helping with the morning program at Open Connections. I knew that she was a writer, and that she was heading up to Cambridge, Massachusetts when she graduated, to work at Holt Associates. (Holt Associates is the organization founded by well-known educator John Holt, which publishes the bimonthly homeschooling magazine *Growing Without Schooling*.) A short time before she left, I asked her if it would be okay if I sent her some of my writing to comment on. I had really liked her comments as we worked together on my dictated work, and I was hoping she would do the same through the mail.

Several months later, she came to visit us. While she was there, I exclaimed over how nice it was to work with her in person again. Mom picked right up on that. She said to me, "Why don't you call Susannah once a week or something? That way, you could still send things through the mail, but you would also get to talk with her personally, and clarify things if you had to." I thought that was a great idea. We investigated, found a (relatively) cheap time to call, and agreed that I would call her at the specified time each week. Susannah went back to Boston, and we began what became a weekly (or sometimes even twice-weekly) ritual. In the past few years we have gone back to using the mail most often, with phone calls only occasionally.

Amanda discusses
her writing with Susannah

Photo by Susan Shilcock

Susannah offers suggestions for improvement on not only such mundane things as grammar, punctuation, and spelling, but also on such things as historical accuracy. Plus, she makes clear, constructive criticisms: "I think you need to be clearer here—is Mary saying that she hates what her father did, or that she hates her father?"

Susannah offers several things that are difficult for me to get from other people in my life. First, she is not my mother or my sister. Therefore, she is not constrained the way they sometimes are by feeling they should say a story is "nice" just because they're family. Second, she knows when to stop; she doesn't tell me so many things at once that I am overwhelmed. Third, as a writer and as an editor, she knows where I'm coming from. She asks insightful questions and offers her interpretations of what I'm trying to say.

Here's one example of how we work: I received a letter from Susannah saying that she liked a poem I was working on, but thought I might want to reconsider some of my line breaks, since most people, when reading a poem, will stop, if only momentarily, at the end of each line. She suggested that I read it aloud to myself and see whether I agreed with her. So I did, and decided to change some of the line breaks, but to leave some the way they were. This is a great example of our work together: I send something, she reads it, she writes to me about it, I read her letter, I follow (or don't follow) her suggestions, I send her the revised work, and we repeat the process.

Susannah can work with me in a way that most school teachers can't work with their students. Obviously, this is largely due to the fact that she and I are working one on one, and school teachers often have to work with fifteen to thirty students at a time. Also, I lead the way with Susannah: I decide what I want to write, when I want to write, what to write about, and how I want to do it. (As I said before, I use pen and paper and a computer. Sometimes, though, when a story is coming so quickly that I can't think clearly enough to write it down, I just tape-record it and send it to Susannah, and she later types it up for me.)

An offshoot of this work is that Susannah recently wrote a book of her own, *Writing Because We Love To: Homeschoolers at Work* (Heinemann-Boynton/Cook, 1992). In the process of writing this book (which concerns Susannah's apprenticeships/relationships with young writers, including me), Susannah sent me drafts of the manuscript, asking for my input and suggestions. I thought it was neat that *she* was asking for *my* input!

When she sent me the manuscript, I was very busy, and I didn't get to discuss it with her as much as I would have liked. In reading it, though, I discovered so many things that I had unwittingly taught Susannah. For example, she wrote about how my thoughts on the old "write about what you know about" theory had affected her. I had told her, when I was in the process of writing a teenage romance story (as an experiment), that if she had told me only to write about what I knew about, I would be in sore trouble because I, a homeschooler all my life, was writing a story about a girl who went to school! However, I told her, it might have been appropriate for her to question me if that was *all* I was writing about. Maybe then it would have been time for me to ask myself why I wasn't writing about homeschoolers, or even why I wasn't writing neutral stories where school intrudes little, if at all.

I think one of the reasons I was writing about schooled kids, and why I was writing "neutral" stories, was that I felt in my non-fiction articles for homeschooling magazines, I was already writing about a homeschooled child—me! I also think that since the vast majority of children are schooled, I was unconsciously writing for them, assuming they'd want to read about schooled children. (Don't ask me why, with my background, I thought that!) Also, as I discovered in the writing course Patti and I took, my personal view of traditional or non-traditional is slightly skewed. (We did a short assignment on baking chocolate-chip cookies, and I wrote what I felt was a non-traditional story. But since I was unthinkingly deviating only from my family's tradition—my father always bakes the cookies in our house—I had the mother do it in the story, and my piece accidentally ended up traditional.)

Another thing I think Susannah learned from me was that dictating really is writing. Most adults don't think of it that way—they see it as "telling a story" or something, but they fail to see the equivalence of the businessperson who dictates letters, or the author who uses a tape recorder or even that well-known invention, the Dictaphone. I think dictating is just another form of writing: We went from oral history (a form of dictation), to hieroglyphics on stone, to stick and papyrus scrolls, to quill and inkwell, to pencil, to fountain pen, to ballpoint pen, to typewriter, to word processor, and now some of us are back to dictation. Nobody says that the woman who chooses to use an old typewriter instead of a new word processor isn't really writing. I think that since this condescending attitude toward young people's dictation is so prevalent in our world today, Susannah had never really considered it until I and other young writers brought it to her attention.

***

For any young writers who are looking for a mentor/writing apprenticeship (or any kind of apprenticeship, really) I would say five things: First, don't work with anyone you're not comfortable with. Find someone else. Second, if you're having trouble finding what you want, put the word out among *everyone* you know. You never know whose uncle's sister-in-law's daughter is an established writer who would be happy to help a just-starting-out writer. Third, take a writing course at a community college, at summer school, anywhere! If you go where the writers are, you'll have a better chance of finding one to help you. Fourth, write an ad and put it in a homeschooling newsletter, or newspaper, or church paper. Or put a poster at your library, at the supermarket, at a college, anywhere! Fifth, when you do find someone, stress that this is an experiment. You don't want to be locked into something anymore than they do! Try it for a month, or six weeks, or whatever, then reevaluate. Good luck!

Finally, if you are looking for a volunteer position, apprenticeship, or other work situation, don't limit yourself to places with established youth programs. I've worked at many organizations, volunteering my time. I began at a nature center when I was eight, and this turned out to be the hardest place of my volunteering career to get into. The staff was used to seeing large busloads of school children on field trips, and those kids, tired and restless after a long ride, would often run, jump, be noisy, and generally enjoy themselves on their own terms during the staff-led tour. Therefore, the employees were more than a little skeptical about having an eight-year-old volunteer. (All of the other volunteers were adults, most in their thirties and early forties.) My Dad and I met with the head of the volunteers and another top staff member, and at the end of the meeting they were still somewhat unsure. I was finally allowed on a trial basis after one adult volunteer (whom we knew) agreed to "sponsor" me. She drove me to and from the nature center once a week, and worked with me on most of the things I did. These included leading school groups on tours and assisting at various festivals (for which I did research on different subjects—e.g. Easter egg dyeing using natural dyes). I worked at the nature center for several years.

After that, I worked at a home for physically and mentally handicapped children, a local environmental group, and the library. All of these positions were enriching, exciting, and fun. If you are interested in volunteering at a local organization, start by getting as much information as possible about what you'd be doing. Many organizations have strict rules regarding what a volunteer may or may not do, particularly if the person is under age eighteen. Suggest a trial period; try to find someone already volunteering there who can sponsor you; problem-solve with your contact person to try to find a way. Sometimes you can even volunteer out of your own home, helping with mailings and such. People are often wary of a child or teenage volunteer, but once they see that you're a responsible person, they'll probably come around. If you are genuinely interested, you can find a way.

Amanda Bergson-Shilcock
Bryn Mawr, Pennsylvania

This is How I Live

The phone is ringing when I walk into the house, and I hurry to answer. It's Julia. "Two of my friends are coming tonight," she says. "Do you want me to bring anything?"

I look down at the bags I'm holding. "No," I say, "I stopped and got spinach and basil for the pesto, and strawberries for dessert. We're fine."

Photo by Julia Bergson-Shilcock

"How many people are coming? Are you sure we'll have enough?"

She always worries about this. Not for nothing was my sister's childhood nickname the Food Lady. "Nine people," I tell her. "We have plenty. See you at seven."

I hang up, disentangling myself from the phone and offloading the grocery bags, the coat, the backpack, the lunchbag. When I went househunting, I put a good kitchen at the top of my list, and when I walked into this old Victorian I knew I had found what I wanted. Someone had knocked out a wall to make the galley kitchen into an open, sunny workspace and I was the lucky beneficiary.

The kitchen was important because I knew I'd be spending a lot of time there, cooking not just for myself but for friends and family. As a child I remember people being surprised at the strength of the friendships among my siblings and me, as though it was unusual for us not to be vying in a constant zero-sum rivalry for attention. As an adult I took it for granted that when I announced a weekly Sibling Dinner at my new house, they'd be there.

I took it for granted because in my family, homeschooling wasn't a kind of dogma or even a particular set of activities. Instead, it was an orientation toward the world—a way of looking at things. Eating dinner together wasn't a family rule or something we had to plan for, it was just the natural result of how we lived. Maybe that's why today, at age twenty-six, sitting with my siblings and friends around my own dinner table, I still think of myself as a homeschooler.

Officially, my career as a homeschooler ended in the spring of 1993, at a small private graduation ceremony across the street from the middle school I had never attended. By the grace of a progressive superintendent, I received an official high school diploma.

Of the dozen people present that day, ten were my relatives. While my aunts and uncles and grandfather might not have fully understood homeschooling, when the superintendent asked if anyone wanted to speak as part of the ceremony, each one of them offered advice or congratulations. Then I was handed a diploma bound in dark red, and that was that. I was the only graduate.

I was thankful for the credential, pleased to be finished with state oversight of my education, and moved by the small, personal ceremony. But when my mother suggested a graduation party, I was befuddled. What, exactly, would we be celebrating? I was not ready to stop being a homeschooler.

In fact, I was not certain I was ready for any sort of traditional next step. All around me, my schooled peers were enduring the roller-coaster ride of SAT tests and the college admissions process. They were discussing where to go and what to do as though the entire world was laid out before them in the *US News & World Report* college rankings.

But I liked my life the way it was. My dance classes brought me joy and my job at the library was the perfect blend of books and community interaction. I was taking driver's ed and going to my sister's soccer games, hanging out with friends from age twelve to forty, and reading voraciously. I felt as though I was earning my keep and more, both in my family and in the wider community. I did not want to exchange my rich, full life for a dorm room and the *US News* paradigm of education.

When I said as much to my parents, they didn't flinch. To their credit, they tried again to live out the credo they had been practicing since I was a toddler: Respect your child's wishes, and take her seriously even when you disagree. They had managed to do that when I was a seven-year-old who insisted on wearing only clothes that had pockets, and now, with higher stakes, they did it again: They listened, they paid attention, and eventually they made suggestions.

"You don't have to go full-time," my mother reminded me, characteristically looking for creative means to a common end. "You can take a couple of courses, keep your job, even keep taking dance classes. There are a lot of colleges nearby. We'd love to have you live at home if you don't want to live in a dorm."

I didn't make an immediate decision, but I did schedule a few college interviews. After so many years of talking about homeschooling with every person who asked why I wasn't in school, not to mention making presentations at conferences and speaking to the media, I was an old hand at discussing my eclectic background. All of my interviews went overtime, as I explained what I was looking for in a college and how it would fit into the larger picture of my life.

At the end, each admissions person looked at my total lack of transcript and grades, and at the blank spot on the form where standardized test scores were supposed to go. Then they looked at me as I told them I hadn't taken the SATs, and didn't plan to take them.

That had been the most difficult aspect for my parents to swallow. My mother's opinion was that I might as well use my modest talent for standardized tests on the best-known test of all, even if I thought it was meaningless. My father said very little, lending his silent weight to her pointed reminders of each registration deadline and testing day as they passed.

To me, after seventeen years in a household where achievements as diverse as finding crayfish in the backyard creek and building a scanner out of Legos were recognized and celebrated, participating in the academic ritual of the SAT seemed blatantly hypocritical. How could I say that all kinds of intelligence were important, and then capitulate the first time someone wanted to define me as a test score?

Despite my convictions, I didn't tell many people about my SAT resistance, partly because I wasn't sure what would be gained by talking about it. I didn't expect my schooled friends to understand, and even the other homeschoolers I knew were taking standardized tests as a matter of course. I wasn't interested in making them feel judged for their choices.

When one of the few friends who did know what I was doing described my SAT resistance as activism, I rejected the idea. I knew what activism was: lobbying your elected representative, carrying a sign, writing letters, testifying about pending legislation. I had done all of that when my family helped to enact a new homeschooling law.

By the same token, I thought I knew what activism was *not*. And to me, refusing to take the SAT was just my own private choice: something among the colleges, my family, and me. And so instead of talking publicly about it, I wrote pages and pages of essays, outlining the varied activities of my homeschooling years and my principled objections to standardized testing. I mailed them off and hoped the admissions people had meant it when they said they wouldn't reject me just because I lacked test scores.

In December I got a letter of acceptance. And in January 1994, I started classes at the University of Pennsylvania.

It would be a long time—years, in fact—before I spoke publicly about the SAT. I stayed silent on many occasions in college when people made assumptions I could have contradicted, including once in my first semester when a professor referred to "the SATs, which we all presumably took to get in here," his tone indicating that there was no real question.

As time went by, I began to mention my lack of test scores in passing, usually when people asked how I'd gotten into college. It inevitably elicited a reaction: "You *didn't?* And they let you *in?*" At first I felt compelled to point out that I was only a part-time student, and that the university did say they'd be watching my grades for the first year. Eventually I just shrugged and said yes, and by that time I could add that none of my siblings had taken those exams either.

Because my stance on the SAT seemed to me to be so matter-of-fact and consistent with my family's general philosophy, I was always slightly surprised at the curiosity it evoked, even within the homeschooling community. When I appeared as one of a panel of grown homeschoolers at a conference, I was bemused when it turned out that what people were most eager to talk to me about afterwards was the SAT question. It was a revelation to think that you could seriously question the test, they said, and I realized that the ripple effects of my personal decision were spreading further than I had considered.

But it wasn't until I walked into a grocery store in 2002 and was confronted with a towering display of the Sunday paper that I fully understood how much my individual choice was part of a larger mosaic. I was twenty-five by then, and seeing headlines proclaiming "Colleges Moving Away From the SAT" was a pleasant shock. It was clear from the article that the changes were incremental at best. Still, it felt like a victory just to see a public acknowledgment of the SAT's failings.

It was the kind of victory that I hadn't always been able to visualize during my years in the university's world of assumptions, and I went home and wrote an e-mail. *Now I feel like an activist,* I said. *And now I see that activism is not just lobbying and testifying, but also all the choices about how I live my life.* Of course, that was true of homeschooling itself, just as much as the SAT decision, but somehow it took the concrete issue of the test for me to really grasp the concept.

I sent that e-mail to Susannah Sheffer, the friend who had first identified my conscientious objection as a kind of activism. It wasn't unusual for Susannah to have been able to identify something I was too close to to see myself. In fact, she had been doing that for me for over a decade, while we had worked together as writing mentor and apprentice.

Throughout my childhood and into my teenage years, Susannah had embodied one of my family's basic tenets of homeschooling: the value of adult resource people. Because of our geographical locations, our interaction was largely by mail and phone, and it was usually informal. There was certainly no curriculum or set of activities we were trying to accomplish. I just wrote, and she responded.

I didn't realize how much I was unconsciously absorbing from our interaction until I began writing for college classes. Amidst all of the new technical tricks that my classmates and I struggled to master, there was also the challenge of obtaining and providing feedback. It was a surprise to realize that many of my professors knew very little about giving feedback, although they understood evaluation well enough. Searching through a ten-page paper for evidence that the professor had done more than assign a grade to it, I realized how well working with Susannah had educated me for *thinking* about writing.

As I grew into my twenties, my contact with Susannah underwent a slow metamorphosis from mentorship to adult friendship. Of course, we had always talked about other subjects, but now our sphere of conversation widened even further. And our writing-related conversation became even more of a dialogue, as she sent me her own works-in-progress and I scribbled copious notes in the margins.

As a young person, I had known that my apprenticeship with Susannah was rare. Indeed, I had very few age-mates who had adult mentors. But I was less aware that it was also unusual for a such a friendship to continue and flourish as time went on. It's probably a legacy of my upbringing that it never occurred to me that there would be a time that Susannah and I *wouldn't* be friends.

And yet that was a radical assumption. I was certainly not surrounded by models of successful cross-age friendships. College pressures worked against forming friendships outside the campus community, much less across age barriers. My friendship with Susannah was a real-world tether, a reminder that there was someone who could give me feedback more substantive than a score. I rarely discussed my thirty-something friend with my teenage classmates, but on some level I was aware that just by nurturing our relationship I was making a private statement about its importance.

Most of my statements during the first few years of college were private, because being a homeschooler in college at first meant being incognito. Much as I had loved speaking publicly about homeschooling, now I relished the opportunity to lose myself in Penn's huge urban campus and be just another student. I was there on my own terms: a part-time, commuter student who took a mixture of day and night-time classes, declined to declare even a potential major, and chose courses based on how interesting they looked rather than their value as graduate-school stepping stones or résumé-builders.

It didn't take long to realize that while college had plenty of new information to offer, I already had many of the tools to shape and interpret it. My parents had been scrupulous in their respect for each person's opinion, and I took that respect for granted in college. I didn't assume that my opinion about a book or an idea was any less valid than another student's, but nor did I assume they had nothing to teach me.

I loved the variety of people I encountered. During breaks in my history class I chatted with a sixty-something couple who had been active in the civil rights movement. In a writing course I bonded with visiting high-school students who shared my taste for Roald Dahl. After Spanish classes I hung out with an eclectic group of adult students, listening to stories of crazy travel adventures, single parenthood, job angst.

And slowly I became more outspoken. When people asked about my background I brought up homeschooling; when they challenged me, I countered with the evidence of my own experience. Bea, who would become one of my closest college friends, was a union tradeswoman who frankly admitted that she assumed homeschoolers were elitist. Our shared political perspective helped build common ground, and our after-class debate sessions went on so long that I often had to run for the last train home. Soon I was channeling this passion into a weekly opinion column for the college paper, taking on issues as broad as world politics and bioethics, and as personal as grading and age segregation in schools.

When I had spent two years balancing college, library work, and everything else, my sister Emily started classes at Arcadia University. She went the mainstream route, complete with dorm room and a full-time course load. I looked at the stack of bills on my mother's desk, and the minimum-wage salary of my library job, and I decided to go job hunting.

I was clear about what I wanted: This would be a pay-the-tuition-bills job, not my life's work. Knowing my own tendency to stick with things until the bitter end, I promised myself I would take a full-time job, but continue college at night, and quit the job when I graduated.

On my first day as a receptionist at a legal publications company, I learned the ropes: Answer sixteen lines, greet whomever walked in the door, and sort the mail. By the end of the first month I was so bored I was using my trash can for basketball practice, and making ninety percent of my left-handed shots.

I begged for more work. When I didn't get enough, I studied my Spanish textbook, conjugating verbs under my breath. I made friends with the temporary workers, the cleaning staff, the Fed Ex driver (she was going to college at night too). I tried to develop empathy for people whose entire lives were spent in work that bored them.

Most of all, I paid attention. I watched the marketing staff bend over backwards to meet artificial sales targets, I listened to the editorial staff gossip about Supreme Court rulings, I heard all about the personal lives and ambitions of most of my thirty co-workers. I hatched plots for how I would run things differently (if my parents could trust a seven-year-old to know what she wanted to wear, certainly adults could be trusted to write down their own vacation days on our communal calendar).

And after two years, when I was in the midst of my last semester, I learned firsthand what a corporate takeover looked like. By that time I had worked in four departments, and the new owners had lots of plans for my new role with the company.

But I resigned. Whatever they were interested in offering—a nicer office, more money, a window—it couldn't compete with my promise to myself. I took a break, and wrote a new list of what I wanted in a job. This one would be more than just a paycheck.

I took my time, exploring a slew of possibilities and coming close to taking two jobs that seemed almost right. It was hard to say no without being able to say why, but my memories of an ill-fitting job were still too fresh to allow me to just say yes.

When I did say yes, it was to a career I had never envisioned: in the nonprofit sector, as I had wanted, but as a grants manager, overseeing grants to local social services organizations. The first year was a blur of moving along a steep, fast learning curve.

But since the initial rush, I have been struck by how much the fundamental tenets of my childhood hold true. Respecting others, listening, being alert to the inner ethical voice—my job is not just a fascinating source of information, but an endless series of opportunities to continue living as I have always lived. Every day, I can make choices that are consistent with how I want the world to be. Often, I have the chance to be stubborn on behalf of something I believe in, and just as often, the chance to back down and admit I was wrong.

Because my co-workers know my background, they occasionally ask whether I will homeschool my own children. I don't know how to answer, although when I imagine my future children, I am quite clear that I want for them the same thing that I had: loving, respectful parents who care enough to create a protected space in which each child can thrive.

I don't know if that space will be created by homeschooling. Indeed, how can I possibly know what would be the best learning situation for a child I don't yet have? And at the same time, how can I believe that an institution which requires you to obtain permission to engage in basic bodily functions can create a healthy learning environment? I am grateful that new organizations, such as the resource center my parents operate, have helped create some specks along the schooling/homeschooling continuum.

Of course, all of my musings are just speculation until I find a spouse who is committed to the same general ideas as I am. It is funny to hear the way that so many people talk about this issue, because so little of what they want in a partner is about shared values and philosophy, and that's pretty much the *only* item on my list. How can I know if I want a guy who is tall or short, athletic or subdued, when what I most care about is that he believe in respecting the integrity of people of all ages?

I am standing in the kitchen chopping basil when I hear the front door open. "I'm here!" calls Julia as her bookbag thuds to the floor. "Let me just wash up, and then tell me what can I do to help," she says, coming into the kitchen. "Do you mind if I put on some music?"

"No," I say, hearing more voices at the door, the muted hum announcing the arrival of my teenage brother Nicholas and his girlfriend, and Emily and her husband Chris. The CD player comes to life, the music of Julia's favorite jam band filtering through the house.

"We need some air in here," Julia says, opening a window to the warm summer night and expertly adjusting my curtains to suit her discerning eye. "Cail called. She's going to be a little late. And Andrea's just going to walk over from the train station. She says we can start without her."

"Sounds good," I say, as the kitchen fills up with energy and conversation. Nick and his girlfriend are quizzing each other in preparation for an upcoming Latin exam, Julia is offering counsel as Emily describes a complex interpersonal dynamic in her office, and Chris is telling me about a marvelous history of funk music that he heard on the radio.

He pauses for a minute, and I look around the crowded room at these people I love, who care so much about each other's lives and are so curious about the world. *This is my life*, I think. *This is how I live.*

"Okay, everybody, let's sit down," I say. "It's time for dinner."

Do you Have to be a Genius to Unschool?

The main reason I put this book together—which encompasses most of the reasons discussed in the introduction—was the same reason I wrote *The Teenage Liberation Handbook*: in order to give young people the confidence, inspiration, and knowledge they need to unschool themselves. I expected that the writers who share their lives here would serve as guides and role models, making others feel that living with freedom would be more possible for them.

And then it occurred to me one rainy day that for some readers, this project might backfire. Most self-directed unschoolers I've met or heard of, including the writers of this book, have more confidence, expertise, interesting experience, and *apparently* more intelligence than most of their schooled peers. This is of course a generalization—many schooled teenagers have lots of expertise, whether because of or in spite of their particular school situation. And conversely, some unschoolers have yet to delve passionately into anything.

But as a generalization it is solid, and the essays in this book support it—and so I was afraid some of you might be intimidated. Therefore I want here to defend Pessimistic Readers against their own fears that This Would Never Work For Them (or for their offspring, who apparently lack not only genius but also motivation).

Some of the essayists offered me their viewpoints on this often-confused issue, and Kevin got cleanly at the heart of it: "I think that, rather than needing to be a genius *in order* to unschool, unschoolers are likely to *become* geniuses."

Of course. School destroys genius (by not recognizing most varieties of it, by punishing extreme forms of it, by stealing time from its development, by converting it into obedience or "well-rounded" mediocrity). Unschooling builds genius (by allowing people to fully explore what they love, enough that they often become experts).

That is the catch, of course: Many people, young and old, love nothing. In other words, they are "unmotivated" except perhaps by the fear of flunking or losing a job.

But lovelessness is learned, not innate. It is taught/caused mainly by school, and also by dysfunctional relationships, extreme poverty, guilt, loneliness, physical disease, etc. To the extent that school causes it, unschooling can remedy it, although not, in most cases, overnight. If you get out of school and allow yourself to flounder for a while, eventually some long-forgotten desire will push up from below like a freshwater spring, a fountain, or even a volcano.*

Some of the essayists—and a few of their parents—told me what they thought of the question at hand—"Do you have to be a genius to unschool?" Here are excerpts of their answers:

Amanda Bergson-Shilcock:

No. Most emphatically, no.

Actually, I hate this whole label business. Labeling seems to be the entire reason we have schools. Schools label active kids "ADD" (Attention Deficit Disorder); bored or unenthusiastic kids "learning disabled"; and kids who are willing to play the straight-A game "gifted/talented/top stream/honors students/ academically talented"—take your pick.

Don't fall for the labels. Everyone is talented. Let me cite two examples. The first occurred when I testified for the State House of Representatives. We were trying to pass a bill more favorable to homeschooling, and after several years we had finally gotten to the point of testifying before the House Committee on Education. While I was waiting for my turn, I listened to other homeschoolers testify. I was particularly impressed by one girl, who was sixteen at the time. She related how in school she had been labeled "learning disabled." When her parents approached the school officials to get permission to homeschool, they were told that since the girl was LD she needed special attention that she could get only in school. After a battle, the family got permission to homeschool. Three years later, she took a mandatory state test. When the school got the test results, they told the parents that their daughter was gifted, and should not be allowed to homeschool, because at home she could not get the special attention that she would receive in school! (Just for the record, she stayed at home.)

The other example is a girl I know who is fourteen years old and has never been to school. Alicia (not her real name) is a dear friend of mine. She

---

* For a more thorough discussion of this phenomenon, see "The importance of the vacation," chapter twelve of *The Teenage Liberation Handbook.*

didn't read until age ten and still hates to read. To her, the phrase "reading for pleasure" is an oxymoron. Had she gone to school, I'm sure she would have been tagged immediately as learning disabled, and then it would have been well-nigh impossible for her to shed that tag.

Yet Alicia has written daily (yes, daily) to a friend for eight months—real letters, too, not "Hi, how are you, I'm fine." She's been balancing a checkbook of her own for four years. She works part-time as a sales clerk in a small retail shop, and she does far more than sell. Fully sixty percent of her marketing and publicity ideas have been adopted by the owner of the business.

Ayanna Williams:

No, you do not have to be a genius to unschool. If you are labeled dumb, homeschooling would most likely be really good for you before you start *believing* you're dumb and stop trying. I know a guy who was a good student until the third grade. He got good grades. Then, in the third grade they found out he could not read! He had not been cheating; he just had a great memory. (They figured it out when he was in a play and memorized his lines so fast they wanted him to help other kids.) At that point they put him in a special remedial class and his grades went way down. From then on he was considered dumb—rather than clever for being able to get along fine without reading skills.

I think homeschooling allows you to grow and be something very few can be after thirteen years in the system. I know my story would have been totally different if I had stayed in those classrooms another five years.

Vallie Raymond:

No, people don't have to be anything besides themselves to do what they have their hearts set on doing. That's one thing I've noticed that some schooled kids don't realize. Not only does unschooling give you the freedom of learning what you are interested in without having a teacher peer over your shoulder, but it lets your true genius come through.

I can't speak for everybody because I don't know everybody's situation, but a lot of school kids I know would do just fine homeschooling, even if their parents worked or didn't help them.

Speaking for myself, one thing that makes unschooling work is that I am able to be myself without having to worry about being unpopular or have teachers hate me. The world is full of things to worry about. I'm glad that I'm not using my time to worry about something I don't have to.

Kevin Sellstrom:

No! I am not a genius by any stretch of the imagination....but I remember what I am interested in and what I think is important. For instance, although I once studied it, I am no longer familiar with the methods of working with chemical formulas—adding, subtracting, multiplying them; I don't intend to be a scientist or someone who would need to have these skills. (If I ever do need them, of course I can look them up.) I am, however, quite familiar with the formulas for finding specifications and dimensions necessary to build radio antennas—and also with the construction techniques themselves.

I am not "super intelligent;" rather, I have the opportunity to follow my interests as far as I want them to take me. I think this is what makes people see unschoolers as geniuses; many unschoolers are highly knowledgeable in interesting fields, instead of slightly knowledgeable in many boring areas. Because of the many options you can offer yourself as an unschooler, you can become much more knowledgeable than your counterpart who is still stuck in the ratrace of school. I believe everybody has the potential to become a genius, but public schools stifle many opportunities and in the end only a relatively few students get pronounced "intelligent."

I think the biggest requirement to succeed in unschooling is that a person have the freedom to do what they want to do. Under these circumstances, people may not automatically become "geniuses," but they stand a good chance of satisfying their interests and living a fulfilled life.

Bonnie Sellstrom (Kevin's mother):

One question we are frequently asked is how come our children are so smart. When we started homeschooling, we did not have gifted children. Our state often puts gifted and talented children in special classes; the requirements for participating include high scores on standardized tests. Neither of our children qualified.

We have let our children use their strengths to gain knowledge in all areas of life. By emphasizing these strengths, we have seen their weaknesses disappearing. This approach to learning makes it appear that many homeschooled children are more knowledgeable than their peers.

I often refer back to the Native Americans. They knew how to use nature's resources as food and medicine. They knew when to move to new lands because of weather conditions. They knew how to make nature work for them to grow crops. They knew how to preserve these crops for future use. Other ancient people, too, have shown their abilities to learn without schools. Pursuing your own interests, doing your best at all times, is what makes a person educated. A piece of paper with your high school grades on it will not fix a flat tire. A piece of paper marked "College Diploma" will not explain how to build a house.

I have seen Kevin's autobiography develop into a 13,000 word project. It has been interesting to see such a large project written by a person who has not been required or encouraged to write much in the past seven years. In fact, neither of our children have ever written much more than thank you notes. Yet they have both been able to express themselves in writing when needed.

Anyone who pursues their own interests will become qualified to share their knowledge. You can bring out the best in almost anyone by asking them to share their talents and knowledge with you.

Jeremiah Gingold:

Ask a stupid question...! Of course you don't have to be a genius to homeschool. Case in point: Do I strike you as a genius? (Don't answer that!)

Seriously, you don't have to be in any way a uniquely special person to unschool yourself. The only real requirement is a desire to learn and live in the real world. And, perhaps, the permission and help of your parents, legal guardian, or whatever. Of course, if you happen to be a genius, that's great too!

Serena Gingold:

Don't be ridiculous! The reason people sometimes think that we are geniuses is because we are allowed to focus our whole attention on one subject that we're interested in. Then we can excel in that area and we seem smarter than a kid who goes to school and has to be good in everything.

I have had a couple of opportunities to compare my work with that of other kids. One time was at our local National History Day contest. Except for a few other projects by well-known "A" students, Jeremiah's and mine really stood out. We were shocked because we hardly ever do any regular schoolwork at home, and somehow didn't think our work would be up to par. Instead, we each won first place in our categories with really high scores.

I don't think we won because of our IQ's, but rather because we cared about what we were doing and we wanted it to be the best we could make it. My project was called "Separate But Not Equal: The African American Struggle for Education Rights." I became really involved in the subject because black history and civil rights struggles are very important to me. It was obvious that to most of the other kids this was just another assignment, while to me and Jeremiah it was an opportunity to share what we care about with others. The other kids tried to get away with as little work as possible. I don't think that had anything to do with their IQ's either—I think that's just a school survival skill that I've never had to learn.

Pam Gingold (Jeremiah's and Serena's mother):

Of course you don't have to be a genius to homeschool, any more than you have to be a genius to grow your own food, cook, raise a family, or do anything else that is natural and life-sustaining. Much more important than your IQ is courage, faith that you really do know what's best for yourself, and a willingness to accept responsibility for your own life education, failures included.

You should possess a sense of adventure and be willing to experiment. Like raising a family, it's all a matter of trial and error. There are no rulebooks, no easy paths to follow. Each and every one of us do it in a different way, by seeing what works for us.

I see homeschooling as more of a lifestyle choice than an educational option. It is difficult to break the chains of a lifetime of being told that others know what's best for you, but it *is* possible to learn to trust in yourself. All of life is an experiment, but homeschooling is living life to its fullest potential because you get to determine what potential that is.

Homeschooling is certainly not a decision to take lightly, but there are no tests to pass or anything to "qualify" you, like having to be a genius. All that's required is a genuine desire to try!

Gwen Meehan (Patrick's mother):

The experience we have had to date has convinced me that it is not the student's IQ that is important to homeschooling. It is his or her personal desire and commitment that will spell success. Also important is the parents' determination to shake off their overawe of educators and claim their personal power to direct their own lives and facilitate the lives of their children. We humans are innate problem-solvers. That's what we do best.

Erin Roberts:

No, of course not! The purpose of unschooling is to learn about the real world and about real life in a way that no textbook could ever teach you. However, a lot of people think you do have to be a genius to unschool. When I mention that I learn at home I can almost hear the mental gears whirring—"She doesn't go to school at all? Wow, she must be really smart." Then comes the question: "What are you, some kind of genius?"

Am I? Everyone is, in their own way. Some people are geniuses at fixing cars or broken TV's. Others are geniuses at solving math problems or writing or painting. Others are geniuses in working with animals or getting people to agree with one another.

Adults in particular perceive me as being intelligent. I always score very high on standardized tests, not necessarily because I know the subject but because I know how to take tests and enjoy taking them. Being thought of as smart usually works to my advantage. Adults and kids are more willing to listen to me. They are also more willing to put me in charge of things and assume that they will be done correctly.

On the other hand some people think that I'm either A) too smart for my own good, or B) lying. In second grade (my last year of school) I had a teacher who told me that I couldn't possibly be doing the kind of math I was doing (long division and high school algebra). She made me do it in front of the whole class until she found a problem I couldn't do.

No, you don't have to be a genius to unschool, but unschooling will help you bring out your own particular genius.

Craig Roberts (Erin's father):

I have another question I would rather answer but I'll get to that. Homeschool advocates like to point out the unschooled success stories like Einstein and Edison and by association infer that from the rank of unschooled children will come the next modern day geniuses. If you are in school without a "gifted and talented" label, you may quickly conclude that you need school.

The question I prefer to answer is "Does unschooling bring out the genius in you?" I make the assumption and firmly believe there is genius in every child, even if only an "idiot savant." Idiot savant is one label I have given myself though informally I have been given many other labels in my life. My saving genius happens to be an ability to take standardized tests. In 1967 while in tenth grade, I took a standardized aptitude test and scored in the ninety-ninth percentile. That qualified me as a genius by the standards of MENSA, the organization for the superintelligent. So I guess that for four hours of my life while I took that test I was a genius. That score also qualified me for a visit to the school guidance counselor to see what my problem was. The counselor thought with a score like that I should be an A student with maybe an occasional B. I was, in fact, a C student with an occasional A and frequent D's and F's. School also labeled me lazy, an underachiever, a smart alec, immature, etc. If I was diagnosed in the late seventies or early eighties, I would have been labeled dyslexic and other various forms of learning disabled and could have ended up in special education. I recently read that the current label for me is "work inhibited." I was definitely schoolwork-inhibited. I did virtually no school homework assignments until my fifth year in Engineering School. By then I'd had sixteen years of school, was married, and wanted to make sure I did not stay in school any longer. I ended up on the Dean's List which, of course, totally blew the image of my many labels.

Despite my labels, I never felt lazy or work-inhibited when there was something I enjoyed doing. For ten years I would spend hours with my stamp and coin collections. I would sort, catalog, and semi-annually record my inventory. I cataloged every penny, nickel, dime, quarter, half dollar, and silver dollar I owned, where they were made, and how much they were worth. I also knew the occasion for every commemorative stamp ever issued.

In many ways I appeared to be a "normal" teenager. I was an Eagle Boy Scout, played sports, belonged to clubs, worked summer jobs, and had a girlfriend. I also sat in the back of every classroom, slept in class, goofed off, was sent to the principal's office at least twice a year, and was totally bored by school.

Basically, school was a waste of my time and the teachers' and principal's time, too. I learned and remembered more that I use in everyday life from Boy Scouts, sports, my summer job, and long talks with my girlfriend's parents and my grandmother. School just happened to occupy a disproportionate amount of my time and my life.

I am a classic case of opposites attracting. My wife had a very different experience. Sandi loved school, was the teacher's pet, got mostly A's with an occasional B, sat in the front of the classroom, and was extremely active in a variety of school activities.

Although Sandi thoroughly enjoyed school and certainly had the system figured out, she has since realized that she didn't learn anymore than I did. She spent her school years getting grades but really did not get an education.

Despite our different educational experiences, we both agree that school wastes a lot of time. Also, we both enjoy our five children too much to send them off to a stranger for six hours a day.

What does all this have to do with whether unschooling brings out the genius in you? Our family has one "genius" and one straight "A" student who both believe the best school is no school. What difference does it make if your child is a genius? There is no correlation between being a genius and being a happy, confident, and competent individual who is able to get along in the world. We want our children to get a meaningful education by being in an environment that is conducive to growth without the meaningless labels and grades that schools provide.

There were many reasons we thought of as to why our children should unschool. In fact, almost every day we realize many opportunities would be missed if our children schooled. However, there is only one deciding factor why Erin and her four siblings unschool. We ask them, "School or unschool?" They answer, "*Unschool!*" That is enough of a reason for us.

Kyla Wetherell:

If I wasn't so certain that everyone would benefit equally from unschooling, I would probably go so far as to say that students who are not labeled talented/gifted—and especially those whom school considers stupid—would succeed through unschooling even more than the academically talented.

Students who are made to feel smart in school at least have some encouragement and sense of achievement, however artificial it may be. But the "average" and "underachieving" often believe themselves to be just that. They are constantly convinced to sell themselves short. Yet, their labels are usually the mere result of their admirable refusal to submit, or do busywork, or memorize something that has no meaning for them.

I was always encouraged by school people and labeled as talented and gifted, but all that this meant to me was that I was good *at school*. I've had friends who got C's and D's in school—even when they tried—but they could explain how a space shuttle worked, or why the French Revolution was so bloody, when I knew close to nothing about either. For years, I spent too much time on school to learn anything. I was good at it; I was told I was smart, but I can't think of anything valuable I've done that I couldn't have done without all the labels.

Unschooling allows both "successful" and "unsuccessful" students to search for real, meaningful achievement, and to realize that whatever they enjoy doing is surely more worthy than being able to make the grade in school. In fact, many of the people I know who have recently quit school to get on with real living were considered failures by the school system. Grades are unrelated to intelligence, and intelligence is subjective anyway. Don't let others' opinions of your so-called "potential" get in your way. If you know what you want to do, unschooling will allow you to do just that. (And if you don't, unschooling will give you a chance to find out.)

I suppose that if I were in the position of an "average" or "below-average" high school student, bored and disgusted with school and impassioned, say, with skateboarding and calligraphy, my greatest concern would be about how to support myself when the time came—with not even a diploma to show for myself. Well, as long as you stay in school that's the fearful angle you're going to have on the "real world." After all, how would schools survive if everyone knew about all the opportunities out there—like the chance to sell skateboards with poetry etched in calligraphy, while skating everywhere from Phoenix to Uganda?

I speak from experience that whatever you want to do, you can do it better and more successfully outside of school. And actually, this is even more true now that unemployment is rising. With or without a high school diploma you'll be lucky to find a minimum wage job; with a college degree you'll be lucky if you find above-minimum wage work in your field. Yet, in my experience and that of friends, it's not nearly so difficult to find a rewarding, high paying job if you have *experience*. (I know many college freshmen who have recently left school in order to apprentice, since they have realized that school is just a long road to nowhere special.)

I have even found that most of the academic things I felt I needed to pursue once I quit school, in order to "keep my doors open," were completely unnecessary. As far as I can tell, there's no reason to work on academic stuff out of obligation; just by pursuing your interests, you're already doing the best thing to set yourself up for doing them more and on a larger scale in the future.

Unschooling is all about getting experience. And in the real world, rather than having your IQ or your academic ability haunt you every day, you'll find that both are irrelevant.

Recommended resources

I put an extensive bibliography in the original edition of this book, but there are so many resources now available for unschoolers, and you can hunt them up so easily on the Internet, that I'm including just a short list this time. Please don't consider this a definitive list of the "best" stuff, because I no longer keep up with everything that comes out on homeschooling or even unschooling. But I definitely stand by what I recommend here.

Organizations

Clonlara, which is still run by its visionary founder, Dr. Pat Montgomery, continues to help homeschoolers all over the world earn diplomas, interact with officials, and otherwise legitimize themselves. Clonlara School, 1289 Jewett, Ann Arbor, MI 48104, www.clonlara.org.

Also, many of the organizations that the writers described in their original essays are still thriving. Consider looking into 4-H, Habitat for Humanity, National History Day, Odyssey of the Mind, the South American Explorers Club, and any of the others recommended. All can be easily tracked down on the Internet or with a librarian's help.

Books

Cafi Cohen, *And What About College? How Homeschooling Can Lead to Admissions to the Best Colleges & Universities.* Cafi's son went to the U.S. Air Force Academy (after also being accepted at many other institutions, and offered numerous scholarships). Her daughter entered a selective liberal arts college with a substantial scholarship. Cafi tells what their homeschooling was like (*not* "school-at-home"), how they kept records, and how they conveyed it all to college admissions people. She also offers well-researched information for other college-bound homeschoolers. Really solid, helpful material. Cafi has two newer books that I imagine are also good, but I haven't read them: *Homeschooling: The Teen Years*, and *The Homeschoolers' College Admissions Handbook: Preparing Your 12-to-18 Year Old for a Smooth Transition.*

John Taylor Gatto, *Dumbing Us Down: The Hidden Curriculum of Compulsory Schooling*. Gatto is one of the most exciting people I know. After teaching for twenty-six years in New York City public schools, and winning numerous awards including New York State Teacher of the Year, Gatto—like Holt before him—has turned his energy toward speaking out against traditional schools and in favor of more dignified ways of learning: homeschooling, radically alternative free schools, and apprenticeships. This book is a collection of thoughtful, caustic essays. Also see his *Underground History of American Education*.

John Holt, various works listed below. Holt was *the* visionary pioneer of the unschooling movement. After decades of trying hard to improve schools by working as a teacher and urging educational reform, he turned his energy instead toward encouraging families to leave the system altogether, and toward supporting them in their efforts. He started *Growing Without Schooling* magazine and wrote many books. His writing delights me with its fresh, honest, unassuming way of observing young people. What follows is not a complete list, but any of these will make a good beginning; you'll want to keep at least one around for moral support and a wise, logical reminder of why you should be out of school. In chronological order:

Freedom and Beyond. Freedom, choice, authority...this book first raised the question of whether we need schools at all.

Escape From Childhood: The Needs and Rights of Children. Going beyond educational issues, this compassionate and radical book explores many areas where young people face unnecessary discrimination and oppression.

Instead of Education: Ways to Help People Do Things Better. This book builds on the concept that meaningful learning and doing are inseparable, and you can't have one without the other.

Teach Your Own. An overall guide for parents taking their children out of school. Despite the title, the book does not really advocate that parents *teach* in the strict sense; rather, it encourages them to support their kids' learning, largely by staying out of their way. A good one to give hesitant or confused parents if you're a young person who wants out of school.

A Life Worth Living: Selected Letters of John Holt, edited by Susannah Sheffer. This collection provides a warm, personal introduction to Holt's ideas and work.

Grace Llewellyn, *The Teenage Liberation Handbook: how to quit school and get a real life and education,* revised edition. This is the first and only complete (more or less) guide to unschooling for teenagers. It discusses why to quit school and how to do it—from large issues like dealing with the law and reluctant parents, to specifics like finding exciting ways to learn history and Spanish.

Video

Grown Without Schooling, by Peter Kowalke. This is a heartwarming and unpretentious documentary in which ten grown-up homeschoolers talk vulnerably about, and let us observe, their lives. Our very own Erin is one of them. Available at www.grownwithoutschooling.com.

Events

Not Back to School Camp
This is my annual gathering for unschooled teenagers. It's affirming, inspiring, and way too much fun. We run sessions in Oregon and West Virginia. Details at www.nbtsc.org or from NBTSC, P.O. Box 1014, Eugene, Oregon 97440.

Quo Vadis
My good friend Evan Wright directs this wonderful annual gathering for self-educated adults. Details at www.quovadis-gathering.org.

Magazines

Growing Without Schooling. Unfortunately, the best homeschooling magazine ever has gone out of business. The back issues are still relevant, though, and you can order many of them from Fun Books, www.fun-books.com, (888) FUN-7020. The letters from parents and kids that pack *GWS* explore every conceivable subject, from young children's play to teenagers working on archaeological digs to parents who disagree with each other about educational choices. In addition to letters, *GWS* has short essays, articles, book reviews, and excellent interviews with people working on the cutting edge of education (Ivan Illich, Herbert Kohl, etc.).

Home Education Magazine. Another excellent magazine, especially for parents. Includes good information about resources and legal issues, but the best attributes of this magazine are its long, thoughtful essays, its well-researched articles, and its regular columnists. Their web site has lots of helpful information too. P.O. Box 1083, Tonasket, WA 98855, www. http://www.homeedmag.com.

Life Learning Magazine is very good also. It's relatively new, though created by long-time unschoolers, and it helps to fill the void left by *GWS*. Box 112, Niagara Falls, NY, 14304-0112, http://lifelearningmagazine.com.

Web sites

There are tons, and I'm only familiar with a few. It helps to search for "unschooling" rather than "homeschooling."

http://info.nbtsc.org/schoolfree/
School Free includes a list of unschoolers in their early twenties who are happy to answer questions from younger people who are considering unschooling, or just starting out.

Jon's homeschool resources, www.midnightbeach.com/hs/index.html.
I believe this is the most comprehensive non-commercial homeschooling site on the Internet. It offers lots of excellent content and will point you to other good sites.

Unschooling.com
Created by the folks at *Home Education Magazine*, this is a clear and helpful site.

Index

Unschooling T Shirts

Original design by Grace Llewellyn,
printed on 100% cotton sweatshop-free shirts.

"unschooler \un-skül-er\ *n* : one who learns from life and love and great books and late morning conversations and BIG PROJECTS and eccentric uncles and eyes-wide-open and mountains and mistakes and volunteering and starry nights—instead of from classrooms and exceedingly dull textbooks and sedative lectures and interfering homework. *Synonyms*: HOMESCHOOLER, SELF-SCHOOLER, AUTODIDACT, RISE-OUT." Black ink on a long-sleeved raglan baseball-style shirt, white with black sleeves.

Modeled by Gabriel Lester: Not Back to School Camp dish queen, guitarist and singer for Abandon Ship, circulation manager for *All Round* Magazine, snowboarder and all-around athletic and sweet guy.

"I have become a walking billboard with my unschooling shirt! It's wonderful! Makes me feel well read! But most importantly, it tends to put people in the frame of mind that is excited and curious about what one would do if not spending all their time at school. I end up having more enthusiastic philosophical conversations, rather than upsetting, one-sided, floods of invasive, accusatory questions."

*"The unschooler T-shirt was fabulous!
It has started many interesting conversations!"*

*"My 13-year-old son loves his unschooling T-shirt
and always wears it to his once-a-week public school class."*

To order, see the order form at the back of this book, or for more T-shirt styles go to www.lowryhousepublishers.com/t_shirts.htm

Not Back to School Camp

for unschoolers ages 13-18

Meet 100 people as free and brilliant as you. Frolic in the sun and rain. Share your talents and learn from others. Talk until the sun comes up. Gather strength. Play soccer or tag. Teach a workshop. Walk in the forest. Swim. Drum. Encourage each other to new heights. Laugh. Prepare for a year of joyful, creative, meaningful, challenging, and excellent work.

NBTSC usually happens in Oregon and West Virginia, summer and early fall. For complete information, send $2 to NBTSC, Box 1014, Eugene OR 97440, or see www.nbtsc.org.

Campers say

- *"This camp totally changed my life. I feel confident and proud to walk the path I chose."*

- *"The atmosphere surrounding a big group of unschoolers like this is the most life-giving energy I have ever experienced, and I've become addicted to it! Ever since camp, which I left with the determination to incorporate this energy into everything I do, I've been enjoying life much more. I've felt more free, more passionate, and happier!"*

- *"NBTSC is the only place where I have met so many totally inspiring, giving, caring people in one week—let alone people my own age. As soon as I got off the bus, all these people came up and hugged me—that's completely the spirit of NBTSC. I didn't hear a single negative remark or put-down about another person the entire week! Instead everyone was constantly building each other up and helping one another out. I'm just sad I didn't find out about camp sooner."*

Parents say

- *"My son returned from your camp with renewed enthusiasm for life and learning! Thank you so much for having this get-together of, apparently, some of the most gifted and interesting people on earth!"*

- *"[Our daughter] returned full of self assurance, excitement, and positive loving energy. The revelation that there are other teenagers out there with her unschooler ideas was a delightful awakening for her."*

The Teenage
Liberation Handbook
how to quit school
& get a real
life and education
by Grace Llewellyn

This is a very dangerous book. It contradicts all the conventional wisdom about dropouts and the importance of a formal education. It is funny and inspiring. Do not, under any circumstances, share this book with a bright, frustrated high-schooler being ground into mind fudge by the school system. This writer cannot be responsible for the happiness and sense of personal responsibility that might [result]. -Bloomsbury Review

Packed with information for young people who want more than schools can offer....an invaluable and unique resource....Llewellyn presents a credible and appealing case for becoming self-taught....fascinating, frightening, and exhilarating.... -Voice of Youth Advocates Magazine (VOYA)

Bursting with clever strategies, valuable resources and wise guidance on how to design an interest-driven self-education. It was the sole inspiration for our family to take on an endeavor we thought was out of the question. -Whole Earth Review

Anyone who follows this clear blueprint is certain to meet the future with courage, enthusiasm, resourcefulness and the abundant love of life that the author has. She demonstrates brilliantly that school and education are two very different things, defining the latter with such a wonderful zest the reader is left dazzled with his own rich possibilities.
-John Taylor Gatto, former New York State Teacher of the Year, author of *Dumbing Us Down*

Freedom Challenge
African American
Homeschoolers
edited by Grace Llewellyn

"Strong stuff...A collection of revelations about the power of learning and love."—Bloomsbury Review

"An inspiring read...16 African American homeschoolers from all across the country, telling how homeschooling has challenged and inspired and renewed and blessed their families."—Home Education Magazine

Sunshine apprentices at an herb nursery and learns about architecture and astronomy from family friends. Khahil and Latif collect bugs and read physics books. Indira challenges herself far more than school ever did. Tunu wins piano competitions and joins with other Black homeschoolers to learn robotics from an engineer. At six, Maya taught herself to read; at seven, she decided to learn to row a boat... Unique, inspiring words on self-directed learning, healthy socialization, how single parent families homeschool, how parents can be their children's best educational allies, how homeschooling continues the work of the Civil Rights movement, much more.

Grace Llewellyn taught school for three years before unschooling herself and writing *The Teenage Liberation Handbook: how to quit school and get a real life and education,* which she followed up by editing and co-writing several other books including *Real Lives*. She now directs the annual Not Back to School Camp for unschooled teenagers, has a small bellydancing career on the side, and gets her hands into numerous other projects. She lives in Eugene, Oregon.

Grace's web site includes current information on her projects, ways you can be involved, links to interviews with her and articles about her work, links to helpful resources for unschoolers, and more: www.GraceLlewellyn.com.

How to order another copy of ***Real Lives,***
The Teenage Liberation Handbook, Freedom Challenge,
or an **unschooling T-shirt**

Use our order form or any old scrap. We accept U.S. funds: checks and money orders. (If you want to pay with a credit card, you can order online at www.LowryHousePublishers.com.) Include your name, shipping address, phone (in case we have questions), list of what you want, and payment. **Shipping** is $5 for each U.S. address, regardless of the number of items. Shipping to other countries is $5 for the first item and $2 for each additional item.

The Teenage Liberation Handbook	$20
Real Lives	$18
Freedom Challenge	$17
Unschooling T Shirt	$20

Mail or phone in your order to Lowry House Publishers, P.O. Box 1014, Eugene, OR 97440-1014, 541-686-2315. *Thank you!*

You can also order online *at www.LowryHousePublishers.com*

PLEASE SEND

____ copies of *The Teenage Liberation Handbook* @ $20.00

____ copies of *Real Lives* @ $18.00

____ copies of *Freedom Challenge* @ $17.00

____ Unschooling T shirts (white with black raglan sleeves) @ $20

Enclosed is a check or money order for _____ (be sure to add shipping
—see above).

SHIP TO

name_____ phone_____

Street address_____

city, state, zip_____

Send to: Lowry House Publishers, Box 1014, Eugene, OR 97440.